<u>The Dell War Series</u>

The Dell War Series takes you onto the battlefield, into the jungles, and beneath the oceans with unforgettable stories that offer a new look at the terrors and triumphs of America's war experience. Many of these books are eye-witness accounts of the duty-bound fighting man. From the intrepid foot soldiers, sailors, pilots, and commanders, to the elite warriors of the Special Forces, here are stories of men who fight because their lives depend on it.

D1008045

DEATH AT THE RUBBLE PILE

Weldon was firing again and the Marine on his left was in the process of clearing his weapon when—*clack-clack-clack-clack*—there was one big burst from the rubble pile, an AK47, and Weldon's feet flipped out from under him, and he was suddenly face to the sky. Half his left biceps was gone (he was left-handed). But he was in shock, stunned; the pain was not registering yet. His feet were propped upon some rubble in the trench—an odd, uneven position—and he knew that the NVA would be rushing the trench.

His M16 had landed on some of the shattered concrete in the trench near his right hand, and his fingers wrapped around the pistol grip as he realized there was an NVA standing atop the rubble pile, looking down on them with his AK47. He saw the man's pith helmet and fatigues—everything was happening in the eternity of a few seconds—and he saw that the NVA was laughing and shouting excitedly in Vietnamese. . . . In that flash, Weldon, still on his back, lifted the M16 up one-handed, swung it in the right direction, and firing with the wrong hand, squeezed a burst into the NVA's head and chest. . . .

Other Dell Books by Keith William Nolan

BATTLE FOR HUE: TET 1968
INTO CAMBODIA
INTO LAOS

* * *

OPERATION
BUFFALO

* * *

USMC Fight for
the DMZ

Keith William Nolan

A Dell Book

Published by
Dell Publishing
a division of
Bantam Doubleday Dell Publishing Group, Inc.
1540 Broadway
New York, New York 10036

The trademark Dell® is registered in
the U.S. Patent and Trademark Office.

ISBN: 0-440-21310-X

Reprinted by arrangement with Presidio Press

Printed in the United States of America
Published simultaneously in Canada

December 1992

10 9 8 7 6

OPM

To Mary Celeste Anderson, Kelly Lynn Williams,
and (of course) to my former Marine of a dad,
William Francis Nolan

★

★

Operation Buffalo was a motherfucker. —Cpl John D. Musgrave, Medically Retired (Rifleman, 3d Platoon, D Company, 1st Battalion, 9th Marines, 1967–1968)

I was laying in the hospital a day or two after getting hit on Operation Buffalo, reading the newspaper. Secretary of Defense McNamara was visiting South Vietnam and the paper said, "McNamara visits DMZ, everything under control." I just laughed. From my lowly position as a platoon commander, things couldn't have been more chaotic. —Col Frank Libutti (2d Platoon Commander, C Company, 1st Battalion, 9th Marines, 1967)

After all these years, I still have bad dreams about my experiences and they are always punctuated by a vision of poncho-covered Marine KIAs with their boots sticking out waiting for a bag and helo evacuation. —LtCol D. Curtis Danielson, Retired (Executive Officer, 1st Battalion, 9th Marines, 1967)

Being a Navy Cross winner, a lot of people expect me to say I'd do it all again. I wish I could, but I can't. The thought from Operation Buffalo of a field, about half the size of a football field, littered with dead Marines from Bravo Company, will not permit me to say I'd do it all again. I can never forget stacking their bodies three and four deep on top of a tank to get them out and home. My willingness to swear blind, undying allegiance to this country's foreign policies died in Vietnam. I have not deserted my country, but rather my country deserted me when I needed it the most. This government allowed thousands of young men to place their lives on the line in a war in which the government knew there was never a strategic plan to win. Surely our leaders would not let us die for nothing. But they did. I gave all I had to this country in Vietnam. I have no more to give. Maybe the ones who died are the lucky ones. Their suffering and pain are over. —Cpl J. Larry Stuckey, Medically Retired (Fireteam leader, 2d Platoon, C Company, 1st Battalion, 9th Marines, 1967)

Contents

★

Contents

Introduction

★

Operation Buffalo, fought in July 1967 by the U.S. Marine Corps in the desolate, blow-torched, and shell-pocked wasteland in the shadow of the DMZ, was unique in the terrible combat one of the rifle companies saw in the opening hours of the campaign. No other Marine rifle company in the entire Vietnam War suffered as much in a single afternoon as that command. Operation Buffalo was not unique for the other companies and battalions that rushed to the aid of that one decimated company. What they endured was typical of DMZ combat from 1966 to 1969. Undermanned, underequipped, undersupplied, underrested, and undertrained Marine companies went up against not only booby traps and snipers but numerically superior North Vietnamese regulars in nose-to-nose fights in which both sides brought mortars and artillery to bear. The Marine war along the DMZ was devastating in its intensity, numbing in its length, appalling in its casualties, and inspiring in terms of individual heroism.

That Operation Buffalo and other similar DMZ campaigns have not been properly recognized for the gallantry they produced is profoundly sad. Leadership at the highest levels was not as inspired among the Marine commanders in Vietnam as it was in WWII and Korea, nor did the units on the DMZ (having no rear to pull back to for group training and refurbishment) operate with the same cohesion as their counterparts on Iwo Jima or in the Chosin Reservoir. But on a man-to-man, platoon-to-platoon level, these Vietnam Marines performed with a bravery and endurance that would have made their forebears proud. I purposely selected this campaign, set before the 1968 Tet Offensive and the resultant disintegration of morale and performance, so that these pages would not be muddied with tales of drugs and race riots and fraggings. The Marine Corps, true to its Spartan ways, awarded few personal decorations to the Marines of Operation Buffalo and the other DMZ campaigns except for Purple Hearts, which were often awarded in multiples of two or three per man. This omission caused one of Buffalo's company commanders, Al Slater, to comment, "Of the many injustices perhaps the worst was my inability to get deserved combat awards for our grunts. I wrote as much as I could in the field and sent the write-ups to the rear for processing. Very few of my write-ups materialized into commendations."

When Slater and one of his young riflemen, Larry Stuckey, were both pinned with a rare reward soon after Operation Buffalo, Slater wrote to Stuckey, "Even though the Navy Cross is awarded for personal gallantry, I'll accept mine with a silent feeling that it is for the efforts of all our Marines. I wish that I could subdivide it and issue a share to each man."

This book is offered as that long-delayed share.

Those who contributed to this book in terms of interviews (mostly by mail and phone) with the author are sincerely thanked. Considering my youth and nonveteran status, I especially appreciate the time, effort, and frankness put into the interviews by those who were there. Those who were interviewed (or who reviewed the rough draft) from the 3d Marine Division and miscellaneous units include LtGen Louis Metzger, Ret; Col Joseph Kelly, Ret, and James Stockman, Ret; LtCol Ralph Brubaker, Ret, Bill Masciangelo, Ret, and Barry O'Neil, Ret; Maj Stephen Hartnett, Ret, and Billy Hill, Ret; ex-Capt Jim Coan; and ex-Cpl David Gotham.

From the 1st Battalion, 9th Marines: Col Frank Libutti and Henry Radcliffe, Ret; LtCol Robert Bruner, Ret, Charles Budinger, USMCR, Curtis Danielson, Ret, and Albert Slater, Ret; Maj Edward Hutchinson, Ret; ex-Capt Al Fagan; ex-Lt Wallace Dixon; SgtMaj Tom McGuigan, Ret; MSgt Bob Gossen; GySgt Leon Burns, Ret, and Tony Santomasso, Ret; SSgt Ronald Hutchinson, Ret; ex-Sgt Marshall Belmaine, James Gallagher, and Harvey Geizer; ex-Cpl George Blough, Mike Bradley, Robert Carpenter, Dave Miller, Harry Montgomery, John Musgrave, Richard Payne, Ron Power, Louis Robesch, Phil Rothberg, Larry Stuckey, Brian Tuohy, James Toy, and Steve Weldon; ex-LCpl Larry Bennett, Bob Burkhardt, John Flores, Dave Hendry, and Lee Strausbaugh;* and ex-Hospital Corpsmen Greg Favorite and Tom Lindenmeyer.

From the 2d Battalion, 9th Marines: Col William Kent, Ret, and John Peeler, Ret; Maj Frank Southard, Ret; and ex-Sgt Gary Davis.

From the 3d Battalion, 9th Marines: Col George Navadel, Ret, and Willard Woodring, Ret; Capt Lester Westling, USN, CHC, Ret; LtCol Bill Collopy, USMCR, and Jerry Giles, Ret; 1stSgt Bryce Lee, Ret; GySgt John Hatfield, Ret; ex-Sgt Roger Ford, David Gomez, and Charles Saltaformaggio; and ex-LCpl James Manner.

From Battalion Landing Team 1/3: Capt B.D. Cole, USN; Col Burrell Landes, Ret, and Gerald Reczek, Ret; Maj James Daley, USAR, Dennis Kendig, Ret, Norman Kuhlmann, Ret, and Tom Santos, Ret; Capt Ron Burton, Ret; ex-Capt Charles Jordan; ex-Lt Keith Gregory; SgtMaj

---

* Unwilling to discuss such brutal memories with a total stranger, Strausbaugh was "interviewed" instead by his old friend Bennett, who then (with his permission) passed the information on to the author.

William Head, Ret; SSgt Ken Bouchard, Ret; ex-Sgt John Steiner, William Taylor, and Stanley Witkowski; ex-Cpl Mike Brugh, Mark Chartier, Ed Kalwara, Raymond Kelley, Steven Lind, and Larry Miller; ex-LCpl Duane Dull, Jim Groeger, Wayne Pilgreen, and Billy Rusmisell; and ex-PFC Robert Law.

From Battalion Landing Team 2/3: Col Robert Bogard, Ret, John Broujos, Ret, and James Sheehan, Ret; LtCol Raymond Madonna, Ret; Maj James Cannon, Ret, and Richard Culver, Ret; Capt Ralph Jenkins, Ret; MGySgt Charles McWhorter, Ret; SSgt Dean Caton, USANG; ex-Sgt Richard Backus, Tom Huckaba, and Jim Mason; ex-Cpl Arthur Hofer and Tom Small; and ex-LCpl Ray Miskell.

Also my deepest thanks to Mrs. Lillian Sullivan Perry, who provided the letters her son, Cpl Charles Sullivan (C/1/9), wrote home before he was killed below the DMZ. Great assistance was also provided by the Marine Corps Historical Center, Washington, D.C. (in particular by Benis Frank, Danny Crawford, Joyce Bonnett, Joyce Conyers, Evelyn Englander, and Sheila Gramblin). Additional help came from the Records Branch, Personnel Management Division, Records Service Section (MCB Quantico, Virginia); Cmdr Roger Pace, USN (Chaplain Corps), Chaplain Resource Board, Norfolk, Virginia; James Plate, National Order of Battlefield Commissions, Rockford, Illinois; SgtMaj Bill Krueger, Ret, 3d Marine Division Association, Springfield, Virginia; Roger Liggon, 1/9 Veterans Association, Plainfield, New Jersey; David Zaslow, Marine Corps Tankers Association, Oceanside, California; Doug Wean, K/4/12 Marines Reunion, Villa Park, Illinois; Michael Triner, Chairman, HMM-164 Reunion Committee, Chicago, Illinois; and Joe Klein, Contributing Editor, *New York Magazine*.

Keith William Nolan

Prologue:
12 October 1967

★

Three more Marines were dead. Covered by olive-drab blankets, they lay on stretchers outside the entranceway of the medical bunker, one with his arm resting on the ground. It was the wristwatch of this dead man that Lieutenant Coan noticed as he passed by. He wore the same type of black band as did his old Basic School compadre, Ted Christian, who had come to Con Thien only two days before when his battalion, 1/9, relieved 3/9 of their Time in the Barrel. Coan, with the tank platoon permanently posted to Con Thien, wanted to walk away from that covered, anonymous corpse who wore his friend's wristwatch. Ted Christian was a good man, a slow-talking West Virginian who'd been known as the Warthog in Basic School due to his stocky build, pug nose, and acne-scarred face. Ted Christian could not be dead.

Coan had spoken to Christian only a few hours earlier, sitting on the cots in Coan's bunker of mud-coated board flooring and sandbag walls. Over C-ration coffee heated in empty fruit cans, Coan had asked, "So, Ted, what's goin' on with you these days?"

"Well, you're lookin' at the new XO of Alpha Company. I just moved up today! No more friggin' patrols, and no more walkin' the damn lines at night."

"What's this stuff I hear about One-Nine being jinxed, Ted?"

Christian had inhaled sharply at that one. His eyes had narrowed and some sixty uncomfortable seconds had passed before he spoke solemnly. "Bravo has had more than their share of bad luck, and now they got mostly new guys—and new guys make dumb-ass mistakes. But the rest of One-Nine is okay. We got us a number one CO, Colonel Mitchell. That crap about bein' jinxed really bugs me, Jim. Our guys hear that and it hurts their damn morale."

Christian had stared into his cup then for another long moment before deliberately changing the subject. "I guess you heard about Duke Jory and Spanky Dineen?"

"I heard they bought the farm."

"Yeah."

"Remember Tom Barry? I took over this tank platoon after he got two Hearts in one week up here."

Finally, Christian had stood. "Got to let the rest of Alpha see their new, hard-chargin' XO in action. Thanks for the coffee, Ice Cream."

"Sure, Ted. But like I said—this is a bad place. You never know when they'll drop a few in on you. Keep alert for incoming, okay?"

Christian hadn't looked convinced, and when Coan had bumped into him again after lunch, neither Christian nor his company commander (nor the battalion chaplain at the Alpha CP) had on his helmet and flak jacket. Coan had just left the group when the NVA fired an artillery airburst round that left a greasy black cloud hanging above the Alpha CP. A single round, no more, and as Coan had watched through the vision blocks in his tank cupola, a handful of corpsmen had responded to the shouts for help from the CP, followed by a dozen other grunts, new-guy dumb about what was probably coming next. What had come was another airburst round in the same spot as the first, catching rescuers and spectators alike in the open. Coan had counted ten teams of stretcher-bearers coming back before he had had to look away.

Now, Coan saw that corpse's arm with the black wristband, and he walked into the medical bunker. He collared the nearest corpsman not working on the wounded inside and pointed back out to the body. "Who is that man?"

"We don't know. He didn't have no dog tags on when they brought him here. I heard that he was with a bunch of guys who took a direct hit down by the LZ this afternoon."

"Let me take a look, I think I know who he is."

The corpsman followed Coan back out as Coan reached down with trembling hands to draw back the blanket. The corpse's waxy, gray face belonged, of course, to Ted Christian. Later, back in the medical bunker, the chaplain recognized Coan and approached, saying, "Don't worry, Lieutenant, I was able to reach Lieutenant Christian in time before he died."

"In time?" Coan lashed out wildly, "In time for what? He's dead and you got to him in time!" The chaplain recoiled, embarrassed, just as Coan was immediately embarrassed himself by his thoughtless, outburst. Tears in his eyes, he ran out toward his tank, passing along the way on the footpath a clump of yet-to-be-policed-up human brains. He was barely conscious of the mortar rounds beginning to thud in.

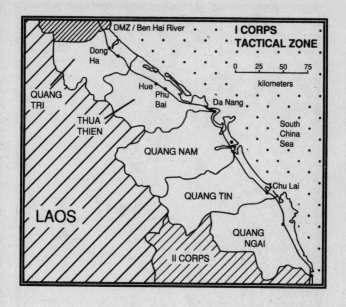

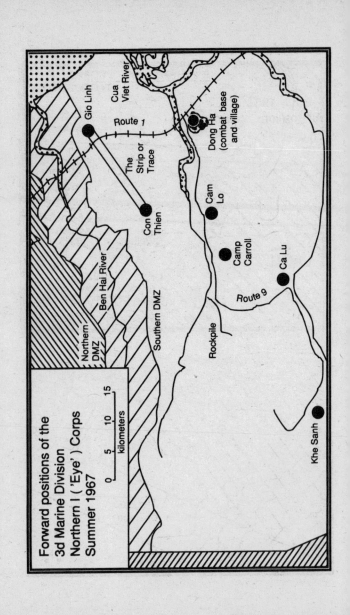

Forward positions of the
3d Marine Division
Northern I ('Eye') Corps
Summer 1967

0   5   10   15
kilometers

Northern DMZ

Ben Hai River

Southern DMZ

Gio Linh

Cua Viet River

Route 1

The Strip or Trace

Con Thien

Dong Ha (combat base and village)

Cam Lo

Camp Carroll

Ca Lu

Route 9

Rockpile

Khe Sanh

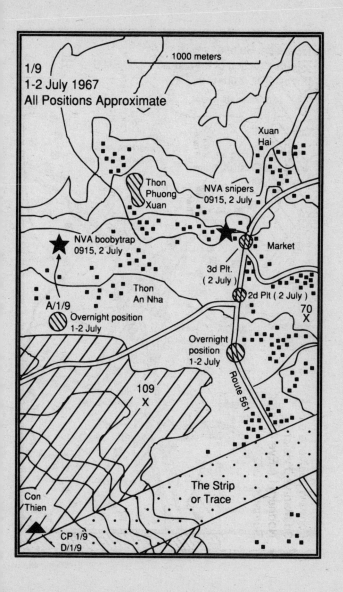

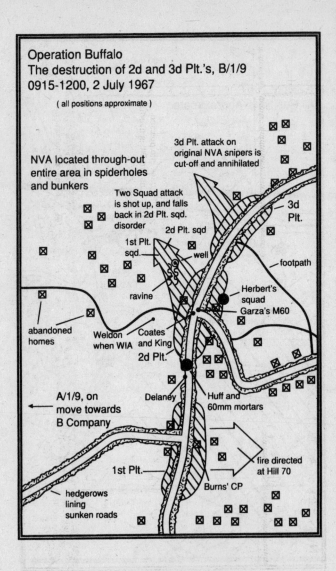

Operation Buffalo
The destruction of 2d and 3d Plt.'s, B/1/9
0915-1200, 2 July 1967

(all positions approximate)

3d Plt. attack on
original NVA snipers is
cut-off and annihilated

NVA located through-out
entire area in spiderholes
and bunkers

Two Squad attack
is shot up, and falls
back in 2d Plt. sqd.
disorder

2d Plt. sqd.

3d Plt.

1st Plt. sqd.

well

footpath

ravine

Herbert's squad

Garza's M60

abandoned homes

Weldon when WIA

Coates and King

2d Plt.

Delaney

Huff and 60mm mortars

A/1/9, on move towards B Company

fire directed at Hill 70

1st Plt.

Burns' CP

hedgerows lining sunken roads

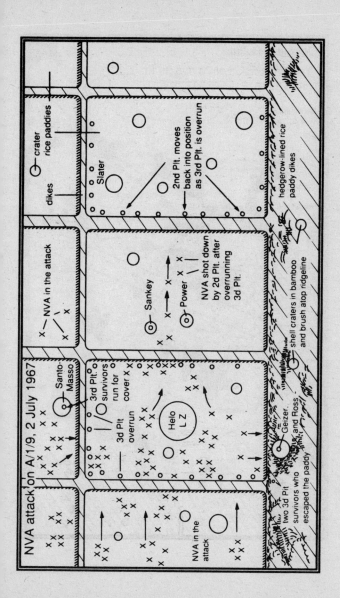

NVA attack on A/1/9, 2 July 1967

x — NVA in the attack

○ — crater
○ rice paddies
dikes

Santo-
Masso

NVA in the attack

3d Plt Plt
overrun

3rd Plt.
survivors
run for
cover

Helo
LZ

Geizer,
Krenz, and Ross

two 3d Plt
survivors who
escaped the paddy

Slater

2nd Plt. moves
back into position
as 3rd Plt. is overrun

Sankey

Power

NVA shot down
by 2d Plt. after
overrunning
3d Plt.

NVA in the attack

hedgerow-lined rice
paddy dikes

shell craters in bamboo
and brush atop ridgeline

Operation Buffalo
3 July 1967

0   1000   2000
meters
(all positions approximate)

Southern edge
of DMZ

Thon
Phoung Xuan

Huan
Hai

Route 561

Thon An
Nha

Gia Binh

B/1/9 MIAs

70 X

The Strip
or Trace

109 X

158

BLT 1/3 in
position
by 1945

3/9 and
A,C/1/9

Con
Thien
(1/9)

Thon
Nam Tan

Route 561

BLT 1/3 lands in LZ Hawk;
marches to Trace
up Route 561
(1025-1400)

Van Kim

Phu An

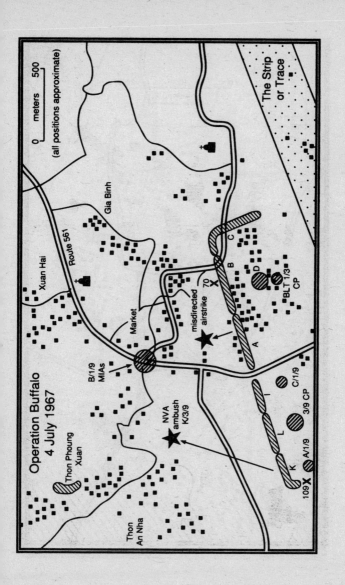

Operation Buffalo
4 July 1967

0   meters   500

(all positions approximate)

Thon Phoung
Xuan

Thon
An Nha

Xuan Hai

Route 561

Gia Binh

Market

B/1/9
MIAs

NVA
ambush
K/3/9

109 X

K

L

A/1/9

3/9 CP

C/1/9

misdirected
airstrike

70
X

A

B

C

D

BLT 1/3
CP

The Strip
or Trace

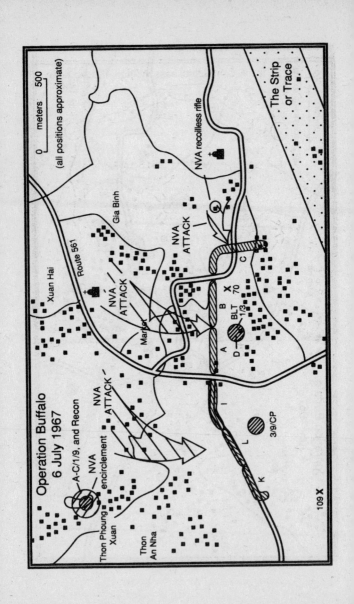

Operation Buffalo
6 July 1967

0 meters 500

(all positions approximate)

A-C/1/9, and Recon

NVA
encirclement

NVA
ATTACK

Thon Phoung
Xuan

Thon
An Nha

Xuan Hai

Route 561

Gia Binh

Market

NVA
ATTACK

NVA
ATTACK

NVA
ATTACK

NVA recoilless rifle

The Strip
or Trace

A
B
C
D
I
K
L

BLT
1/3

X
70

3/9/CP

109 X

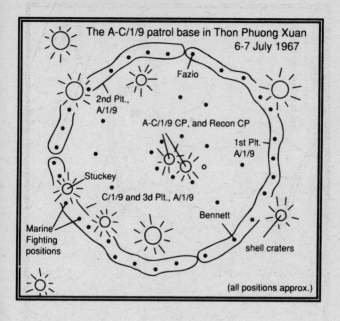

The A-C/1/9 patrol base in Thon Phuong Xuan
6-7 July 1967

Fazio

2nd Plt.,
A/1/9

A-C/1/9 CP, and Recon CP

1st Plt.
A/1/9

Stuckey

C/1/9 and 3d Plt., A/1/9

Bennett

Marine
Fighting
positions

shell craters

(all positions approx.)

PART ONE

THE Z

★

The 3d Marine Division (of Bougainville, Guam, and Iwo Jima fame) was headquartered on the island of Okinawa when its lead elements splashed ashore at Da Nang, Republic of Vietnam, on 8 March 1965. They were the first American infantry units committed to South Vietnam. By July 1965 the 3d Marine Division's three infantry regiments (the 3d, 4th, and 9th Marines) were in position in the middle and southern provinces of the I Corps Tactical Zone (South Vietnam was divided into four such corps), tangling primarily with the ubiquitous yet invisible guerrillas of the Viet Cong. As of 15 July 1966, however, their war would be with the regulars of the North Vietnamese Army. On this day, elements of the 3d Marine Division, with elements of the 1st Marine Division (the only other Marine division in Vietnam), launched Operation Hastings along the northern edge of I Corps at the narrow joint where North and South Vietnam were divided along the Demilitarized Zone. To avoid the long, debilitating march through Laos (along the Ho Chi Minh Trail), the 324B NVA Division had attempted a direct invasion across the DMZ. Operation Hastings smashed this attempt. The NVA maintained their efforts. In October 1966 the 3d Marine Division Command Post displaced from Da Nang north to Phu Bai, and a Forward Command Post was established at Dong Ha in the shadow of the DMZ (the 1st Marine Division, meanwhile, moved into Da Nang). Joined by the 26th Marines, 5th Marine Division, in April 1967, the 3d, 4th, and 9th Marines, 3d Marine Division, as of Operation Hastings, conducted a running series of campaigns along the DMZ and in northern I Corps against repeated NVA forays from the DMZ and Laos. These included Operations Prairie, Prairie II, Prairie III, Beacon Hill, Prairie IV, Beacon Star, Beau Charger, Hickory, Belt Tight, Cimmaron, and in the beginning of July 1967, Operation Buffalo.

1
Saddling Up

★

"Hello, girls, how's it going today?" S Sgt Leon R. (Lee) Burns, the 1st Platoon Commander of Bravo Company, 1st Battalion, 9th Marine Regiment, 3d Marine Division, III Marine Amphibious Force, directed his innocent-voiced (and Maine-accented) sarcasm toward their sister platoon, the 2d. At this time, the morning of Friday, 30 June 1967, the company was forming up at the southern gate of the battalion's hilltop strongpoint at Con Thien, Quang Tri Province, Republic of Vietnam.

Staff Sergeant Burns's harassment was good natured, competitive, and delivered with a grin, for he was, in fact, as close to the men of the 2d Platoon as he was to those of his own 1st Platoon. His initial assignment with Bravo Company had been as platoon sergeant to 2d Platoon. He had moved over and up to command the 1st Platoon only after their very sharp lieutenant had been mortally wounded northeast of Con Thien. That had been on a sweep as routine as the one they were to begin this morning. The routine was in the regularity of the maneuver—not that contact with the enemy hadn't been, and wasn't now, anticipated. Con Thien was, after all, less than seven thousand meters south of the Ben Hai River, which divided North and South Vietnam. There was nothing between this lonely, little outpost (*an ugly morsel of high ground,* the battalion exec called it) and the main-force regulars of the North Vietnamese Army but the waves of waist-high and head-high, razor-edged elephant grass that partially carpeted the area's rolling terrain. There were also brush lines and tree lines and the hedgerow-lined dikes of rice paddies, into which the NVA had spent years digging spiderholes, bunkers, and trenches, the construction so subtly a part of the natural contours of the terrain as to be almost invisible. The villagers, whose fields the Marines patrolled and the North Vietnamese ambushed, had been evacuated less than two months earlier, during Operation Hickory, so that, unhindered by innocent bystanders, Marine supporting arms could be more liberally employed against whatever section of the labyrinth the NVA had slipped across the Ben Hai to occupy. However, the Marines (who liked to refer to themselves as LBJ's Hired Killers) were constrained by presidential order from mounting their own operations across the Ben Hai to strike decisively at the heart of Hanoi's invasion.

This was thus the battalion's fourth stagnant month around vulnerable Con Thien, a circumstance not to be pondered by these outnumbered Marines. Staff Sergeant Burns instead made them laugh, calling out again to 2d Platoon, "What are you guys, Reservists out here for the afternoon?"

Bravo Company loved Staff Sergeant Burns. *Court-martial him one day and sober him up the next,* joked one of his company commanders—*and put him back in because he was a Marine's Marine.* He was the most respected member of the outfit, a short, stocky, overfed, cocky, mouthy, eleven-year veteran with a Winchester 12-gauge shotgun and a Colt .45 pistol in a shoulder holster. Even the bush did not trim his excess—though Burns sweated off a good fifteen pounds during each two-week patrol. *He may have looked like a sack of potatoes,* thought that captain, *but you'd bust your ass keeping up with him.* The company wouldn't be back at the rear long enough to brush their teeth (as another of his captains put it) before Burns would be the new owner of a gut-enhancing case of cold beer. The captain didn't know how Burns did it. Usually they considered themselves lucky just to collect their individual ration of two warm beers, the supply picture was that bad. Burns, however, was not actually performing magic. On his way to Vietnam in December 1966, he had been part of a staging battalion at Camp Pendleton, California, made up exclusively of staff NCOs, so that when they arrived in-country together and were assigned to different units, he had a tremendous number of contacts throughout the war zone. That made all the difference in getting what few extras were available. His Marines appreciated him for that, but more than that (commented these captains), they worshiped the ground Burns walked on, because he had a sense for trouble and he was, most important of all, fearless.

Staff Sergeant Burns's talents were not initially recognized. Before joining Bravo 1/9, he had been a platoon sergeant with Mike 3/3 on the Razorback, an isolated mountaintop outpost. There he served a second lieutenant who, like many mustangs (officers with prior enlisted service), did not feel he needed a right-hand man in the form of a platoon sergeant. This mustang, however, had spent much of his career in the military police, and as far as Burns was concerned, he didn't know his ass from a hole in the ground when it came to the infantry. After much head butting, the mustang requested Burns's transfer, and it was in April 1967 that he joined Bravo Company at the Khe Sanh Combat Base (where they had been detached from the rest of 1/9), the westernmost anchor of the division's line of strongpoints below the DMZ.

It was in the jungled mountains of Khe Sanh, where Bravo Company was the sole rifle company at the time, that the legends about Burns began. On the first night of his first patrol with his new company, he approached the overweight, inexperienced 2d Platoon commander, Lieutenant King, after he had passed the word to dig in for the night in the shadow of Hill 861. Said Staff Sergeant Burns, "Well, you can dig in, but I'm not staying here tonight."

"What do you mean?"

"You don't think anybody can see us out here?"

King looked around with a gesture that said *like where?* Burns continued, "There's somebody watching us. I know there is."

After dark, Burns approached King again. "Well, you ready to move?"

"Move where?"

"Lieutenant, I'm not staying here."

Burns was the new guy here, but he talked King into moving. They settled back down in the brush three hundred meters away, deciding not to reveal their clandestine exit by banging around and digging-in in the dark. They just sat quietly, and at midnight an NVA mortar barrage rained down on the spot they had just vacated.

Six days later, on 24 April 1967, King and Burns's platoon was ambushed on Hill 861, sparking a two-week meat grinder that became famous as the Khe Sanh Hill Fights. As the initial reinforcements were rushed in, Bravo Company had by day three been rendered combat ineffective with excessive casualties that included a wounded skipper. Surrounded and cut off, with their dead and wounded unevacuated (between the fog and the antiaircraft fire, helicopter medevac attempts were frustrated), Bravo finally accomplished a late-afternoon rendezvous with the rushed-in Kilo 3/9. They all then started back toward the newly assumed positions of 3/3 with their stiff, bloated, and decomposing KIAs in litters fashioned from bamboo poles and ponchos. It was an ugly, slipping, sliding march in the mud, fog, rain, and black of night, with the dead occasionally rolling down the brushy hillside. Each time, the column stopped and they were recovered. The Marine Corps never leaves its wounded. The Marine Corps never leaves its dead. The Marine Corps never leaves anything. Bravo Company reached 3/3 at dawn; then, after finally evacuating their casualties, they marched back to Khe Sanh.

From the lung-popping ridges of Khe Sanh (where Staff Sergeant Burns had been recommended for a Bronze Star), Bravo Company rejoined the rest of 1/9 in the brushy fields of Leatherneck Square, that quadrilateral defined by the Marine strongpoints at Con Thien, Gio Linh, Dong Ha, and Cam Lo. Leatherneck Square had also been the scene of action unprecedented for 1/9 in its intensity.[1] and following reunification, the cycle continued with Operation Hickory, another vicious slugfest that included the first Marine incursion across the southern DMZ up to the Ben Hai River. Hickory was followed by Cimmaron; and talk in 1/9 was that the battalion gave the 3d Marine Division its highest enemy body count but that they, in turn, took the highest casualties in the division.

War is Hell, but combat's a motherfucker. In fact, 1/9's operations were known for such obscene casualties and tragic twists of fate that they became famous throughout the division. *That's the word on them—they step into shit wherever they go. Everything they touch turns to shit.* That's why the grunts of 1/9 called the DMZ the Dead Marine Zone. That's why they called their battalion Walking Death and themselves the Walking Dead. *If something can go wrong, it will go wrong with them poor bastards. They're jinxed.*

"Okay, saddle up."

"Saddle up, saddle up . . ."

---

1. Having originally come incountry in June 1965, 1/9 experienced many frustrating days of booby traps, snipers, and ambush (VC style) around Da Nang. Late '66 and early '67 were spent on the special landing force (the highlight being an amphibious raid in the Mekong Delta called Operation Deckhouse IV), followed by a brief respite on Okinawa. During February 1967, 1/9 conducted Operations Chinook II and Bighorn near Phu Bai and along the Street Without Joy; then, on 1 March 1967, the move to Leatherneck Square commenced, and there was nose-to-nose battle (NVA style) during Operation Prairie III. It continued into May 1967 with Operation Prairie IV.

The sun was a scalding yellow on the horizon as Bravo 1/9 began moving off Con Thien that last morning in June. Their initial objective was a grid coordinate two thousand meters southeast into Leatherneck Square, and they had no way of knowing whether this patrol would make them feel like the victorious Bloody Bastards of Battlin' Bravo or, as they called themselves on the bad days, Fucked Over Bravo. FOB Company.

Only 150 figures hiked down the barren Con Thien hill, a full 50 short of the assigned strength of a Marine rifle company. The constant turnover of personnel because of casualties and end-of-tours had robbed them of this manpower, just as it had relentlessly drained them of experience. Staff Sergeant Burns, for example, was the only staff NCO in his platoon (which should have been run by a lieutenant anyway) and one of only two sergeants. His platoon sergeant was a young three-striper, not the experienced staff sergeant called for in the table of organizations; and likewise, his fireteam and squad leaders were privates first class, lance corporals, and corporals, instead of corporals and sergeants. FOB Company, undermanned and underexperienced, had many a replacement wounded or killed before his greenness had been weathered off. There was a superstition in Bravo Company that if you got new boots, you also got dead; so there were helmeted, flak-jacketed, sweat-slick, and pack-humping grunts in this downhill file whose jungle boots were frayed and flopping but who had refused replacements. They kept their old ones together with white tape from the corpsmen, which they then camouflaged by rubbing with dirt.

2

Indian Country

★

Because of wounds, deaths, reassignments, and the policy of keeping an officer in a combat command for no more than six months, company and platoon commanders went through 1/9 like sand through fingers. On 30 June 1967 Capt Sterling Kitchener Coates, a 1961 graduate of the Naval Academy, had served as the Commanding Officer, Bravo Company, 1st Battalion, 9th Marines, for a mere week. He had originally joined 1/9 as the S-3A (Assistant Operations Officer) at Con Thien, but less than two weeks into that job had volunteered to replace the outgoing skipper of Bravo Company (who had himself replaced the one wounded at Khe Sanh). Coates had joined them at Dong Ha, where two days of fried chicken and free beer had been their reward for thirty-eight straight days in the field. At age twenty-nine, Captain Coates (a family man) was an impressive, dedicated officer, confident without being overbearing, a man well respected and liked by his fellow officers.

Down at the cutting edge, where the grunts judged
their officers most harshly, Staff Sergeant Burns also liked
what he saw of their latest company commander. The man
was deliberate, precise, methodical—*level headed,* Burns
thought, and in Captain Coates he reckoned they had the
makings of an outstanding skipper. Bravo Company
needed nothing less at the time. Between the enemy, the
elements, and the endless patrols, these Marines also had
to contend with a company gunnery sergeant whose spe-
cialty (besides finding reasons to remain inside the wire
when patrols went out) was inane, petty, morale-busting
harassment. *A complete alcoholic and a fucking asshole* was
Burns's widely seconded opinion of this gunny whom they
called Chicken Bone for his scrawny, sunken chest, or the
Irish Pennant for his long, lean frame. Between his drinking and chain-smoking, the gunny looked like the grim
reaper in jungle utilities. Already antagonized at having to
police up and bury rocks at the gunny's pleasure, the
grunts' hatred of the Irish Pennant was capstoned when the
story got around that during a memorial service for their
dead at Khe Sanh, the gunny was overheard saying to the
officer beside him in formation, "Oh well, they're replace-
able."

There was much talk among the grunts in Bravo Company about how long the Irish Pennant would survive if he
ever went on patrol with them. The mood was such that the
letters home from PFC David J. Hendry (which had reflected timeless Marine esprit during Operation Hickory:
"Even tho this has been a real bitch, we are still cracking
jokes and messing around") sounded like this by the end of
Operation Cimmaron:

One of my buddies lost his leg the other day. He had
a minor cut & they sewed it up. The damn 1st Sarg.
won't let anyone rest so had him out filling sand bags.
The leg got infected & now he has ganagrene. . . . Last
nite the Lt. [King] told the squad leaders that today we
would re-build bunkers & put up barb wire. The squad
leaders asked why we couldn't rest while we could. The

Lt. said, "We can't give them any rest, no slack, we gotta keep pushin them." Yo, he's gonna get his ass shot too. . . . We are starting to do some dangerous things now because we are tired of being messed with. Last nite an ambush of 10 & two l.p.'s of 4 apiece went out. We all joined up instead of going to our designated points. We then had 18 men. So we fixed it so we would have nine changes of watch with two men up at a time. This no slack is making us really mad so this is how we retaliate.

Enter, then, the idealistic, intelligent Captain Coates. No model Marine, PFC Hendry nevertheless wrote home from Con Thien:

We've got a new Capt. & he really seems alright. He fixed it so that everyone could fire 1,000 rds yesterday to loosen up their rifles. Plus he got us beer yesterday and today. I really like my M-16 much more now. It only jammed once which was surprising by comparison. I was firing offhand at a 50 gal. barrel at 500 meters & hit it every time on semi & with about 3–4 rds. auto before the barrel would rise . . .

Humping to the southeast of Con Thien on the morning of 30 June 1967, Bravo Company's staggered column moved with Captain Coates's headquarters behind the lead platoon. Radio aerials marked their place in the line. There were the two PRC-25-equipped radiomen shadowing Coates (who was Bravo Six in radioese); plus the two with 1st Lt. William F. Delaney, the company executive officer (Bravo Five), and those with their forward air controller from the 1st Marine Aircraft Wing and their forward observer from the 12th Marines (Artillery). Last, but not least, with them was the company gunnery sergeant, one Staff Sergeant Ritchie in place of the Irish Pennant who (lucky him) happened to be on R&R.

The 1st Platoon, or Bravo One, was under SSgt Leon R. Burns, the shotgun-toting heart and soul of the company.

The 2d Platoon, or Bravo Two, was under 2d Lt Thomas G. King, who, after Khe Sanh, was turning into a good (albeit still chunky) platoon commander, as long as he had a good NCO guiding him. At least Burns thought so. The grunts (too weathered to sympathize with the intense pressure placed on a factory-fresh, boot brown-bar taking over a combat-wise platoon) disagreed. PFC Steve Weldon elaborated: "King was immature, inexperienced, and very aloof. He wasn't listening to anybody that had been incountry, and he liked volunteering his troops without going out with them. He had no common sense about how to survive, and he was killing people with his stupidity. Marines were not noted for fragging officers, but this guy (and it was an unspoken feeling) would have probably been shot by his troops eventually."

The 3d Platoon, or Bravo Three, was under SSgt Alfredo V. Reyes, who was brand-new to his rank and his command.

The Weapons Platoon, or Bravo Four, was under Sgt Richard Huff, a big, jolly guy who in reality commanded only two 60mm mortars and their crews since the heavy platoon's M60 machine-gun teams and LAW rocket men had already been divided among the three rifle platoons.

After humping two thousand meters (two kilometers) to the southeast of Con Thiên, Captain Coates established a patrol base with Staff Sergeant Reyes's platoon and Sergeant Huff's mortars, while Lieutenant King and Staff Sergeant Burns prepared to conduct independent, contact-seeking platoon patrols.[1] In Lieutenant King's case, he

---

1. HM3 Thomas Lindenmeyer (D/1/9) explained why they fought. "It was a bit of patriotism. It was a great deal of gung ho. It was some 'Payback is a motherfucker'. But mostly it was just that every man knew what he had to do, and every man knew that he had to do that thing for the group, and that if he didn't, everybody in the group was in jeopardy. And every man owed every other man in the group the loyalty of doing his job and doing it the best he could. And that crossed all lines. It crossed wealth, it crossed education, it crossed race. It bound all men together. If you didn't do your job, you weren't people—you weren't part of the unit."

called up his three sharp squad leaders—Sgt Kenneth R. Clopton, Cpl Robert L. Haines, and LCpl Harry J. Herbert —and after explaining that they would be continuing generally southeast on the trail they'd followed thus far, he told Herbert to put his squad on point. Herbert put the excellent point man, LCpl Frank T. Lopinto, up front, and with four flankers provided from Clopton's squad—two off the road on each side of Lopinto to form a five-man front —off they went. The four flankers set the pace, as they had to deal with the off-road obstacles of hedgerows thick with banana trees and dilapidated barbed-wire fences. Eight hundred meters down the fork they followed in the road, they came upon a square of four structures, pastel-painted, concrete buildings. A haystack beside the buildings was searched, as were the first two structures, revealing only battered furniture and cobwebs. The third house was three stories high with an upstairs balcony—a beautiful spot for an NVA forward observer—and sure enough, in the disarray of clay pots, work benches, and rolls of colored decorating paper on the ground floor, they found three hundred 9mm pistol rounds as well as a scattering of spent cartridges. Wrote PFC Hendry (one of the flankers provided by Clopton) in notes he compiled while recuperating from the wounds that ended his tour, the fourth building.

was the most beautiful Catholic church I have ever seen . . . blue and white and covered with statues of all the saints. Most of the benches on the inside were still upright. However the floor was covered with litter and most of the windows were broken out. Beautifully colored paper decorations hung everywhere in the church. This explained the rolls of paper in the building next door. The little workshop must have been used to make decorations . . . the alter . . . was still intact, tabernacle and all. We moved to the storage room behind the sanctuary where we found quite a few statues. Most of them were damaged, missing limbs, etc.

The platoon took a break near the church, then swung north to complete their counterclockwise sweep back to the captain's patrol base. Three hundred meters north of the church was the graveyard for the evacuated hamlets in the area. Lieutenant King passed the word to take a twenty-minute break, and PFC Hendry sat atop a burial mound. Helmet off, sweat dripping, and his rifle across his lap, he drew pensively on a cigarette; he noticed something new then on the package, namely, a warning that seemed wonderfully ironic, "cigarette smoking may be hazardous to your health."

The North Vietnamese Army had approximately 35,000 troops positioned above the DMZ. They were organized into four divisions (the 304th, 320th, 324B, and 325C), with one of them, 324B, most active in the Con Thien area. The primary mission of the 1st Battalion, 9th Marines, during the summer of 1967 was the defense of the Con Thien Combat Base. It was known to the Vietnamese as the Hill of Angels and to the Marines as the Bull's-eye (duty there was called Time in the Barrel), in deference to the fact that its sun-baked, bald knobs rose into view only six kilometers from the NVA artillery batteries above the DMZ. Con Thien was actually three hills, the highest only 158 meters high. It had originally been occupied by the U.S. Army Special Forces and their Nung mercenaries as an outpost to monitor NVA infiltration across the DMZ. The outpost had been converted into a strongpoint by the Marines early in 1967 as part of the obstacle system known as McNamara's Wall for its champion, Secretary of Defense Robert McNamara. The idea was to bulldoze a swath twenty-four kilometers long across the eastern DMZ (the western DMZ, where Khe Sanh was located, was jungled mountains and valleys), along which would be installed strongpoints, mine fields, sensors, etc., and across which the NVA would have to move in full exposure to the Marines' overwhelming firepower. The 3d Marine Division had resisted the concept. The strongpoints along the bulldozed swath would tie down an intolerable number of

units, and the NVA could always exercise the option of
infiltrating instead through Laos to the west. It was an elec-
tronic Maginot Line. But with reservations or not, during
May and June 1967, 1/9 had secured the bulldozers of the
11th Engineer Battalion, 3d Marine Division, for the completion of the first leg of McNamara's Wall; a swath 600
meters wide cut the ten kilometers from Gio Linh west to
Con Thien. It defined the terrain like an immense dirt runway and was known to the troops as the Trace, the Firebreak, or most commonly as the Strip or the Death Strip.
Maintaining the defense of Con Thien shackled 1/9 to a
static and targeted position, robbed them of one and, more
often, two of their four rifle companies to secure that position, and, in sum, put them in a defensive rather than an
attack posture. Considering that the Ben Hai River was
inviolate because of political considerations—at least south
to north by the allies, not north to south by the communists
—the initiative around Con Thien belonged not to the 1st
Battalion, 9th Marines, but to their old friends in the 324B
NVA Division.

Humping was their word for patrolling, and the Indian
Country around Con Thien in which 1/9 humped was
gently rolling flatland easing here and there into hillocks.
Terraced rice paddies were cut into the slopes, property
lines demarcated by dikes on which had been planted
hedgerows and bamboo thickets. Slit trenches further defined the dikes, having been dug by farmers to keep the
bamboo roots from growing into the fields themselves.
Both Marines and NVA used these agricultural trenches.
With all the civilians having previously been relocated, the
property lines had a new meaning; the hamlets were now
burnt and rubbled, and the fields pockmarked by shell craters from a succession of firefights and full-blown battles.
    What had been a dirt-road-connected community of
field and farm and market was now a mean, ugly place of
wilting heat ("I mean your water boils in your canteens,"
Cpl Charles E. Sullivan of C/1/9 wrote home, "and you can
blister your hand by grabbing your rifle barrel"). A place

where the Marines controlled only the ground on which
they stood and where NVA reconnaissance teams almost
always had them under observation. LCpl J. Larry Stuckey,
also of C/1/9, commented:

> Our company movements in the field were very rou-
> tine, noisy, and much too predictable. The NVA always
> had a pretty good idea of where we were and our
> strength on any particular day. They hit us a whole lot
> more than we hit them. My fireteam set up many am-
> bushes trying to hit the NVA. Not once did we ever am-
> bush an NVA unit.

About this time, the Marines' old reliable M14 rifle
had recently been replaced by the M16, which was lightweight and modern and liked to jam up when you needed it
most. Specifically, the brass cartridge tended to expand inside the chamber when fired so that the extractor would
tear off the cartridge's base but leave the spent cartridge
itself. The next round would then be double-fed into the
uncleared chamber. When this happened, and it happened
a lot, a Marine would have to push the magazine release,
pull the ammunition magazine out, and pull the charger
handle to the rear and lock it; then, produce his cleaning
rod, beat the mangled brass out of the chamber, slide the
magazine back in, allow the bolt to go forward, roll back
over, fire another round—then push the magazine release,
pull the ammunition magazine out. . . . The Marines
were not amused. When the defects of the M16 were pub-
licly exposed after their first major test, the Khe Sanh Hill
Fights, the powers that be refused to acknowledge the in-
trinsic flaws of the weapon. The official line was that any
problems with the M16 were the result of the troops' im-
properly maintaining and cleaning their pieces. Such explanations were meritless. Still, the grunts wished to believe
they exercised some control over their lives, so (noted
HM3 Lindenmeyer of D/1/9) whenever a rare three or four
toothbrushes arrived in a sundry pack

there was a spirited discussion amongst the Marines as to who was to get the toothbrushes. They used them to clean their rifle. They cleaned the chamber of their rifle three, four, or five times a day, and they cleaned all the ammunition at least once a day, in the superstitious hope that if everything was all nice and clean it might actually work. More than one Marine, however, died sitting there screwing together the ramrod for their M16 so as to pound a jammed cartridge out of the chamber. The M16 was indeed a piece of shit and everybody hated it.

There were other problems. When PFC Dade D. Henderson, a radioman with the 1st Platoon of Bravo 1/9, originally drew his equipment at the battalion rear in Dong Ha, the deuce gear he ended up with (belts, packs, canteen covers, etc.) was just shot, the oldest he'd ever seen—he didn't even have foot powder—and the plastic pouch containing his one and only sterilized battlefield dressing had already been opened. Worse, he was issued only seven magazines for his M16 and was told that if he put in the twenty rounds each magazine was designed to hold it would overfeed and jam. It was ridiculous, but he never could scrounge up any more magazines. The Marine riflemen along the DMZ were, in fact, so habitually short of things that replacements often ended up with the gear of the most recently killed or wounded. The motto back at supply seemed to be "You Can't Waste What You Don't Have."

The next bad sign for Henderson came on day four when he and three other replacements caught the morning convoy to Con Thien. The Irish Pennant turned them over to Staff Sergeant Burns, who divided the four new guys among his three squads, and Henderson was shrugged off as just another boot by his new comrades and told that he would be point man on the next day's patrol. They kept their word and Henderson found himself in the absolutely insane position of walking point on his very first jaunt into

Indian Country.[2] When they stopped to set up an ambush near the Strip, Henderson, a stocky, muscular, squared-away kid, set down the radio battery they had had him carry and laid out his grenades and magazines before him. Shortly, there was a rustle of bushes, and Henderson was stunned to see an NVA—a real live *gook*—coming into view, a perfect target except that the safety on Henderson's M16 would not budge. As he struggled with his uncooperative rifle, a short-timer lance corporal let out a panicked scream, *My God, there's thousands of 'em,* then simply got up and ran away. The rest of the ambushers played follow the leader as Henderson scooped up his grenades and magazines, grabbed the radio battery, and chased after them.

Another example of malfeasance, and then, an explanation. One evening at Con Thien, Cpl Harry Montgomery of the 3d Platoon of Bravo 1/9 was approached by a fellow squad leader, a corporal whom he liked. It was his turn to take out the night ambush, but he was reluctant. "Hey, Monty, you know, I really don't want to go out there to-night. I got a funny feeling. You know, could you stand some help standing perimeter?"

"Well, first we're gonna have to persuade the lieutenant and the captain not to send you out. I'll tell you what I'll do. I'll have one of my men with the infrared scope fire a couple tracer rounds out, and I'll have my line open up. Then, when the lieutenant comes over, I'll tell him we saw

---

2. HM3 Lindenmeyer (D/1/9) explained, "You never even learned a man's name until the man had stayed alive for a month. Nobody counted, nobody was part of reality unless they'd stayed alive that long. Then, if they had, they'd learned the tough lessons, and they'd proven themselves, and you could count on them to do their job. If they were just fucking new guys you didn't know what the hell they would do, because they didn't know what the hell to do, and you couldn't explain it to them. They just had to know. It was really tough when you were a fucking new guy, of course, and when I was new I thought that was the shits at the time, but I began doing it myself later. I wouldn't learn a Marine's name until he stayed alive long enough to be worth it."

some motion or activity along the perimeter. And I don't think he'll send you out then."

"Oh man, Monty, that'd be great!"

The hoax worked, and with two squads manning the holes instead of one, everyone was able to get twice as much sleep as normal. Fatigue motivated most of the misconduct. Such was the relentless pace of operations, and Capt Frank L. Southard, CO, H/2/9, noted:

> We were under the gun to do three patrols a day, and although you had been humping through the bush all day, two ambushes a night—they were asking for more than anybody could possibly deliver. When the troops get exhausted you really have to stay on top of them because they don't stay "tactical" during operations. They fall asleep on listening posts, they go out on night ambush but don't really go out on ambush—they go out a hundred yards and find some place to sleep. It was very, very draining, to the point that we had one man that was really lightly wounded—but he was so exhausted his body wasn't up to fighting off the shock, and he died in the helicopter being medevacked.

In addition, the supply system was such that the grunts basically wore rags. Because I Corps was the end of the supply line, and the tons of ammunition, food, fuel, and construction material for McNamara's Wall all had to be landed across a hundred-meter beach at Dong Ha, even socks were a luxury item at times, and the troops ate virtually nothing but C rations.

BrigGen Louis Metzger, Assistant Division Commander, 3d Marine Division, at Dong Ha, was well aware of these problems. Metzger had served as a battalion commander in the Marshalls and on Guam and Okinawa during WWII, as well as in Korea. But nothing he saw in those two wars matched the demands (in terms of terrain, climate, and days in combat) placed on the individual Marine rifleman in Vietnam:

Due to the overcommitment of the division, it was necessary to move battalions from their parent regiments in order to meet the changing tactical situation and the enemy actions. The result was that the teamwork that results from training and working together was disrupted. The troops were exhausted and pushed to the limit. If you are going to fight a protracted war of attrition, you have to have the resources to sustain your people in the field. We were not able to rotate units and provide them with proper rest during this period of time.

There were many frustrations to be found along the DMZ. Not only was the 3d Marine Division facing a superbly equipped foe (thanks to the Soviet freighters allowed to dock in Hanoi and Haiphong) but they were combating these regulars along a sparsely populated frontier that the Marine Corps would have preferred to have ignored for the time being. At this stage in the war, the Marines wanted to concentrate their efforts on the densely populated coastal regions where (before Operation Hastings had spurred them northward) they had been enjoying potentially lasting and meaningful successes in the pacification arena. Hanoi wanted the 3d Marine Division on the DMZ so that villages once secured by them could again be controlled by the VC, and so that by challenging the Marines in open battle (in circumstances favorable to the NVA) they could deliver casualties that would eventually demoralize the American homefront.

The 3d Marine Division was spread thin along the DMZ because Gen William C. Westmoreland, the theater commander, was impatient with the slow, but steady, progress of Marine pacification programs and because he believed that, given the political shackles with which they had to operate, victory lay in seeking open battle with the NVA/VC anywhere, anytime, and grinding them into bone dust with overwhelming U.S. firepower. This premise was flawed in that it overestimated the village security the ARVN could or would provide and underestimated the punishment the NVA could absorb. But even if one were to accept it, its practice provided the 3d Marine Division with one more frustration. General Westmoreland, faced with the demands of four corps areas, limited his forces in I Corps. Later, after the 1968 Tet Offensive—when the NVA/VC had been battered into temporary submission throughout much of South Vietnam—Westmoreland would deploy substantial elements of the 1st Air Cavalry, 5th Mechanized, and 101st Airborne Divisions (U.S. Army) to augment the 3d Marine Division's war in northern I Corps. The situation as it stood in the summer of '67, however, was further commented on by Brigadier General Metzger, "Obviously, the division was grossly overextended. There was no way we could control the territory that we were assigned. We did what we could with what we had."

From the graveyard where Lieutenant King's platoon from Bravo 1/9 had rested not far into their patrol of 30 June 1967, their sweep continued due west. Several hundred meters of humping brought them into a small hamlet where they found what was not supposed to be there, namely, three men, three women, and a boy of about five or six. Since freshly whittled punji sticks were also discovered, these people were taken with the platoon as Viet Cong suspects as the patrol route now turned to the south. En route, they approached another hootch, and when the flanker on that side, PFC Hendry, was within a dozen paces, someone suddenly appeared from behind a mud wall. On instinct, Hendry whipped his M16 to his shoulder, but he let the trigger go slack when he realized he'd trained his rifle on what was only a terrified boy of about thirteen years. With an apologetic look, Hendry moved on. The point team returned to the road that led back to the captain's patrol base. There, Lieutenant King halted them and called back Sergeant Clopton, who then went back up the column to retrieve Hendry and the other three flankers originally detached from Clopton's squad. The whole squad was to escort the prisoners back to Con Thien. Clopton put Hendry on point and told him to step it out because it was already late afternoon and there was no time to waste before darkness closed in. This he did, and additional time was saved because they were met five hundred meters from the perimeter wire by the battalion intelligence officer, who had come out with a small patrol.

As PFC Hendry would write in his notes, "He had several interpreters with him, and they immediately pounced on the prisoners with an onslaught of demanding questions. . . . The squad did an about-face and headed back."

Meanwhile, as Lieutenant King's platoon swung back toward the patrol base from the east and Staff Sergeant Burns's did likewise from the west, Captain Coates supervised the offloading of their helo-delivered evening resupply. The C rations were then divided up, three cases per squad, so that as the platoons humped back in each man could quickly pick up his three meals, stow the cans in his pack, and reshoulder his gear. Bravo Company moved on then to a final night position further southeast and dug in as various fireteam patrols reconnoitered the paddied surroundings. Like all their actions on this hot, wasted day, this reconnaissance was part of the routine, and other rituals were observed as Bravo Company battened down for the night. Captain Coates called together his platoon commanders (Burns, King, Reyes, and Huff) to discuss their resupply needs, the likeliest avenues of potential enemy approach, the placement of their machine guns to cover such approaches, etc., etc., and to pass along word that they had been designated the reaction force in the event of a ground probe or assault on Con Thien. Afterward, the platoon commanders returned to their portions of the company square, and Lieutenant King called up his squad leaders (Clopton, Haines, and Herbert) and told Herbert to make a fireteam available for their listening post while Clopton's squad had the ambush. The LPs went out 100–200 meters to monitor those likely avenues of approach and to give early warning by radio should any bad guys actually appear in the night. The ambushes deployed further from the perimeter and, with a full squad, their mission was to engage whatever NVA night travelers might pass by. One LP and one ambush per platoon. One awake and two or three asleep on the LPs, three awake and the rest asleep on the ambushes. Routine. Routine.

The only good thing about being stuck with the ambush, thought PFC Hendry of Clopton's squad, was that they didn't have to dig fighting holes on the perimeter like everyone else—although Weldon, Francis, and Waterson, also of the ambush squad, got so jumpy about mortars that they dug in for the two hours they had to wait between getting the word and actually leaving the perimeter. They stepped off at nightfall, going cross-country to the northwest back through the location of the daytime patrol base so as to reach the road they had taken out of Con Thien that morning. Their ambush was to be along that road, and Hendry, once again bringing up the rear as tail-end-charlie (which was almost as bad as walking point), was glad they were concealed by a no-moon night. But—*the noise of our gear hanging from us would tip off any goonie for a hundred meters or so.* Five hundred meters out they came to a tree line that ran on a ninety-degree angle from the road, and Sergeant Clopton, who was an excellent squad leader, set in one fireteam on each side of the tree line and his third to the rear. After a whispered discussion regarding the watch sequence, everyone but the three with first watch settled into as comfortable a sleeping position as one could. No one got any real rest, though. The artillery at Cam Lo, some distance to the southwest, began firing illumination rounds then—no one in the ambush knew why—which burst almost directly over their ambush position, turning the road and field a sickly, eerie white as the flares swayed toward earth on their parachutes. The sudden stadium glare completely exposed the Marines in the ambush. *Playing games,* thought Hendry, who knew they were in for a nervous night thanks to their own artillery. Sometimes it seemed that's all they were doing out here.

3

Caged Lions

★

LtCol Richard S. (Spike) Schening, the latest CO of the 1st Battalion, 9th Marines, 3d Marine Division, was the oldest battalion commander these men had ever seen. With a gray crewcut, he was short, skinny, and out of shape, as well as being gruff, crotchety, and hardnosed, a man who approached everything like a pugilist. Behind this, however, was a hard-eyed, stiff-upper-lipped stoic who, as a sergeant of Marines, had been wounded at Cape Gloucester and Peleliu. He had been wounded again as a mustang platoon commander in Korea. He would be wounded a fourth time, as a battalion commander in Vietnam, at about the same time that the troops (at least most of them) were coming to understand that this irascible old bird of a colonel was also an intelligent, creative, and brave combat leader.

Lieutenant Colonel Schening had assumed command on 22 June 1967, soon after 1/9 had relieved 1/4 at Con Thien; 1/4's Time in the Barrel had included a two-battal-

ion NVA ground assault on the thirteenth anniversary of
the fall of Dienbienphu (8 May 1967), which penetrated
the perimeter and disintegrated into hand-to-hand combat.
Forty-four Marines were killed before the outnumbered
Marines sealed the rupture and proceeded to kill or capture those NVA still inside, while artillery fléchette rounds
shredded those NVA moving away in retreat. The NVA
lost 197 killed (and 8 captured), their bodies hastily and
shallowly bulldozed into a mass grave in the perimeter
wire. Complete with decaying limbs protruding grotesquely
from the thin surface, these dead NVA extracted their re-
venge if the wind was right to blow their smell across Con
Thien. This grave (and the usual Marine garbage) also
brought to good old Con T the rats that had a penchant for
C rations, for pipe tobacco, and for biting sleeping Marines
in their bunkers.

Moving in, 1/9 occupied two of the three small hills
that made up Con Thien—the two that sat side by side,
east to west, with a low saddle between them—while the
third knob (directly south of the eastern of the two northern hills) was occupied by a detachment of Green Berets
and their Nungs. The Marines had so little faith in the
Nungs' loyalties and abilities that they erected a barbed-
wire barrier between their positions and their allies. More
coils of concertina ran all around the three hills, and a ring
two hundred meters wide had been cleared by bulldozing
around the perimeter. Through the employment of perimeter mines and phougas (napalm-filled oil drums fixed with
a detonating charge), as well as seismic devices and ground
radar that allowed grenade launchers, mortars, and artillery to be placed upon unseen but electronically detected
enemy night attackers, the NVA were kept out of Con
Thien during 1/9's tenure. Major Danielson remarked:

> The enemy made repeated attempts to penetrate
> the Con Thien perimeter during hours of darkness and
> were rebuffed in every case as a result of the outstanding
> defensive network plan which Colonel Schening had de-
> veloped. We will never know precisely how many enemy

casualties resulted since the enemy always carried away the bodies. There was enough blood on or near the outer wire, however, to indicate that the NVA suffered more than a few casualties.

Lieutenant Colonel Schening's Command Post (CP), on the western knob of 1/9's two-hill front, utilized the good, solid timber-and-sandbag underground bunker originally built by the Green Berets they had displaced. While Major Danielson (XO) maintained the battalion rear in Dong Ha, Schening had with him at Con Thien 1st Lt Gatlin J. Howell (S-2 Intelligence Officer), Capt James H. R. Curd (S-3 Operations Officer), and 1st Lt Wallace Dixon (CO, Headquarters & Service Company), whose ammunition and supplies were stored adjacent to the CP in the only other timbered, underground bunker on the hill. On the line, Schening had (as of 30 June 1967) four career-minded officers serving as his rifle company commanders:

Capt Albert C. Slater, Jr., had Alpha Company; Capt Sterling K. Coates had Bravo Company; Capt Edward L. Hutchinson had Charlie Company; Capt Richard J. Sasek had Delta Company.

Con Thien's two-hill front required only two rifle companies. The other two could not be, as Major Danielson put it, "profitably and safely employed inside the defensive perimeter without creating targets of opportunity for the constant enemy rocket, artillery, and mortar fire"; so on a rotating basis, two companies "were employed outside the perimeter in company strongholds from which patrols and sweeps were conducted."

Day to day, the riflemen of 1/9 preferred duty outside Con Thien to life in a slit trench on a bald hillside that the NVA artillery batteries had had years to zero in on from their emplacements above the Ben Hai River. The Soviets and Red Chinese had delivered to the NVA an arsenal of 85mm, 100mm, 122mm, 130mm, and 152mm artillery pieces, as well as 122mm Katyusha rockets, that the NVA gunners used most profitably. For example, a correspondent described one ingenious technique employed by the

NVA heavy-mortar crews which involved burrowing a narrow shaft into the slope of a ridge facing a Marine position. "Chambers were hollowed out at the bottom of the shaft for the mortar and its crew so that weapon and men would have the whole of the earth above as protection. The fired mortar round flew up and out the camouflaged opening of the shaft. A variation of the technique was often used for the howitzers."

The NVA fired their guns at irregular intervals, often in the late afternoon when their muzzle flashes were most difficult to spot, and they pulled their camouflage back over each emplacement after each shot. They built far more artillery emplacements than they had artillery pieces, and they moved their guns every day. They constructed phony artillery positions to be detected by their foe's aerial photography. They detonated harmless explosive charges to simulate muzzle flashes to confuse Marine observers as to where to direct their counterbattery fire. They installed a gauntlet of 12.7mm, 37mm, and 57mm antiaircraft guns, augmented by Soviet-built surface-to-air missiles (SAMs) to protect their artillery against air attack. The situation was completely intolerable. Denied the obvious infantry solution by the politics of the DMZ, the Marines could respond only with their own artillery. Regarding the results of their bombardments of phony enemy positions, empty enemy positions, and real enemy positions nestled under tons of rock and earth, Brigadier General Metzger commented:

> You throw it in the breech of a gun, pull the lanyard, and it blows up and plows the earth and you haven't hurt anyone . . . it was just unproductive. . . . The enemy can stand any number of misses. . . . We were taking a pretty good licking . . . they had us pinpointed and everything pinpointed. . . . I mean they were killing Marines and we couldn't locate them. . . . Eighteen and nineteen year old kids were getting killed because we couldn't locate this artillery. Our ammunition dumps, our helicopters were driven out; our fuel was burning,

and we had to sit and take it because the enemy can stand any number of misses.

The Marines of 1/9 were hacking it. One of the games at Con Thien was to sit at the edge of your slit trench and see who had the balls to fall backward into it last as the artillery roared in; but beneath the brave surface of spitting in death's face, there were deep morale problems, and many a morning Lieutenant Colonel Schening and his sergeant major would move around the perimeter to talk with and cheer up the young Marines. One day, with the same purpose in mind, Gen William Childs Westmoreland, COMUSMACV, helicoptered into lonely, little Con Thien. Major Danielson escorted Westmoreland around the perimeter. When a Marine pointedly asked, "General, I lost my best buddy to incoming yesterday—why can't we go into the DMZ after those bastards?" Danielson said, "The general's response was, 'Son, I wish we could, but the politics of the situation are such that we can't violate the DMZ.' Can you imagine how frustrating that response was to a young, dirty, unshaven, bleary-eyed, thirsty Marine?"

4

Across the Death Strip

★

In the 1/9 CP bunker at Con Thien during the evening command conference of 30 June 1967: As Lieutenant Colonel Schening noted, when Bravo Company (Captain Coates) had swept southeast of Con Thien that morning it had left Delta Company (Captain Sasek) the sole guardian of the Hill of Angels. Delta Company had marched back to Con Thien after a ten-day patrol north of the Gio Linh-Con Thien Strip. Charlie Company (Captain Hutchinson), which had operated in tandem with Delta Company above the Strip, was still in position but was due (the next morning) for a helo-lift to the battalion rear in Dong Ha for a three-day stand-down. Alpha Company (Captain Slater) had departed Dong Ha that morning after an abbreviated stand-down of their own and had assumed positions west of Con Thien.

Come 1 July 1967, Lieutenant Colonel Schening continued, Bravo Company was to continue patrolling southeast of Con Thien until approximately noontime, when they were to sweep north on Route 561, a sunken cart trail that ran all the way from Route 9 to the Ben Hai River. They were to establish a patrol base north of the Strip. They were to be joined in the vicinity by Alpha Company, which was to sweep north in the morning so as to place themselves a kilometer west of Bravo Company's patrol base. Alpha and Bravo 1/9 were then expected to spend ten to fourteen days crisscrossing the three kilometers between the Strip and the invisible southern boundary of the DMZ, just as their sister companies had recently done. Such patrol activity was designed to detect the first movements of the latest NVA push and guide the placement of the 3d Marine Division's limited manpower. Although the Marines had come to the DMZ unwillingly, and though once pushed there they would have preferred a mobile defense of the region as opposed to the stronghold-and-barrier approach, the strategy that locked them into place at Con Thien also demanded that they hold Con Thien at all costs. The concrete had been poured, so to speak, and a regimental commander explained:

> Con Thien was clearly visible from the 9th Marines headquarters on the high ground at Dong Ha ten miles away. . . . Although Con Thien was only 160 meters high, its tenants had dominant observation over the entire area. Visitors to Con Thien could look back at the vast logistics complex of Dong Ha and know instantly why the Marines had to hold the hill. If the enemy occupied it he would be looking down our throats.

Given this assignment, Captain Slater of Alpha Company discussed the area with Captain Sasek of Delta Company. Slater was the most aggressive company commander in the battalion, but Sasek (the most experienced) cautioned him that Delta's last sweep above the Strip had resulted in a running series of contacts. Perhaps what Delta had encountered was the advance or reconnaissance party for another NVA assault on Con Thien, and Major Danielson remarked on the remainder of the staff meeting:

There was a discussion concerning the use of platoon versus company patrol bases. As I recall, Captain Slater wanted to cover more ground through the use of platoon patrol bases. Captain Sasek thought the risk of separation was too great, especially when operating north of the Trace. The decision reached by Colonel Schening was that platoon patrol bases were okay south of the Trace but not north of the Trace.

Since 1/9 did not have the numbers needed to sweep and resweep the same areas around Con Thien continuously, the NVA—who stood their ground to fight only when they had numerical superiority or a terrain advantage —would reappear as soon as a sweep ended, secure in the knowledge that this particular area would lie fallow the few days they needed to lay in supplies or prepare an ambush before the Marines would reappear. To counter this, Alpha and Bravo Companies were being sent above the Strip hard on the heels of Charlie and Delta Companies' withdrawal to surprise an enemy accustomed to Marine routines.

On the evening of 30 June 1967, as Captain Slater prepared for their sunrise sweep, he was well aware that the measure many of the troops had made of him was negative. It did not surprise him. Although he was, in reality, an intelligent, idealistic, soft-spoken man of twenty-seven, he was also a hard-charging taskmaster. He was a tall, blond, hard-jawed ox of a man who had been terribly disappointed when, upon assignment to Vietnam, his secondary MOS as an AO had waylaid him into a Bird Dog for five months. Then assigned as aide-de-camp to the CG, 3d Marine Division, he had chafed in the rear with the gear for another four months before going directly to the general to explain that he was getting no infantry experience. The general appreciated his élan ("Pick any company you want. I suggest you go for a company that's up to its armpits all the time so you can get that experience"); and the mask that Slater then wore for the troops of his new command reflected his determination that in Alpha 1/9 he had inherited (and intended to square away) a mediocre example of what a Marine Corps rifle company was supposed to be about.

Leadership was one of the problems. Slater was supposed to have five lieutenants, but in fact he had only two; and his best one, 1st Lt Al Fagan (2d Platoon Commander), had left for R&R just as the company had been saddling up to depart Dong Ha. Fagan had said to him (out of bravado, and in an attempt to get closer to this introverted skipper), "You know, Captain, my girlfriend is a stewardess from Pan American so she's in Hawaii all the time. I can put this off for a couple weeks if we're going on a big operation."

"Nah, you go ahead and go."

"I hate to miss all the fun."

Fagan had also hated to leave Slater with Johnson, his platoon sergeant, and Jones, his right guide, honchoing the 2d Platoon in his absence. Both were buck sergeants on their first enlistments, and both were combatworn—*as long as I was there to kick 'em in the ass, they were okay but left on their own I would have little confidence in them. These guys had had enough.*

Between Fagan's departure and the company's movement, a new man, S Sgt Michael S. Richardson, had arrived to take over 2d Platoon.[1] Slater's only other lieutenant, 2d Lt Stephen P. Muller (3d Platoon Commander), was not only the product of an abbreviated Basic School—such were the manpower needs of Vietnam—but he had only a month or so in the bush. Muller was a good man and a helluva nice guy, but he knew nothing of the Marine Corps except the pine trees of Quantico, Virginia. His first command was this one. Luckily for Slater, at least his 1st Platoon was in able hands, namely, those of SSgt H. C. Leslie, a big man and a great, unflappable leader.

Captain Slater's three months with Alpha Company

1. No one knew Richardson, so for this reason and because he didn't pass muster during Operation Buffalo, a pseudonym is used.

(he had two weeks remaining on his tour) had prepared him to expect the worst. He had joined Alpha A Go-Go, as the company called itself, aboard a resupply helo into Leatherneck Square to replace a captain who'd been concussed by a NVA mortar round. The captain had been injured during a 24 March 1967 assault on Phu An (a hamlet south of Con Thien where 1/9 went nose to nose with the NVA on a regular basis); and Slater arrived as Fagan, the only lieutenant left of the four who had started the assault, was in the process of medevacking the last of their wounded. The company had fought bravely at Phu An,[2] but they had been decimated; and as Slater, just off the bird, expressed his unhappiness with the ragged positions they had hastily assumed, Fagan thought bitterly that *the army wouldn't even let a company like this stay in the field.*

The introductions got worse. Captain Slater, understanding none of what had come before, knew only that he was finally where he wanted to be. He immediately made the mistake (as he later recognized it) of bringing his tatterdemalion company together and proclaiming, "Okay, now we're going to go back out on patrol—*and let's make contact!*"

The grunts stared back at him. "No, we really don't want to make contact."

"This is what we're here for."

"Well, it doesn't do any good. You make contact, people die."

"Well, what the hell are we here for?!"

"You'll find out, but listen to us. . . ."

Slater thus picked up the nickname Captain Contact, and he quickly came to understand that as far as the grunts

2. And one of Alpha's own, Sgt Walter K. Singleton, won the Congressional Medal of Honor when he "made numerous trips through the enemy killing zone to move the injured men out of the danger area. Noting that a large part of the enemy fire was coming from a hedgerow, he seized a machine gun and assaulted . . . through the hedgerow directly into the enemy strongpoint. Although he was mortally wounded, his fearless attack killed eight of the enemy and drove the remainder from the hedgerow."

of Alpha Company were concerned, officers and staff NCOs were good only for getting you killed. The men were possessed of a salty, weary, don't-tread-on-me attitude. There was little talk of mission (no one could see the point of these nickel-and-dime contacts), certainly none of victory, and their single goal was to survive their tours. They hated anyone who did not see the wisdom of taking the path of least resistance. It was an attitude that ultimately could get its followers killed, and it horrified, angered, frustrated, and disappointed Slater:

> The company had been out of training for so long, and had such a terrible turnover of personnel for so long, and they were so tired for such long periods of time, they just picked up these horrible habits. They threw everything out as far as the book is concerned. They took shortcuts. We couldn't get them to do the fundamental things of fire and maneuver, reaction as soon as you got hit, etc. Lots of times I discovered they weren't going out on LPs—they would go out maybe a couple of feet and sleep. It totally floored me. I just could not believe what was happening, and I was looking all around me, saying I know in my heart this is all screwed up. It wasn't like the Marine Corps.

There were Marines in Alpha Company who agreed, including Sgt Harvey N. Geizer. Geizer thought part of the problem was overconfidence. Individual NVA camouflage, for example, stood in masterful and stark contrast to the lackadaisical approach taken by many Marines. Geizer was disappointed—"since camouflaging is taught and stressed in fundamental Marine Corps training. This very important combat principle, like some others, seems to have been neglected as a result of the tragic belief that sloppiness was tolerable because, after all, we had far superior air, naval, and artillery firepower for protection."

Captain Slater came on hard discipline-wise (though it did seem futile, for example, to be upbraiding an LP-sleeper upon return to Con Thien only to have the office hours interrupted by incoming artillery); but it was not until 13 May 1967, during Operation Hickory, that he had a chance to prove that he was not all talk combat-wise. When Alpha Company swept into Phu An again and was cut to ribbons (again) in a murderously efficient U-shaped ambush, Slater became (as Sergeant Geizer put it) *all leader—he lived up to everything a Marine captain is supposed to be.* When a certain NVA bobbed up from a spiderhole to fire his AK47, Slater personally talked a tank forward over the hole, which confused the NVA and allowed Slater to run out and kill the man with a head shot from his .45 pistol. When he was shot in the arm, he refused evacuation until the end of the two-day engagement. Then he was in Dong Ha for only a few days before he shunned a medevac out of Vietnam and rejoined Alpha complete with metal stitches holding his injured muscles together. He had a corpsman paint the area every day with antibiotics to prevent infection.

For some, Phu An was where Captain Contact became Captain Slaughter (and an unimpressed Gunny Santomasso remained stubborn, tight-mouthed, and frustrating to Slater); but Lieutenant Fagan (one of their walking wounded) came to understand, as did most of the grunts, that though he did not like Slater, the man was an excellent, dynamic officer. *He had brass balls.* And yet . . . and yet Fagan could not forget the moment when with one platoon lieutenant already dead, and Fagan's own platoon reduced to eight effectives, Slater had insisted on another assault into the machine guns to recover two dead Marines. A staff sergeant had given his wedding ring to another NCO as they coordinated with their tank support; he had known what was coming and he had indeed been killed following Slater out into the killing zone. As Fagan commented:

> For Slater to do that was an act of great courage for himself, but to lose the lives of five, six, seven, eight—even one guy—to retrieve those bodies (we were going to get them the next day anyway) was an absolutely stu-

pid thing to do. That kind of stuff he would do, and he scared the shit out of the guys.

Likewise, after the Second Battle of Phu An, Captain Slater's opinion of Alpha Company began to change:

Before Phu An, I thought I was indestructible. I wanted experience, I wanted contact, I wanted to kill enemy. When I first came under artillery fire I would stand up and belittle the people around me—"Ah, those are just a bunch of stray rounds, you don't have to worry about that kind of stuff"—I was trying to act like a hero. Then, at Phu An, it hit me. I had gone out with the forward elements, with the tanks that were firing, and then all of a sudden it hit me: I was out there all by myself and it just scared the hell out of me. And, after that, I had much more of an appreciation for the grunts' emotions and what they were going through. It was like you go out and make contact, and you don't hold any ground, so you don't gain anything by it. You trade rounds, take casualties, hopefully make a lot of kills, and everybody goes back their different directions to meet another day. Kind of worthless. I guess I understood that the grunts were a kind of victim of circumstances, a victim of the system as it was out there.

Slater revealed none of these inner reservations, for they did not alter the reality of Alpha Company's situation, which was that they were a Marine rifle company at war. They had a job to do, and to do it—and to survive—they had to be aggressive and adhere to the fundamentals. This Slater stressed again to his company leaders on the evening of 30 June 1967, and the measure he took of Alpha A Go-Go then as they prepared for his sixth operation with them was that "they were clean, they weren't into drugs in the field. The brothers were into knocking knuckles, but Alpha had spent so much time in the styx that everyone was dependent on each other. They respected each other, and especially respected the ones that were good, but they

wanted to finish their thirteen months and get out of there
alive, and that's what they talked about. I was still working
on reorienting their thinking and discipline when Operation Buffalo began."

The night of 30 June–1 July 1967 had been one of
anxious, quasi-sleep for Sergeant Clopton's squad from the
2d Platoon of Bravo 1/9, as they supposedly waited in ambush while artillery illumination (fired from Cam Lo in
support of someone else's war) revealed them to any interested passersby. At first light, 0530 on Saturday, 1 July
1967, Sergeant Clopton and crew started the thirty-minute
hike back to Bravo Company—as did all the unsprung ambushes and listening posts—and, upon arrival, there was
time for breakfast in cans and gun oil and cleaning rods
before saddling up for the day's hump.

At that time, 0830, PFC Hendry said his good-byes to
Clopton's squad and, as ordered, walked over, pack on
back and rifle in hand, to join the even more undermanned
squad of Corporal Haines. Clopton's squad had the point
this morning, but Haines told Hendry that he and three
others from Haines's squad—Cpl Arthur E. Demers, Cpl
Delma L. Reed, and LCpl Jeffrey S. Hatison—were going
to accompany the point man, LCpl Claude C. Francis, as
flankers. Francis walked the trail with Reed and Hatison on
his right flank and Hendry and Demers on his left. Their
sweep took them back east past a schoolhouse they had
noticed the day before; this time Hendry could see numerous pockmarks in the red-and-yellow building, as well as
obscenity-peppered graffiti in both English and Vietnamese on the walls. They also passed the four cement buildings they had searched earlier, as Hendry sweated and
cursed his way through the same barbed-wire fences and
bamboo thickets that had hindered the flankers the previous day. This time as they paused to re-search the buildings, Hendry took a few Instamatic shots as proof that
there really were concrete structures this close to the
DMZ. Instead of turning north as they had at this point in
the patrol twenty-four hours earlier, on this day the patrol

route continued east. Several hundred meters beyond where their east-west road intersected north-south Route 561, they came upon another empty Catholic church and a catty-cornered schoolhouse, which PFC Hendry described in his post-tour notes:

> Demers and I checked out the church and it was in a hurt, 106 M.M. shell casings lay about the entrance. . . . The church was a real mess. Most of the pews were over-turned, C-ration cans lay everywhere and a field dressing caked with blood lay in the aisle. A half eaten fruit cake lay on the floor along with myriad pieces of stained glass from the once beautiful windows. Demers and I walked back into the sunlight. I noticed a chair overturned under a tree down by the road. I walked down to the chair and righted it. It felt good to sit in a chair with my pack supported by the back of the chair. Naturally as soon as I got comfortable we were given the word to saddle up and get ready to move.

Bravo Company continued east on the road, until Hendry and Demers on the left flank could no longer see point man Francis because of the high, thick hedgerows. They had to shout back and forth to make sure they were keeping abreast of Francis, until Francis called to them that word had been passed to take a thirty-minute break. The Marines were too wasted by the sun to be tactical. Hendry and Demers simply lay in the weak shade of a small tree. Hendry took a few swallows of warm canteen water and lit up a C-ration Winston as they compared photographs of family and friends. Flies and gnats irritated the large blisters-of-unknown-origin on Hendry's arms, so he produced a plastic bottle of insect repellent from his pack and spread on the oily, model-glue-smelling bug juice. It tingled through his scabs (which he hoped would get bad enough to get him out of the field for a while) and drove off the bugs for a few moments, until it was washed away with the sweat dripping from him.

"Flankers up!" Hendry and Demers reburdened themselves under their packs and gear and passed through a farmer-made opening in one of the hedges to reach the road, where they fell in with Reed and Hatison to walk past the column of men crapped out on either side of the road and reach Francis on point. There, Lieutenant King told them to turn around and walk back to the rear of the column, because they were reversing directions and the tail was now the head. The company was spread out down the road all the way back to the church and schoolhouse, so down to there they trudged; and then they turned north on Route 561 with Reed and Hatison on the left flank, Francis on point, and Hendry and Demers on the right. The flankers stumbled through increasingly thick vegetation, eventually passing through a small clearing where Hendry noticed a U.S. hand grenade in the dirt. Forgetting about the possibility of booby traps, he picked it up and added it to the five already packed into his grenade pouch.

Not far beyond this clearing, Captain Coates called a halt and sent Staff Sergeant Burns's 1st Platoon back on patrol the way they'd just come, while deploying Lieutenant King's 2d Platoon and Staff Sergeant Reyes's 3d Platoon in a three-sixty around his CP. Coates further directed King and Reyes to dispatch observation posts; and Hendry, Demers, Hatison, and Reed ended up in the OP sent due east to a tree line 200 meters beyond their perimeter. Once in the tree line (after crossing a field littered with expended M16 and M60 cartridges), they set up along a ribbon-thin trail and immediately checked the area out. Demers discovered an NVA bunker, but the entrance was laced with cobwebs that indicated its inactive status, so instead of being worried, they were relieved to have the handy shelter in case of a surprise mortar attack.

At that point, back on the trail, their OP became one in name only as Reed and Hatison sat back—packs, flak jackets, helmets, and web gear removed in the heat—to write letters, while Hendry and Demers wolfed down a C-ration lunch, then redonned their gear to hunt up a water hole they had spotted during the hump north. Hendry wasn't too hot on just the two of them moving over 400 meters away from everyone else, and they had no idea when the company would be moving again—but what the hell, a cool drink would hit the spot. The water hole was actually a shady natural spring around which a meter-high cement wall had been built on three sides. Not bothering with purification tablets, Hendry drank without stopping until his first refilled canteen was empty, then he drained another canteenful of spring water flavored with some children's drink mix that Demers had. Next, they stripped off their gear and cleaned up with their around-the-neck sweat towels, and in the process Hendry overturned a rock in the spring to reveal a four-inch-long leech. Commenting unconcernedly that they had probably gulped down a few baby leeches, Hendry and Demers got their gear back together. Demers insisted that he knew a shortcut and Hendry reluctantly tagged along, thinking angrily that they should go back the way they'd come since they knew that route was free of booby traps. The route Demers chose was blinded by vegetation, and it was with great relief that they finally made it back to Reed and Hatison on the trail.

Shortly thereafter, Corporal Haines, their squad leader, came walking across the field to retrieve them. The company was moving north across the Strip. As Haines explained it, a spotter plane had reported a company-sized NVA movement and Bravo Company was to attempt to intercept them; but as Hendry wrote, "The news of there being large numbers of N.V.A. near didn't bother us much but all the walking in the heat of the day made us groan. We had reports like this many times and most of the time they were false alarms."

A note about the NVA: the Marines hated, feared, and respected them in roughly equal parts. Like the Japanese the Marines had faced in the Pacific, the NVA were expert at the basic warrior skills of cover and concealment, and fire and maneuver, and they enjoyed a reputation for bravery, aggressiveness, ingenuity, and discipline. The NVA also conducted themselves with a take-no-prisoners savagery, and stories did circulate in the 3d Marine Division of dead Marines being recovered who had been castrated and whose USMC tattoos had been flayed off. The Marines on the DMZ responded much as their forebears had on places like Peleliu and Okinawa, where the paucity of Japanese prisoners belied the battlefield reality of scared men willing to surrender and grievously wounded men unable to commit hara-kiri. A rifleman from D/1/9 explained, "I probably hated them as a way to fight my fear. You'd get real scared, then you'd get real angry, and you couldn't wait to get your hands on one of those slimy bastards. We didn't take prisoners. Anybody that came to us was just a sorry fucker."

Early in Captain Slater's tenure with Alpha Company, one of their battalion sweeps finally came up with a prisoner, who was then loaded aboard a helicopter. Lift-off, then someone hit Slater quick-like and pointed—a figure was plummeting from the helicopter at a high altitude. Slater then monitored battalion's horrified call to the aircraft commander, who responded, "That wasn't us. That was that injured Marine that you put in, the walking wounded, with the prisoner. The crew chief couldn't stop him—he just went crazy."

In April, Alpha Company policed up a slightly wounded NVA while coming in to assist Charlie Company, which had been partially overrun along the Street Without Joy. Slater assigned two Marines to escort the prisoner to the CP, but battalion radioed that the man never reached them. Slater questioned the two escorts, who said they had handed the NVA over to some Charlie Company survivors. Needless to say, the prisoner's body turned up beside the road with a bayonet rammed into him. An appalled Slater harped at his platoon commanders, "Somebody has got to control these Marines. It's all right to hate and fight, but you gotta draw the line."

Their hatred came to encompass all things Vietnamese ("Rest assured," remarked Captain Southard of H/2/9, "many a Marine died due to the efforts of some 'innocent kid' or 'harmless old woman' "), including their ARVN allies. At one time, there was an ARVN detachment at Con

Thien adjacent to the trenches occupied at the moment by Alpha Company. Each day a certain NVA howitzer would occasionally fire a single round toward the hill. Its long, whistling approach gave everyone time to seek cover, but knowing their chances of getting hit by this single round were slim, the ARVN would indulge in cheap bravado by remaining above-ground to laugh at the ducking Marines. One day, one of the howitzer rounds landed amid the sauntering ARVN. It killed almost a dozen, and Slater couldn't stop his Marines from cheering the scene. The ARVN were lazy, scared, and inefficient, thought Captain Slater (and he knew it devastated his Marines to see whom they were fighting for), while "the NVA were people we had the greatest amount of respect for, even though we hated them. Right in the thick of it, you could see that there was something wrong."

On 1 July 1967, as Alpha 1/9 humped north from their overnight positions west of Con Thien, Captain Slater could sense the general uneasiness in their extra-cautious column. There was an electricity, an uncanny feeling that contact was imminent, and Slater kept them moving at a good clip toward a stopping point that he knew was defendable and offered cover and concealment. Despite the heat (it was like opening a stove on a sweltering summer day back home), Alpha Company handled the pace.

Except for one man. He was their newest replacement, a black sergeant named Jefferson,[3] who was a cherry in the 'Nam but a lifer in the Corps with enough time in to give him a round gut that bulged over his belt from his unzipped flak jacket. Unacclimatized, he stumbled along, his steel pot of a helmet boiling his brain and his pack and flak gear reducing him to a bent-kneed packmule. Marines kept passing him, none feeling the strength or desire to help: "Fat motherfucker."

"New guy."

"Piss on 'im. Let him keep up."

3. Not his real name.

Meanwhile, farther up the column, Cpl Ronald G. Power's attached S-2 scout team, consisting of L Cpl Terry L. Quigley and Staff Sergeant Xuan (their NVA-turned-Kit-Carson-scout), were also feeling the effects of the stunning heat. They were humping heavy loads *(this was the big woods,* Power thought, *you didn't go unless you had a lot of bullets, a lot of rocks to throw),* but Power was too primed to be anything but a paranoid, head-turning, brush-scanning machine. He too could feel it, and he finally dropped back to walk beside Sergeant Geizer, their attached FO from the 12th Marines and a man whom Power greatly admired. Power and Geizer had come incountry aboard the same troopship, both had sixteen months in the bush, and both had been wounded twice; so now, Power said to Geizer, "I bet them motherfuckers are following us along. Let's drop back here a little bit, see if anything's going on back here."

Geizer did not like Power (he was too loud and wild), but he trusted Power's bush sense; so Power, Geizer, and the artillery radioman, PFC John Ross, started drifting to the tail of the column, slowing down to let people pass. When they got back to the rear elements, there was this guy they really didn't know—it was Sergeant Jefferson—lying semiconscious to one side of the trail being made by the company's passage in the brush (which was pretty bad but, fortunately, not quite machete-thick). Jefferson had already lost touch with his own squad, and none of the anonymous grunts passing him now gave a shit; so Power, Geizer, and Ross stopped with Jefferson as the column simply kept on moving. Finally, when the last man passed them, Geizer turned to Ross. "Run up the column. Catch up with the captain and you tell him if he wants artillery, he best stop because we're staying here with this guy. We're not leaving him, and if he wants his artillery support he damn well better stop."

Ross disappeared into the bushes, and it became deathly quiet as Geizer, kneeling with Power beside the unconscious Jefferson, suddenly felt totally alone in the middle of nowhere. No, not alone. They could both feel a hundred eyes on them, and Geizer had that back-of-the-neck sensation that translated into a frightful cadence in his brain. *We-are-in-trouble.* Ross crashed back to them through the bushes, open-mouthed and gulping air thanks to the twenty-five-pound radio on his back, as he told them that Captain Slater was not stopping. Slater could not allow one man to slow down and jeopardize the rest (especially now that he'd been assured that that man was in good hands), and a medevac would only broadcast their location to every interested NVA.

Power, Geizer, and Ross had no choice but to get Jefferson's gear off him and force him to his feet; then with Ross bringing up the rear, and Power and Geizer on either side of Jefferson to hold him up, they got moving, stumbling now themselves in the white-hot glare, their hands full not only with 200-plus pounds of semiconscious Marine but also with his pack, flak jacket, ammunition, web gear, canteens, and rifle. Sergeant Jefferson was moaning, "Leave me, leave me, just leave me . . ."

The man wanted to lie down and *die.* It seemed the company was at least 200 meters ahead of them, and they were not closing the gap. They stopped, and Geizer took the radio handset from Ross. He spoke directly to Captain Slater. "Look, we've got a heat casualty back here. The guy's in bad shape, and we can't keep up with you. Skipper, you gotta slow down."

"Is he conscious?"

"Yes."

"Is he on his feet?"

"Yes."

"Okay, keep him moving. It won't be far."

Uptight City, thought Power as they got Jefferson to his feet again—*the bad boys are around here. I know it.* They were sitting ducks and were beginning to resent Jefferson for their vulnerability. *I don't know this guy from shit,* Power was angry out of his mind, *but I got his gear hanging all over me and I'm toting his rifle.* Even calm, mature, unshakable Geizer was muttering curses at Captain Contact as they wheezed along. "This motherfucker, man, he's going to get our ass killed. He's fucking leaving us. This shit ain't cool. Man, you don't do that shit . . ."

When Staff Sergeant Burns's platoon from Bravo Company returned to the company patrol base around 1300, they were none too happy about moving right back out again without a break. It was a 2,000-meter hump north to the Strip from where they were, but fortunately for the winded 1st Platoon, Captain Coates selected Lieutenant King's 2d Platoon to lead the way. King put Herbert's squad on point, and their perennial point man, Lopinto, stepped out in front on north-south Route 561 with the sweep's perennial flankers—Hendry, Demers, Hatison, and Reed from Clopton's squad—grumbling along again.

By the time these five reached the southern edge of the Strip, they were blinking constantly from the stinging sweat pouring down their faces.

A cream-colored cement building with a red tile roof was at the edge there, half-covered with the earth and debris the bulldozers had pushed off the Strip. The uncovered half looked like shrapnel-made Swiss cheese. The Strip stretched 600 open, vulnerable meters from its southern to its northern edge. Crossing would put Bravo Company in view of the NVA artillery observers along the DMZ, so Lieutenant King gave the word to spread it way out with seventy-five meters between men and to really make tracks. Lopinto got moving along the remnants of Route 561 that ran north-south across the east-west grain of the bulldozed swath. Hendry, Demers, Hatison, and Francis were trying to keep up on the flanks where the dirt was plowed and rippled, high and then low and soft, with cut-down trees further obstructing their route. The thought of incoming artillery was the incentive that kept them hustling, and the thought of ambushers in the downed trees and brush pushed up along the northern edge kept their eyes darting into every conceivable position where an NVA could be waiting, looking for a bush in the wrong place, an unnatural outline, a reflection of sunlight off metal. . . .

There was nothing, and point man and flankers reached the low brush and bamboo on the north side, followed by the rest of Herbert's squad, which set up a hasty perimeter into which came Lieutenant King with Clopton's and Haines's squads.

King deployed the platoon in a one-eighty that extended north a hundred meters with their backs to the Strip, then took the handset from his radio operator, LCpl David M. Bradley, to advise Captain Coates that security was out and that the company could proceed across.

PFC Hendry, for one, dropped his pack and sat on his helmet to wait for the rest, but he had scarcely burned half a cigarette when they started filing into the hasty perimeter. *They really must have moved out,* he thought. He picked his gear back up as the line expanded with the new arrivals —2d Platoon to the west, 3d Platoon to the north, 1st Platoon to the east—and Lieutenant King assigned each of his squads a sector to cover. The squad leaders set in the specific two-man positions. Haines placed Hendry and Reed closest to the Strip on the western flank, but they shifted their position a bit when Haines moved on so as to take advantage of an old machine-gun hole. They dropped their gear again and talked about all the people who would be rotating home in August and September so that, as Hendry wrote, "We figured that if things stayed as they were he would be the squad leader and I would be the squad. We thought it would be pretty funny if we went to the rear and Reed called for third squad and attachments to fall out and I came busting ass out of a tent and stood at attention in front of Reed."

Following the bent elephant grass in Alpha Company's wake, Power, Geizer, and Ross managed to push Sergeant Jefferson close enough to where the company had stopped that Captain Slater sent back a half-dozen men to help them in. They arrived with a poncho into which the fat, delirious sergeant was rolled. Marines were digging in as they dragged in. Power was so pissed off with Captain Slater that he didn't volunteer to man a position on the line as he usually did (with Quigley and Xuan) but instead dug in near the CP, hoping that each angry swing of his entrenching tool transmitted what he couldn't say—*Hey, fuck you, we ain't going out on no fucking perimeter.*

Actually, Captain Slater and Corporal Power were about as tight as their rank allowed. Power had been grunting with the Walking Dead for sixteen months, and that meant something. Slater would ask Power for advice, and they would occasionally talk about things more personal. Slater was certainly experiencing the loneliness of command; so it was after digging in and cooling off that Power walked over to Slater. "We'll help with the radio watch tonight."

Captain Slater had to call in a medevac to end Sergeant Jefferson's first inglorious hump, and two other helicopters arrived to drop off a lieutenant and first sergeant—this was payday and they were there with the money orders and other paperwork—as well as water cans and cartons of C rations. Going out on one of the choppers was the company's senior hospital corpsman, HM3 Wood (better known as Woody), a black sailor who'd been well beyond his rotation date out of the bush. As a rule, corpsmen spent only half their tours in the bush in recognition of the unique psychological pressures of the job. Woody's replacement had recently joined them. Although Woody was scared to death to go out one more time (he told his buddy, Sergeant Geizer, that if he went out on this one, that was it—*he wouldn't come back),* he had nonetheless bucked up and decided to tag along to show his replacement the ropes. Woody was that kind of guy. Geizer was pinned down one day in a paddy with Woody, who would flinch and cry out loud—*unh, unh*—at each round zipping past. But when somebody hollered for a corpsman, his whole personality transformed and he ran through bullets like a movie hero. Geizer had been among those who wrote witness statements for Woody's Silver Star recommendation for the miracles he performed during the Sec-

ond Battle of Phu An; and Geizer was now among Woody's
compatriots who shook his hand, slapped his shoulder, and
wished him luck before he climbed aboard the helicopter
that would carry him up and away from Indian Country.

5

Shadows

★

Shortly after deploying above the Strip on 1 July 1967, Bravo 1/9 spotted two NVA coming south toward them on Route 561 from an area of abandoned, rubbled buildings designated "Market" on their topo maps and known to the Marines as the Marketplace.

It was the sweep's first enemy contact. Marines were quickly dispatched to eliminate them, but the NVA disappeared at the sight of them. Captain Coates pursued the issue by putting Staff Sergeant Burns's 1st Platoon and Staff Sergeant Reyes's 3d Platoon on line and sending them up Route 561 into the Marketplace. Meanwhile, two UH34 helicopters (obsolete machines known as Sea Horses or Ridgerunners) appeared from the southeast. They flew past Lieutenant King's 2d Platoon, maintaining the perimeter, to land some eight hundred meters to the west where Alpha Company was setting up. Burns's and Reyes's platoons advanced about three hundred meters north to the southern edge of the Marketplace where a

trail cut in from the west and ended, forming a rightward
leaning T-shaped junction. They scouted the area for some
fifteen minutes, then returned empty-handed at just about
the time the two helicopters were swinging east after
resupplying Alpha Company.

It was about 1800 now. A green smoke grenade was
tossed into a clearing off Route 561 to mark Bravo Company as one of the '34s orbited at a thousand feet to watch
for enemy movement while the second '34 roared in at
treetop level. Everyone had donned helmets and flak jackets to watch the resupply from their holes—the NVA liked
to mortar helo landing—as the chopper touched down
lightly on its rubber wheels. The crew quickly tossed water
cans and ration cases from their side door, and then the
pilot brought the helicopter up, lowered its nose, raised its
tail, and charged back across the treetops, remaining low to
restrict the enemy's observation of them.

PFC Hendry and his buddy Reed sat back up on the
edge of their hole, relieved that the first helicopter had
come and gone without incident. *Punk-punk-punk.* The
sound of NVA 82mm mortar rounds exiting its tube was
distinct, and Hendry and Reed exchanged nervous glances
before dropping back into their holes—all of Bravo Company were making like moles—to count the thirty or so
seconds between exit and impact. *Punk-punk-punk-punk*
. . . The waiting was the worst part about mortars to Hendry, and this time he was acutely aware that the tube was
still belching out rounds even before the first one had
arched in on them. *Christ, won't they ever stop!* The first
explosion was 300 meters north of them, around that road
junction, and within two minutes the NVA placed forty or
fifty rounds in that area. The NVA were obviously firing
without a forward observer, guesstimating the distance between their tube and where they had seen the helo alight,
but no Marine took satisfaction in their foe's misjudged
bombardment. The NVA were usually too damn good with
their mortars, and even this raid was in a very effective
pattern that surely would have caused casualties had it
been on target.

The second helicopter touched down, unloaded, and took off within thirty seconds, and as the noise of its engine subsided, the thumping of the enemy mortar began again. Everyone was already down in their holes. *This time the goonies will be on target,* Hendry thought, as did his hole partner, Reed, who seemed to be on the verge of freaking out as they waited for the impact. But what can you do, Hendry mused—*a mortar round doesn't have eyes. If it lands in your hole, that's that. If it lands outside your hole, all you get is a good scare and maybe a few bells ringing in your head.*

The explosions began (it was the same concentrated pattern of forty or fifty rounds), closer but still more than a hundred meters off target. When this mortaring ceased, Captain Coates gave the word to saddle up and move out quickly. It was already dusk, and they still had to move to their night position and dig in. As each man passed the landing zone, he grabbed either a case of C rations or a five-gallon water can. PFC Hendry, for one, ended up with a case of C's under his left arm and his M16 swinging in his right as he followed the line up Route 561 straight toward the mortar impact area—*what the hell's the captain think he's doing?*

A 300-meter hump brought them near the Market-place's first road junction into a flat, brushy area with good fields of fire, and here they deployed, letting the main road slice through the middle of their perimeter. The area was already dotted with old fighting holes, as well as the junked remains of an Ontos (a tracked vehicle mounted with six recoilless rifles), which sat as a reminder inside their lines. The evening rituals commenced. Burns, King, and Reyes got their platoon sectors from Coates, then they assigned each of their squads a portion, and the squad leaders got down to placing their men. In Corporal Haines's squad, Hendry, Reed, and a third man, L. Cpl. Cesar Eduardo Carvallo, were assigned a position near what looked to be a 155mm artillery crater. Dropping their gear, they got down to shoveling the shell crater into a three-man fighting hole. They were finishing up when Corporal Haines decided to move Hendry from this position to one with Demers. Hendry picked up his flak jacket, only to discover it was covered with red ants (as was the rest of his gear) so carrying it instead of wearing it, be trudged over to Demers's position. Demers was sitting beside an old fighting hole, and Hendry threw his gear down and broke out his E-tool so the hole would accommodate his six-five frame. By the time Hendry was finished chopping at the sides and scooping the loose dirt out, they were joined by a man from rockets. This Marine (a lazy guy) wasn't too hot on digging a larger hole, so he said that if anything happened he'd use the artillery crater about fifteen meters away.

It was then that an NVA fired into Bravo Company's position. One shot, no casualties. The NVA was probably a scout sent to determine what damage (none) the mortaring had wreaked.

This is something different, thought Staff Sergeant Burns, who had never known the NVA to waste more than ten rounds to harass a Marine patrol; and as the Marines divided their watches, one man up, two asleep (each man sacked out until his turn came with his flak jacket for a pillow and his poncho liner pulled over him), even the usually skeptical PFC Henderson doubted whether anyone was screwing off (sleeping) on watch this night. They all knew something was up. The ambushes were the most alert. Lance Corporal Herbert's squad had the ambush from Bravo Two, and they set in along Route 561 south of the perimeter, between their lines and the Strip. During the night they could hear noises to their rear—south—like cans rattling; but Herbert, a young, smart squad leader, brushed it off as the scurrying of nocturnal animals in a pile of old, unburied C-ration cans. Cpl Michael D. Pitts's squad had the ambush from Bravo One, and they set in along Route 561 north of the perimeter, between their lines and the DMZ. During the night they could hear noises to their front—north—but Pitts could not brush them off. They were voices. Vietnamese voices. Pitts and squad were set in at the rightward-leaning T junction. The

NVA were up at the next crossroad, which was a leftward-leaning T junction because the trail ran into Route 561 from the east and ended there. The NVA did not venture south into Pitts's ambush.

PART TWO

THE WALKING DEAD

★

From the "Command Chronology 9th Marines, July 1967": "Operation Buffalo commenced at 1000H, 2 July 67, when B/1/9 made contact with two battalions of the 90th NVA Regiment [324B NVA Division] in grid squares YD 1272 and 1372."

From the comments of Col George E. Jerue (CO, 9th Marines) made during an interview with the 3d Marine Division Historical Section: "It is felt by most of the people that were close to the operation and those who actually took part in it, that we had surprised the NVA and we still believe that they were preparing positions from which to launch an attack, quite probably towards Con Thien."

From the "Operations of U.S. Marine Forces, Vietnam, July 1967": "The action developed rapidly into a well-coordinated attack by five NVA battalions. The enemy, for the first time in the war, employed both light and medium artillery in mass and in close coordination with his ground attack, in addition to using both mortars and flamethrowers. The remaining companies of the 1st Battalion, 9th Marines, maneuvered rapidly both overland and by helicopter to reinforce and relieve the pressure on Company B. They came under heavy mortar and artillery fire as they entered the action, and the battle throughout was intense and at close quarters."

6

Sunday Morning

★

PFC George M. Blough of the 2d Platoon, Alpha Company, 1st Battalion, 9th Marines, 3d Marine Division, greeted the sunrise of Sunday, 2 July 1967—the first official day of Operation Buffalo—through fatigue-hooded eyes.

It had been a long night. Blough was on watch when he heard something in the bushes beyond their perimeter. Something—someone—was moving out there in the dark, not too far away. Blough was a new guy, one of their replacements after the latest Phu An tragedy, and not sure how to handle this, he slid back to Corporal Solomon, leader of the squad to which he'd recently and temporarily been attached. Blough woke Solomon who, in turn, told him to wake everybody in the immediate vicinity and alert them that a grenade was going to be thrown at a possible movement; Blough was then to return to his hole and await Solomon's signal to throw the frag. This Blough did, but when he turned back toward Solomon after dropping back in his hole and scooping up a grenade, he saw that Solomon was asleep again. Solomon had been there a long time, and it was obvious now to Blough that he hadn't taken this cherry's report very seriously.

PFC Blough put the grenade down and picked up his M16, staring into the dark with his heart in his throat. He could hear something rustling the bushes again. He didn't know what to do. You couldn't fire at night because the muzzle flash would reveal your position, and you could only lob out an anonymously delivered grenade with permission. Blough, the uncertain new guy, was reduced for the next forty-five minutes to whispering loudly into the black whenever he heard the brush rustling again, "If you understand English, don't move or I'll fuckin' kill ya."

When Blough's watch was finally over, Corporal Solomon was up next. Blough had just lain down and had been asleep for what seemed like five minutes when Solomon crawled back to him: "Hey, there is somebody in the bushes! Where's the grenades?"

"I don't know."

Blough did know, but as he thought (with new-guy dumbness) *he fucked with me, I figure I'll fuck with him.* Solomon's dark eyes flashed with anger, and he was still pissed off—so was Blough—when their twilight patrol discovered trampled vegetation out in those noisy bushes. Now you see (or hear) them, now you don't.

As Alpha Company saddled up, Lance Corporal Quigley of the attached scout team brushed his teeth just as he did every morning. Quigley had this thing about clean teeth, but although he used only two or three capfuls of canteen water, Corporal Power, the senior scout, bit into him as he did every morning, "Quigley, *goddammit,* you're wastin' that fuckin' water. A little scuz on your teeth, man, *fuck that shit.* Live with the scuz. You're gonna *need that water.*"

"Fuck, man, bitch about something else. *It's my water.* Bitch when I ask you for *your* water."

Corporal Power had played this game with Quigley

many a morning, as he had played similar games with the man who was his partner before Quigley, and the man before that. The scout section had lost four of eight men in March, two or three of the remaining four in April, and (after replacements) three of five in May. Through it all, Power had remained a constant, having originally joined the battalion's 106mm Recoilless Rifle Platoon in February 1966 (his baptism of fire had actually been in April 1965 with the 6th Marines in the Dominican Republic) when 1/9 was down around Da Nang. He had shrapnel scars from a booby trap down his back, the reminders of a mortar across his chest, and a battalion-wide reputation so that guys who had been there four or five months (that was considered a long time with the Walking Dead) would nudge guys who'd been there a few weeks and motion toward Power: "You see that guy over there? That's the motherfucker who came over here and started this war, man. It's all his fault!"

Corporal Power, who was a natural born actor and bullshitter—a very intelligent young man of twenty who had joined the Corps to escape the blue-collar drabness of Lavonia, Georgia—did not let his audience down. During the Buddhist Uprising in Da Nang, when ARVN tanks battled each other in the streets, Power and a buddy could think of no better time to steal a jeep and, packing grenades and .45s, go pussy hunting amid the gunfire. The result of that jaunt was a bust to private first class. When snipers popped off at them, Power would stand up (as long as they were in VC land and not up against NVA) to beat his chest and roar; and when new officers rotated in, he would go into his salty, I've-seen-it-all routine, "Hey, whoa, you're gonna tell *me* what to do. I was here when you were a junior at fucking Auburn somewhere. When you were fucking sorority sisters, *I was killing gooks!*"

Corporal Power was a definite piece of work, but Captain Slater (for one) considered him a definite asset in the field with his extensive bush-culled experience. With Power's S-2 team this time around were Lance Corporal Quigley, the son of a sergeant major and a solid scout (*you had to be pretty goddamn gung ho to volunteer for this shit,* as

Power thought), and the Kit Carson Scout Xuan, a good soldier though a slightly built man as his Marine-sized helmet and flak jacket emphasized. Power, Quigley, and Xuan waited with Captain Slater's command group as helicopters landed in their perimeter this Sunday morning to retrieve the water cans from the previous resupply and to take aboard the lieutenant and first sergeant who'd arrived the previous evening to pay the troops. Power was glad to be with Slater. For all of his Captain Contact behavior, Power still had a lot of confidence in Slater's unflappable presence and he'd rather go out with Alpha A Go-Go than with any other company in the battalion.

When Lance Corporal Herbert of the 2d Squad of Bravo Two brought his ambush in and reported the night's activities to his platoon commander, Lieutenant King informed him that they would be continuing north that morning. Specifically, Herbert's eight-man squad and Cpl Margarito Garza's two-man machine-gun team were to walk point for 2d Platoon into the Marketplace on Route 561, and 2d Platoon was to walk point for Bravo Company. They would be followed by the company headquarters and by the 3d and Weapons Platoons, while the 1st Platoon remained in their overnight position with the entire company's packs and overnight gear to await the morning resupply. Once the helicopters had delivered it, 1st Platoon would have to pay for their day of relative inactivity by humping the resupply, plus all the packs and overnight gear, to a predesignated area that 2d, 3d, and Weapons were already expected to have reached, and where they would dig in for their second consecutive night above the Strip.

With that (and by now it was about 0800), Lance Corporal Herbert placed his best point man, Frank Lopinto, who also happened to be his best friend, out in front. Lopinto was a tough mother. Shirtless beneath his flak jacket and slung with an especially heavy load of grenades and ammunition, he moved down the dirt cart trail they called Route 561. The trail was eight to ten feet wide and

bordered by hedgerows that grew along the trail's embank-
ments and were actually above the helmets bobbing on the
road, especially where the trail was worn three to four feet
below ground level.

Behind Lopinto and Herbert's squad, Lieutenant King
tramped in line with Sergeant Clopton's and Corporal
Haines's squads. Stretching out then behind 2d Platoon
from their overnight position (with its burnt Ontos) came
Staff Sergeant Reyes's 3d Platoon, tailed by Captain
Coates and his command group. Bringing up the rear on
the road was Sergeant Huff's 60mm mortar section. While
they humped past the first shattered, pockmarked concrete
buildings of the Marketplace, Staff Sergeant Burns's 1st
Platoon carried the company's packs and overnight gear up
the road a bit to an area that would accommodate resupply
helicopters. With two squads securing the landing zone, the
third squad recovered the water cans and rations kicked
from the doors of the hovering choppers, tossed aboard the
empty cans from the previous resupply, and saw the pay
officer who'd choppered out the day before go off.

Bravo Company's initial objective was the rightward
leaning T junction up Route 561. Lance Corporal Herbert's point squad (which had worked this area before and
knew the location of every NVA spiderhole and trench)
was surprisingly preceded to the junction by a squad from
the trailing 3d Platoon. Herbert's radio was beginning to
blink out; but the message did get through about this squad
moving up on the flank, which was lucky, Herbert thought,
because if uninformed they might have ended up killing
each other. The 3d Platoon squad had already secured the
crossroads and were down along the side of the road when
Herbert's people arrived. They reported that they'd seen
nothing. Herbert halted his squad and called up Lieutenant
King, who told him to deploy in a wedge formation on the
right flank of the road, then, get down and wait for the
other squads in the platoon to move up and get on line
with them. When they did, King gave the word and the 2d
Platoon swept several hundred meters forward to the leftward leaning T junction. To their right-rear some distance

away was Hill 70 (hills were named for their heights in meters), which was actually two adjacent little knobs with a connecting saddle, and which was bald except for its blanket of waist-high elephant grass.

The 2d Platoon halted at the second junction, and Herbert set his squad in on the right flank, facing Hill 70 to the southeast, with Garza's attached gun team. Lieutenant King explained to them that 3d Platoon was going to pass through their perimeter to assume the company point. The 3d Platoon would then continue north another 300 meters on the road and sweep that area, while 2d Platoon secured the CP and the 60mm mortars and sent elements east on the east-west trail intersecting their north-south road to sweep that area. After 3d Platoon had completed their clockwise sweep of several hedgerow squares with 2d Platoon standing by to reinforce if contact should be made, they would secure another spot on the road for 2d Platoon to leapfrog through to conduct the next sweep while, this time, 3d Platoon stood by. Another long, hot day of routine misery and boredom. They never found anything, that is unless the NVA wanted to be found.

After the helicopters had bounced in and out of Alpha Company's position for their water cans and rear-echelon types, Captain Slater gave the word and their hump to the north commenced. They were some fifteen hundred meters west of Bravo Company, and their sweep was generally on the same axis and at the same foot-plodding speed. Alpha Two was on point, followed by the company headquarters. Slater meant to have 1st and 3d platoons uncoil next from their overnight rice paddy, but the 2d Platoon was only eight hundred meters into the hump (it was 0915) when there was a sudden explosion from the point.

It had started. Corporal Solomon's squad, screening the flank of the point squad, had tripped a booby trap (a grenade from the sound of it) and the lead man in their file was down. This was a black Marine, and one of his legs had been blown off below the knee; the other leg was shredded by shrapnel. While two corpsmen, one a vet and the other a cherry, moved to this man, the rest of the squad halted in place. The second man in the line, an Hispanic, sat on a paddy dike along with the third man in line, namely PFC Blough, where they were joined by Corporal Solomon. Word was passed for Solomon's squad to move out on the flank so as to provide security for the helicopter. PFC Blough waited for the number-two man, the Hispanic Marine, to take the point; but then Corporal Solomon pointed his M16 at him in what might have been a careless gesture, but which seemed intentional and threatening. Solomon was still pissed, "Blough, you're walkin' point."

Hey, fuck, you know! Blough stood up, wishing he were back with his squad. He didn't know these Marines and this Solomon character seemed a real prick. He wondered if the fact that the number-two man was an Hispanic like Solomon had anything to do with the squad leader's decision to put him, the third man, up front. *Fuck it,* Blough thought, *I'll go.* It was about time he found out what walking point was all about. *What the fuck.* Blough had just started off through a patch of scrub brush—and was suddenly sprawled out—the echo of a booby-trapped grenade ringing in his head.

Blough's legs were mangled.

Corporal Power, back with the command group, stared up the staggered (and now halted) column, the desiccated paddies shimmering under the unrelenting sun. He had recognized the explosions as grenades. There were shouts from the point. Marines down. Nearby, Captain Slater was on the radio with 2d Platoon, and a voice crackled through the bitch box of the company radioman: "We hit something else up here. I'll let you know."

Silence. Slater tried again, "This is Alpha Six Actual. What's going on?"

A different voice answered, presumably the radioman of the previous speaker (who had presumably headed for the scene of the crime): "I don't know."

Slater turned to Power and told him to find out what was happening, so leaving Quigley and Xuan, Power moved up the column. Marines passed the word as he passed them.

"Mines."

"Mines."

"Mines are up there."

Power made it to the point elements, alert all the while not only because he'd been warned but because the feeling was on him again. *These fuckers, man, they're here. They are fucking here.* He knew what the NVA knew, that heat-wilted Marines tended to ignore their training and use the paddy dikes and farmer-carved hedgerow breaks. As such, Power avoided more possible booby traps by going through the hedges wherever they looked weak enough to push through bodily. Confronted with another hedgerow, he started through a spot of thinning brush in the thorny obstacle—and there on the other side was a goddamn U.S. 105mm artillery round. Power froze. The NVA were experts at converting dud rounds into booby traps. He knelt and bent forward to inspect the heavy, squat projectile. It was partially hidden and dirt was scraped up around it, but he could clearly see the missing component in the base plate through which the NVA had removed the shell's explosives. Only the metal casing remained.

Power had seen this trick before. The idea was to place a shell with just enough showing so that an alert Marine would spot it, then back up thinking it was booby trapped and bump into the real booby traps on the flanks of this paper tiger. Power proceeded past the howitzer round without trouble. *That's clear. I'm on their path.* On the other side of the hedgerow, he saw the Marine he took to be the point squad leader (presumably this was Solomon, but Power did not know the man); there was another hedgerow between the squad leader and where the booby traps had gone off.

"Get up there and see what the fuck they're doing," the squad leader called to the man in front of him, pointing to a man-made hedgerow opening.

Power called to the squad leader, "Hey, don't send

that guy through there. Bring him over here, run him through here."

The squad leader shot Power a look that translated into *hey, man, this is my fucking squad, who the fuck are you?* He said nothing to Power, then looked back at his rifleman, "Get the fuck up there."

The squad leader returned his attention to Power and they were looking each other right in the eye when the Marine went through the opening and—BOOM!—he hit another one. He was wounded, not dead, but Power was raging pissed—*sixteen months,* he thought, usually when he said something people listened—and he maintained his glare at the squad leader. Then, without a word, he passed on to push through the hedgerow. The corpsmen on the other side were most concerned with the one-legged black Marine who lay there with his open eyes glazing into shock. Power paused to look down—the man was coherent enough to look back up at him—and he tried to sound encouraging, "All right, brother, it's going to be all right, we're gonna get you outta here."

Power found the trip wire of one of the booby traps, or rather he found the end that had survived the explosion. *Brand spanking fucking new,* he thought as he examined the wire. *Ain't roughened, ain't corroded, ain't weathered, ain't nothing.* The NVA had probably rigged it last night or this morning. They knew the Marines were there. They could anticipate what route they would follow north. Power looked out at the terraced, hedgerow-lined rice paddies and the intersecting brush and tree lines. *I know these motherfuckers are looking at me right now. They are right up here.*

When the second of the three trip-wired grenades blew PFC Blough off his feet (mangling his left leg, and ripping his right leg and left arm with white-hot shrapnel), he instantly flashed to Corporal Meyer and Lance Corporal Saunders. Meyer was his short-statured, field-wise hell-raiser of a squad leader, and Saunders was an equally seasoned black grunt. Both men were short-timers; because

Blough had been the only one of five replacements who did not require medevac for heat exhaustion during their first hard hump, they had decided he should take over the squad when they rotated. They had spent many a night telling him what he needed to know. Saunders, in particular, had stressed to Blough that he was in Alpha 1/9, and he really didn't know what that meant, "but it means you're going to get hit. What kills guys over here is shock. Do you know a lot of songs? If you get hit, this is what I want you to do—start singing every song you know."

Which is just what Blough did as he lay bleeding on the dirt. Blough stopped singing when their two corpsmen got to him, asking instead, "Am I going to live, am I going to live?"

The vet corpsman answered, "Yeah."

Then Blough kept asking if his balls were all right and the corpsman muttered, "Yeah, yeah," but Blough was getting freaky about it, so the doc finally took Blough's unwounded right hand and cupped it against his groin. "Your balls are there."

Meanwhile, the vet corpsman had his cherry corpsman working on Blough's left foot. As instructed, he cut away the frayed jungle boot, and the horror of the sight suddenly dribbled from his mouth, *"Oh my God,* look at his foot!"

I must be pretty fucked up, Blough thought. He couldn't tell. He was in pain, but mostly he was numb, especially after the senior corpsman thumped a morphine Syrette into his leg. Gunny Santomasso appeared at his side, and after answering his question regarding what type of booby trap it had been ("Gunny, I wouldn't of stepped on it if I saw what the fuck it was"), Blough was lifted into a poncho. A Sea Horse landed in their smoke-marked clearing-turned-landing zone. The one-legged black Marine, who was in bad shape (but who would survive), was hefted into the cabin; and the other wounded man was being helped in when Blough, waiting his turn, thought he heard the soft exit of a mortar round from its tube over the slap-slap-slap of the vibrating chopper's propellers.

"Gunny, there's mortars!"

"No, no, you're just delirious—"

Then Gunny Santomasso also heard the pops of a 60mm mortar and he roared, "GET HIM ON THE FUCKING CHOPPER!" as Blough, inside his poncho, was swung through the doorless door frame. The Sea Horse, nose down, roared out of the LZ with its three bloody, bandaged Marines as the first shells began exploding around Alpha Company.

Corporal Haines's squad from Bravo Two had taken up positions to the rear of their platoon, and while waiting, PFC Hendry thought again of the premonition he'd had as he woke up. It had been so strong that he had turned to his buddy Demers to announce that "Today, PFC Hendry is going to get his second Forty-Eight."

A Forty-Eight was a wound that required at least two days in a hospital, and two Forty-Eight-Hour Hearts (as in, Purple Hearts) qualified a Marine for immediate reassignment off the line. Hendry already had one such wound, picked up over three months ago on his first day in the field when the helicopter taking him there was shot down. Now, waiting, Hendry and Demers toyed with the various pieces of shrapnel laying around the old bomb crater at whose edge they sat. The area was tree shaded, and they had removed their helmets and web gear with its attached ammunition pouches, grenades, and canteens. Holding up a large chunk, Hendry asked his buddy how he'd like to catch that across his knee or arm. Demers grunted. He was only three months away from normal rotation and had no desire to have his departure speeded along by a serious wound. Hendry and Demers sorted through the bomb fragments, finding a few marble-sized ones, and Hendry joked that he needed to get hit by one like that for his second Forty-Eight. The one that would get him home.

Suddenly, a shot. More shots (it had been fifteen minutes since Bravo Three had filed by, and that's where the firing was coming from); then one of the rounds flickered through the tree branches above Hendry and Demers. They triple-timed back into their gear and flattened behind the tree. More shots cracked past. Up ahead, there was even more firing, and Staff Sergeant Burns of Bravo One (sitting with the company's packs back down Route 561) literally got ice chills in his stomach. This was where his predecessor had been shot and mortally wounded while crossing a zigzag slit trench. The whole area was an NVA brier patch, a hall of mirrors in which they watched everything the Marines did from their camouflaged entrenchments. Burns had hoped for better this time around: July 2d was, after all, his wife's birthday.

The firing on Bravo Company had begun beyond the second crossroad on Route 561, the leftward leaning T junction in the Marketplace. The 3d Platoon's very first casualty was Staff Sergeant Reyes, their platoon commander; his trigger finger was shot off by one of the first sniper shots. He started back down the column to be medevacked as his platoon wheeled to the left flank (west) to assault what appeared to be a squad of snipers in a trench of some sort. The NVA had originally been firing SKS carbines, but when AK47 automatic weapons joined in, Captain Coates radioed Staff Sergeant Burns of 1st Platoon. Burns was instructed to load one of his squads with M60 ammunition and rush them and a machine-gun team up Route 561 to reinforce the contact, and have his other two squads stand by if needed.

Captain Coates then moved forward to the point elements of 2d Platoon to observe what he could of the 3d's fight, leaving his XO, Lieutenant Delaney, back with 60mm section, about a hundred meters behind 2d Platoon.

In his haste to advance, Coates neglected to inform Delaney that he was moving his command group, but even if alerted, Delaney was in no condition to follow. Almost overcome by the heat as he lay on the west side of the road, Delaney had been helped across the cart path by his two radiomen to a clump of bamboo whose shade offered some relief. The bamboo, however, seriously obstructed their view up the road. Lying there, Delaney got the sudden word from Coates about his advance toward the contact.

Coates explained that 3d Platoon was heavily engaged and 2d Platoon was under some sniper fire. Meanwhile, Sergeant Huff had assembled his two 60mm mortars on the road behind the 2d and 3d, and Delaney, tucked in the bamboo behind them, told Coates that they had no more rear security. He requested permission to move 1st Platoon up, leaving the packs and resupply where it was, and when Coates agreed, Delaney got Staff Sergeant Burns on the radio. Coates's instructions to Delaney were to maintain the rear half of the company perimeter at the crossroad using Huff's and Burns's people, while he, Coates (in his first firefight), dealt with the NVA firing on them from the left flank.

The NVA carried light 60mm mortars with which they were mobile and expert shots. In the space of some three minutes, the NVA placed thirty to forty mortar rounds onto Alpha Company. Captain Slater, however, was among those who could see the flash of one of the tubes. It was visible in a nearby tree line, and Slater called up their best M79 man, a country boy who carried a rucksack full of rounds. The kid was an expert at hitting the target with his first shot—thus giving the enemy no time to react—and sure enough, he dropped his first one right on the money. For good measure, he broke open and reloaded the single-shot M79 three or four more times. As Alpha Company began to unscrew itself from the ground, there was gunfire to the east where Bravo Company was moving. *Pa-pow. Da-dow. Da-da-dow.* There were single shots, short bursts, then a rushing together of automatic-weapons fire and explosions, *da-da-da-dow, da-da-da-da-vrrrrrRRRRRRRRRRR-RRRRRRRRR.* Corporal Power, for one, had never heard a firefight reach such a shattering crescendo so quickly, nor had he ever heard the decibels just peak like that and stay there. *VVVVRRRRRRRRRRRRRRRRR.* No lulls. *This is deep shit.*

7

Clay Pigeons

★

The doctrine of the Marine Corps is that the only way to survive an ambush is to counterattack instantly, to close with the ambushers and overwhelm them. Cpl Leon E. Bell, radioman for the 3d Platoon, Bravo Company, 1st Battalion, 9th Marines, tried to orchestrate precisely such a response in the absence of Staff Sergeant Reyes, their platoon commander and first casualty. Up against what appeared to be a few NVA with SKS carbines in a trench, Bell had two of his squads lay down a base of fire while his third squad maneuvered off Route 561 to assault the snipers from the flank. His young voice cool and authoritative—he was just *super people,* thought Staff Sergeant Burns, who was monitoring the radio—Corporal Bell guided his squad leaders by radio. "Okay, baby, you gotta get up, you gotta go, you gotta get a base of fire down."

With M79 grenadiers lobbing rounds toward the enemy trench from the road, the assault squad made its move with Corporal Bell constantly pushing over the radio, "Keep your base of fire up . . . keep going, keep going. . . . Pin 'em down, pin 'em down. You gotta go. . . ."

They assaulted right into a *platoon's* worth of AK47 fire. Stunned, the assault squad leader radioed back that he was pinned down, but it was too late and Bell responded forcefully, "Well, it's times like this you get off your dead ass and go. You got no choice."

There was no place to go. The number of AK-firing NVA multiplied again—they just seemed to materialize inside spiderholes and bunkers in the elephant grass and hedgerows—and the entire 3d Platoon was soon engulfed. The NVA were utilizing those pre-dug ambush positions that invisibly dotted the Con Thien countryside. And as experience had taught them, they had held the bulk of their fire until their foe were within a few dozen meters, so that the soon-to-be-pinned-down Marines could not employ air or arty support without endangering themselves. From their concealed positions, the NVA trained their AK47s down prepared fields of fire, squeezing point-blank bursts into confused Marines seeking cover and brave Marines desperately rising up to find something to shoot back at. Noise and chaos and screams, and Corporal Bell no longer answered the radio.

Lance Corporal Herbert, the intelligent, articulate, and very able leader of the 2d Squad of Bravo Two, was right behind the monster erupting around Bravo Three. Herbert's platoon sergeant, Sgt William E. Hilliard, moved over to Herbert at this time with their 81mm mortar forward observer and radioman. Hilliard, a recently promoted but solid NCO, asked Herbert if he knew what was going on. No, Herbert said; his radio, which had been giving him trouble all morning—it would receive, but not transmit—had finally just shut down completely. They could hear 3d Platoon's war on the left flank but had no idea what was happening.

At the time, Lance Corporal Herbert had his point squad deployed on the right flank of 2d Platoon, facing Hill

70 to the southeast, with his six men in widely spaced positions along with a two-man machine-gun team. Because they were short of men, Herbert and his radioman had also assumed a position on the thin line. There was an explosion then on Hill 70, and Herbert saw that 1st Platoon, marching up the trail to reinforce them, was lobbing in rounds from their rearward position.

They were indeed. Fifteen minutes after Captain Coates, Bravo Six, had instructed Bravo One's Staff Sergeant Burns to send a squad and a machine-gun team to reinforce the contact, Lieutenant Delaney, Bravo Five, ordered the other two squads forward. They left the company's packs and the supplies just taken off the helicopters, picked up machine-gun ammunition (about a hundred rounds per man), and were moving up Route 561 when the point squad leader, Corporal McGrath, called to Staff Sergeant Burns that they had movement on their right flank on Hill 70. Burns told McGrath to take them under fire, so the corporal had a LAW put into action. Its 66mm rocket roared to an impact in the elephant grass of Hill 70.

The result was a chain reaction of firing. Lance Corporal Herbert, for one, kept his eyes open after the explosion on Hill 70, and then, he too saw the figures moving on the high ground. There were five of them, and although it was too far to see faces, Herbert held his fire because they looked unusually tall and were wearing (it appeared) helmets with branches or something sticking from them. They could have been Marines. But 1st Platoon was continuing to fire on them, so Herbert joined in with his M16 sighted on those five coming down through the elephant grass.

All five fell as he opened up. He couldn't tell if he'd hit them or if they'd ducked. Then two of them jumped back up, and he shot again and they fell again. Herbert waited; then he saw two more figures rushing down the grassy slope. He shot at them, and they, too, all went down.

At least temporarily. Some of the NVA bobbing over Hill 70 (using the same hand-and-arm signals and fire-and-maneuver tactics as the Marines) were wearing Marine flak jackets and helmets,[1] which was designed to cause great confusion, especially if they closed with the Marines. Sergeant Huff had his two 60mm mortars on the trail behind 2d Platoon and Staff Sergeant Burns, coming up from behind, called for a fire mission on Hill 70. Sergeant Huff already had one tube pumping rounds at the trench line that 3d Platoon had been assaulting before commo was lost with them, so he had his other gun crew fire on the hill, which was actually out of sight to them because of the thick brush along the road. They put four rounds down the tube, but because of another frazzled radio, their radioman had to run up the trail to see if the riflemen were satisfied with their aim. He ran back to report that they were, so the mortar crew placed twenty more rounds on Hill 70.

The NVA kept coming amid the explosions in fireteam-sized rushes, and Lieutenant King, Bravo Two, decided to tighten up their perimeter along the road. Getting a hold of Sergeant Hilliard through the 81mm FO's radioman, he told him to pull Lance Corporal Herbert's point squad back with him.

"Let's *go!*" Hilliard turned, shouted, and started back.

Herbert yelled to his Marines, and they started running to the rear in a loose file, Herbert up with Hilliard and their corpsman. They made some thirty meters; then suddenly, Hilliard jumped toward a hole just as a Chicom grenade landed beside him. BOOM! Herbert was sent sprawling. Then he instantly crawled into a small hole that his radioman had already found. The corpsman ran to the hole too, bleeding from a small shrapnel wound to the head and shouting that Sergeant Hilliard had been killed instantly by the grenade. KIA. Automatic weapons began scything the grass from all directions. The NVA were already upon them, and as the squad returned fire, Herbert passed the word up and down the line to see if anyone was in contact with the other squads. No one was. Herbert's radio was

---

1. Or at least, noted an after-action report, headgear "made of strips of bamboo, paper, plastic and camouflage type material . . . obviously designed to look like the USMC helmet."

already kaput, and the 81mm FO's radioman had taken a big chunk of shrapnel in his. So they had no more commo with anyone. Herbert reckoned his position to be about twenty meters east of the road, but he didn't know if his platoon was dead, still in position, or if they'd pulled back and left them. He did not know how many NVA were in the area. He did not know anything.

There was another AK47 burst and, instantly, an inhuman scream, followed by shouts to Herbert that one of their guys was hit. Herbert sent his superficially wounded corpsman in that direction, but he was shot in the legs as he ran and sent sprawling.

The next shot was to his head. KIA.

There was a shout to Herbert that it was the point man Lopinto who had screamed. That was Herbert's best friend, and he shouted back to ask how bad he was hit. The return shout was that he was dead. KIA. Everyone was basically facing forward, except for a few who had turned around to return the fire coming from their rear. Herbert called again for the men on the right and left flanks to see if they could make contact with any other friendlies. Again, they could not, so the 81mm FO told his radioman to take off his useless radio, crawl back, and reestablish contact with the platoon. The man came running back very shortly, saying that no one was behind them but NVA. *Here we are,* Herbert thought. *NVA to our front, NVA to our rear, and the NVA we can't see who are all around us.*

Lance Corporal Herbert passed the word for the squad to pull back into a tighter perimeter so they could at least all see each other. He didn't need any NVA getting in the brush between his squad's two-man positions. He then told his radioman, who had unshouldered his twenty-five pounds of malfunctioning junk, to take the radio with him and pull back to the left as he, Herbert, went to the right around a tree in their path. The radioman got up and started crawling on all fours, dragging the radio behind him, while Herbert went on a belly crawl—and there was an AK47 crack and the radioman collapsed, killed instantly by a square shot to the neck. KIA. *Slowly but surely,* Herbert realized, *they're pickin' us off.*

At the same time that Lieutenant King had directed Lance Corporal Herbert's point squad to fall back toward his roadside CP (at the leftward leaning T junction), he had also called forward Corporal Haines's squad, which was on rear security. From there, King wanted them to move forward into the fray developing around Herbert's squad, and leading the way, Haines sprinted some thirty meters up Route 561. Haines then knelt along one side of the road and waved his squad on by ones and twos to a bomb crater across the trail from him. The first two Marines made it to the crater, then crossed on to a deep ditch on Haines's side of the road. Haines motioned the third man, Reed, to come on, and for a fat man Reed moved out, canteens flapping at his hips, his run speeded along by the AK fire now beginning to crack at them.

Under fire, Reed made it to the crater, then over to the ditch, followed in turn by Harshman. The fifth man, Hendry, jumped to his feet and began the road run in a crouch, pausing for an instant (near the command group) when he passed Corporal Garza who had his M60 pointing north from the left side of the road. Hendry dropped his hundred-round belt of machine-gun ammunition there with a (forced) cool, "Here's a present for ya, T.J."

Garza just nodded, his face as uptight as Hendry's must also have been. Hendry completed his up-the-trail sprint with a leap toward the crater. He landed on the steep side of it, hit loose dirt, and rolled to the bottom, then clambered back up and tailed Harshman to the ditch across the road. One at a time like this, Haines got his squad in the ditch as NVA fire continued to snap by, mostly from a tree line across a fairly barren field to their left at about the eleven o'clock position. When the fire slackened a bit, Captain Coates (who was walking up and down Route 561 and occasionally firing his .45 into the brush) shouted at Haines to get his 2d Platoon squad on line with the first squad that had come up from 1st Platoon. Together, they were to assault the enemy-held tree line at eleven o'clock. Haines slid over to Hendry to tell him he would be point for the squad—Hendry's guts knotted even tighter—and that he should first go for a dead tree thirty meters ahead. The rest of the squad assault line would follow.

Hendry, tensed, waiting, hoped that air support would precede their assault. It didn't. Nor was artillery being directed onto the enemy.

Captain Coates hollered at Haines to get his people moving, and Hendry ran to the dead tree in a terrified zigzag, then hit the deck the instant he reached it. To his left, he could see the 1st Platoon squad. They were pinned down. To his rear, he could see Reed cautiously crawling toward him, followed by the rest of the squad who all made it to the dead tree without casualty. The NVA had not spotted them as they poured their fire into the other squad.

When Haines got close enough to Hendry to be heard, he shouted at him to run the twenty-five meters more to a hedgerow across their front. Terrified again, Hendry was up and moving again, but this time the NVA saw him. And as he bellied down, rounds kicked up dirt all around, sending him head first over the lip of a nearby bomb crater. He exposed only enough of his head then to watch the flank while—somehow—the rest of the squad wormed their way through the fire and crawled into the safe haven of the crater. Their job, however, was not to hunker down but to assault, and Haines now told Hendry to crawl through the short elephant grass to tie in with the squad from 1st Platoon. This Hendry did, going prone beside a Marine from the other squad at about the time Captain Coates could be heard bellowing from the road, "FIRE FOR SUPERIORITY!"

The 1st Platoon Marine beside Hendry opened fire. But an NVA machine gun quickly returned the fire, and he caught a round in the jaw. An RPG flashed in, the explosion hitting several more in that squad, and any man who exposed his position in the brush by firing, instantly had that NVA machine gun blasting at him. The NVA were dug in and could see everything. The Marines did not have a single target to square their sights on. Nothing in the NVA tree line could be seen moving. *Fire for superiority?* Hendry thought with anger and horror, *What in the hell is this! We need some shit here, man! We don't need to be flingin' rocks. We need stuff. Napalm, five-hundred-pound bombs. Then maybe we'd have something going on.*[2]

The Marines' fire petered out. A sergeant yelled back that the NVA fire was too heavy to advance any further, and Captain Coates gave the word to pull back. Too late. The two squads were pinned down.

Now the NVA tried to surround them. Hendry had eased back to where Haines was, to find out what he should do, when Hatison started yelling about NVA going around their right flank. Hendry looked up and there the little bastards were, streaking through the brush and on across the road to take up positions about a hundred meters north of their pinned-down situation.

They could hear Corporal Garza, back at the crossroad with Lieutenant King, placing M60 fire on the suddenly exposed NVA, but it was not enough. There were too many NVA, and they kept coming. With NVA now on both sides of the road and nothing but open field between them and the rest of the company on the road, Hendry, Hatison, and Harshman jumped into another crater. They opened fire on the NVA still dashing across the road. They fired on the NVA in the brush on their flanks too, but with elephant grass secured to their pith helmets and bush hats as well as on their packs and web gear, and around their arms and legs, the NVA were almost impossible to see.

Finally, Hendry made out three of them running into a particular patch of brush to the east, on the opposite side

2. Col John P. Lanigan (CO, 3d Marines, January–May 1967) commented during his post-command debrief, "We need additional supporting arms training for NCOs and our officers. We need to get them so familiar and used to calling supporting arms and using it that it just becomes automatic to them. If there's one weakness that we had over there, it was . . . a time lag between the time they got into contact and the time they were able to call in fire."

of Route 561. It was about a hundred-meter shot, but M79-man Harshman dropped his first round directly into the brush. After the explosion, one shrapnel-peppered NVA hobbled out of the brush. Hatison shot him—and then, of course, an NVA's shot hit the crater edge beside Hatison's head. The assholes were everywhere.

After having his platoon sergeant, radioman, corpsman, and point man all killed in the first moments of the attack on 2d Platoon, Lance Corporal Herbert scrambled into a small bomb crater where three other Marines had also sought shelter. He had no idea what was going on except that two of his men, a grenadier and a fireteam leader, were off away from the crater and were yelling to him, "Can we come over, can we come over!"

Herbert responded in the negative. He knew there was an NVA near them because the last shot that had killed his radioman had apparently come from a dugout near the crater. They had to knock that NVA out before those two Marines could make it over, but the M79 man didn't understand this and, despite Herbert's shout, he got to all fours to make his move.

The NVA shot him in the face.

Herbert heard the shot but had no idea his grenadier had been hit until the man came scrambling into the crater on all fours, screaming, *"I'm hit, I'm hit!"*—and, just then, the NVA fired again, shooting the man in the side as he tumbled into the crater. Herbert thought the guy was dead, and the guy thought he was dead too. But upon examination it turned out that the last shot had deflected off his flak jacket, and although the face shot had gone through his cheek and shattered half his teeth, it had exited through his open mouth. The M79 man was in a lot of pain but could still function, and Herbert turned his attention to the fireteam leader who was still stuck out there and hollering to see if it was okay for him to come over.

"No! Wait!"

Herbert pulled the pin on a grenade, shouted at the team leader to come running as soon as the grenade went

off, then threw it toward the dugout where he thought the
NVA was. The team leader made it to the crater safely, but
an NVA behind some bushes heaved a Chicom grenade at
them. It landed near the crater and they ducked down,
sweating until they realized it was a dud. One of the Marines threw a grenade back. It too was a dud, but his second grenade roared. No more Chicoms. No more anything,
actually, except an occasional AK47 burst. Herbert concluded that the NVA must have considered his craterful of
survivors too meaningless to do more than keep pinned, as
their main body pressed the attack on the rest of the platoon.

There were NVA climbing up in the trees to fire down
on the pinned-down squad from 1st Platoon and the
pinned-down squad from 2d Platoon, and PFC Henderson
of the 1st was among those firing back at them. This was
insane. A fury of M16, M60, and M79 fire would shatter
tree branches and vegetation, and if they were lucky, a
body might crash heavily back to earth—but more NVA
kept coming, and one by one, Marines were being picked
off. Then the NVA began mortaring them, and Henderson,
squeezing flat, suddenly felt something heavy hit him and
his radio was blown off his back, landing as twisted scrap to
one side. Henderson hadn't gotten a scratch. Insane. He
saw the brush move then, and he started laying down M16
fire until, almost immediately, he was shot in the back, the
round punching through his flak jacket and into his shoulder and the blood instantly gushing from a severed artery.
Henderson rolled away to where he thought he was
unseen on a little footpath, but he was just starting to put a
bandage on the bullet hole when he was shot again. The
bullet hit him high up on his leg like a paralyzing sledgehammer. *They got me spotted so I best be still.* Now the
bushes were moving, and NVA were suddenly becoming
visible. It was too much to take. Marines began running
back toward the road, running for their lives, and Henderson, a bloody mess, was ignored. It was the final disillusionment, and he thought bitterly that all the indoctrination in

boot camp about Marines never leaving their wounded, never leaving their dead, was a bunch of *shit. Everybody's running!* All were running except one man, PFC Maurice K. Mock, from Henderson's squad, who saw Henderson and exclaimed, *"Oh my God!"* Mock knelt quickly beside Henderson and used his K-Bar knife to cut away Henderson's trouser leg so he could bandage the wound. But Mock never got the chance to stop the bleeding and heft Henderson onto his shoulders. Mock was shot in the back of his head, the exit of the round grotesquely blowing his face away and dropping his body atop Henderson. KIA.

Up ahead, in the eye of Bravo Two's storm, Corporal Haines got the attention of Hendry, Hatison, and Harshman. They crawled from their crater with rounds snapping all around them; then, they jumped up to follow Haines. They ran top speed to their left toward the Bravo One squad, but with AK47 bursts continuing to crack and ricochet all around them in the open, Hendry and Haines dived into the dirt behind a log. Hendry, looking around, could no longer see several of the men from his squad, including some who just moments before had started this run behind Haines.

Cpl Delma L. Reed was KIA.
L Cpl Cesar E. Carvallo was KIA.
L Cpl Stephen W. Harshman was KIA.
L Cpl Jeffrey S. Hatison was KIA.

Hendry had no idea. All he knew was that the NVA fire was increasing until he and Haines had no choice but to get up and start running again. Demers and a grunt from 1st Platoon joined them as they sprinted south past several dead Marines and several wounded Marines too. They did not stop for them. *Two men helping one wounded make three dead,* Hendry thought. They made it to a cement well and knelt beside it, only to have more rounds ricochet off it in showers of concrete, and again they were up and running, this time into a nearby north-south gully with large stalks of bamboo along the sides.

The 1st Platoon Marine was in the lead, followed by

Demers, and then Hendry. Thirty feet to their front, a bush suddenly leaped to its feet—it was another camouflaged enemy soldier—and emptied his AK47's thirty-round banana clip into them. The lead Marine was shot in the head —KIA—and Demers in the arm, as Hendry dropped and came back up with a grenade from his grenade pouch ready in his hand. The NVA had disappeared. Hendry tossed the grenade over a small knoll, hoping their ambusher had sought shelter there. Then he tied a dressing around Demers's arm as Haines came forward with eight or nine other survivors from the two mixed-up squads.

The rest of the company was to the east, somewhere on the other side of a fifteen-foot-high embankment. They all started scrambling up it. Hendry and two other Marines crested it first—and were horrified to see eighty meters of naked, coverless earth between their embankment and Route 561. Immediately after popping up, the Marine on Hendry's right was hit from behind, and he arched his back and flipped over onto it, screaming the whole time, *"Oh my God, no, no, oh my God!"*

Hendry ducked back down. Two Marines crawled past him, trying to make their break to the right, but another invisible NVA opened fire from the bamboo twenty meters away. KIA. KIA. The NVA had anticipated the direction of their retreat. Hendry looked back at a man getting up on his hands and knees to make a run for it. He was hit in the jaw and arm, then in the side. KIA. Corporal Haines called to Hendry to get back up the embankment.

"Get fucked! I'll go if you go!"

Barking back that if they lived he intended to have Hendry court-martialed, Haines did indeed make his own move, and Hendry jumped up to follow him straight across that eighty meters of open field. Rounds hit all around them. They crawled. Hendry felt terrible. He could hear wounded buddies screaming in pain, screaming for help from the other side of the embankment. He knew the NVA would kill them. He kept crawling until halfway across Haines stopped to catch his breath. Lying flat behind him, Hendry looked around from under his helmet brim and noticed a dirt clod a foot or two to the front-right of his head. Another shot, the dirt clod disintegrated, and Hendry was spurred on, pushing himself forward while staying as flat as possible, cheek to the ground, every muscle straining to move. A round grazed his arm, leaving a streak of red, but he hardly felt it. It only drove him faster. Haines and Hendry were crawling, but a machine gunner suddenly flashed past them, running at an astonishing speed and jumping over the berm and down to safety on the road despite a hail of fire.

When Haines got to within ten feet of Route 561, he leaped to his feet and ran, making it, even as Hendry behind him kept crawling with bullets smacking into the dirt so close his ears were ringing. Finally, he too shot to his feet and jumped over the berm with enemy fire roaring past. He'd made it. Back down on the sunken road, Hendry passed Garza and his still-blazing M60 and scooted across the road to Lieutenant King. He was feeling good; he knew they were out of it now. He gave the lieutenant a little wave and asked where Haines had gone. King started to answer—and the instantly numbing, sledgehammer impact of a bullet caught Hendry full in the hip, knocking him down. He rolled off the exposed road into a shallow ditch on the northern edge of the east-to-west trail running into Route 561. He was feeling no pain (despite the through-and-through bullet wound) and was plenty happy. He joked to the Marines in the ditch with him, Hughes and Pigott, that he'd just gotten his second Forty-Eight-Hour Heart. He was going home. He'd made it through hell to get back to the lieutenant, and there was no way a medevac wouldn't be forthcoming. He was going to see his family again. Pigott hollered for a doc, but as the corpsman started for their ditch, he was shot in the back. KIA. The NVA were pressing their attack onto Route 561. Nowhere was safe.

PFC Weldon of Bravo Two, having lost contact with everyone in his squad (and unaware that his superb squad leader, Sergeant Clopton, was a KIA), was zigzagging south through the brush west of Route 561. In something of a panic, hoping to find somebody else in olive drab, Weldon passed a twelve-foot-high pile of concrete junk, the remains of a demolished hootch. The rubble sprawled on into a nice, deep L-shaped trench occupied by two Marines. Weldon thankfully piled in with them: "What's goin' on? Where are you guys from?"

"We're from First Platoon."

No other Marines were visible to Weldon, but almost immediately, he spotted an NVA some fifty meters to their rear. The pith-helmeted, camouflaged NVA was moving in a bush-to-bush crouch, west to east, toward Route 561.

Weldon and his two new buddies opened fire, and the surprised NVA pivoted, firing back. And then he spun, hit, and fell out of sight. Another NVA appeared, rushing into the brush where his comrade had fallen, but he was forced to jump out of sight as the three M16s were turned on him. More NVA appeared, including some to the left of the rubble pile, whose virtually point-blank AK47 fire sent dirt kicking up along the edge of the trench as the Marines bobbed up to return fire. Weldon kept his M16 blasting rearward, while the other two concentrated on the NVA rushing into positions beyond the rubble pile to their front. An M16 jammed and, angry and panicked, the Marine screamed to see if either of the other two had a ramrod. Weldon did, and slipping it from its compartment in his rifle's stock, he handed it over to the defenseless Marine.

Weldon reshouldered his M16. He was firing again and the Marine on his left was in the process of clearing his weapon when—*clack-clack-clack-clack*—there was one big burst from the rubble pile, an AK47, and Weldon's feet flipped out from under him, and he was suddenly face to the sky. Half of his left biceps was gone (he was left-handed). But he was in shock, stunned; the pain wasn't registering yet. His feet were propped upon some rubble in the trench, higher than his head—an odd, uneven position —and he knew that the NVA would be rushing the trench. He knew he had to respond. His M16 had landed on some of the shattered concrete in the trench near his right hand,

and his fingers wrapped around the pistol grip as he realized there was an NVA standing atop the rubble pile, looking down on them with his AK47. He saw the man's pith helmet and fatigues—everything was happening in the eternity of a few seconds—and he saw that the NVA was laughing and shouting excitedly in Vietnamese. The NVA was not looking directly at his victims; and in a flash, Weldon, still on his back, lifted the M16 up one-handed, swung it in the right direction, and firing with the wrong hand, squeezed a burst into the NVA's head and chest. The man tumbled out of sight over the back end of the rubble pile.

Weldon realized then that the two Marines with him in the trench were not moving. He reached over to one—KIA—then the other—also KIA—both of them shot across their chests. He crawled from the trench and up the rubble pile to make sure no more NVA were there. He saw the dead one on the other side. Suddenly and utterly alone, he decided to head south again. Crawling through the brush and running across the open areas, Weldon could hear tons of firing, here, there, and everywhere, but he didn't know if any of it was meant specifically for him. And he was too sun beat and blood splattered to really care—up until the next dash across an open area when he felt a sudden sharp pain across his ass cheeks that hurled him off his feet. He landed facedown in the dirt, and wildly relieved to see his helmet and M16 lying right in front of him, within arm's reach, he scooped them back up and scrambled to his feet. He charged on into the bushes with a new wound, a bullet-torn crease across his butt.

Lieutenant Delaney's attempts to make sense of the cacophony to the north and west of his bamboo thicket were interrupted by a sniper shot thumping into one of his radiomen, the one on the other side of the road. KIA. The radio aerials that brought in the fire support were a favorite NVA target, and it seemed to Delaney that every Marine with a radio basically had a bull's-eye strapped to his back. He eventually lost all radio contact with Bravo Two and Bravo Three, had only intermittent contact with

Bravo Six, and as he told the 3d Marine Division Historical Section five days later, "Different people were on the phone at different times, it sounded like they were wounded, and each time they came on they didn't know what the situation was, all they could say is, 'Somebody get down here and help me. They're all around. They're running through us, throwing grenades.'"

8

Run in Circles, Scream and Shout

★

Sergeant Geizer, the artillery spotter with Alpha Company, had the PRC-25 riding on the back of his radio operator, PFC Ross, turned to the arty freq so that they could eavesdrop on the conversation between their counterparts in Bravo Company and Con Thien. Shouting to make himself heard over the constant automatic-weapons fire and explosions—a real nerve-ripping wall of sound—Bravo's FO described a scene of disintegration, of utter chaos and fragmentation. Geizer could have pulled his teeth out in frustration as he listened. This was no skirmish; this was a major battle. And Geizer knew from experience that such realities took time to sink in with higher-higher. So he stood and waited, and listened some more to Bravo Company dying, while his mind raged. *When the hell are they going to give us directions to turn east and join them?*

Sergeant Geizer, who was twenty-three years old and about as squared-away a Marine as one could hope to find, had come to the Marines only because he hadn't received a satisfactory assignment in the Peace Corps. Tinkering with the idea of a career in the Marine Corps, he had volunteered for Vietnam and had talked his way out of a behind-the-wire job with an artillery battery and into the field as a forward observer, originally with 1/4. When 1/4 departed Vietnam for Okinawa to train for redeployment to the combat zone as an amphibious landing team, he had volunteered to join 3/4 so as not to miss any time in the bush, and when 3/4 similarly departed for Okinawa, he had volunteered for 1/9. He had extended his tour in Vietnam and had even refused his R&R.

Artillery spotters were supposed to be lieutenants, but Geizer (who, incidentally, had no formal training as an FO) was a sergeant, and his assistant forward observer, David H. Sankey, was only a private first class. PFC Sankey was a full-blooded Arapaho from an Oklahoma reservation, a quiet, likeable, trustworthy man in the field, but also a man who struck Geizer as serious and melancholy. When he spoke, which was not often, he gave the impression he was hungry for something he wasn't finding. Sankey was straight as an arrow in the bush, but in the rear he was an alcoholic and resister of authority to the point that his escapades with his partner in crime, Corporal Power, kept his sleeves bare of chevrons. Geizer and Sankey had two radiomen assigned to them, PFC Ross and PFC Russell Duckworth. Since Ducky was the sharper of the two (he was a tough, wiry, little fireball), Geizer gave him to Sankey, while Geizer, with sixteen months of bush experience to lean on, kept the quiet, unassuming Ross.

Finally, Captain Slater got off the radio with the CP at Con Thien. Alpha Company was to turn around and hump back south through the overnight position they had not yet completely uncoiled from, then turn east and reinforce Bravo Company's fight from the rear. By the time they were into their forced march, the man on the arty freq that Geizer was listening to over Ross's bitch box was literally crying his eyes out and begging for help.

"Hey, what the fuck's going on over there?"

Radio operators, even ones who were not supposed to be on Bravo's nets, were changing their freqs over as they walked. One radioman said, "Bravo says there's a million of them motherfuckers over there."

The word spread mouth to mouth. "Bravo's gettin' the shit bad, man. They're beggin', they're pleadin', they're gettin' fuckin' rubbed out, man."

"Bravo is fucking dying over there, boys. *Let's go.*"

Everyone in Alpha was getting real nervous, real up-tight, but they moved it out, walking a rapid single file through dry, waist-high grass and scattered brush, making their own trail. *There is a shitload of gooks over there and these motherfuckers have got a shitload of ammo.* Corporal Power's mind was racing, even as the other half was locked like radar on his surroundings—he was ready, ready, ready—as he strode toward the cacophony to the east. *They are not trying to conserve ammo, they are throwin' shit on Bravo.*

Bravo Company's fight was audible, if not visible, to Lieutenant Colonel Schening, et al., in the CP bunker atop Con Thien. And despite only intermittent radio contact with Captain Coates, it became obvious to these blind men that this was a battle Bravo Company might lose. Schening told Coates to hang on. He had directed Alpha Company to move overland to them, he had alerted Charlie Company at Dong Ha to helicopter into the Strip, and he had directed Delta Company at Con Thien to organize a tank-infantry relief force. The temptation for Spike Schening, of the gruff manner and thrice-wounded experience, to join his Marines in the field was strangled by his primary mission to hold Con Thien. It was impossible to calculate whether Bravo Company had encountered an NVA company, battalion, or regiment. It was impossible to anticipate whether Bravo Company could hold and, if they could not, whether waves of NVA would then be darting through the wire at Con Thien. As Major Danielson noted, Lieutenant Colonel Schening "would have been conspicuously in violation of his primary mission had he abandoned Con Thien. He had no choice. Despite the poor communications, though, he had better control from Con Thien than he would have ever had from the Trace or with one of the companies involved."

PFC Henderson of Bravo One lay aching and momentarily apathetic on the footpath with the body of PFC Mock sprawled atop him. With a bullet wound in his hip and another in his shoulder, it took much effort for Henderson to finally push Mock off. It was time to start thinking about surviving this debacle, and after retrieving his M16 and his dead buddy's K-Bar knife, he forced himself to crawl back down the footpath toward Route 561.

Ten painful meters later, Henderson realized he had found a little perimeter of fellow survivors. They had pulled in tight with their backs to a big, thick, protective clump of bamboo; several seriously wounded Marines gathered there with four slightly wounded Marines spread out in a half-circle away from the bamboo as a perimeter of sorts. No one was bandaged yet. There were other Marines spread out here and there in the area, which was under intermittent mortar attack from tubes firing from so close that they could hear the pop of each outgoing shell. Luckily, the NVA ammunition was full of duds, which the Marines could hear thudding into the dirt near them.

It was nerve-wracking, and Henderson soon realized that these Marines were in a state of panic. There were a lot of boots in Bravo Company, and they were so scared they wouldn't shut up. "Can we get out of here now?"

"No, stay put until Charlie gets here."

"What do we do now? What do we do?"

Fools, Henderson thought as he whispered harshly to the closest of them, *"Shut up, shut up."*

But they kept babbling, and Henderson finally saw the inevitable Chicom grenade come over from some bushes, tumbling end over end to land near him. The Marines with him scurried away, but Henderson couldn't move anymore. BOOM! It hurt so bad that when he looked down at his right leg he half expected to see that it had been blown off.

It hadn't, but a large chunk of shrapnel had smashed bloodily into his calf.

Someone blasted the brush from where the grenade had come and shouted that he'd gotten that gook. That shut the new guys up for a while, and since no one else seemed to care enough anymore, the bleeding, enraged Henderson tried to honcho the group, telling them to keep quiet and stay alert. These Marines had no idea who Henderson was, and when they answered him, they called him sarge.

Other Marines were going absolutely apeshit. One rushed around in front of the bamboo, fired off a magazine, then dropped it to the ground, and thumped in a fresh magazine as he rushed to a new position. In one squeeze of the trigger, he emptied that magazine, then jumped back down. Henderson, watching him, wanted to scream that they didn't have that kind of ammunition to waste. Insane. They were also supposed to police up their empty magazines—not just drop them in the dirt—because they didn't have very many. And if they ever got the boxed rounds out of their packs that had been left behind, they'd need them to reload.

Bushes were moving around them, so there was reason to fire. At least for as long as one could: *"Dammit, my rifle jammed!"*

This pissed-off curse became a chorus in the little perimeter; before long it seemed that every other Marine had an M16 in his hands rendered useless by unextracted brass, which could only be cleared with a ramrod. Problem was that, though every man was supposed to have one, the supply system had not provided them in such abundance. *A guy would give his left leg for an M16 that was working,* Henderson thought, as he watched Marines without ramrods frantically bang their rifles against trees to dislodge the jams. That didn't work, and it didn't work when they tried to pry the brass out with sticks.

Insane. Insane. Insane.

★

PFC Weldon of Bravo Two ended his rearward running and crawling in a crater marked by the small, up-
rooted, and upside-down banana tree in it. He bandaged
his shot-away, badly bleeding left biceps (by sitting in the
dirt he also unknowingly stopped the bleeding from his
bullet-creased ass), then took a solid hit from his canteen.
He realized he was getting weak, so he crawled to the bottom of the crater and propped himself up against the tree,
rising up every now and again to look around.

Weldon heard someone coming. He pointed his M16
toward the noise. Luckily his reflexes were good because
what came into view (with his weapon also at the ready)
was one of the company's attached combat engineers. They
knew each other. The engineer, a lance corporal, piled into
the crater, tied Weldon's bandage a little better, and appraised their situation. "Well, we're not doing any good
here."

Weldon followed the engineer out of the crater and
back toward the crossroad where Bravo One was deployed.
They found some Marines on the west side of Route 561,
but they wanted to get across the road to join the main
body on the other side. An NVA machine gunner was firing
on those who exposed themselves, but other Marines were
returning his fire, and Weldon and the engineer were able
to make their move. They joined the others hiding behind
various pieces of cover (Weldon rolled into a roadside
trench), but even here, he realized, there was no real perimeter. *Helter-skelter,* Weldon thought as NVA mortar
crews worked the crossroad area, putting (it seemed) a
round every five meters. *Anything that walks or moves,
they're definitely putting a hurting to.*

Shot in the leg and chest, LCpl J. Skinner of Bravo
Three, lucky enough to have had survived the massacre
that had occurred on point, was also lucky enough to happen upon Lance Corporal Herbert's ignored little group
from Bravo Two. One of Herbert's men jumped out of
their crater to grab Skinner as he came past. Skinner was
hurting bad, and they gave him all their canteen water to

keep him up, as they waited and waited and waited. Lance Corporal Herbert finally couldn't stand it any longer. On the verge of heatstroke from the direct sunlight pounding the crater, he crawled out to lie in the miserable shade of a nearby tree. There was a rim of raw, upturned earth about fifteen feet away and Herbert didn't understand that it was a bomb crater until an NVA stuck his head up from it, looking around. He was probably keeping tabs on the crater for the return of his comrades. The NVA was to his right, and being a right-handed shooter, Herbert had to switch his M16 to his left hand before he could trigger a quick burst to the right. The NVA dropped back down, and no idea whether he'd hit the man or not, Herbert immediately wheeled around to face the crater. He waited. Every now and then, an NVA would shoot at him from another location now that he'd exposed his position with that burst. But he stayed flat and motionless, and eventually, that NVA decided to stick his head up again from the crater. The NVA looked around again, but he didn't see Herbert who, thus, had time to square his sights on the man's head. Then he squeezed the trigger.

Finally, PFC Hendry thought when looking up from his trailside ditch to see the first two F4B Phantom II jets and two UH1E Huey gunships. A prop-driven 01E Bird Dog observation plane dipped in to mark targets with white phosphorus rockets, and the Phantoms roared in to place their 250- and 500-pound bombs where the white smoke roiled up from the greenery. Marine Air thus killed some of the NVA, while terrifying most of their grunt counterparts only a few meters removed from ground zero.[1] In Hendry's trench, he, Hughes, and Pigott plugged their ears and opened their mouths so their eardrums wouldn't burst as dirt clods and debris from the explosions showered down on them. Over and over again. The Hueys

1. PFC Weldon commented, "We knew it was getting quite warm because you could see the numbers on the Phantoms when they were pulling up out of their runs—lot of shrapnel flying through the air."

also skimmed low, their M60 machine guns firing incessantly, pursuing NVA who sought cover in the hedgerows and, in the process, tearing apart brush where Marines themselves were huddled. The Bird Dog marked NVA targets all around Lance Corporal Herbert's isolated crater. The impact of the closest bomb was unreal. Herbert felt like he'd exploded from within. He thought he had a concussion. Bombs and napalm seemed to suck the air right from the lungs of anyone nearby; then, the Hueys rolled in again. One of Herbert's men had a machine-gun round glance off his flak jacket. Herbert popped a green-cluster flare, anything, but it didn't do any good. So he tore a yellow smoke grenade from his web gear and threw that from the crater. No result. *Either the platoon's dead,* Herbert thought, *or they've pulled back and given us up for dead.*

As Alpha Company hurried through the waist-high brush, trying to close that 1,500 meter gap with Bravo Company, NVA snipers fired on them from concealed positions to the north and east, though not from the long, gradual slope to the south, which ran east-west and at whose base the column marched. And the closer they got to Bravo, the heavier the fire on Alpha. These AK- and SKS-toting snipers, all poor shots, did not slow Alpha Company down, but the claymore mine that the point team walked into did. The explosion sent the point man, a radioman, and a rifleman sprawling with shrapnel wounds and sent a fourth man (who had rejoined the company only two days earlier after recuperating from Phu An wounds) into shock. Captain Slater decided that Bravo could not afford the time it would take to medevac these four, so he ordered the point platoon to pick up their casualties and to keep moving. Closer still, Alpha Company could see the Phantoms supporting Bravo Company. They made their passes from east to west at a slow drag to release their bombs; then, regaining speed and altitude as they completed their passes, they flashed past Alpha's line to their north, flying west as the grunts humped east. As the Phantoms came out of their bombing patterns, the grunts could

hear a considerable number of NVA heavy machine guns
open fire on them from a tree-lined ridge far to the north.
The NVA were swarming all around Bravo Company but
also had units all the way north to that ridge line. The
distant, muffled reports of those machine guns made everyone realize that this fight was going to be worse than anything originally imagined. That was confirmed in short order when a pair of Huey gunships supporting Bravo peeled
off at Alpha Company's approach and proceeded to strafe
their point element. Luckily, there were no casualties.

When the point man for the 1st Platoon of Bravo
Company had made it up Route 561 to where he could see
the most rearward man of 2d Platoon, Staff Sergeant Burns
was at the first crossroad. An embankment ran along the
right (or eastern) side of the road at this point, and bamboo grew thickly among the hedgerows running down the
left side. Burns placed the remaining two squads from his
platoon in at this location. An old cement building, which
had been reduced to its foundations and four rubbled walls
no higher than four feet, was on the right side of the road,
and Burns established his command post in a small crater
at one of its corners.

The fighting was at the next crossroad, and it was from
there in the thick of it that Captain Coates radioed Staff
Sergeant Burns to alert him to Alpha Company's arrival.
Coates assumed Alpha would march in on the west-to-east
trail that joined north-south Route 561 at Burns's location.

Burns saw no one coming.

"Where is Alpha Company?" Coates finally radioed
Burns, "God, we need 'em! Send two platoons down here
as soon as they get here."

Burns was beginning to wonder himself where old Alpha A Go-Go was, and he wasn't sure Coates could survive
the wait. Stray rounds from the battle ahead occasionally
skipped down the road, and one of Burns's Marines
shouted over to him that an NVA sniper was looking right
down the road. Every time a 2d or 3d Platoon Marine tried
to cross he got zapped. The Marine said the sniper had

gotten a half-dozen people. Coates did not order Burns to enter the fray with his two squads. He needed them to hold open the back door should Alpha not arrive in time, and Bravo needed to back out under fire.

It was fortunate for what remained of Bravo Company that Lance Corporal Herbert's smoke grenade and Lieutenant Delaney's shouts into the radio were basically ignored by Marine Air, because by bombing practically atop the company, they might have scared hell out of the grunts (apparently no Marines were hit by friendly fire), but they also gave pause to the North Vietnamese attack.[2] Bombs and napalm did not, however, end what was an infantryman's fight, and in the hour or so it took the NVA to regroup—and (presumably) move reinforcements into place—the grunts of Bravo remained hunkered down and played cat 'n' mouse with the snipers in the bushes.

"Second Platoon help, Second Platoon help!"

No one moved because the call was obviously coming from an English-speaking NVA trying to entice a Marine to come running to help, so he could shoot the man for his trouble. No grunt would talk that way, Hendry thought as he lay in his roadside ditch listening to a genuine casualty, his buddy Weldon, bellowing for a "GODDAMN CORPSMAN BEFORE I BLEED TO DEATH!"

No one moved for Weldon either.

Glancing to their rear, Hendry and Pigott caught sight of a man in Marine gear walking across a field. They held their fire, then realized too late that no Marine would be crazy enough to stand up by this stage in the fight. By then the NVA imposter had disappeared into the bamboo, and Hendry and Pigott were mad enough to spit, especially

2. This was not accomplished without cost to Marine Air. The first hit was scored against Capt Ray Pendagraft's Phantom, which made a crash landing in the South China Sea that killed both pilot and copilot. Later in the afternoon, an F8 Crusader piloted by Capt Bruce Martin was similarly brought down, but this time the pilot of the one-seater aircraft parachuted into the ocean and was immediately rescued by a USAF Jolly Green Giant helicopter.

when a Chicom thumped into the dirt on the edge of their ditch. It was right above Hughes's head. Hughes already had three dents in his helmet from where rounds had ricocheted off, and now the steel pot saved him again, although the explosion did deafen him and give him a concussion.

More shrapnel filled the air from four mortar tubes the NVA had employed, pumping a near constant stream of rounds on all of Bravo Company except, by oversight, Lieutenant Delaney's bamboo thicket in the middle of their scrambled perimeter. Somewhere in all of this, Captain Coates was hit and his FAC, Capt Warren O. Keneipp, got through on the radio to Lieutenant Delaney who, as the company exec, should have taken command. He was, however, in no position to do so. Out of the sun in his bamboo clump, Delaney no longer seemed on the verge of passing out; however, after Keneipp's call, when Delaney and his surviving radioman LCpl Lawrence G. Cromwell, crawled from their cover so as to move up the road and take command, NVA fire instantly sent the brush shuddering around them. They scurried back. With one of his radiomen already shot dead on the road, it didn't take much to convince Delaney to stay where he was. He radioed Keneipp to take command of Bravo Company while he, Delaney, would hold his position in the middle and send up reinforcements from Alpha and Charlie companies as soon as they arrived. Keneipp, who had only been with the company about two weeks after combat duty as a fighter pilot, answered that he too had been hit and that his radioman was the only Marine he was really in command of. Five days later, Delaney explained the situation like this to the 3d Marine Division Historical Section:

> From what I could gather it was complete disorganization down in front with two platoons and the Six CP. The platoon commanders were either dead or wounded. The company commander was hit or dead. The only one running the company down there was the Forward Air Controller and he didn't have communications with the 2d or 3d Platoon. So what we had was fireteams in little

pockets with no control. They were just on their own, set up their own little perimeter, and, of course, we had the dead and wounded mixed in with them all over the place.

Delaney and Cromwell, the only ones still in radio contact with battalion (they probably knew more about the big picture than anybody else in the company), expected Alpha Company to arrive any moment, and comparing maps, it seemed that Alpha had made it to within several hundred meters. Then word came to Delaney and Cromwell that Alpha had been ground to a halt and that they had in excess of thirty casualties. Salvation, it appeared, rested with Charlie Company, which was Bald Eagling in from Dong Ha.

Corporal Power was now moving with the lead of Alpha Company. The column was strung out, west to east, across three hedgerow-separated rice paddies. The NVA were waiting beyond the last hedgerow of the easternmost paddy. An RPD machine gun opened fire, then two or three more. There were also a lot of AK47s and a lot of Chicom grenades, and as the point halted to return the fire and the column spread out to move up on a firing line, Power fell in with them, closely followed by the artillery team of Sankey and Duckworth. Beyond that last hedgerow, there was a monstrous fallen tree lying in the elephant grass and brush, covered with vines, and it defined the farthest advance of Alpha Company. Power made it to that tree with a buddy, Garrett, as did Sankey and Duckworth a few minutes later. Power began heaving grenades over the log toward a particular machine gun he could hear; then, he rolled into the elephant grass to fire his M16 blindly through it toward where he could hear NVA firing and moving. He did not dare rise above the waist-high grass to look around. The air was so electrified with NVA fire that to do so seemed suicidal.

9

Into the Meat Grinder

★

The light infantrymen of the North Vietnamese Army were highly indoctrinated, highly motivated, and well trained in the basic warrior skills, while their commanders, veterans of victories against the French, were intimately familiar with the terrain of the DMZ and had learned through trial and error how to fight the 3d Marine Division. These lessons had become doctrine because there was no rotation in the North Vietnamese Army to short-circuit the institutional memory.

That was why the NVA, using their expertly situated entrenchments, had been able to ambush and annihilate the lead platoon of B/1/9. That was why they had moved with a mobility and aggressiveness that seemed amazing, swarming into the next platoon in line and mixing with their foes, so that the Marines could not effectively employ their superior fire support. The tactic was known as Grabbing the Belt, and with their superior numbers, the NVA now planned to destroy piecemeal each fragmented group of Marines. Likewise, the NVA had halted A/1/9 in its tracks, waiting to commence fire until the Marines were so close that they would have extreme difficulty pulling back to employ air and arty. Meanwhile, NVA artillery was shelling Con Thien (hoping for a lucky hit on the CP bunker) while additional columns of foot soldiers rushed south to reinforce the effort to overrun B/1/9 and to begin the effort to overrun A/1/9.

The NVA tactics were tried and true.

Lieutenant Colonel Schening, who had commanded 1/9 for exactly ten days, had responded by immediately alerting C/1/9 to helicopter (Bald Eagle, in the nomenclature) from Dong Ha to the Strip. This would take time, so meanwhile, he had directed D/1/9 (on the bunker line at Con Thien) to make one platoon available to attempt an overland relief with a four-tank platoon from A/3d Tank Battalion. This would reduce the defensive force atop Con Thien to the remaining two rifle platoons from D/1/9 and a pair of Dusters (tracked vehicles with twin 40mm automatic cannons) from the U.S. Army. These would hardly be adequate should the multibattalion NVA force in the Marketplace push through A, B, and C/1/9 and assault up the slopes of Con Thien.

Such a possibility was transmitted to regiment and on to division, where the decision would have to be made regarding the commitment of the Northern I Corps Reserve (for the past several weeks it had been 3/9) from Dong Ha.

On 2 July 1967, the closest that Captain "Mac" Radcliffe, the S-3A (Assistant Operations Officer), 1st Battalion, 9th Marines, had come to the enemy was to observe several at 700 meters through field glasses at Con Thien. That was a frustrating circumstance for he sorely wanted to command a Marine rifle company in combat. This he had made abundantly clear upon arrival at the 3d Marine Division CP in Phu Bai exactly six days earlier, the day after he touched down in Da Nang. The division personnel officer behind the field desk in the hot, dusty tent was a mustang captain, a man resembling Radcliffe's father who was a gruff up-from-the-ranks Old Corps captain. Radcliffe knew how to talk to him. The captain tried to oblige this young hotspur. The mustang checked the division's company commander slots and finally looked up. "Well, how about One-Nine?"

"Captain, I don't give a shit where I go. I came over here to command a rifle company. You can put me in Dong Ha to command a rifle company, or you can put me up in Hanoi. Just give me a Marine rifle company. I'm an infantry officer and that's all I want to do."

"Okay, you're going to One-Nine. The convoy leaves from here."

"Thanks."

Radcliffe put his cover back on upon exiting the tent. There, coming down the road, were five or six buddies, fellow captains just off the plane who had also just received their orders. They fell in together on the road like raucous fraternity brothers, heady with the anticipation of adventure. They knew they were invincible, and they did not yet understand the true meaning of their question, "Where you going?"

"One-Nine."

They laughed, and Radcliffe rejoined, "What the hell's so goddamn funny? Where you guys going?"

"Two-Nine."

"Three-Three."

"Fine, so what the hell you laughin' about?"

"Mac, goddamn One-Nine's at Con Thien."

"So what. They told me I had a good chance to get a rifle company."

More laughs from these hot dogs, then, "Yeah, you'll have one for about three fuckin' days with those guys. Christ, you never heard about One-Nine, the Walking Dead? You never heard about One-Nine's reputation?"

"Naw, what the hell's the difference?"

The next morning's convoy took Radcliffe to Dong Ha where he found the tents housing the battalion rear, and he presented himself to Major Danielson. The battalion exec sat shirtless and fleshy behind his field desk, using forty words when four would suffice. Radcliffe could just tell he was a Boat School guy, a ticket-punching bureaucrat.[1] He explained that indeed a company commander's slot had been opened but that the S-3A, Captain Coates, had just filled it. Danielson added that Radcliffe would most likely fill Coates's place as the Three Alpha and that, as far as being a company commander, he would just have to wait until somebody rotated. *Or somebody gets hit,* thought Radcliffe. Two nights at Dong Ha, then Radcliffe caught the convoy to Con Thien where he met Lieutenant Colonel Schening and was turned over to Captain Curd, the S-3, to be snapped in, briefed, and oriented. Con T was miserable and dusty, and hotter than he knew anything could be. He couldn't sleep at night. He could barely control his fear and self-doubt as he anticipated his first contact. *Can I hack it?*

On the morning of 2 July, Captain Radcliffe had been waiting an intolerably long time at the southern base of the CP knob for a helicopter that was to give him an overview of the battalion area, when he noticed a Marine waving at him from the top of the CP hill. Getting the idea, Radcliffe trudged up the hill to the CP. Everyone in the bunker was in a great state of agitation. Lieutenant Colonel Schening and Captain Curd gave Radcliffe a quick briefing, mapping out the approximate locations of Alpha and Bravo companies and explaining that Bravo was in heavy contact but that details were foggy as radio communications were intermittent. Apparently, as they explained, Captain Coates had been wounded and his FAC, Captain Keneipp, had assumed command. Schening appeared concerned about having an aviator in charge out there and concluded, "Radcliffe, you're going to take a relief force out there. Sasek is

1. Such was the major's reputation throughout 1/9, and Lieutenant Fagan (soon to serve as the S-2) commented, "Danielson was a little paunchy, a little jowly, and that's very unbecoming in a Marine officer. He wasn't particularly outgoing. He was more of a Southern gentleman than he was a yelling type Marine, and the guys didn't like him. It was more because of his physical aspects and mannerisms because he was, ultimately, a very capable officer. It's a shitty job anyway, being the XO. Because a good XO does all the dirty work."

going to give you a platoon from Delta Company and some tanks. You go out there and take charge of Bravo Company, find out what's happening. Pull them back to the Strip."

"Aye, aye, sir."

Radcliffe was ready. His mind was clear. Only after the event would he comprehend that years of training and practice had exorcized those demons of self-doubt the moment he got his marching orders.

Captain Sasek, the CO of Delta Company, was also in the CP and Radcliffe was overjoyed at his presence. They had gone through OCS together and had most recently served together as tactical instructors at the Basic School. Sasek was a short and stocky athlete who came across as a good old country boy *Dumb, yeah,* Radcliffe thought. *Dumb like a fox.* Sasek exited the CP with Radcliffe, giving quick advice as they headed for the tanks. For one thing, Radcliffe carried only a .45 pistol. This was in accordance with the directives he had read that officers should only carry side arms so they would remain true to their positions as firefight directors, and not give in to the temptation to become participants with an automatic weapon in hand. That was all nonsense, and Sasek gave Radcliffe his M16 and a bandolier of ammunition. Radcliffe strapped it around his waist, then took eight more magazines that Sasek produced and crammed them in a baggy thigh pocket of his jungle utilities. He had his helmet and flak jacket on and was now packing an M16, a .45, a K-Bar knife, two canteens, a compass, and enough ammo, he thought, to last him his whole tour.

Captain Sasek explained that 2dLt Thomas P. Turchan, the 3d Platoon Commander of Delta Company and the one who would be accompanying the tanks, was brand-new. But, Sasek said, he could offer compensation in the form of Cpl Charles A. Thompson. He was Sasek's own senior radio operator, and as he told Radcliffe, "You take Thompson. The guy's good, he knows the territory."

Captain Sasek had gotten the word before Radcliffe, so Turchan and the 3d Platoon—the Third Herd—were

already sitting all over their four M48 tanks. Radcliffe and
Thompson climbed into a jeep (with driver), as did Lieutenant Howell, the battalion intelligence officer. He, too,
was going. Howell, a gentleman and a warrior, was stocky
and muscular with a black flattop and a dark complexion.
He had done a hitch as an enlisted man. Then he had
completed his degree and gone on to a high-school teach-
ing position and a family. When the Marines had landed at
Da Nang, though, he had felt honor bound because of his
Reserve commission to request an active-duty assignment
in Vietnam. The man was committed, he was smart, and he
was incredibly brave. He had commanded the 3d Platoon
of Bravo Company for more than eight months and his
years as a high-school teacher and coach had served him
well. Always calm, never abusive—and always an officer—
Howell had instinctively known how to handle these young
Marines. They, in turn, had worshiped him as *the only goddamn officer worth his salt* (at least in Bravo Company).
And although he was only weeks away this July morning
from rotating back to his wife and children and the safe life
he had never had to leave, Howell had volunteered to accompany the inexperienced Radcliffe and Turchan. Those
were *his* Marines dying in the Marketplace, and there was
no way he could abandon them. That's the kind of man he
was. That's the kind of Marine he was.

The jeep and tanks started out.

When Charlie 1/9 was alerted to Bald Eagle to Bravo
Company's rescue on the morning of 2 July 1967 (the second day of their Dong Ha R&R) it was a tired grunt company badly in need of rest. This did not distinguish Charlie
from Alpha, Bravo, or Delta 1/9 but it was a fact reflected
in the letters of Corporal Sullivan, a fireteam leader in the
2d Platoon and one of the best Marines in the entire company:

4, March, 1967. . . . I saw Alpha Company come
back in carrying 10 dead V.C. and 2 live ones. . . .
These V.C. up here aren't rice paddy farmers, they're

N.V.A. regulars and you have to kick their teeth out before they run. No problem. This battalion's been waiting a long time to do just that. . . .

13 March 67. . . . Well, we got creamed. About 40 casualties in the company. My squad—Tony Orlando—dead—old "Mac" Matturri, schrapnel up and down his spine and legs, Martin, a plate in his knee, Jackson, legs and back, Charlie Marlow, shot in the shoulder, Frank Bignami, schrapnel in the neck . . . "Doc" Kline got wounded, "Doc" Jessop and "Doc" Tessier got wounded trying to patch Tony up. He got shot in the leg by a .50 and as they were trying to patch him up a gook threw a grenade which rolled up against Tony's back and went off. The company Gunny got hit, so did a photographer, Lt. Dixon, 5 guys out of 60 mortars, 3 guys attached to 2d Plt with machine guns, Sgt. Cantu got killed and a lot more. Charlie Company isn't taking any more slant-eyed prisoners . . . we killed 400 (about) of them. They found out this wasn't 2/3 or 3/4 they were messing with. They met the hard guys.

The meat grinder of which Corporal Sullivan wrote took place on 5 March 1967 in the one and only Phu An, and their incumbent skipper, Captain Curd (currently the battalion operations officer) was one of the wounded. Their new skipper, Captain Reed, was killed on 5 April 1967 when some elements were overrun along the Street Without Joy. One of the platoon commanders, Lieutenant Dixon (currently the headquarters company commander) took the company for several weeks until Captain Hutchinson transferred in. Corporal Sullivan was made squad leader; and the 2d Platoon got a new platoon commander, 2dLt Frank Libutti (a darkly handsome Citadel graduate and an excellent officer for a boot brown-bar), and a new platoon sergeant, Sgt Anthony Lefefe (a tough, soft-spoken Samoan with a temper if pushed). They also got a few new guys to fill out their depleted ranks, including Larry Stuckey, a volunteer. Libutti and Lefefe were under a poncho shelter having C rations when he knelt down to look in, "This is Lance Corporal Stuckey reporting in, sir."

"Oh, relax, relax."

Libutti assigned him to Sullivan's squad. He wanted him to take over a fireteam of three PFCs, Smith, Smitty, and Alabama, but Stuckey spoke up, "I'm hesitant to do that, sir, because I have no experience whatsoever. I've never been with a division. I'm fresh off Sea Duty. I've been leading the good life the last couple years, and I really need some time to learn what I need to know about the field. Can I report back to you when I feel ready?"

"Sure, no problem."

Stuckey got a good workout because squad leader Sullivan was tough and demanding. *But he always took care of his men,* Stuckey thought. *Everyone felt safe being around him because he knew what he was doing.* Being the best, Sullivan and squad pulled a disproportionate number of ambushes and point duty. Two weeks and one firefight later, Stuckey approached Libutti, "I'm ready now."[2] Libutti, Lefefe, and Stuckey thus became veterans of the hot, dusty, nickel-and-dime contacts that grindingly filled the void between the big battles (with Stuckey losing Alabama along the way to an AK47 graze wound across the neck), while old salt Sullivan recorded their ups and downs in his letters home:

22 May, 1967. . . . We was in this real thick growth and this guy who was the point walked right up on a gook sleeping in a hole. He pulled the trigger once and nothing happened. Then the gook woke up and watched while he pulled the bolt back and got another misfire, then he went and jumped in a bunker with another gook and they jabbered at each other all the while that the grenade that sent them to hell was being sent "sealed

---

2. Stuckey commented, "It was terribly hot and tempers sometimes ran a little short, but when the unit made contact with the NVA we pulled together and did what we were trained to do. After a contact, morale always seemed to be high."

with a kiss" to them, compliments of Dick's fire team. We also had one guy wounded a few hours before that by a gook grenade thrown by a gook dressed up like a tree. . . .

May 25, 1967. . . . My squad keeps getting smaller and smaller. I got one guy with heat exhaustion and another (a niggar) with a fake foot injury. I let him go because I don't rightly appreciate niggars nohow. . . .

2 June, 67. . . . We are at Con Thien . . . One of my men got killed in a minefield the other night. I told the idiot about it. I found his body the next morning. He was after a parachute which was hanging on the barb wire. . . . Damn shame—18 years old with 30 days left in Vietnam. . . . Please send 3 lbs. of sugar and some yeast cakes. It's a special project. I got a hillbilly in my squad who says he can make grape wine. We got plenty of grape juice.

29 June 1967. Delta Company was hit near the Marketplace and as they closed with the dug-in NVA, under air and arty cover, Charlie Company swept in under fire to help with the mop-up. Of this firefight, the letter to the Sullivan home came not from their son, but from a grieving buddy:

One of his men was hit by a burst of fire from a machine gun and he was helping Dick turn the man over so they could dress the wound. This man that was hit made it out okay. Your son was hit through the back and was conscious for about 30 seconds at the most. . . . Out of the four men who went to try to help get him out three was hit. . . . The corpsman tried every possible way to save him. If we could have gotten him out sooner I think we could have saved him. But the enemy had us pinned down for about twenty minutes at least. When we finally got him out his pulse was very weak and he didn't make it to the landing zone for the choppers.

Nickel and dime. Nickel-and-dime bullshit.

The water ration above the Strip allowed no shaving and barely enough to drink, so on 1 July when Charlie Company assembled in a clearing for the helicopters, they were one bearded, dirty, scruffy, tatterdemalion group of grunts that stank to high heaven. It was in this condition that the helicopters delivered them to Dong Ha for their R&R.

Freshly shaven and in clean utilities on this lazy Sunday of 2 July 1967, Captain Hutchinson answered the EE8 field telephone ringing in his CP tent. The caller was from the 3d Marine Division Forward CP. "Have your company ready to move out, and report to the Division CP."

In the relatively brief time that Hutchinson had commanded Charlie Company, he had impressed his riflemen as a calm, deliberate, and straightforward skipper who knew his tactics and got to know his people. Their last commander, Curd (Reed hadn't survived long enough to make a strong impression), was a hard-core, hard-nosed man whose fighting skills and personal bravery were matched only by his ego. Hutchinson in comparison was soft-spoken and did not appear to be eyeing his future oak leaves at the expense of his men. Everybody loved Cap'n Hutch. What they did not know was that he had come to 1/9 under a cloud from 2/26. There had been an incident involving then-Lieutenant Hutchinson's platoon outside Da Nang that included a pitch-black night and a plan to surreptitiously leave one platoon behind while the other two noisily departed their overnight position. The idea was to ambush any VC who came to look over their supposedly vacated bivouac, but the stay-behind platoon ended up ambushing Hutchinson's platoon. In the confusion, he lost physical contact with his rear squad, and they did not rejoin until dawn. Shortly thereafter, Hutchinson was relieved of command and—promoted to captain, nonetheless—shuffled off to the DMZ where the war really started for him.

Briefed in the underground, sandbagged, and fluorescent-lit bunker of division forward, Captain Hutchinson was told that the sweep being conducted by A and B/1/9 (in the area C and D/1/9 had just departed) was in heavy contact, with Bravo taking the worst of it. And that a tank platoon with a platoon from D/1/9 was proceeding toward where Route 561 entered the northern flank of the Strip. C/1/9 was to Bald Eagle onto the Strip, rendezvous with the tanks, and proceed north on Route 561 to the farthest point of Bravo and then recover their dead and evacuate their wounded. *Why are you sending another company into the meat grinder,* Hutchinson found himself thinking as he listened incredulously to the various briefers. To begin with, he didn't want the tank support—they were nothing but big, lumbering targets, he thought, prone to break down[3]—and he was amazed that the tanks seemed to be the extent of the fire support he was to be provided. Then there was the fact that Charlie Company numbered in the neighborhood of a hundred riflemen. At the very least, if Alpha and Bravo were in as much trouble as the briefers indicated, Hutchinson thought, all of Charlie Company and all of Delta Company should be committed, along with Lieutenant Colonel Schening and a jump CP to control all the firepower that they could muster. *They want me to do this alone? The people at Division should know better than that.*

They probably did. Con Thien could not be abandoned, and lean reinforcements like C/1/9 had to be shoved into the fray while the decision was made regarding the commitment of 3/9. There really was no choice, so Hutchinson swallowed his reservations. "Aye, aye, sir. I'll do my best. I'll try to get them out."

Meanwhile, Charlie Company was being rounded up by the gunny and his runners. Lieutenant Libutti, for example, was at Mass (he was, after all, from a nice Italian family on Long Island) when someone interrupted the cel-

3. Actually, tanks were needed to evacuate the KIA and WIA from the Marketplace to the Strip. Additionally, in the event of a massed attack on the relief force, their 90mm main guns and .50-caliber machine guns could be decisive.

ebration by calling from the back of the chapel-tent, "Everybody from Charlie One-Nine get to your CP and get to the LZ. Charlie Company members please get back to your area, get your gear, and get down to the landing zone."

Lieutenant Libutti and several others jogged back to the company tents in minutes; and when Libutti stuck his head in the CP tent to find no Hutchinson, he headed for the nearby tents of the battalion rear. "What's going on, I just got word for everybody to get down to the LZ?"

An officer there explained that commo had been lost with Bravo Company and that Alpha was in trouble too. "Get Charlie Company ready to go. Get down in the LZ. Fly in and do what you must. Make sure that you have your gas masks because we think they may be throwing gas."

By the time Captain Hutchinson jeeped to the helozone, things were getting typically hectic. The gunny had about eighty or ninety riflemen formed up by fireteams and squads, but of Charlie Company's three rifle-platoon commanders, only Libutti of the 2d had been located in time. The 1st and 3d platoons were to be led by NCOs. The grunts were angry about their aborted R&R, and they were scared. So there were some long faces as Captain Hutchinson gave them the frag order. "Frank, you and Second Platoon will be in front. First and Third will be on the flanks, and I'll be in the middle with the CP. We're going in a formation roughly egg-shaped, and move down to the area where Bravo Company is, set up, see what's there, and then take it from there."

The four M48 tanks from A Company, 3d Tank Battalion, were commanded by a staff sergeant, and they moved east from Con Thien along the southern edge of the Strip at a good pace. In the jeep, Lieutenant Howell and Corporal Thompson kept changing to various radio frequencies hoping to pick up a communication from Bravo Company. Nothing. Still, the situation didn't yet seem real to Captain Radcliffe who was also in the jeep. This was his first day in the bush. The situation was very real to one of the anonymous tank-borne riflemen who was on his sixth month in the bush. Everyone's gear was individualized, and this Marine had taken a black pen to the camouflaged cover that was sealed like a second skin to his steel pot. On one side he had drawn a Confederate flag, and on the other was his girlfriend's name, his blood type, and "1/9." On the back was:

Missouri Is The State I'm From
But
Misery Is The State I'm In

This Marine, however, had volunteered for this misery, and from day one at Camp Pendleton, he'd been taught that the lowest thing on earth (besides a Marine recruit) was a nonhacker, a buddy-fucker, somebody that didn't pull his load. *Anybody that wears the uniform is your buddy. If he's a Marine, he's family—and if you back out on him, you're lower than shit.* Twice, he had turned down his R&R because they were scheduled on the eves of major operations, and good old Dying Delta needed every swinging dick. *I'm not a brave man. The idea of embarrassing myself in front of my buddies is probably what kept me going.* Now, he was jostling along on the back of a tank, heading toward the sounds of the guns once again. *Marines never leave their dead. Marines never leave their wounded. The loyalty is the main thing. You're loyal to the Corps and the Corps is each individual Marine.*

The tanks and jeep made a left turn onto Route 561 and headed north across the 600 meters of Strip. They stopped on the northern side just short of the trees and bushes, and the infantrymen dismounted to reconnoiter and secure the area. They did so without difficulty. There was a half-moon of old, partially back-filled fighting holes tied into the Strip with Route 561 running north-south through the center of the arc. Captain Radcliffe was beginning to think that the situation was not as grave as had been indicated. They had not seen a single enemy soldier, had not taken a single round. And he decided to deploy Lieutenant Turchan's platoon here to secure a medevac landing zone, while he went forward with Howell and Thompson and the tanks, to take charge of Bravo Company and bring them back south. Radcliffe told Turchan not to move for any reason from this position. "Spread your platoon out as much as you can in this half-moon and dig in. We're going to go up and find out what's going on."

Lance Corporal Stuckey of the 2d Platoon, Charlie Company, who was tall, muscular, and bespectacled, an intelligent twenty-one-year old, was at the Dong Ha helozone with Smith and Smitty of his fireteam. Fragmentation grenades, packed individually in squat tubes, were being uncased and passed out two per man, and there was a sense of urgency in the proceedings that had quickly turned their anger to fear. Combined with the concern they all felt for their fellow Marines in Bravo Company, it bound them together as a fighting unit like nothing Stuckey had ever seen. The nickel and diming was over. Their helicopters began landing then (it was about noon), and Stuckey ended up sitting beside Sergeant Lefefe. He glanced at Lefefe as they approached the Strip for their landing. Lefefe the usually happy warrior was looking unusually grim, and Stuckey chewed gum in cadence with his pounding pulse as the back ramp began its motorized reopening.

10

What Sixty Mike Mikes Do

★

Kneeling behind the monstrous, vine-wrapped fallen tree that marked the limit of Alpha 1/9's advance, Corporal Power's grenade duel with the invisible NVA continued until he finally told Corporal Garrett, behind the tree with him, that he was going to pull back to hunt up some more grenades. With fire snapping overhead, Power shoved off on his belly and headed for the bogged-down Marines spread out in the three side-by-side paddy fields west of these NVA entrenchments.

Only several hundred meters west of Bravo Company, Alpha Company had been stopped cold while still crossing these three overgrown, shell-pocked paddies. They had been carved into a slight ridge line that ran east-west, so that their southern flank rose up into trees and bushes and bamboo, and their northern flank fell away into brush-dotted flatlands carpeted with elephant grass. It was far to the north across this shallow valley that another low tree-lined ridge rose into view, atop which NVA machine gunners fired on the jets supporting Bravo Company to the east.

As Corporal Power pushed himself along, he bumped into a Marine whom he did not know who'd been hit in the upper arm. The man was already crawling back toward the easternmost paddy's hedgerow, so Power grabbed onto his gear and, remaining flat at all times, got him through the shrubbery and into the paddy. There, they ran into Sankey and Duckworth, the assistant forward observer and his radioman, who also lent a hand in pulling the wounded man back. They felt safe enough now to get up a little bit as they moved toward the casualty collection point the corpsmen had established at the southeastern corner of the paddies.

The first NVA 60mm mortar round arched from its tube then. The three paddies that Alpha Company was strung across had been preregistered so that of the hundreds of rounds the NVA mortar men would pump out, not a single one would fall wide of the mark.

BOOM!

BOOM!

The second round had fallen closer to them than the first. It was obvious where the third would be, so Power and Sankey dropped the wounded man and went flat to his left and right. Duckworth started to hurtle a log to their front. Power was looking up at him from under his helmet brim and—BOOM!—he saw an explosion of smoke and dirt a millisecond before Duckworth completed his dive. *Aw fuck, that had to get him!* It did. But Ducky was a tough little dude, and he crawled back to them under his own power, shouting not in pain, but in anger, *"Fuck,* I'm hit! Got me in the ass! Fuck, of all goddamn places!"

BOOM! BOOM! BOOM!

Captain Slater had made it to the northern hedgerow of the easternmost paddy, and from there he could hear the NVA mortar tubes thunking from somewhere along that ridge across the valley to their north. To neutralize them with counterbattery fire, Slater needed a firm fix on their position; so he stood at the edge of the perimeter, hands on hips, looking and listening. Power could see Slater from where he was flattened with Sankey and Duckworth and their wounded charge, and he was amazed once again at their skipper's cool. Good old Captain Contact. The only other man not on his belly was one of Slater's radiomen, LCpl Robert W. Genty, a slim, blond, tight-muscled dude who stood beside the skipper now with apparent nonchalance as they studied the ridge line to the north.

BOOM!

BOOM!

BOOM! BOOM!

Alpha Company had a three-tube 60mm mortar section whose crews had begun setting up as soon as it had become clear that they had a fight on their hands. They got their tubes up in three separate shell craters in the middle paddy, but they were not firing and Captain Slater told Gunny Santomasso to find out why. Santomasso simply stood up, then strode down the dike and into the clear, and disappeared through the hedgerow separating the easternmost paddy from the middle paddy as he bellowed with gravel in his throat, "WHERE ARE THEM GODDAMN MORTARS?"

BOOM!

BOOM!

BOOM!

Power and Sankey dragged the man with the arm wound to where the corpsmen were at the southeast corner, then, during a brief lull Power took off toward Captain Slater. More mortar rounds crashed in, and he ended up in an old bomb crater with Corporal Garrett, both of them nervous because their crater was a large one, the size of a small room, which increased the chance of lightning striking twice. The crater was five or six feet deep, and Power looked over its edge, searching for a smaller, safer shelter he could dash to during the next lull.

It was then that a round exploded in the casualty collection point. Garrett, a good old hot-rod-driving Alabama boy, completely flipped out with an anguished cry, "Jesus fucking Christ, it hit right in the middle of them guys! I gotta go help 'em!"

"Don't go!"

Garrett was a new guy. He started out of the crater and Power made a grab for his legs. He missed. Garrett was up and over the lip of the crater; he made it three or four strides—BOOM!—and then he was down, his ass and leg torn up. Power jumped out of the crater to drag him back in. He lay at the bottom, wiggling and kicking, hurting bad but hanging tough. Power began to realize just how deeply they were all in trouble. *We are in a bad fight and it ain't being looked after. It ain't being run right.* Captain Slater was concentrating on pushing through to Bravo Company, and Power could only think that the skipper was so aggressive, so intent on completing his mission that, like at Phu An, he was throwing haymakers with both hands instead of keeping one up to guard.

Alpha Company was scattered across the three paddies with little tactical coherency, except at the point where Slater was pushing, pushing, pushing. *Everything is geared toward Bravo, but we're in bad shit here and we ain't takin' care of business.*

Captain Slater knew that Alpha Company was in trouble, but he also knew that Bravo was in much more desperate straits. He had managed to make radio contact with somebody on the Bravo tac. It seemed to be a young radioman, and Slater had never heard anything so pathetic and heart rending. "My God, they're everywhere. Everybody that I can see is dead. Get to me fast or we're all gone. Every time we raise our heads, we get blown away. They're shooting right down our throats. Please get here. Right now!"

"We're going to be there in just a couple of minutes. Hang on, keep your head down."

There was a long lull in the mortaring. Alpha Company had accumulated too many casualties to fight and move simultaneously, but Bravo could not survive the wait for Alpha's medevacs. Hating to do it, Slater decided to split his command. He would immediately send Staff Sergeant Leslie's 1st Platoon north (to get around the NVA line to their east) with instructions to swing east to join

Bravo. Taking the time to muster fire support, he would then personally accompany Staff Sergeant Richardson's 2d Platoon in the trace of 1st Platoon. Meanwhile, Lieutenant Muller's 3d Platoon was to establish a medevac LZ in the westernmost of the three paddies they now occupied. After the medevacs, which Slater was presently requesting, Muller was to fold up his all-around defense and follow them to Bravo. Thus decided, Captain Slater collared Staff Sergeant Leslie, "You guys get to Bravo. You get down to Bravo. Go."

Staff Sergeant Leslie, their best platoon commander, was a kindhearted, lionhearted moose of a man. He cracked a big, unflappable grin, "All right, sir. You mean high-diddle-diddle, right-up-the-middle?"

"Goddamn right that's what I mean. Don't delay with the wounded. Take your wounded with you and leave your dead. *You get there.*"

Captain Slater also turned to LCpl Ronald W. Fazio, one of the company's perennial point men, and told him to catch up with Gunny Santomasso who was off hunting up their mortars. Slater wanted their 60mm's, plus as many M79-men as he could round up to join him and 2d Platoon. Fazio found Santomasso all right, but as the gunny had already discovered, their mortar section had only one tube left. One crew had been put out of commission with wounds from a near miss, and another crew had been snuffed out by the direct hit of an NVA mortar round in their crater. Fazio looked in to see that one of his best friends was among the mangled dead. Fazio had just rejoined the company from the hospital. He wasn't ready for this. *Everything's mixed up, hopeless.* He hustled back toward the skipper with the bad news, almost muttering what he was thinking—*We're not making it out of here!*

When Captain Slater and Gunny Santomasso rejoined each other, Slater explained that he was going to try and push through to Bravo Company. He was going to keep his primary radioman, Lance Corporal Genty (who had done a hell of a job at his side in Phu An), while he wanted Santomasso to take the other company radioman, LCpl

Thomas T. Crisan, and assist the inexperienced Lieutenant Muller: "You stay here with the Third Platoon. Get a medevac in . . ."

Meanwhile, during the long lull as casualties were carried to the westernmost paddy, Slater (who was still standing along the northern hedgerow-lined dike) told Sergeant Geizer and his radioman, PFC Ross, to place artillery on the ridge to their north. This Geizer did, blanketing both the forested ridge line with explosions and (because he suspected that NVA reinforcements were humping through the tall elephant grass) the shallow valley between them. As Geizer adjusted the fire, he actually edged off the dike and into the paddy, disregarding potential sniper fire so as to see his targets without any brushy obstacles. After the fire mission, he continued scanning the terrain to the north, and he happened upon a movement 200 meters out. That didn't pose a problem because he was easily an expert shot within 300 meters, but when he shouldered his M16 he realized he was staring down the barrel at a man with a flak jacket carrying another flak jacketed man over his shoulder. *Whoa, that's got to be a Marine.* Geizer lowered his M16, then thought, *dammit, it can't be. It can't be Bravo 'cause he's too far away from Bravo—and it's not Alpha.* He raised his M16 again and literally put the sights on the back of the head of the man who was carrying his comrade. *Dammit, I don't want to live with myself if I kill a Marine.* Again, he let the barrel dip in his hands, but this time, just as the man was about to enter a thicket of bamboo, Geizer realized that he wore no helmet and had almost shoulder-length black hair. *Dammit, why didn't I notice that first?* Geizer sighted in a third time with definite intent to kill, but the figure disappeared into the bamboo before he could squeeze the trigger.

11

Alpha a Go-Go

★

Lieutenant Muller of the 3d Platoon, Alpha Company, 1st Battalion, 9th Marines, had a wife and child and, in civilian life, had been a lawyer; but upon assignment to Vietnam his patriotism had demanded of him that he request a line unit. Slater had been glad to get him, and mostly he thought well of his performance. Likewise, Cpl James J. (Chink) Toy, a Chinese-American and a squad leader in the 3d Platoon, had been impressed when Muller first came aboard and said that he, Muller, realized he was inexperienced and that he wanted advice from his squad leaders and old-timers. That was the first and only time that Toy had seen a new lieutenant who didn't come on like a gung ho prick, and in stocky, chubby, personable Muller, he sensed they had an officer who genuinely cared. *Just a wonderful man,* Toy thought.

Most of the old-timers, however, were absolutely impatient with Muller as he learned on the job (to the point that some even approached Slater, "Hey, sir, the lieutenant's no good, he's going to get us killed"); and rejected and depressed, Muller had come to Slater shortly before Operation Buffalo and commented that regimental legal had offered him a job. "They'd like me back in the rear to run some courts-martial. It's up to you."

Slater still had faith in Muller, "You know, you're coming along. You're doing well. Hang in there a little bit longer. I think we're just about ready to bring that platoon of yours around."

Lieutenant Muller stayed, but he simply had not had enough bush time by the beginning of Operation Buffalo to have absorbed all the lessons. His medevac LZ perimeter around the westernmost of the three paddies was proof of that. *Really ragged,* thought even Corporal Toy. The line was thin because men were needed to rush the casualties to the center of that overgrown paddy—medevacs were on the way—and of the men who remained along the hedgerows, some were in positions that allowed them good fields of fire and some were not. No one had been assigned specific areas to cover, everyone had just been told to face outboard and watch out, and in the confusion, some Marines were even facing the wrong way.

The goddamn Third Platoon perimeter is not for shit. So thought Corporal Power as he and PFC Sankey helped the wounded Garrett into it. They came back again with Duckworth and another walking wounded leaning on them for support, then Power and Sankey headed back to the middle paddy. They were just on the eastern side of the hedgerow dividing the two paddies when two helicopters were seen approaching from the southeast.

Smoke was popped in the LZ.

The first Sea Horse settled down on its rubber wheels, the priority evacs were loaded aboard, then it was up and out. Power had been wounded at Phu An when the NVA mortared their medevacs. That old feeling hit him as the second Sea Horse began its descent, and he told Sankey to get down. They dropped into separate shell craters. The Sea Horse landed on the western side of their hedgerow.

BOOM!

BOOM!
BOOM!

The NVA mortars abruptly began a renewed barrage, at the same time that several NVA machine guns opened fire on the LZ from the west and north. Power could see the old '34 Sea Horse shaking as it came out of the LZ, taking hits but still making it up and away. The two medevacs had gotten all of Alpha Company's wounded except for seven with minor injuries and a smaller handful of shell-shocked Marines.

BOOM! BOOM!
BOOM! BOOM! BOOM!
BOOM!
BOOM! BOOM! BOOM! BOOM!

Sergeant Geizer and his radioman, PFC Ross, were positioned about seven feet up the low ridge line that ran east-west and defined the southern edge of the three paddies that were terraced into its slope. Specifically, Geizer and Ross were above the westernmost paddy LZ in a shell crater that had been scooped out of a small open area in the bamboo atop the ridge, a perfect spot from which to adjust artillery fire. Their wounded partner Duckworth was also with them, and they had just been joking enviously about his million-dollar wound. But Ducky reacted instantly to the renewed firing, jumping from the crater and running to where he thought he might find Sankey (who now carried the radio) so as to keep the two FO teams separate. Far to the north, Geizer could see puffs of smoke in what he knew was North Vietnam, and the muffled kettledrumming of outgoing artillery soon became the whistling rush of incoming.

CRASH! CRASH! CRASH!
BOOM!
BOOM! CRASH! CRASH!
CRASH! BOOM! BOOM! BOOM!

After sixteen months of hearing U.S. artillery going over his head, Geizer was finally hearing NVA artillery coming down on his head. It was a terrible experience and an ominous sign for, although the NVA regularly shelled fixed positions like Con Thien, they rarely expended their artillery shells on the Marines' bush positions. That they did so now meant that the NVA foot soldiers around them had their own forward-observer teams with radio communications back to the firing batteries in North Vietnam. Meanwhile, wildly relieved that their medevacs had gotten out despite the ring of fire, Captain Slater started off with 2d Platoon, following 1st Platoon's path. He had a final radio conversation with Lieutenant Muller of 3d Platoon, "Make sure that perimeter's secure now. I'm going to leave with the rest of the company, and we're going down the hill and join Bravo."

The NVA light infantrymen used the cover of their artillery and mortars to move into position for a ground assault on the solitary platoon in their hedgerow-encased LZ. The NVA moved in teams of four, carrying AK47s or RPGs, plus as many as twelve grenades apiece and a very occasional flamethrower. They were expertly camouflaged with elephant grass slipped through bands around their pith helmets and bush hats, on their backpacks and ammo vests, and around their arms and legs. The NVA were absolutely invisible when they knelt in the three- to four-foot-high elephant grass, and they stole right up to the edge of the LZ perimeter. The NVA were basically coming in under their own artillery and mortars—hard core—and since the Marines were heads down under this fire, they were undetected. When the NVA were close enough, they sprang up in the elephant grass and came running and firing toward the hedgerows. Only then did the NVA artillery and mortars cease firing. The sun was blazing above these open paddies.

This is happening too fast! thought PFC Charles Ragland, a black member of a machine-gun team who, along with LCpl Jack Rush and PFC Paul Forbes, raked the elephant grass in front of their hedgerow position. There had been nothing one moment, then a swarming rush of NVA had materialized from nowhere. *Lot of people think a ma-*

chine gun can take care of itself, but all a gunner has on his mind is knocking out what's in front of him. Ragland wished a fireteam had been sent in with them as security. *We can't be lookin' all over the place!* Ragland was terrified of their unprotected position and nervous about some of the Marines deployed along the hedgerow on either side of him. *Lotta boots in Alpha, they don't know what's comin' off, they don't know what to expect, they don't know how to work together.* An NVA was screaming in English to cease fire, and although Ragland, Rush, and Forbes kept their M60 blazing, some of the new guys stopped shooting. Their confusion was compounded by the fact that some of the NVA charging through the tall grass wore Marine helmets and Marine flak jackets. *These guys they had never saw nothin', they just out here, and some of 'em are actually freezing.*

Most weren't. It appeared to LCpl David J. Dishong, a rocket man, that the NVA were unaware of the hedgerow position occupied by him and Corporal Alonzo's squad. Alonzo threw several grenades into their ranks—several NVA appeared to go sprawling in the elephant grass—then he directed artillery fire in as close as possible to the hedgerow edge of their perimeter. More NVA went down. They finally caught sight of Alonzo's squad, and thinking they'd be *pretty swift about it,* as Dishong sarcastically phrased it, the NVA started a brushfire. The wind drove the fire into the hedgerow, and with the NVA coming right behind the flames, Alonzo passed the word to fall back. Dishong unslung his four LAW rockets, hurled them into the fire, then started off, turning to watch with great satisfaction as they exploded just as the NVA reached the hedgerow.

The LZ perimeter disintegrated.

The NVA were coming through the hedgerow to the right of the M60 team and before the crew could shift their fire, the NVA shot Rush and Forbes to death.

The gun team's sole survivor, Ragland, played dead as the NVA overran the position. One NVA picked up his M16 and threw it to the side, and another grabbed him and fired three shots beside his head. Ragland played his role well, though, and the NVA let him go as his team rushed on. Ragland watched through barely opened eyes as the next team of four NVA came through the hedgerow *(walking trees,* he thought), then knelt for a moment to get their bearings before moving out smartly. The first group had ignored most of the Marines lying around the hedgerow, including the immobile wounded, but when the second team moved through, Ragland saw them shoot at least one Marine in the back as he lay there. Then an NVA in the third team through picked up that Marine's M16 while others tore through the pockets and packs of the dead, and the other gear that had been left behind, taking canteens, rations, and ammunition.

As soon as the assault had begun on 3d Platoon, Captain Slater had turned around with 2d Platoon, leaving 1st Platoon to make its own way east to Bravo Company. He knew that Charlie Company and elements of Delta were on the way and that 1st Platoon could find sanctuary with them. The intensity of fire on 3d Platoon, however, demanded immediate reinforcement. Slater tried to raise Muller on the radio as he moved back. He got no answer. Lieutenant Muller had, in fact, been killed. The story that Corporal Toy later got was that Muller's radioman cracked up and dove into a crater (or maybe the radioman had been hit and had rolled there for cover, in the confusion, who knew). Muller was running to him so as to regain radio contact when he was shot in the leg. The leg wound severed a major artery, and Muller bled to death (or maybe he was shot again) as the NVA overran his platoon.

As the NVA swarmed into the westernmost paddy, Sergeant Geizer, up on the southern ridge with radioman Ross, had them in sight amid the stray rounds that snapped through the bamboo around him. He wasn't able to call in a single artillery round before one of those stray bullets caught him in the right side just below the rib cage. The sensation was as if a jackhammer had been held to that spot and punched one time—that was how Geizer visual-

ized it. The burning pain was worse than anything he'd
known was possible, and his first coherent thought was a
laughing scream: *John Wayne, you sonuvabitch!* In the movies you get hit but can still blow away ten Indians, but in
real life Geizer could barely breathe. *This sonuvabitch has
tore me up!*

Ross, beside him in the crater, immediately got on the
radio to the Con Thien CP. "Six One Actual has been hit,
Six One Actual has been hit."

There was intense pain for an intolerably long moment; then Geizer realized he could cope with it. His mind
flashed to the terrifying chance that he was paralyzed, that
his spine had been hit. He was afraid to try to move, but he
finally did and it was okay. He could move. Ross started to
patch him, then exclaimed, "Hey, it came right out the
other side, it came right out!" And Geizer realized that the
bullet had blown a second hole in him, an exit wound out
his back only (he would later learn) a half-inch from his
spinal column. Forever an NCO, though, Geizer gave Ross
hell as he patched him, for the radioman had used his own
field bandage, forgetting that they had been trained to use
the bandage of the wounded man they were helping.

Armed with only a Colt .45, the short, flinty, and
highly respected Gunny Santomasso stood in the drainage
ditch just below the east-west hedgerow of the paddy's
northern edge. A veteran of Korea, he had been Alpha
Company's big-nosed, black-mustached, and shillelagh-car-
rying gunny for four months; and now (again) he was the
calm in the storm as he shouted over the din, directing the
survivors of 3d Platoon to a large crater on the other side
of the hedgerow, actually outside their original lines.

Men made it toward the gunny any way they could, as
Santomasso shouted at one of the Marines to retrieve an
M79 from a dead Marine some ten meters away. The man
was scared and refused to go. Santomasso got on the kid's
ass and decided to get the M79 himself—and immediately
thought better of it for he could suddenly hear Vietnamese
voices. He couldn't see any NVA, but he could hear them

coming up the hedgerow in the drainage ditch. He had already directed his radioman, Crisan, to the refuge of the bomb crater—he was basically alone out there—and he tossed a grenade toward the voices even as he shouted at the young Marine with him to get to the crater. Then he lobbed out his second and last grenade and sprinted for the good, deep hole himself, the final one in.

Gunny Santomasso shouted to one of the radiomen who'd made it to this last-stand position, "Get on your phone and call artillery!"

The kid was near tears, "I don't know how—"

"I don't give a shit if you know how or not. You get your FO and tell 'em where we're at and put it on us—this is it—or we've had it!"

As the radioman got cracking, Gunny Santomasso squeezed .45 rounds into a crawling NVA who was about thirty meters away in the rice paddy. He dropped back down, reholstered his .45, grabbed a young Marine's M16, and raised up again to shoot a second NVA crawling through the grass. Almost immediately, other NVA pulled their comrade to cover as more NVA rushed past, trying to surround the crater. The Marines killed any NVA who exposed himself, and Santomasso turned his sights on his third NVA who came out from behind a bush and went to one knee behind a little, stunted tree.

Simultaneously, this NVA swung his AK47 toward him.

Gunny Santomasso squeezed the trigger—nothing, no shot—and then, it was like a branding iron had been laid against his skin, a real shocking blow, as an AK47 round caught him at belt level on his right side.

He jumped down into the crater and looked to see that the round had torn through his flak jacket. He pulled out a battle dressing expecting to find a bullet hole in his guts, but it was only a nasty, painful, uncritical graze. Santomasso grabbed a young Marine with an M60 machine gun and told him to fire up the gook behind the tree with single shots. They had no ammunition to waste, and Santomasso didn't want the NVA to hear their M60.

Santomasso organized a hasty, all-around defense from the six or eight able-bodied Marines in the crater. He had them take ammunition off the wounded and dead they had dragged in. He shouted that there would be no rapid fire. He bandaged himself (trying to shake off the shock), then secured a second, working M16, and crouched for a moment beside the two corpsmen in the crater. One was in a paralytic state of shock with his eyes rolled back—at first Santomasso thought he was dead—and, ignoring him, he turned to the second corpsman. This man, too, had been stunned into inaction, but he had not disappeared yet. He slowly came out of it as Gunny Santomasso slapped him and shook him by the front of his flak jacket. "We gotta have you, we gotta have you, we got too many wounded kids in here."

Corporal Power unshouldered his pack (which was a more utilitarian NVA type previously taken off an NVA body) and tossed it aside so that he could better fit into the small crater he had sought cover in when the shelling had begun again. He was in the middle paddy about fifteen feet east of the hedgerow that separated the middle paddy from the westernmost one. The NVA were coming through 3d Platoon. *Like shit through a goose,* Power thought. He readied himself like an upsidedown turtle in his miniature crater, feet against the rim, shoulders tight against the opposite rim, helmeted head trying to hunch down. He had his M16 aimed between his knees at the hedgerow. His buddy Sankey was in a similar predicament in another crater some ten meters to his right. There were other Marines here and there in the middle paddy, but most of 2d Platoon was setting up to their rear behind the dike-hedgerow separating the middle paddy from the easternmost paddy.

Sergeant Jefferson broke through the hedgerow.

This was the same hefty new guy who'd been medevacked with heat exhaustion the previous evening, only to be returned to the field this morning, and he was running now, stumbling for his life. Jefferson was already bandaged from wounds received earlier—he'd apparently missed the medevac—and now, Power watched incredulously as Jefferson took more hits. He got hit and he got hit, and his run turned into a slow-motion 180-degree turn, head bent, body leaning in, until he just collapsed dead before completing his little circle in the grass.

The NVA were right behind Sergeant Jefferson, coming through the hedgerow, and Power's life flashed before his eyes. He saw it all in a second, and he realized then and there that everything he had ever done, every decision he had ever made, it had all been to get him in this hole on this day. *I'm dying' right here. That's it. It's over.* Power shot an NVA who burst through the hedgerow with his AK47 at port arms, jumping from the dike to the paddy. He shot the man before he even landed. He was feeling sharp. He was catching every movement. He shot another NVA who came through the bramble. He could hear Sankey to his right similarly placing short bursts into charging NVA, but in his peripheral vision he could see some NVA getting past them. The Marines along the dike behind him opened fire, dropping those NVA dead in their tracks in the high grass.

The NVA stopped charging.

Another stood up from behind the dike to throw a stick-handled grenade right at Power like a line drive. He exposed himself for only a second, but Power, still on his back with his M16 between his knees, shot him. He saw the fucker jerk and drop, just before the Chicom hit him right in the chest where his flak jacket was unzipped. It bounced away.

Other grenades thumped into the dirt an arm's length away and went off with brain-jarring blasts. There was a cross-fire steel storm above Power's head with the Marines behind him getting the upper hand, and the NVA-occupied hedgerow in front of him was shuddering and disintegrating under their unrelenting fire. Power could hear an NVA shouting commands on the other side of that hedgerow. The voice moved up and down the dike, and he hated that man for such a strong, fearless voice. He hated him for keeping his men firing even as their hedgerow cover was shot to pieces. Power knew they were going to kill him. They were going to kill him as he changed magazines. He was trying to keep his bursts short. They were going to kill him with a burst to his head or chest. *I hope it's in the chest. I hope it ain't in the face.* Thoughts flashed through his mind even as he kept shooting. *I hope the motherfucker who kills me is something of a poet, who has a little sensitivity in his soul and will realize what he's done. I hope it won't be some fucking redneck gook who's going to rub me out and think nothing of it.*

When Cpl Sammie K. Peterson, a mortar man and salty veteran of Operation Hickory, first saw the NVA coming through the elephant grass, the helmets and flak jackets some of them wore gave him considerable pause. *Might be Marines.* He hesitated an additional moment before firing from his crater. *If I shoot him, he's going to shoot back.* Training, of course, took over, but so did hatred. The very sound of the NVAs' high-pitched singsong jabber drove him into a fury. It sounded like they were laughing, fucking laughing about the Marines they had killed in the LZ.

Little slant-eyed bastards, Peterson thought. He opened fire and *dinged* a couple of them, as he put it, before the ones he could see dived into the elephant grass. He enjoyed their deaths. He wanted to crush them. He wanted to slit their throats.

The NVA had the same intentions. First, the ammo man to Peterson's mortar crew got shot in the hand; then, their assistant gunner got shot in the leg. The NVA were firing toward the team's 60mm mortar, the only one left in the company, which was on its bipod beside their holes, and Peterson finally got balls enough to rush out and tip it over. The NVA fire on them slackened a bit then. The wounded A-gunner was, meanwhile, sitting in a tight hole with his wounded leg cramping up until, insane from the pain and the sun scorch, he leaped from his cover. He stumbled around, trying to ease the knots in his bleeding leg and crying for water, while everyone hollered at him to get back in his hole. Peterson thought to throw something at the man to knock him out so he could be dragged back to cover, so he slung a full canteen with all his might for a perfect hit on the man's head. It had no effect, so he finally dashed out and physically threw the wounded man back into his hole. Peterson jumped back and called to his squad leader, two holes down, to crawl over and massage the man's gun-shot leg to keep him from flipping out again. The squad leader shouted back, "You're crazy as hell!"

The NVA artillery commenced firing again. By this time, Captain Slater had reached the northern hedgerow of the three paddies. In no good position to organize or direct anything (the situation had him and his radiomen at the prone ready to blow away anything that might pop up), Slater at least tried to coordinate artillery support. It was impossible. He couldn't distinguish the incoming NVA artillery from the incoming USMC artillery, and shells were impacting here, there, and everywhere. It was a madhouse. There was no way he could adjust the fire. Slater could see NVA rushing through the elephant grass to the north, and he realized there were Marines, including Gunny Santomasso, who he recognized, bobbing up from a crater out there to shoot them down. The NVA were maneuvering past this crater to assault 2d Platoon's northern positions (all hastily assumed), who were also responding with well-aimed shots. The NVA were thus totally vulnerable to the gunny's half-dozen, who would pop up one or two at a time to drop another NVA from a few feet with M16 fire. The NVA appeared totally confused by these bursts that seemed to originate from nowhere, and their attack from the north fell apart.

On the low ridge overlooking the overrun LZ, Sergeant Geizer, all alone up there with PFC Ross in their bamboo-surrounded crater, was dying a million deaths. The pain of the gunshot wound that had punched through his side and out his back had become unreal. Intolerable. He bit through the chin strap of his helmet. He broke off pieces of the bamboo that he could reach, the reeds were only as wide as his little finger, and chewed them to splinters in his agony. He was still coherent enough, though, to see the new puffs of smoke from the north when the NVA artillery again commenced fire, raining steel on Marines and North Vietnamese alike in the paddies.

CRASH!

CRASH!

CRASH! CRASH!

Choking back the pain, Geizer took the radio handset from Ross and made contact with the Con Thien CP. He tried to call in a mission on the NVA artillery he could see in North Vietnam, but was told, "You can't call in a mission. Your assistant has a mission in progress."

Either Sankey or Duckworth was bringing in the rounds, so Geizer got off the radio and concentrated on his more immediate circumstances. Seven feet down the ridge line and across a dozen meters of rice paddy there were NVA foot soldiers. The whole LZ paddy was full of them. Geizer could see them, or to be correct, he could see a paddy in which clumps of elephant grass moved. There were two Marines at the base of the ridge at the southwest corner of the paddies who had hopped the hedgerow dike, so they were actually outside their old perimeter. They rose at intervals to spray the LZ with M16 fire. They weren't aiming, but it was almost impossible to miss considering all the grassy clumps in the LZ. From his meager perch, Geizer could see several of the clumps heading toward the two isolated Marines. They approached slowly, gradually raising their heads—their pith helmets and bush hats were completely covered with elephant grass—until just their eyes were above the real grass. Then having looked around, they crept a bit closer. Geizer turned to Ross, "Get over there and tell those sons of bitches to get up on the high ground."

Ross moved out, going left down the ridge.

Geizer gritted his teeth to keep from crying out in pain. Ross crawled back into the crater. He apparently could get no response from the stranded Marines, but once back under cover, he did join the downhill shooting into the paddy. He said he got one—and then his rifle jammed.

Ross couldn't believe it; he was beside himself. He was defenseless.

It was Geizer's turn. He'd been feeling guilty because he had an M16 and 200 rounds of ammunition, more than he needed as an artillery spotter, as well as four fragmentation and two tear-gas grenades, and he had never seen such a potential turkey shoot in all his sixteen months in the bush. But he was in such pain he had not fired a single shot. Again, he choked down the pain, lifted up, shouldered his rifle, and squared his sights on a clump of grass about seventy feet away that was moving toward those two Marines. The NVA had his face above the wave of real elephant grass. Geizer squeezed the trigger once—the shot blew away most of the NVA's head—then slumped back into the crater. He was so wretched, so miserable with pain that he couldn't bring himself to fire again. *All this ammo and grenades,* he chided himself.

His one shot had been enough, though, because now rounds kicked up around him so closely that he knew they weren't more stray shots. Somebody had him in his sights. There was another shot and Geizer knew he'd been hit. He had felt the impact under his shoulder, but when he rolled away onto his bandaged right side, he saw that the bullet had actually furrowed into the ground underneath where he'd been lying.

Geizer rolled back onto his stomach, looking up with his M16 ready in his hands. He could tell from the trajectory of the impacting shots that the NVA must be in a tree. He did not, however, begin firing randomly and rapidly into the treetops. He had, after all, been raised around guns and had always been taught to conserve ammo. *One of the worst things Marines do is when one enemy bullet zings in, that selector goes to automatic and, boy, they let loose.* Usually to no benefit. Geizer held his fire and scanned the treetops for the sniper. But then, there was a tremendous whack to his helmet, which remained on his head, and immediately, he felt blood running down the left side of his face. The round had drilled through the left-rear of his steel pot, the burst-open metal slicing through hair and skin down to the skull in a splatter of blood. The pain was not excessive, and Geizer scrambled away again. This time, he hoped, completely out of the target zone.

His mind formed words meant for Ross that he shouted, or thought he shouted, or at least meant to shout. It was hard to tell, his brain was all wobbly. "Hey, this guy's had his three tries for a quarter, and he's just getting too close. We're getting out of here!"

<u>12</u>

Banzai

★

It was the North Vietnamese who ended the stalemate between them and Bravo Company, 1st Battalion, 9th Marines, 3d Marine Division. They ended the stalemate by overrunning the Command Post and the 2d Platoon of Bravo Company.

PFC Henderson, lying in front of the bamboo with his .45 in hand and a dozen grenades hanging from his web gear and flak jacket, could hear NVA moving in the bushes. In fact, he'd tossed a couple grenades where he could actually hear them jabbering. Suddenly, there were shouted commands in Vietnamese, and just as abruptly, NVA came swarming out of the brush. Banzai. Because of the bamboo wall, which would have broken the momentum of their assault, the NVA did not charge into Henderson's little group, but they streamed past the flanks. They just ran through screaming and shooting those Marines they could see, intent on reaching the main road where the Marines with the radios were hunkered down. Henderson lay there stunned, unable to bring himself to fire, amazed that no one seemed to notice him. He thought the NVA looked crazy. They were just a wild mob, some of them with insane faces as they ran firing into trees, bushes, and men so indiscriminately that Henderson was convinced that NVA were accidentally killing other NVA. Others stumbled along vacant-eyed, rushing right past him without pause. He was so bloody, maybe they thought he was dead. The NVA shouted to each other as they ran past, little guys in green with grass sticking from their helmets and gear, so that in moments the brush had swallowed them back up as they streaked on for the main road.

It seemed that some of the NVA following the main assault line hadn't gotten the word about this stranded group of Marines. Henderson had his M16 sitting atop the little berm that bordered the footpath where he lay, and he looked beyond that into a coverless stretch of field into which came strolling three NVA atop a dike. They were walking close together, and the one at the tail even had his AK47 slung over his shoulder instead of in his hands ready to use. Henderson meant to kill them, but when he propped himself up against the berm, his shoulder wound, which was unbandaged but kept nicely shut by his tight-fitting flak jacket, spread apart in a flush of hot blood down his back. Gritting his teeth, Henderson quickly sighted his M16, emptied the eighteen-round magazine in one burst, then slid back down onto the footpath to resume the position that had kept his shoulder wound sealed. It looked like his sweeping burst had caught all three NVA, but he really couldn't be sure. And after having gone through this procedure of bleeding and firing several times before this banzai, he decided to just let it go. They were all going to die anyway. He just resigned himself to it as did, it seemed, the other wounded Marines sprawled here and there around him. It was as if the pain of their wounds had slapped them into reality; so while the unwounded ran around like crazy men, screaming and wasting ammunition, there was no yelling among the wounded. There was only the unspoken feeling that when the NVA came back for

them they would keep killing North Vietnamese until they
themselves were killed.

The main body of NVA reached the intersection of
Route 561 and the east-to-west trail in a screaming, shooting fury. They were met there by Corporal Garza who,
already wounded twice but still in position in the sunken
road, wouldn't stop firing his M60 machine gun. Chicoms
came over the roadside hedgerows, followed by AK-firing
NVA; and Captain Keneipp, only days away from reassignment to the astronaut training program at NASA, provided
Bravo Six's last words to the CP at Con Thien; "I don't
think I'll be talking to you again. We are being overrun."

Captain Coates was killed.
Captain Keneipp was killed.
Lieutenant King was killed.
Corporal Demers was killed.
Corporal Garza was killed.
Corporal Haines was killed.
Lance Corporal Bradley was killed.

Some fifty feet east of this terrible crescendo of fire
was the twice-wounded PFC Hendry, still huddled in the
trailside ditch with Hughes and Pigott. They could hear a
Marine screaming back on Route 561, *"No, no, please don't
kill me, oh God, please . . ."*

A shot, a final scream.

There was no more Marine fire from the CP area.
Fuck this! Hendry thought as the situation became abruptly
clear, and Pigott looked back at him, equally horror-
stricken. *"We gotta get the hell out of here."*

Hendry tried to pass the word to Hughes, but he was
still deaf and stunned from the grenade that had gone off
above his head. So they had had to kick him to get the idea
across. The NVA were still not visible to them around the
elbow of their trail, but they were now so close on the main
sunken road that they could be heard plainly as they spoke
to each other. Pigott led the way, running north to south
across their east-west trail and crashing through the brush
to a footpath that led south in a course parallel to but east

of Route 561. Pigott was followed by a limping Hendry and a concussed Hughes, and they made it about forty meters before sudden and heavy fire sent them sprawling.

Meanwhile, PFC Weldon followed his engineer buddy out of their trench when they heard the shouts to pull back. It was mass confusion, made worse by the burning bamboo and elephant grass, and in the smoke, Weldon lost sight of the engineer. He panicked. He had no idea where he was going. He picked a direction in the choking smoke and moved that way.

"No, we gotta go back this way!"

The engineer had doubled back for Weldon and was waving him back in the right direction. "No, come this way, we gotta get outta here!"

In Hendry's group, Pigott jumped up to run again, and from out of nowhere, Hendry's buddy Weldon bounded into view about twenty meters ahead. Relieved to see people standing upright and surviving, Hendry (with Hughes tailing him) followed Weldon. Within moments, Hendry saw several Marines huddled in a bomb crater so he leaped in, looked around, and realized that good old Weldon was sitting beside him. Weldon explained how he'd gotten shot and how he'd gotten the laughing bastard that did it. Sergeant Huff of the mortar section was in the crater, and it seemed, at least temporarily, to be the safest place around. So when Hughes stumbled by, they screamed at him to get in the crater with them. Hughes's concussion was still too much, and he wandered past them in a daze. Somehow he made it to safety on his own.

The last radio contact that Lieutenant Delaney had with whoever was on Bravo Six's radio was a whispered voice, which explained that he was the last man alive around the command post. The whisper said that he had been hit four times and that there were NVA within five feet of him. The perimeter had collapsed and Lieutenant Delaney, realizing that their bamboo hideaway was now the front, told his radioman, Lance Corporal Cromwell, to lie down in the tall grass. If the NVA proceeded through their position, Delaney said, they were to hold their fire and more or less play dead.

One of the radiomen with the Six CP, Cpl. Domingo Trevino, lost consciousness after being shot in the leg. When he awoke, everyone around him was dead, and an NVA machine gun was firing from nearby. Trevino responded with his M16 and managed to empty the magazine before the return fire tore up his flak jacket and right shoulder. The NVA did not finish him off, but tied his hands behind his back and began dragging him across the fields east of Route 561 as he blacked out several times. Finally, as he lay bleeding and exhausted, they tied another rope around his waist that they then secured around a tree before moving off into the bushes. Presumably they had left Trevino in the open there as bait for an ambush within an ambush.

Even before the situation had completely deteriorated for Bravo Company's road-bound 2d and 3d Platoon, Staff Sergeant Burns and his tail-end 1st Platoon had had their hands full with reinforcements being fed into the fray from Hill 70 to the east. Conducting business from the crater beside the demolished concrete hootch on the eastern shoulder of Route 561, Burns had his machine gunner, LCpl Peter Talmon, hose down every rush visible to them in the elephant grass. Talmon seemed to hit at least two of the bastards and a new man, PFC Watson, did an equally outstanding job, exposing himself to fire seven LAWs into Hill 70. Burns saw at least two more NVA go down from the LAW explosions. The rest kept working their way in until they had gotten within range to add a captured M79 grenade launcher to the mortar barrage landing around the platoon's crossroad positions. The NVA fired their M79 from so close that the Marines could hear each shell's outgoing pop, though they could see no one in the hedgerows and elephant grass around them.

Then the NVA got within hand-grenade range, and an NVA charged them on the heels of the first Chicom explosion. The man wore a recon-style bush hat and what Burns took to be a large pack, and he ran across Burns's front and hit the deck. Burns realized the pack was really a Soviet flamethrower just as the NVA let go with a stream of fire in the direction of Talmon and his M60 machine gun.

A flamethrower! Swinging his 12-gauge shotgun on the flamethrower operator, Burns kept his finger back on the trigger and pumped off four shells with such speed that it sounded like an automatic weapon. The NVA had not been aware of Burns until Burns popped from his crater to fire, and, blasted and bleeding, the NVA did not fire again. A few minutes later, a Chicom bounced off the rifle barrel of one of the Marines and exploded nearly at his feet, not injuring the rifleman but starting a grass fire on the right flank. Burns gave the startled Marine a hand-and-arm signal to move back and cover the rear of his crater. Then, he noticed another NVA trying to follow the fire into the platoon's perimeter. The NVA came over the embankment with bush hat, ammo vest, and automatic weapon, and Staff Sergeant Burns stood up again from his cover. This time his shotgun barked with lethality. In fact, the 12-gauge blew away most of the man's head.

Bravo One's platoon sergeant (in reality a young buck sergeant) was in position at the rear when he saw a man in helmet and flak jacket moving through the trees. Realizing that their reinforcements had finally broken through, he hollered, "Hey, Alpha Company over here!" The man, another NVA in USMC gear, wheeled and fired in response, dropping the platoon sergeant. Excited, the NVA did not rush to cover, and the sergeant, though shot in the leg, was able to M16 the NVA into the ground.

The platoon sergeant was hit in the company of the most rearward squad, under Corporal Pitts, which was taking the brunt of it. Afterward, Pitts would discover that only he and two others had come through unscathed, while three in his squad had died and eight had been wounded. Pitts lost his squad one or two at a time as the hot afternoon dragged on. First, two of his fireteam leaders got wounded; then, his grenadier got shot through the arm near the elbow so he could no longer handle his M79. Two fearless NVA—unusually large men made bigger by helmets, flak jackets, and web gear—dashed across Route 561 to the south, firing bursts right into the squad as they ran. They killed two Marines. Other NVA, unseen in the bush, further confused the situation by shouting orders in English at the Marines.

Corporal Pitts and his squad did not crack. The M79-man, who'd been doing a great job until shot in the arm, ran to help with his good arm when he saw Pitts dragging a wounded team leader to cover. At that time, they took an automatic burst, and the grenadier had two fingers shot off. He simply crawled over to Pitts and asked him to chamber a round in his .45 for him since he couldn't do it with his mangled hand. Another wounded man, a team leader, kept his M16 in action despite being shot in the arm, and then in the leg, then in the other leg, and finally in the other arm. He never got shook up. He would just holler to Pitts to let him know he'd been hit again before resuming fire.

Soon after the crescendo of fire up Route 561, Staff Sergeant Burns could raise neither Captains Coates nor Keneipp. He had likewise lost all commo with 2d and 3d Platoons. Lieutenant Delaney was no longer on the net either. Burns did not think Delaney was dead; it did not appear that the NVA had reached the exec's bamboo hideaway. But he rated the lieutenant's leadership skills as *zippoint-shit,* and his next thought was *hey, that's it—you're in charge.*

Burns told his radioman, a bespectacled kid who was nearly incapacitated by the direct sunlight filling their crater, to switch to the air freq; then he took the handset. "Bird Dog, Bird Dog, this is Bravo One."

Finally, a response: "Who are you?"

"This is Bravo One, Two, Three, Four, Five, and Six, and I need all the help that I can get. If you don't get somebody in here pretty soon this is going to be the Lost

Command. I don't care if you get the Army in here, but we gotta get somebody in here."

The voice in Burns's ear belonged to a Bird Dog spotter pilot, orbiting the battlefield as a flight of A1 Skyraiders came on station. "We're trying to get somebody in. I can see 'em coming."

Not good enough. The tank-infantry relief force, whose progress the Bird Dog was presently reporting, had only just started north from the Strip; meanwhile, Burns could no longer see up Route 561 for all the smoke filling the sunken road. The grass fire started earlier by the Chicom had spread out of control (perhaps fueled by another NVA flamethrower), engulfing the hedgerows between Burns and Delaney's group. The NVA continued firing through the smoke and flame, and Burns's growing casualties included their heroic machine gunner Talmon who was mortally wounded. The survival of those who remained rested on superior firepower to squash the numerical superiority of the NVA; so, calmly conferring with the Bird Dog pilot, the one and only voice he could get on the radio, Burns, who had just seen another NVA squad in the elephant grass atop Hill 70, called for the first air strike there.

Burns watched the NVA squad drop out of sight on the eastern slope of Hill 70 just as the Skyraiders' napalm burst on impact and sent streaming fingers of fire splashing across the hilltop. Right on target. Marine Air really was the best. And, although Burns could see none of the NVA who were firing on his platoon (between the brush, the fire, and the smoke, he really couldn't see much of anything), he could sense their positions. So he told Bird Dog to have the Skyraiders next expend their ordnance no more than fifty meters from the road. Again, the air strike was dead on target, breathtakingly so, frightfully so,[1] splashing the

---

1. And surprisingly so, considering Staff Sergeant Burns's imprecise method of marking targets. The company's 3.5-inch rocket launchers, capable of firing WP marking rounds, had been replaced by lightweight, prone-to-misfire LAW rockets, so Burns had been reduced to

last of the flight's napalm to within fifteen meters of Burns and his Marines. The jellied fire boiled up right before them, sucking the air from their lungs, the heat on them like paint, while the air swirled with ash and dust. Beautiful, perfect, but although the NVA fire did lessen, Bird Dog immediately reported to Burns that he could see forty NVA at the crossroad farther up the trail. That had been the center of Bravo Six's position. Burns, realizing the worst had probably occurred, made a decision that he relayed to Bird Dog: "Okay, you know what to do. There's nobody firing down there, they must all be dead. I want an air strike on that area."[2]

Two survivors were trying to make it back down Route 561. One of the assistant mortar gunners, PFC Ronnie B. Fields, watched as one of the survivors who was already wounded stumbled and fell on the road. His buddy went back to help him, and on that spot they both died, shot in the head. Horrified, Fields asked Sergeant Huff, the mortar section leader, if they hadn't better pull back to where Burns's platoon was set up behind them on the road. Huff agreed. The first order of business, though, was to retrieve LCpl Simon Cull, a mortar gunner who had found himself

---

throwing WP grenades to mark targets. Very imprecise. This was another reason he regretted the recent replacement of their M14 rifles with M16s, for not only was the M14 more dependable, a better sniper rifle, and capable of firing M60 ammunition (which eased resupply problems), but it could also be fitted with a grenade-launcher mount that would fire WP shells. This was the most precise way to mark targets for close air support, and as soon as Burns returned to Con Thien he requested that at least one M14 be reissued to each platoon.
2. Back at Con Thien, Burns discussed this air strike with Ritchie, their acting gunnery sergeant, "Ritchie had a bad case of shell shock. He was shaking like a dog shitting a peach pit. Ritchie said he was in a hole, and he was playing dead, and there was a North Vietnamese standing at the top of the hole getting ready to shoot him. They came in with the close air, and either the close air got the North Vietnamese or else he took off running. I felt very badly that I might have killed some of my own people, but Ritchie told me, 'If you hadn't of done what you did, none of us would have got out alive.'"

pinned down by one particular sniper. Huff popped M16
cover fire toward the NVA's dugout, and Cull made his
scramble back to the soon-to-depart main group.

Nearby, Lieutenant Delaney and his radioman, Lance
Corporal Cromwell, were also planning to make their bird.
They had survived unscathed so far because of the dense
bamboo thicket overhanging the part of the shallow roadside ditch where they had sought cover. It shielded them
and deflected what rounds did come snapping through.
And with Huff's Marines deployed around them, they were
tucked in the middle of the fight and had probably felt the
safest of any of the participants. Which was negligible comfort, especially when several Marines appeared from the
smoke and ash and burning hedgerows ahead and ran past
them on the road. They looked like the last survivors of the
lead platoons. And so with smoke rolling into their bamboo thicket (the brushfire was bearing down on them), Delaney said to Cromwell that it was time; they had to move.
Delaney was humping his gear and Cromwell his radio;
both of them were weak from the sun and could barely
move. And with the trail slowly being consumed by fire
around them, their first thought was that it would take too
long to crawl back through the underbrush along their side
of the road.

The fire hadn't reached the opposite side, though, and
Delaney attempted a quick crossing. He immediately drew
several automatic bursts and several individual sniper
shots, one round of which grazed his left forearm, and he
instantly spun around and jumped back down in the ditch.
Cromwell wrapped a bandage around Delaney's arm, and
with Delaney leading the way, they began clawing and
crawling their way south through the hedgerow on their
side of the road. Their fear was so great as they heard the
NVA firing from closer and still closer, that they felt neither the thorns nor their fatigue. They had not gone far
when NVA fire converged on the bamboo they'd just exited, and then, the NVA moved a captured M60 to the
trail. Cromwell wiggled the brush as he crawled, drew a
quick burst from the M60, and was grazed in the arm just

enough to draw blood. Five minutes and a few meters farther on, still crawling and still shaking the brush, he was
knicked in the shoulder from behind by what sounded like
an M16 rifle in NVA hands.

Meanwhile, Sergeant Huff of the Weapons Platoon,
also intent on pulling back, left his cover and moved to the
other side of the road to ensure that he was leaving none of
his men behind. He saw no one, but before they made their
move, a man in the brush between Huff's position and acting gunnery sergeant Ritchie suddenly opened fire with his
M60 backward toward 1st Platoon. Huff jumped up again,
screaming to stop; but when the helmeted, flak-jacketed
man swung the M60 on him (once more, an NVA had
gotten into their lines by wearing Marine gear), Huff instantly shot the gunner to death with a short burst from his
M16.

That was it. Sergeant Huff shouted a command, and
the next thing Delaney and Cromwell knew, men of the
Weapons Platoon emerged from the brush to run past
them on the road. A bomb landed then, fifty meters up-
trail, and the sunken road was awash in smoke, dust, and
ash—a real smoke screen. So Delaney jumped out onto the
road, "Cromwell, everybody's going! Let's get out of here!"
Cromwell, following, the radio an extra twenty-five-pound
burden on his back, finally succumbed to the heat, passed
out on the road, as Delaney, half dead himself, stumbled
along with his eyes forward.

No one noticed Cromwell as he lay unconscious.

PFC Weldon came out of Huff's crater with neither his
M16 nor his ammo bandoliers. They had been given to an
able-bodied Marine because Weldon had previously been
fading in and out of consciousness. Now, though, despite
his shock and blood loss he was moving fast to save his life
(*surprising what the human will does,* as he later put it),
following the helmet bobbing ahead of him as they raced
through the scrub brush. The first five Marines out of the
crater ran through a hedgerow and disappeared into a
bamboo thicket about thirty meters away. *No sweat,* PFC
Hendry thought, but when his turn came, he discovered

that his through-and-through shot leg had stiffened up. He
limped toward the bamboo with rounds kicking up dirt
around him, and upon reaching this cover, he promptly fell
down.

One at a time, more Marines crashed into the bamboo. Some paused to put down covering bursts for Corporal Warren and PFC Wiggams of the Weapons Platoon
who'd been wounded after clambering up the crater side
and out into the open for the run to the bamboo. The reeds
snapped above their heads from NVA firing on full auto,
and the brushfire shimmered toward them. The Marines
took off again through the bamboo stalks, streaking
through both fires to reach the main road. Hendry ran as
well as he could, then dived into a hedgerow next to a man
who'd been shot in the elbow, so his forearm just hung
uselessly. He asked Hendry to bandage him, and Hendry
was just finishing the job when another mortar round
landed on the road, this time only fifteen meters away so
that Hendry was suddenly slapped and stung. He'd taken
two chunks in his leg and thirteen smaller pieces in his
hands and arms. The elbow-shot man had also picked up a
few additional wounds.

Upon reaching Bravo One, PFC Fields and another
Marine from the Weapons Platoon were directed to take
up positions on the left flank. They had no more gotten set
in than there was the report of a .45 pistol, and Fields
twisted around only to see that the pistol shot had missed
an NVA coming out of a nearby hedgerow. The NVA shot
first with his AK47, drilling Fields in his left arm and left
leg, but Fields still managed to swing his M16 around and
dropped the NVA dead on the spot with a burst to the
chest.

After being peppered by the mortar round, Hendry
suddenly realized no one else was around, and he took off
in as much of a flat-out run as his wounds would allow.
Twenty meters farther south was Bravo One, and reaching
them, he fell completely spent into some bushes. He hung

suspended there, watching the blood run from his new wounds, and for the first time all day he lit a cigarette— then another, and another. He drank from his canteen, and he prayed. He prayed *very* hard, as NVA fire continued to crack around them. Then he heard a thud, and glancing toward the road, he saw a grenade sitting there smoking. He couldn't do anything. He didn't have the energy to spring up and run, and the bushes holding him up wouldn't let him press down any lower. *This is just what I need, god-dammit!* He put his arms over his head. The grenade did not explode. It was another dud.

Hating to do it but not sure they would survive otherwise, Staff Sergeant Burns passed the word to pull out of their crossroad perimeter. If anyone in 2d and 3d Platoons who had not already made it back was still alive, he did not know. But the number of NVA now bearing down on 1st Platoon's positions was too great, so with Burns at the tail covering his men with his shotgun, the survivors began stumbling south on Route 561. They had not gone far when they could hear tanks approaching, coming north toward them from the Strip. *Charlie Company.* Sergeant Huff began to cry in relief.

13

Better Late Than Never

★

Starting north on Route 561 from the Strip toward the sounds of explosions and automatic weapons, Captain Radcliffe, who was going into battle for the first time, could not believe how drained he already felt. During training exercises at Camp Lejeune or Vieques Island, he had prided himself on his water discipline. Even on the hottest of days he never needed to go into his second canteen. But the sun above Con Thien was unreal in its intensity. It was also dry as hell, and every step on the dirt road produced another little powdery cloud (Radcliffe thought of the comic character Pigpen) that began to coat his face and forearms gleaming with sweat.

Behind Radcliffe, Lieutenant Turchan of Delta Three was setting his people in against the Strip, facing north. Alongside Radcliffe on the dusty trail were Lieutenant Howell and Corporal Thompson, who humped the radio as the three of them hiked north. The tank-platoon commander, the staff sergeant, had been reluctant to get on the main trail and reluctant to advance without infantry security, so only two of the four tanks advanced initially. The group had gone up the road about thirty or forty meters when they bumped into the first two or three of Bravo Company's wounded survivors staggering south. Lieutenant Howell, late of Bravo Company himself and very anxious to reach his former compatriots, recognized the men and asked them what was happening. *No real help here,* Radcliffe thought as he listened to their semicoherent answers. He sent the men on down the road then, and as they continued on, Howell recognized another familiar face coming toward them: Lieutenant Delaney.

"Hey, Delaney, where the hell's Bravo Company?"

"I don't know. I couldn't get up to 'em."

Rightly or wrongly, Radcliffe made the snap judgement (there is no other kind in combat) that Delaney really meant *wouldn't* and that the man would be of no value to them.

As Radcliffe tried to question Delaney, he responded with a vacant stare and rambling explanations that became a bit incoherent. The heat, that terrific, brutal heat, had wilted Delaney. Radcliffe told him to get to Turchan's position; there he was to let Turchan know who he was, organize the Bravo stragglers there into fireteams and squads, and to stand by to assist the relief force. "Flesh out Turchan's perimeter, and do the best you can to account for the men we're going to send back to you."

Another ten to twenty meters up the trail, Radcliffe, Howell, and Thompson ushered back another few of Bravo's walking wounded; then they knelt behind cover as AK47 fire began to crack from some trees off the road. It was the first enemy fire directed at the relief force. Anxious to keep pushing and to avoid getting tied down in a squad-sized squabble, it was then that Radcliffe noticed two men in the field to the right, twenty meters or less from him. One of them was lying down; the other was kneeling, starting to get up. Radcliffe thought it was a Marine and a wounded Marine; then, he realized the one getting up was shouldering an AK47. Bap-bap-bap-bap-bap-bap-bap-bap.

Before Radcliffe had time to think, he dropped both of them with his M16. He saw the kneeling one get hit, saw him spin and collapse over the prone man, as Thompson rushed up from behind to also squeeze off a burst. Radcliffe was not confident about his shooting (he had never fired expert on the rifle or pistol) and he rushed toward the NVA to make sure they were both really dead. He pushed the one NVA off the other. Both dead. He had put about five rounds in each man. He was incredulous.

Staff Sergeant Burns, covering the rear of Bravo Company's retreat with a shotgun in one hand and a LAW in the other, had only backed up some forty meters from the junction where his platoon had fought all afternoon. He was on the west side of the road, moving cautiously, when he bumped into Captain Radcliffe and Lieutenant Howell who, along with Corporal Thompson and several functioning survivors of Bravo Company, were near a roadside crater. Radcliffe approached this obvious leader to ask who he was.

"I'm Staff Sergeant Burns, the First Platoon Commander."

"Who's the company commander?"

"Right now it looks like it's me."

Burns gave a look of greeting to Howell, whom he recognized and considered manna from heaven, then glanced back to Radcliffe. "Who are you?"

"I'm Captain Radcliffe, Bravo Company's new commander."

"Well, welcome fucking aboard, skipper. Welcome aboard."

"Burns, where's Bravo Company?"

"This is it."

"What?!"

Burns's emotions were suddenly strained, "Sir, this is your command. This is it. This is First Platoon and that's all there is left."

"Well, I want to know where the rest of my people are."

"They're up forward, sir."

"Well, we gotta go up and get them. What do we gotta do to get up there?"

"Get another battalion on line and sweep this area."

Actually, it probably would have taken another regiment, and Captain Radcliffe was coming to understand what a hopeless, desperate situation he was walking into. *Like being spun around and dropped in the middle of the Amazon,* he thought. He had no communications with the people he had come to save; he didn't know what in the hell was going on; and the relief force he was leading seemed suddenly like a piecemeal, helter-skelter response to the situation. *Christ.* He had to start somewhere, so he asked, "Where are the NVA?"

"Skipper, they're every-fuckin'-where. You can shoot anywhere you want. Take your pick, skipper."

"We're going up there and get 'em [the survivors of Bravo Company, not the North Vietnamese], you going with us?"

"Yes, sir, but I want my people to stay here because they've had it."

Captain Radcliffe had noticed earlier some twenty individuals coming south along a tree line that ran north-south about ninety meters east of Route 561. Not sure who the hell was who, Radcliffe had held his fire. But now as they continued forward again, this time with Burns along, they had not gone ten paces when a multitude of AK47s erupted from the direction of those previously unidentified figures. Radcliffe and crew ran back into their crater. He was looking to the rear for their tanks when radioman Thompson told him that Bird Dog was making a pass over the tree line. They had radio contact with the pilot who informed him that he could see approximately a hundred NVA in the tree line and that he had air on station. Hearing this, Burns looked at Radcliffe, "You ever call in an air strike?"

No, he hadn't, so he passed the handset to Burns with the comment, "Call the sonuvabitch in."

This Burns did, saturating the tree line with bombs

and napalm from several passes, which dissolved the enemy fire from that location but did nothing about the NVA still firing from the field between the road and the tree line. Those NVA were in prepared positions, spiderholes and trenches, and Burns instructed Bird Dog to bring the next strikes in even closer to their road. Radcliffe was amazed that napalm could land so close and not also burn them up alive. But they survived, and it was the NVA who ceased firing. Bird Dog kept running strikes until he ran out of fuel. ("I've got to bingo back to base—you got about seventy to ninety dead over there.") And as their air support banked off and they dug themselves out of their crater, Burns sarcastically asked Radcliffe, "Was that close enough?"

Shortly thereafter (sometime after noon), Thompson handed the radio handset to Radcliffe: Charlie Company had just started landing back at the Strip. The point of Charlie Company was presently humping into Turchan's perimeter as their CO, Hutchinson, spoke with Radcliffe via radio: "Bravo Six, this is Charlie Six. We're in the zone. You know what the situation is. I'm putting my company in your hands. Whaddya need?"

Radcliffe was elated. He hadn't known that Charlie Company was inbound, that hadn't been part of the CP briefing, and he told Hutchinson, "I need a platoon up here ASAP to give me some protection on that right flank with these tanks and to keep these assholes off my back. We got NVA everywhere up here." Hutchinson rogered that. He meant to send Libutti's platoon forward to Radcliffe, but they had not all landed yet. It would be some thirty minutes before all of Charlie Company was on the ground from Dong Ha.

A raggedy column of figures approached Lieutenant Turchan's Strip position from the north. The corpsmen attached to Delta Three, Doc Lindenmeyer and Doc Shade (a pair of skinny, bespectacled young men), studied their approach, and when they saw black faces in the group, they knew they were Marines and not NVA in USMC gear.

They all appeared to be wounded to some degree, and one of them approached Lindenmeyer. "Doc, I'm a Bravo Company doc, but I've lost my Unit One.[1] I've a casualty here I want you to see. He has heatstroke."

Lindenmeyer followed him over to the heat casualty who happened to be a black Marine. The man was not sweating, and his skin was hot and dry except where the Bravo doc had been rubbing him with a handkerchief dampened with the last of his canteen water. Lindenmeyer gave the Bravo doc one of his canteens as he instructed, "Strip him naked, boots too. I'll get more water."

Lindenmeyer climbed aboard one of the tanks and yelled to be heard over the roar of the engines, "I need your water can! I have a heat casualty who'll die without it!"

"Okay!"

As far as Lindenmeyer could tell the tank had only a single five-gallon water can, so the crew was making a great sacrifice. Jumping down with the water can, he returned to the Bravo doc, and they immediately began to wet the man down from head to toe. Afterward, Lindenmeyer made his way over to Lieutenant Turchan's radioman who, considering the brown-bar's greenness, almost appeared to be running the platoon. Lindenmeyer reported, "I have three emergency medevacs and five priorities, and the rest are routine. Call in some choppers."

"Okay, doc, I'll call you when they're inbound."

Sgt Thomas L. McGuigan, Right Guide for Delta Three and as new as Lieutenant Turchan, saw two Marines from Bravo struggling with another wounded Marine down Route 561. McGuigan ran out to help carry the man in; then, he put a battle dressing around the bullet hole in the man's stomach and the exit wound out his side. He helped the man to the casualty collection point, threw his helmet off, and rushed back outside their lines to assist any other wounded he could find. The first man he ran into was a Marine who had streamers fluttering from his arms and

1. Unit One referred to a corpsman's field medical equipment.

legs, the long ties to numerous battle dressings. As the
Marine continued by on his own power, he tossed McGui-
gan a grenade, the pin safely in place, with the comment,
"You'll need this."

After running the air strikes on their right flank, Captain Radcliffe took the lead on the right side off Route 561.
Corporal Thompson was, as instructed, ten feet behind him
("Tell 'em what the hell we're doin', I don't have time to
screw with 'em. When I need you, I'll call you"); while
Lieutenant Howell and Staff Sergeant Burns were almost
shoulder to shoulder on the left side of the road. They had
the area divided up—who was to look low, left, high, right,
etc.—and they advanced a cautious step at a time, tensed
and ready to blast anything that came at them, until it
appeared that the latest air strikes had cleared the way for
them. They began taking normal steps, and Radcliffe
drifted to the middle of the ten-foot-wide road.

Burns, who had relaxed not a bit, called to him, "Get
over to the side of the road!"

"I gotta see where we're going."

"You'll see in a body bag if you don't get over to the
side of the road."

With Charlie Company on the way, Captain Radcliffe
instructed the two tanks that had remained with Lieutenant Turchan to move up and join the two tanks already
accompanying the point of the relief force. Radcliffe
wanted the tanks to protect the right flank, which he considered the most vulnerable. He knew that Alpha Company was on their left flank somewhere and that, in fact,
one of their platoons was also attempting to break through
to Bravo Company. This was Staff Sergeant Leslie's Alpha
One, and when Radcliffe reached the junction where
Burns had fought all afternoon, Leslie appeared on the
trail running into Route 561 from the west with a half-
dozen Marines.

Radcliffe, who'd been expecting a full platoon to reinforce them, approached the big sergeant (he did not know
Leslie's name) to ask, "How many men you got?"

"This is all I could bring you."

Considering the volume of fire to both their east and west, Leslie's platoon had been wondering prior to Radcliffe's arrival if they were the only survivors in Alpha and Bravo both. As Leslie now explained, "We're dug in over there on that side. We got our hands full. Sir, we got so damn much fire over there."

The position of Leslie's platoon allowed them to cover Radcliffe's left flank, so Radcliffe said to him, "Christ, you had better get back and hold your own line. Hold that left flank there and don't let the enemy get between us. Just don't let 'em get south of this goddamn trail."

This isn't the kind of problem you'd show at the Basic School for how things ought to look, thought Lieutenant Libutti of Charlie Two as, pumping adrenaline and moving in a half-crouch for fear of enemy fire, he looked for Captain Hutchinson. He was fresh off the helicopter that had landed his platoon in the Strip as others had rolled in to pump rockets. From above, he'd had a panoramic view of this smoke-billowing zoo of a battlefield, with Marines and NVA alike looking like ants as they moved around the burning hedgerows.

Now, on the ground, Libutti could see Marines heading south from the battle to the north. He assumed they were survivors from Bravo Company, but they could have been disoriented troops from Alpha or Delta. No one seemed to know who was who or what was what, Hutchinson and Libutti agreed when they found each other. Hutchinson had landed with the first lift and had already medevacked eleven of his men from the mortars that had greeted their arrival; so now orders from company commander to platoon commander reflected the newcomer's jaundiced eye: "Frank, take your platoon as point, and get in there and find Bravo Company, and evacuate the dead and wounded. Do not stay and fight. I emphasize, do not stay and fight."

"I understand," Libutti answered.

For no other reason than that he could see Marines

coming south on Route 561, Libutti decided to head north
on it. His platoon was spread out in single file, retracing
Radcliffe's route, and they had not gone far when they
heard tanks off on their right flank. The tanks did not seem
to be aware of his platoon on the trail, so Libutti ran across
the field to the nearest one, an act which terrified him once
his adrenaline had cleared because in this nebulous situation he could have easily run into an NVA squad kneeling
in the high elephant grass. The tank-infantry phone
mounted on the rear of the tank did not work. In fact, all
four tanks apparently had inoperative tank-infantry
phones, so Libutti climbed aboard and banged on the
hatch until someone opened up: "I'm Lieutenant Libutti
and we're moving north to recover the dead and wounded,
and *you follow me!*"

Libutti was joined back on the trail by one of the company's acting platoon commanders (a staff sergeant) who'd
come forward with his people. The platoons, already mixed
up from the pack-as-many-on-as-you-can handling of the
helo insertion, were becoming more intermingled as they
rushed north. Libutti had even lost track of Lefefe, his
excellent platoon sergeant. Up ahead, Libutti could see a
handful of Bravo Company grunts. When he saw a Marine
in gear with his weapon, he assumed the man was still
capable of fighting. As Libutti got closer and looked into
these men's eyes, he realized they had just come out of the
twilight zone. Their faces were drawn and tight, contorted
with looks of shock and disillusionment and especially,
Libutti noticed, *real fear*.

"How ya doin'?" Libutti repeated as he found it necessary to walk up to each man. "Listen, we're moving people
back. Keep going."

Libutti encountered only one survivor who still
seemed wide awake, a kid who'd been seriously wounded.
Libutti was moving forward, loaded for bear with his helmet, flak jacket, and pack on, machete hanging from his
web belt, and his hot little automatic carbine in his hands—
but his flak jacket was hanging open. Since he wasn't wearing any rank insignia, the kid grabbed him like he'd have

grabbed a fellow enlisted man. "Goddammit, zip that thing up and button it. I've been wounded a couple times, and the only way I've survived is 'cause I had this thing on. You make sure you button that thing up, you hear me?!"

Stillness surrounded Lance Corporal Cromwell when he awoke alone and abandoned on Route 561. No firing. Nothing. It took him a while to figure out what had happened, but once his head was relatively clear he started south again. Emboldened that his brush-wiggling crawl drew no fire this time, he picked up his radio and sprinted across the road to the better cover on the other side. His dash was greeted by a short auto burst from the rear, and he threw himself down. *They're still here, so I'll have to hug the bushes.* This he did, crawling south another fifty meters until he came to a tree that had been knocked down and covered most of the road. Afraid that he'd bump into NVA snipers if he left his hedgerow, Cromwell could see no way to get around the damn thing except by going over it. So after screwing up his courage for a long thirty seconds, he bolted from his cover, making a dead run for the fallen tree. The NVA opened fire, and he dived head first over it, fifteen rounds (it seemed) kicking up dust at his heels, his weapon and radio and body coming down with a crash. He'd made it. He shook himself off, picked up his radio, and then (as he told the 3d Marine Division Historical Section five days later) he raised his head at a certain noise:

Here were two great big beautiful tanks coming down the road about a hundred meters from where I was. I also recognized the imposing figure of my First Platoon Commander, about two-hundred-and-ten pounds of Marine, leading another friendly unit back down the trail toward me. At this time I was so happy to see that I hadn't been alone out there that I simply picked up my radio, picked up my rifle, put my helmet on my head, and walked up the trail. I received no enemy fire. I must have been in defilade from the small rise that I finally made it over. But I really didn't care much at the time.

When Staff Sergeant Burns, that imposing figure that Cromwell had recognized, saw Cromwell running toward them on the road, he shouted, "Come up the side of the trail, and we'll give you covering fire!"

Back in safe hands, Cromwell was quickly debriefed by Lieutenant Howell. Radcliffe, listening in, was very impressed with Cromwell's clear answers. The young radioman had really kept himself together. After their quick huddle, Burns continued Cromwell on his way toward the Strip, telling him to find Lieutenant Delaney and to do what he could back there. There were dead Marines on the trail and a few dead North Vietnamese—but not many, and not many more were visible in the fields—and at this point Radcliffe resituated their tanks. He deployed two of them on Route 561 where they could fire into both the vulnerable right flank and, if needed *(to keep the NVA honest,* he thought), into the less provocative left flank. He directed the other two tanks directly into the field on their right flank.

Thus deployed, they cautiously edged forward taking light fire from NVA who were occasionally visible in the tree lines to the left (those NVA were mostly concerned with Alpha Company) and increasingly heavy fire from NVA in the tree lines on the right flank. Those NVA were also visible as they moved into position, and Radcliffe, afraid of being cut off before he could even put the remnants of Bravo back together, rushed to the tank of the platoon commander. The damned tank-infantry phone didn't work, so he pounded on the beast until the staff sergeant popped his head out of his hatch. Radcliffe shouted that he wanted the tree line on their right taken under heavy fire. The staff sergeant dropped back into his turret and four tanks turned on their target with long, slender barrels to deliver 90mm cannister and high-explosive rounds, and .30- and .50-caliber machine-gun fire, from a distance of some hundred meters. Radcliffe stared awe-struck at the results. He saw trees fall; he saw the earthen berm there disintegrate, and—his sigh of relief was almost audible at this—he saw NVA being blown into the air while other NVA began fleeing northward back up the north-south tree line. About a dozen NVA rushed them from across that open field, but they were quickly cut down in their tracks.

As dead Marines were passed on Route 561, Captain Radcliffe, who'd already emptied his two canteens between himself and the wounded, stripped the bodies of their canteens and distributed them to other wounded Marines. Litter teams were organized to get the dead and wounded back to the road, and Lieutenant Howell and Corporal Thompson were seemingly everywhere as they searched the roadside hedgerows and the fringes of the roadside fields. They were later credited with personally evacuating twenty-five casualties. Among those rescued was Corporal Trevino, the twice-wounded radioman whom the NVA had tied to a tree, presumably as ambush bait. Sure enough, the first Marines to approach were taken under fire; but the NVA were quieted with return fire, and Trevino was cut loose and dragged back.

When the relief force reached the farthest crossroad, Radcliffe and Howell finally realized the extent of this disaster. Thirty, forty, maybe fifty Marines lay twisted along both sides of the road, clumped atop each other in spots, their weapons and gear strewn down the middle of the road for the length of the column. It was a slaughterhouse.

How could this happen to Marines? Radcliffe was stunned. *This doesn't happen to Marines. We don't get the hell shot out of us like this.*

After Howell identified Captain Coates's body for Radcliffe, they continued their search for survivors. While Radcliffe covered him from the hedgerow, Howell ran into the field to the left and came dragging back through the elephant grass with a wounded man in tow. Now it was Radcliffe's turn as Howell covered him. He could see a crater in the field that appeared to hold three Marines. He

was about to shove off through a break in the hedgerow
when Howell, kneeling over his wounded man near two
trees near that break, with his M16 up and ready, blurted,
"Look out!"

There were NVA, eight of them, coming out of a tree
line on the left and hiking diagonally across that field, apparently trying to get behind the Marines on the road.
There were more NVA back among the trees. They appeared not to know that the relief force was this far up
Route 561, and before they knew what hit them, Radcliffe
emptied his M16 into them. He quickly changed magazines
as Howell also brought his M16 into play; then he
squeezed a second magazine into the elephant grass. It
looked like they'd dropped all eight NVA, so they raised
their sights toward the other NVA previously spotted back
in the trees. Almost out of ammunition, Radcliffe finally let
up on his trigger, and crouching by that hedgerow break
again, he glanced again at Howell. "Jerry, cover me."

Radcliffe sprinted through the waist-high elephant
grass, then jumped into the crater with the three Bravo
Marines. He shouted as he came in because he realized
one of them was gripping a .45 pistol. "Don't shoot, Marine, I'm one of yours!"

The man with the .45 was a black corpsman, U.S. Navy
type, and he looked at Radcliffe. "I'm no goddamn Marine."

The corpsman had been hit in the legs and stomach
and was, in fact, a bloody mess, but he was still coherent.
"I'm watching my buddies. Fuckin' gooks are all over the
place."

Radcliffe checked the two Marines that the wounded
corpsman had been protecting. They were both dead. Radcliffe had to hold part of the corpsman's stomach in as he
lifted him up, and then, as gently as he could, he carried
the man back to the road and laid him beside one of the
tanks there. Corpsmen went from body to body looking for
anybody still breathing, and when they discovered one,
Staff Sergeant Burns cradled the man in his arms. It was
Corporal Bell. The young black radioman, who had done

so well leading Bravo Three after Staff Sergeant Reyes was originally wounded (the sergeant's body was among the rest), had taken a bad wound near the armpit and had lost a lot of blood. Burns tried to talk with him, but Bell was mostly out of his head. And very soon Leon Bell was dead in Burns's arms.

<u>14</u>

Let's Die Right

★

Corporal Power, stuck on his back in his shallow little crater as automatic-weapons fire, both Marine and North Vietnamese, cracked around and above him, was in hell. The fire the NVA had started to smoke out the Marines in the hedgerow when they overran Alpha Three's LZ was raging closer, moving from west to east, engulfing the seriously wounded who lay in the elephant grass of the westernmost paddy. Power could hear them screaming. He could feel the heat closing in on him. He couldn't move. Some NVA were still behind the hedgerow dike to the west, and NVA artillery and mortar fire were still geysering in and around the three paddies.

To the rear of Power's position in the middle paddy, to the east, Alpha Two was hunkered down behind that hedgerow dike, pouring M16, M60, and M79 fire into the NVA until the return fire of AK47s began to slack off.

"R.G., I'm getting out of here!"

The shout to Power came from his good buddy

Sankey, who was tucked in another little crater to his right. Power didn't think the cross fire was survivable yet, and he screamed back, "Sankey, don't do it! Goddammit, don't go! Stay where you're at!"

Power looked to his right, and Sankey sprang up, took three or four steps, then went down like a rock. Power knew he was dead but the crackling approach of the brushfire left him no choice, and moments later, he too prepared to get out. He unhooked his two remaining grenades from his web gear. He pulled the pin on one and laid it on his chest, the safety spoon popping off, then pulled the pin on the second and also laid that one on his chest—he was working with frantic speed—then he took back up the first one and just flipped it out of his crater. He didn't need to hurl it. The NVA behind the hedgerow were that close. He flipped out the second grenade a moment later, and as soon as the first one went off, he twisted around and went over the back of the crater—just as the second grenade exploded. He felt something sting into his foot, a piece of shrapnel from his own frag, but it was nothing, and he crawled on through the elephant grass toward Alpha Two's hedgerow. Convinced that if the NVA didn't nail him, the Marines would in a case of mistaken identity, he kept screaming at the top of his exhausted lungs, "DON'T SHOOT! SCOUT COMIN' IN! MARINE! MARINE!"

Power made it through the hedgerow and into the perimeter Captain Slater and Alpha Two were throwing together. The Marines there asked, "Where's Sankey? You seen Sankey?"

"He's dead, I reckon."

A while later, during a lull in the NVA automatic-weapons fire, Sankey came into the perimeter. When Power realized that his buddy didn't have as much as a scratch, he barked, "What the fuck's the matter with you?"

"It's an old Indian trick. I went down like I was dead, and they quit shooting at me and all of 'em started shooting at you."

Power balled his fists, only half in jest, *"You mo-ther fuck-er."*

★

Cut off from the rest of Alpha Company on the low ridge to the south, Sergeant Geizer (shot in the side and in the head) and his radioman, PFC Ross, knew it was time to *didi mau*—to get the hell out. Ross wanted to move fast and said something about leaving his jammed M16, but Geizer jumped at that, *"No you don't,* you don't leave that behind! You take it with you!"

Geizer then told Ross to make radio contact with Sankey, their other FO. He told Ross to ask if a hasty perimeter had been set up, and Ross told Geizer that the answer was yes. Geizer took the handset himself, "Where is it?"

"Fifty meters to your east."

"Fifty meters to the east. In other words, toward the Gulf of Tonkin?"

"Yes."

"Ross and I are coming in to the perimeter. Be advised we will be coming in."

Ross put a bandage around Geizer's head wound before they started out, but the scrape was deep, and although it was not terribly painful, it was a terrific bleeder. The blood ran in a continuous stream down his neck behind his ear, then curved along his jawbone and down his bare chest under his flak jacket before being sopped up by the front of his trousers. Ross had previously and haphazardly bandaged the gut-to-back wound (not his fault, it was an awkward wound), and although Geizer was still in considerable pain from that one, he could still walk. He periodically leaned on Ross for support as they started east along the ridge.

After what seemed like fifty meters, they peered through the bamboo that was shielding them, but all they could see were more of those little camouflaged pith helmets and bush hats. The NVA were no longer assaulting, but they were still in position. Another fifty meters east, and Geizer and Ross still could see no Marines and plenty more North Vietnamese. Geizer took the radio handset again, making contact with the artillery officer in the CP at

Con Thien. He explained their dilemma, and added, "I'm turning my compass south and heading out of here to the Death Strip."

"Yes. Get out of there. Do it."

They started south, cross-country, stumbling and panting and pushing through the brush, until they reached a seven-foot-deep ravine in their path. Ross went down and up the other side first, but Geizer, right behind him, began to fall backward as he clawed up the far side. *If I fall, this is it—I'll never get up again.* He grabbed desperately for the thin bamboo reeds leaning over from the top of the ravine and managed to pull himself up as Ross reached down and hauled him up and over. They made it finally, somehow, to the stumps and piled-up trees at the northern edge of the Strip, and there they sat down for the first time. Geizer was completely out of water. Ross still had some in his last canteen. He gave it to Geizer. To the southwest they could see Con Thien across hundreds and hundreds of meters of flat, open, sunbaked earth. *How the hell am I going to make it up there?*

Geizer didn't have to. After radioing his position to the CP, he saw Marines on the Con Thien hill, who appeared as miniatures in the distance, pull away a section of perimeter wire, and through it rolled a covered jeep-ambulance, which headed downhill as the wire was closed again. They were a perfect target on the barren slope of Con Thien, so the driver roared down a hillside trail like a bat out of hell, coming to a halt in a cloud of dust each time one of his fender-riding or door-hanging escorts tumbled off. The miniature figure would then run like crazy to jump back aboard, and the jeep would roar off again, bouncing in the air as it hit ruts in its downhill race.

Keystone Kops, Geizer thought, and then he realized that the jeep was roaring across the Strip in a trail of dust toward them. The jeep and its passengers (all volunteers, Geizer was told later) were coming to rescue them. Ross stood up to wave when they drew near and the jeep swung over and stopped right at the edge of the Strip. One Marine alighted from each fender and one from the door frame—there was another Marine behind the wheel and one more in the passenger seat—and they quickly got Geizer onto a stretcher, which they then slid into its rack in the back of the jeep. They were all business and very nervous.

"All right, let's get the hell outta here!"

Geizer could hear one of the Marines telling Ross, "Okay, go back in. Rejoin your outfit."

These men clearly did not understand what was happening, and Geizer hollered from him stretcher, *"No!* No, he can't do that. There's no way he could find his outfit. We couldn't find it when we were close to 'em."

Ross climbed aboard too, and the jeep then roared off back across the Strip and up the slope of Con Thien. There was more stopping and starting but Geizer, on his back on a stretcher, couldn't see much except the canvas cover above and around him and, out the back, the dust billowing behind them.

As the NVA infantry that had fragmented Alpha Company bogged down at the Marines' savage resistance from their doomed, isolated positions, NVA artillery continued to place steel on target. It fell mostly on the NVA infantrymen, and Corporal Peterson (the mortar man turned-rifleman), for example, saw a satisfying direct hit—*head goes one place, arms, legs, everything all spread out, and there ain't much of that gook left.* It was the artillery (both Marine and NVA) that saved them, Gunny Santomasso thought as the NVA ground fire on his craterful of Alpha Three survivors finally began to relent. He could only hope that the NVA would not come again. They were almost out of ammunition. The heat was terrible and Santomasso, like the rest, had donated his canteens to their wounded. He kept on the able-bodied to stay alert. He told them not to panic, that they would make it out somehow. They waited, and their corpsman moved to check Santomasso's self-bandaged, under-the-flak-jacket wound. The gunny waved him off, "Don't worry about it, don't get the kids shook up."

Eventually, Gunny Santomasso could hear Marines

shouting to him from the east, so one by one he sent his Marines back to Captain Slater's hasty new perimeter. Leaving their dead, they dragged in their wounded. The battle was not over, and this was no sanctuary. *A half-ass little perimeter,* thought Corporal Power, for one, with more men hit than not, it seemed. The injured lay in the dirt, hurting bad but silently gritting it out.

One of their sergeants lay with them, the victim of heatstroke and shock. He had other problems. He was an older man, a Texan who had fought hard to get back in the service and do his duty when Vietnam heated up. But he was a nervous wreck on the line, and he drove everyone crazy, mistaking every shadow for the enemy and causing numerous commotions. Slater had even sent him back for a psychological evaluation, but he had been okayed and returned to the field[1] Now the older sergeant was completely out of it, and for hours he just lay there and laughed and laughed and laughed. The sergeant's weird, monotonous laughing was practically the only sound coming from the casualties.

Sniper shots continued to crack.

Morter and artillery rounds continued to crash in, though not as heavily and not as effectively. Most of the rounds fell in the two paddies that the Marines had vacated.

With Power, for one, returning fire at unseen targets, Sankey directed in counterbattery fire from the northern hedgerow. When they could, they dug in. Their E-tools were on the packs they'd ditched in the middle paddy, so Power used his giant buck knife to chop up the dirt, which Sankey then scraped at and scooped up with his helmet. They were getting nowhere, the ground was baked as hard as a rock, but the occasional incoming spurred them on until they had shallow places to lie down in. *This is it.*

---

1. Gunnery Sergeant Santomasso disagreed: "The sergeant that cracked up was a good NCO; but he was new and he was in such a state of shock it took about six Marines to hold him down and doc gave him a shot to knock him out."

Power had already chalked it up. *There's ten thousand of these motherfuckers, there's forty of fifty of us. It's over.*

Power had already been through a lot with the unflappable Sankey, so he shook his hand and made his peace, "We're going to die here. If I had the chance to pick anybody in the world to die with it'd be you, bud, you know. So I'll tell you what let's do, let's take as many of these little motherfuckers with us as we can. You cover me and I'll cover you. Let's die right."

His face a stoic Indian mask, Sankey agreed. However, the staff sergeant from the weapons platoon who was near them was getting shakey. Understandable, but Power found it highly amusing since the man stood at least six-foot-one and was a big-chested, broad-shouldered tough guy, a real strutter. He couldn't help but fuck with the lifer, "Are you ready to die?"

The staff sergeant's high-pitched response verged on cracking, "I'm married, and I got kids!"

"Boy, that's tough, man. You know, it's hard enough to die here like we are—single—I bet it is going to be tough for you. That's too bad, man. It's a shame you're never going to see your kids and your old lady again."

The staff sergeant started crying, and a suddenly embarrassed Power shut the fuck up. It was catching up with him too. He had no water, his lips were cracked, and his tongue was swelling, making it difficult to breath to the point that he could feel himself panicking as he struggled to suck air past the thick, parched thing in his mouth. Power was sorely tempted to run back out to where he'd been pinned down in the crater and retrieve the canteen in his pack, but he was physically drained and snipers were still about. He settled instead for breaking off a bullet from its cartridge and carrying that under his tongue in a (futile) attempt to work up some saliva.

It's like them cats that were on Iwo Jima, or them cats that walked out of the Frozen Chosin, them dudes are looking over our fucking shoulders. Power was reaching into himself to keep it together. Waiting for the next NVA attack that would kill them all, he had to have something to lean

against. That something was the Corps. One-Hundred-and-
Ninety-One Years of Tradition. Semper Fi, Mac. All that
shit. *We signed on and we said we were going to do something.* Captain Slater walked among his Marines. He
seemed at this moment to be a part of that tradition. *A
rock,* Power thought. Slater went from man to man, group
to group, giving them direction and reassurance in his un-
bothered, unhurried voice: ". . . there's a relief column,
it's coming up behind us. They've got some tanks with
them. They'll be along in a while . . ."

15

Survivors

★

Captain Radcliffe had just re-
turned to the road with the wounded black corpsman and
was standing tall as if he were invincible as he directed
their continuing recovery efforts, when he saw Lieutenant
Libutti and Charlie Two coming up Route 561. Libutti had
been one of Radcliffe's students at the Basic School, but he
had come to Vietnam two months in advance of his former
instructor. He greeted him now with a salty shout, "Hey,
captain, you better get down. You're standin' up here like
at Quantico. Get down."

There were, in fact, NVA still about. Libutti had just
joined Radcliffe beside a tank when there was a terrific
clang of metal against metal as an RPG scored a direct hit
on the tank. Then a stunned Libutti realized there had
been no explosion. The RPG had been a dud. Incredible.
An equally startled Radcliffe did not initially realize he'd
been hit by the fragments produced by the nonexplosive
impact—a small nick to his head. He was already covered

in sweat and his flak jacket and gear were bloody from the corpsman and others, so it took someone else to notice the blood running down his sweaty face: "Shit, you got blood all over you!"

Radcliffe had other things on his mind. He wanted Libutti to advance with Charlie Two to the northern point of Bravo's overrun position, and to hold the NVA there as Radcliffe and Howell got their relief force turned around. Taking along Bravo's survivors, wounded, and dead, they would then fall back through Captain Hutchinson's position in the Marketplace (he had made it to the first crossroad with Charlie One and Three). Libutti would follow them out, rejoining Hutchinson after Radcliffe's group had passed through. As Radcliffe explained, Charlie Two was to come out last. "I'm taking these guys to the rear, Libutti. Cover us up here."

From his pinned-down position in one of the craters east of Route 561, the first man that Lance Corporal Herbert of Bravo Two saw was Lieutenant Howell. Under his direction, Herbert's hobbling crew came dragging from their crater with their wounded, including Lance Corporal Skinner, who was the luckiest sonuvabitch in Bravo Three despite the bullets in his chest and leg, and another lucky man, the M79 grenadier whose teeth had been shattered by the round meant to blow his brains out. Back on Route 561, Herbert began hearing the stories, and looking around him, he realized just how lucky all of them in the crater had been. Everyone else was dead—dead, dead, dead—their bodies strewn now before him on the dirt road. Everyone. Dead.

Numb beyond measure, Herbert sat down on the roadside. He smoked a cigarette and thought of Frank Lopinto, his best friend whose last screams he had heard. Dead, dead, dead. NVA snipers began firing then at intervals. Herbert ignored them; he just sat there with his cigarette burning down until Staff Sergeant Burns appeared before him to break the spell. "Come on, let's go, we're getting out of here. The rest of the company's been annihilated. Charlie, Alpha companies coming to give us a hand."

Like Radcliffe and Howell, Burns was everywhere, trying to reinstate some confidence in these hollow-eyed survivors. In truth, Burns had never been so frightened; having had no water in hours (he did recover an abandoned canteen, but the water was too hot to drink), he was running out of steam. He was becoming so foggy at times that later, back at Con Thien, he would be completely taken aback by a tanker's question, "Did you see that tracer round?"

"What tracer round?"

"The one that missed your head by about two inches."

At the time the NVA sniper had almost removed his head, Staff Sergeant Burns was picking up weapons and ammunition and stuff, and throwing it onto the road. Under Radcliffe's direction, two of their tanks were being piled with the wounded and dead as they were found, situated so the turrets could still move, while he kept the other two free because he didn't know what to expect. Radcliffe also ordered that all USMC and NVA weapons in sight be recovered. But because there were not enough free hands to carry them back, he had them laid under the tanks' treads before calling to the tank commander to "crush the sons of bitches!"

Staff Sergeant Burns recognized Bravo's Kit Carson Scout who lay there with a shrapnel-mauled face, clutching his distinctive scout patch in his hand. The man did not really speak English, and Burns had to rush over when he realized a Marine from Charlie Company was preparing to finish the gook off, "No, he's one of ours!"

Burns collared a couple Marines to take care of the Scout, then he reached down and shook his hand, "You're okay, we'll get you out of here."

The Scout looked up at Burns and smiled. There would have been more survivors if the NVA had not, as it appeared they had, gone back up the line on their way out to finish off dazed and wounded Marines at close range with automatic weapons. There were previously wounded and bandaged Marines whose faces had been shot off, and Corporal Fazio, who'd gotten mixed in with the relief force from Alpha One, found a number of Marines in their holes with their M16s torn down. They'd been trying to clear unextracted brass and double-fed rounds, and they had their hands over their heads like they'd been hoping no one would see them. But they were dead, their heads and spines shattered by automatic bursts. All along the column, jammed M16s were being recovered and Staff Sergeant Burns was raging inside. *The people in D.C., they're not here, and it don't work as good as they say it does!*

Everyone was helplessly angry. Sick. Infuriated. Corporal Fazio sat down at the edge of a big bomb crater. Three NVA were at the bottom, two dead but one still moving, and another Marine moving past stopped to shoot the wounded NVA survivor about sixty times.

"You guys have been in a pretty big mess," Staff Sergeant Burns was now talking to the Marines with PFC Henderson, as he made sure water from the tanks was distributed to these men who'd not had a drink since they'd left their canteens at the morning's resupply area.

"We're going to get you out. I'll get you guys out of here."

Though shot twice and hit by shrapnel, and wildly relieved to see Staff Sergeant Burns after having waited for death on his little footpath in front of the bamboo, Henderson was still clearheaded enough to be critical. Watching Charlie Company coming up the road, he couldn't understand why they still persisted in walking close together on a narrow ribbon of trail after what had happened to Bravo Company. Oh well. A corpsman got Henderson's flak jacket off and tied battle dressings around his three wounds, while telling him not to move around too much, because he'd lost a lot of blood. Two arteries had been opened in his leg, one in his shoulder.

Henderson was also told that tanks were coming to take him back to the Strip where medevacs would come in. Two tanks went by. They did not stop. Another tank did stop about the same time that some Marines finished fashioning him a litter of sorts. A Marine who'd been shot in the ass screamed as he was put up on the tank, *"Oh my legs!"* And for a frightened second, Henderson thought they were under fire again and that the man had been hit again. The man had only been crying out from the pain of his old wound. Henderson held on tight to a scarf hanging down from the tank's antenna, eyes shut against his own pain as the tank started south. The corpsman's morphine didn't seem to be doing much good against this roaring, vibrating machinery.

The relief column was reversing gears, turning around to retrace its way back to the Strip. The dead and wounded had originally been placed on the two tanks as they had been found, but when there was no more room for the wounded, dead Marines were pushed off. All together, thirty-four dead Marines from Bravo Company were left on Route 561 as the tanks started south.

Meanwhile, Lieutenant Libutti and Charlie Two walked all the way to the farthest point of Bravo's advance. Libutti had been completely unprepared for the carnage at the second crossroad, and his first impulse upon discovering these dead Marines was to shut down all systems. His mind went into stop action because what he was seeing was impossible. So many wounded, now so many dead—*dead*. More Marines dead than Marines wounded and alive. He wanted to cry, but he was an officer. He knew people were expecting him to take charge, to lead, to do *something*. Accompanied by his radioman and a pair of riflemen, Libutti kept going, all the while looking for the company commander (unaware that Radcliffe and Howell had already identified Coates's body). They found him, or at least they found someone who they took to be the company commander, lying in a huddle with a radioman, a corpsman, and what appeared to be the body of another officer. Dead, dead, dead, dead. Like the rest, they'd been shot point-blank in the head and upper body. The NVA had been ruthlessly efficient—just as the Marines would have been.

At this point, Lieutenant Libutti began waving back the two tanks that had come up to support his platoon. It was time to head south themselves. Captain Hutchinson, back in an open field near the battered structures of the Marketplace, called Libutti, "Do you have the company commander?"

"No. I found him, he's dead. I'm concentrating now on all the wounded. You won't believe the number of people up here that are dead."

"Go back and get the company commander."

"Yeah, I found him and he's dead, and I've taken all his papers and his dog tags."

"Hey, listen, go back and get him."

Lieutenant Libutti ran back up Route 561 with his radioman and a rifleman, and hefting the body of Captain Coates onto his shoulders, ran back with him. Captain Hutchinson, meanwhile, relayed Libutti's report that they were no longer under heavy fire. Nevertheless, higher command said to leave the dead and exit the area posthaste with the wounded.

Hutchinson had never known the Marine Corps to leave its dead, so he responded, "Look, there are some amtracks at Con Thien. Send them up here. I'll load the dead up and we'll get everybody out."

"*Negative*. Get out."

16

Incoming

★

Unit integrity among the Marines strung along Route 561 had been torn to shreds. Grunts of different squads, different platoons, and different companies were coming out side by side. Despite the confusion, a general scheme of maneuver could be discerned as Captain Radcliffe got the whole show turned around to retrace their march to the Strip:

B/1/9, all forty-or-so shuffling effectives, was in front with Captain Radcliffe, Lieutenant Howell, and Staff Sergeant Burns.

1/A/1/9 (Staff Sergeant Leslie) followed with the four M48 tanks of A/3d Tank Battalion, two of which were stacked with casualties.

1 and 3/C/1/9 (Captain Hutchinson), meanwhile, remained in position so as to hold the door open to the south for the lead elements while 2/C/1/9 (Lieutenant Libutti) guarded their northernmost rear. When 2/C/1/9 followed 1/A/1/9 and B/1/9 back south to rejoin 1 and 3/C/1/9, the

reunited C/1/9 would then come out last, shielding the rest from any renewed NVA action, at least from the north.

The road-bound column's destination was 3/D/1/9 (Lieutenant Turchan), whose perimeter on the northern edge of the Strip would accommodate medevacs. The NVA, however, did not permit an easy exit. The tanks were only about fifteen meters south of the southernmost cross-road when (at approximately 1400) one of them (USMC #202136) ran over a mine. The mine appeared to have been constructed from forty pounds of TNT with a pressure fuze, and it succeeded in jolting one tank tread from its road wheels. The tank-platoon commander ordered another tank to tow the damaged one, and he made sure that it pulled up precisely in the tread marks of the damaged tank, to avoid another possible mine. Towing cable attached, the retreat continued all of another twenty meters (by now it was 1500) when one of the casualty-laden tanks (USMC #201983) ran over another mine. This one appeared to have been fashioned from a dud U.S. 175mm artillery round. The Bravo grunts, ahead of the tanks, deployed as security along the raised banks of the road and waited, waited, and waited as the crew repaired their tracks. It took almost an hour. When they set out again, with two tanks fully operational, and the third towing the damaged fourth, they crushed their way through the brush on the left side of the road to avoid more surprises.

The mortaring started then. The first round landed nearly atop one of the tanks, followed in quick succession by twenty more rounds. Captain Radcliffe was tossed to the ground, and the black corpsman whom he'd been carrying in such a way as to keep his stomach wound sealed, gritted his teeth and made some caustic remark about how well Radcliffe was taking care of him. Radcliffe had, in fact, picked up another superficial wound, this one to the leg. The men of Bravo (ahead of the tanks) and of Alpha platoons (behind them) had scattered at the first explosion, and after what appeared to be the last, they reappeared from holes and ditches and from under some nearby banana trees.

They formed back up on the road and continued south at a fast walk. The mortars began thumping out more rounds.

Again, everyone hustled for the nearest cover, sweated out the explosions, then returned to the road. A third barrage greeted them, and some men took off at a run. But shells began exploding far ahead too, so for a third time everyone went to ground. This time NVA artillery joined the mortars, but as Radcliffe and Burns noticed with satisfaction, most of the artillery fell misplotted along their flanks and among the NVA snipers who had previously been harassing them. Radcliffe, looking for advice from Burns as the artillery shelling became prolonged, commented that according to training, when hit by arty you were to get down and let it pass over you. Burns countered, "When you're in an artillery or mortar attack, you get your ass *out* of there. If you don't you're going to be dead. If you want to stay here, you're going to be here *alone.*"

Corporal Fazio of Alpha One, behind Bravo Company, waited five minutes into the lull of raining artillery before he dared to rise from the shelter of his roadside ditch. He called out for Staff Sergeant Leslie. No one answered. He ran in a crouch down the road, looking into the ditches. Nobody was there. Finally, Fazio saw another Marine behind him and he called, "Hey, they're all gone! There's nobody here!"

"*What?* Nobody here?"

"*Yeah,*" Fazio said, the word coming out as a laugh, because what else was there really to do? "They're all gone. I don't know where they went."

"Well, let's go find 'em."

"You can, but I'm not. I'm going back where the tanks are."

"Okay."

Fazio and the other Marine walked over to where several Bravo grunts, who were drained, thirsty, and looking weak as hell, were trying to help some wounded back onto the tanks. Fazio started dragging one wounded man to a hole near the tanks, and the man was mumbling, "C'mon, man, get me in there, get me in there," just as the mortars began thumping again. There was an explosion—and Fazio was knocked into the hole he'd been dragging the wounded guy to. But he wasn't even scratched he realized as he got back up. The wounded Marine he'd been helping was now a dead Marine. More explosions. Marines were yelling. Screaming. Fazio didn't know what to do. But when he saw the five grunts he'd been helping with the wounded just take off running, he scurried around, picked up a rifle lying near him, and started right after them. A sniper opened fire on him.

The position on the Strip manned by Lieutenant Turchan's Delta Three was not originally shelled, and it was here that lost fireteam leader Stuckey of Charlie Two had taken up position. One of the Bravo stragglers coming in his direction was really a sight—bare-assed naked except for helmet, flak jacket, and bandages—coming back carried in a poncho by six other Marines. This was PFC Hendry. Earlier, Burns and a corpsman had stopped him as he hobbled down the road between two buddies; they had stripped off his torn and bloody utilities, tied field dressings around his wounds, and organized this litter team. Along the way back they had been met by a Charlie Company grunt headed in the opposite direction who'd handed Hendry a soda from his pack.

Lance Corporal Stuckey of Charlie Two, anxious and curious and unaware that the rest of his platoon had already moved out, asked them what had happened. They were still talking when the incoming progressed into the Strip perimeter. Hendry had already been sat beside a hole in case of incoming, so he plopped into it as Stuckey slid in beside him. Stuckey was very aware of the rounds hissing through the air, getting louder and closer, and he was very aware that he was actually praying out loud. ". . . *Oh my God . . . oh my God . . .*"

CRASH! CRASH! CRASH!

Dirt clods, fist-sized, came down on them. The concussion was terrific, ear ringing. Hendry was saying something, maybe screaming, Stuckey couldn't tell. And then they heard the rush of new rounds pushing through the air. *This might be the one!* Stuckey squeezed into the raw earth of the hole, clutching his helmet, remembering again how he'd lost his good-luck crucifix during their last operation above the Strip. Without it, Stuckey felt naked to the world.

"Please, God, please God! Oh my God!"

CRASH! CRASH! CRASH! CRASH! The bombardment on the Strip had caught Sergeant McGuigan, Right Guide to Delta Three, out alone in front of their holes looking for more walking wounded from Bravo Company. Never before under fire, only twelve days incountry, the helmetless McGuigan hit the deck astride a hedgerow and tried to make like a turtle in his flak jacket. *Shit, what if a gook comes up and finds me like this?* When the artillery lifted, he ran back to their lines only to find his platoon sergeant, SSgt Jerry Lee Miller, in a hole, hit bad. Miller was conscious and looked up at McGuigan, but he just sort of gurgled. McGuigan dragged him from the hole, screaming for help all the while. They got Miller to Doc Shade, then a Marine told McGuigan that Lieutenant Turchan had also been hit.

Apparently, the platoon commander and platoon sergeant had been Delta Three's only casualties, and McGuigan found Turchan sitting up along a hedgerow with his radioman. The new lieutenant seemed coherent enough, but he was bleeding, bandaged, and rattled, and McGuigan figured he had better take charge. A young corporal, however, offered that since he was an experienced short-timer, he should be the one to check the platoon lines while McGuigan remained with the radio. New guy McGuigan had to agree despite his stripes.

Lieutenant Libutti of Charlie Company, at the tail of the retreat, could hear the muffled cannonade from above the DMZ. He could hear the whistling, screaming rush of each salvo, and with heads down in a six-inch-deep furrow

he and his radioman had scurried into, he lived each crashing impact. Libutti's body and brain vibrated at the concus-
sions, shards of red-hot shrapnel and pieces of splintered
trees spun through the air or bounded down around him,
and amid the smoke and dust and noise, he'd never felt so
helpless. When it seemed that the NVA artillery had finally
ceased fire once and for all, Libutti stood up from the furrow and realized that despite the smothering heat he was
in an absolute cold sweat. Smoke hung in the muggy,
burnt-smelling air, and people were walking around
stunned. So Libutti tried to get things organized, rushing to
his men and those mixed in from other platoons: "Okay,
Marine, listen, we're okay. Let's turn around and let's get
out of here."

Thus, the withdrawal continued. Down the road,
meanwhile, Captain Hutchinson was thinking, *My God, I'm
probably the only one left.* He stood up from the concrete
pigpen that he reckoned had saved him and his radiomen
while the artillery killed everyone else, and he shouted at
those men he could see to get up and move out. Hutchinson couldn't believe it, but by God, Marines got up from all
over the place! They were still there! Along with the straggling groups from Alpha and Bravo Companies came the
four tanks (big, lumbering targets, Hutchinson frowned
again), and behind them came good old, sharp Lieutenant
Libutti and Charlie Two. Libutti rushed to greet Hutchinson, "Skipper, am I glad to see you!"

Well, Hutchinson thought, smiling back at his one and
only lieutenant. *I'm glad you're glad to see me, but there isn't
a hell of a lot I can do for you right now.* Abandoned,
stranded—pick the word, Hutchinson felt it. In fact, it appeared that even the tanks were preparing to move on.
Libutti ran to one, and called up to the man in the cupola,
"Don't leave, we still have wounded people!"

"Get out of the way, I'm leavin'!"

Libutti stood in front of the tank, "You're gonna have
to run over me, you asshole!"

"Goddammit, get out of the way!"

"I'm not getting out of the way! You're staying!"

"Get out of the way or I'm going to run you over!"

It dawned on Libutti that since he never wore his rank insignia (the better to hide from officer-hunting snipers) the tanker probably thought he was dealing with some crazed lance corporal, so he thought to identify himself. "Listen, I'm *Lieutenant* Libutti and I'll break your neck if you leave!"[1]

Loaded with more casualties, the tanks got moving again. PFC Henderson of Bravo One sat atop one of them (USMC #201983, the one which had already hit a mine and been repaired), holding on for dear life to a scarf hanging from a turret antenna. He kept his eyes closed, he was hurting so bad, and a black Marine who'd been shot in the shoulder held onto him from one side while a black Marine who'd been shot in the jaw held onto him from the other. Henderson was a mess. His helmet was gone, his flak jacket had been stripped off by the corpsman, he didn't know where his weapon and gear had gone, and battle dressings hanging with tie-off streamers were wrapped around his gun-shot shoulder and leg and his shrapnel-gouged right calf. His eyebrows were singed from a near-miss napalm strike. He was telling himself that nothing else could go wrong when, as they passed Captain Hutchinson's position in the Marketplace, the NVA opened fire again. An AK47 round caught Henderson in the finger, the terrific impact knocking him off the tank, spilling the two wounded Marines with him. They scrambled around to the other side of the tank, away from the direction of the automatic-weapons fire, and Henderson also tried to crawl away, terrified that he'd be run over as the tank maneuvered. He hadn't made it two feet in his weakened condition when something suddenly flashed hotly over his back and hit the tank. *RPG.* Three RPGs hit the tank, one penetrating and blowing a track off.

1. Regarding the rumor that Libutti had actually drawn his .45 on the tanker, he commented, "To say the least that was a highly emotionally charged day. I may have pulled it out, I don't remember. If somebody says I did it, I probably did."

Henderson, lying there, watched as a crewman popped out of the tank. He ran around his crippled dragon to inspect the damage, then climbed back inside and, presumably, got on the radio, because their last free tank then backed up to attach towing cables to the rear of the disabled one. Captain Hutchinson, also watching, was exasperated. *We're walking around like a bunch of idiots, and the gooks are down in the cover!* He was about fifteen meters from the disabled tank, and he shouted to the staff sergeant he took to be in charge, *"Leave it! Just leave it! We need to move out!"*

The staff sergeant ignored him.

Several Marines grabbed Henderson and heaved him up onto the front slope of a different tank where three wounded men were hanging on. Henderson pulled a dead Marine atop him so that only his legs, which were sticking across the driver's hatch, were exposed.

"Just get the hell outta here!"

Captain Hutchinson was still shouting when the staff sergeant, who had no intention of leaving his property behind, got the towing cable attached and moved out. Hutchinson stared after them at a sight that freeze-framed itself into his memory: a dead black Marine hanging off the back deck of one of the tanks, the tread running under him and bouncing his body as the tank rolled on toward the Strip.

The two operational tanks were now towing the two damaged ones. The NVA followed their retreat with more mortar rounds, and the first one of the latest salvo landed so close to the tank on which PFC Henderson lay that at first he thought the 90mm main gun must be firing since the tank vibrated so fiercely. Then shrapnel stung his left calf (the shells were landing on the left side of the moving tank) and Henderson abruptly realized they were under fire again. It was his fifth wound this day. *There's no way I'm getting out of here.* Bullets ricocheted off the tank. And Henderson could do nothing but lie there helplessly as the tank roared on, until the NVA fire had petered out. The tank stopped. Henderson raised his head. He could see the other tanks and what looked like a hundred walking wounded Marines as well as another fifty Marines lying about with serious wounds, collected about the Strip in knots. He was still clearheaded enough to notice there were no holes for them, no real cover, and that he wasn't out of it yet. But he'd made it to the Strip and that was good enough for now.

The platoon-sized handful that constituted Bravo Company came back in a stumbling, exhausted, overburdened column. Lance Corporal Cull of the Weapons Platoon, for example, was humping his mortar tube over one shoulder and had his free arm around his partner, PFC Fields, who'd been shot in the arm and leg. When a Bird Dog observation plane fired marking rounds into the brush only a hundred meters off the road, Staff Sergeant Burns remarked wearily to Captain Radcliffe, "We got enemy moving in on the left flank."

That was the last thing they needed. But no sooner had Burns said that when a flight of Crusaders came in right off the deck, supersonic winged darts flashing past the road-bound grunts, placing their bombs and napalm cannisters precisely where Bird Dog had marked his targets. Again, Bravo Company experienced a napalm wall from only seventy-five meters, and again, it worked. Not another AK47 round was fired at them. They reached the area where that morning they had staged their packs and received their resupply, and informing Radcliffe of this, Burns set up some security and went into the area to retrieve their gear. The NVA had already been through, and their precious water cans had been opened and tipped over, their packs and SP packages of soap, toothpaste, candy, etc., looted. Burns happened to see his pack lying there, slung it on, and with most of the men also retrieving packs, Bravo Company continued to march for the Strip.

17

Finally, Medevacs

★

Well, it's finally over for me, anyway, Lance Corporal Cromwell (radioman to the XO, B/1/9) had thought upon being ushered south on Route 561 well in advance of the withdrawing column. He had made no great strides in rejoining Lieutenant Delaney on the Strip, such was the heat and the burden of his radio, when the first mortar barrage began around the tanks far to his rear. Cromwell beat it to a roadside hole, then was shocked to see midair explosions that showered their shrapnel down like darts and eliminated the cover offered by holes and ditches. The airbursts were directly above Route 561, and they were a terrible surprise for Cromwell, who had the understanding that the NVA did not have such sophisticated ammunition.

This is the last straw, they can't do much more to us! During the first lull, Cromwell moved out again, finally finding Lieutenant Delaney. They moved on into Delta Three's perimeter, Cromwell much relieved to see that Delaney was all right, not only because he liked the man but because, having survived a scrap or two together, he considered the lieutenant a good-luck charm. He didn't want to lose Delaney until he knew they were out of this mess.

Lieutenant Delaney and Lance Corporal Cromwell tried to bring some order to the chaos that existed within Delta Three's relatively leaderless lines. They began having the wounded moved to the center of the perimeter for better control and for the administrative work of getting their names, ranks, service numbers, etc., which Cromwell relayed to battalion, even as Delaney borrowed the radio at intervals to update Con Thien on their situation and to request medevacs. As they worked, Cromwell made sure he had a handy hole nearby. After twenty minutes, by which time he was carrying all their radios to that hole to control the medevacs that were presently airborne and in-bound, the NVA artillery began shrieking in. The first shell exploded thirty feet to Cromwell's front, and he made a screeching dive the last six feet to the hole onto Delaney who was already in it. The first round had landed in the middle of their position, as did every one of the next one-hundred-and-thirty rounds that Delaney counted from the bottom of their hole. The whole experience was a frightening example of the enemy's artillery skill made even more personal when one round landed so close that the edge of its crater was only three feet from the edge of their hole. Delaney and Cromwell were slammed and bounced by the roaring impact of that one, with the wind knocked out of them and Cromwell left with a throbbing concussion head-ache.

When the shelling lifted, helmeted heads popped up like moles to find that two Marines too seriously wounded to crawl to cover had been blown to bits. The medevacs broke off, and the decision was spontaneously made to move the wounded to a new LZ on the southern side of the Strip. In addition to possibly being out of sight of the NVA artillery spotters, this would also force the next NVA ground assault, which they all knew was coming, to cross the vulnerably open Strip to reach the wounded. As for the twice-shot PFC Weldon, he had found a little hole for himself (and had yet to be treated by a corpsman) when a Marine stopped near his group, motioned south across the Strip, then pointed at Weldon and a few others; "You—you —you—and you. If you can make it back, you know, make it back on your own. If you need help, just let us know."

About this time (approximately 1500), Lieutenant Colonel Schening, CO, 1/9, alerted Colonel Jerue, CO, 9th Marines, that all his companies were engaged and that he had no more units to commit. Colonel Jerue responded that the area's ready reserve, 3/9 in Dong Ha, would be flown in to the Strip to the aid of 1/9. Meanwhile, Schening ordered Major Danielson, XO, 1/9, to organize a rescue force to meet those fifty or so figures, which they at Con Thien could see coming across the Strip. They were not in radio contact with this group (nor with Delta Three, and only intermittently with Bravo Company), but that the group included wounded and needed help was obvious. Danielson rounded up three vehicles, a USMC jeep-ambulance and a USA jeep and truck from the base's Special Forces detachment (aboard which came some USN volunteers from the Seabee detachment), and they soon departed Con Thien.

Captain Radcliffe and Staff Sergeant Burns finally reached Delta Three's perimeter with the bulk of Bravo Company. *Utter goddamn chaos,* Radcliffe thought—*a malaise had affected people who were just lying around that LZ there stunned, numb.* Before turning to rush back up Route 561 to ensure that no one had been left behind, he grabbed Burns to command hoarsely, "Burns, get out there with Howell, and let's get the goddamn people out of here as quick as we can. Get some kind of priority going. Just get 'em the hell out of here. Don't try to fill out casualty evacuation cards, just get 'em on the damned helicopters and get 'em out of here as best you can."

By the time Radcliffe got back—half jogging and half staggering—a Sea Horse was over the hasty LZ that Staff

Sergeant Burns and Sergeant Huff had organized. Radcliffe, bloody and sweat soaked, dusty and exhausted, stood
in the LZ and directed the helicopter in for a landing with
hand-and-arm signals, something he had never done before. The crew chief in the open side door held up four
fingers to indicate the number of wounded they could
carry, but Radcliffe could see at least six seriously wounded
Marines lying there.

"Take all their goddamn gear off!"

Some of the wounded already had flak jackets that
were half blown off, and with the rest of their accoutre-
ments stripped away, six men were lifted aboard the Sea
Horse. The helo hovered and hovered—Radcliffe wasn't
sure it was going to make it—and then away it went.

Casualties from Bravo Company never seemed to stop
coming, and Doc Lindenmeyer of Delta Three simply
treated one Marine right after another. It seemed there
were sixty of them within view. Bare chested under his flak
jacket and looking out from under his helmet brim with
regular Coke bottles for eyeglasses, Lindenmeyer had
started this exercise with a bulging Unit One hanging from
his left shoulder to his right hip. It contained a small surgical kit, battle dressings, and one unit of serum albumin, a
blood-volume expander in a 50cc bottle with a needle-
tipped rubber tube, all of it in a soda-can-sized container.
Four more units were taped to the medical bag's shoulder
strap, while a sixth was in his pack. Five Syrettes of morphine, each a sort of small toothpaste tube with a hypoder-
mic needle at the end, were kept in a plastic vial in his
pocket. Four canteens were on his web belt (a fifth was in
his pack), along with the standard individual battle-dress-
ing pouch over his ass, and a K-Bar and a Colt .45 on his
hip, which he never fired in anger but whose presence gave
him some comfort.

Now, Lindenmeyer was out of almost everything, including serum albumin which he'd ceased using for the
reason it had been issued:

Its effectiveness relies on drawing excess water from body fluids into the circulating system, a method which relies on the availability of water from these fluids. In that heat there was simply no excess fluids in a man's system. We started serum albumin simply to have an IV going when the casualty got to the field hospital because if he went into shock his veins collapsed; it was virtually impossible then to start an IV.

Mostly Lindenmeyer was dealing with shrapnel wounds, but the rain of incoming mortar and artillery rounds did blow both legs off a man he had previously treated for wounds in both arms. The trauma of the blast had sealed the blood vessels, so there was no excessive bleeding. But Lindenmeyer padded the stumps anyway with battle dressings. There was nothing else he could do. He was completely out of serum albumin at this point, so he gave the mangled kid some salt tablets and a gulp of canteen water, hoping that would be enough. But, of course, it wasn't.

The Marine looked up, "Hey, doc."

Lindenmeyer bent back over the man, thinking he was going to ask for another Syrette of morphine.

"Hold my hand."

Lindenmeyer held both of the Marine's hands in his— *like he was a brother, like I was his mother*—and felt the weight of the world on him. The man went into shock. In minutes he was dead. Lindenmeyer stood back up, covered with the dead man's blood; then, because he had no other choice he moved on quickly to another of his casualties. *His* casualties.

Lindenmeyer had wanted none of this. He was no volunteer. The Marines said that USMC meant Uncle Sam's Misguided Children or Unlimited Shit and Mass Confusion, but Lindenmeyer knew that to U.S. Navy personnel like himself, USMC really stood for U're Shittin' Me Chief?! That was the proper response of a hospital corpsman to his chief petty officer upon receiving the sobering surprise that his Vietnam tour was not going to be in the

air-conditioned sick bay of a ship offshore, but with
Ground Forces, FMF Pacific. The Fleet Marine Force. The
grunts. Hell. Lindenmeyer had joined the Navy to get medical training that might serve him after discharge—and
then only because he had flunked out of college during his
third year. The only thing that helped him after Field Medical School and his assignment to D/1/9 was that the man
he was replacing, Doc Speaks, stayed in the bush three
days to ease his arrival. Among other things, Speaks told
Lindenmeyer that the Marines would watch him, and as
soon as he demonstrated that he could and would perform
under fire, they would accept and protect him: "The corpsmen take care of the grunts and the grunts take care of the
corpsmen, and that's the way of it."

During Lindenmeyer's first contact, he knew that he
could not hesitate one instant, and by God, he found himself running up under fire and helping drag a wounded
man out of harm's way. Thus a real person to the grunts
("They call me 'Doc,'" Lindenmeyer wrote home. "It
makes me feel kind of good, like I'm supposed to be something"). Doc Lindenmeyer found that corpsmen, usually a
bit older and more mature than their comrades, had a fa-
vored status in a line platoon:

I was the father-confessor, I was the priest, I was the
guy everybody went to for advice. Guys would come to
me and say, 'Hey, look, I joined the Marines to get away
from my pregnant girlfriend, and she still wants to have
the baby and, you know, what should I do? Should I
marry her?' What do you say to an eighteen-year-old kid
who's in a situation like that? I sure as hell didn't know
what to say. I did the best I could, but I began to understand what it is that a minister does in society, and it has
perhaps less to do with religion and more to do with just
being the detached observer who can perhaps offer some
sage advice with a certain moral and ethical credibility to
it.

After all, Doc Lindenmeyer was twenty-two years old and had a wife back in the World; additionally, along with the C-ration spoon in his flak jacket pocket, he had a pipe, an appropriate prop for the Old Man of the Third Herd of Dying Delta 1/9.

During the next bout of incoming along the Strip, Lindenmeyer lay beside the man he had just treated until —CRASH!—a huge explosion lifted them both up and threw them back down. Lindenmeyer squirmed against the earth, head down until the next lull. He called to the man he'd been treating. No answer. Thinking the man must be dead, Lindenmeyer moved to him; there was a pulse and shallow breathing, and in a few minutes the grunt opened his eyes and seemed okay. A call then came that a man in their own Delta platoon needed attention. The Marine sat staring off into space, unresponsive to his name or to a slap in the face. Lindenmeyer flashed then to Field Medical School; an instructor had been asked to describe the symptoms of shell shock and his seemingly unhelpful answer had been that you'd know it when you saw it. *Well, he was right.* Other Marines were nearby, talking quietly, and Lindenmeyer heard the words, ". . . faking it . . ."

He pulled the casualty tag book from his Unit One and barked, "This man's a casualty. Take him to the center of the perimeter with the rest."

The official nature of the tag, which Lindenmeyer then filled out and attached to the Marine's flak jacket, seemed to end the muttering. Lindenmeyer shoved off to find Lieutenant Turchan's radioman, whom he greeted with, "Where are those fucking choppers? All my emergency medevacs are dead, all my priorities are now emergencies."

"Doc, we got some casualties on a chopper just before that last barrage. Didn't you know?"

"No. Well, get some more choppers in. I still have men who need evacuating."

"Okay, I'll try."

"Where's the lieutenant?"

"He got on the chopper with the casualties."

"Was he wounded?"

"Just a little ding in the arm. He got hit while walking around inspecting the perimeter during incoming."

"Serves him right." Then Lindenmeyer reconsidered, "Who the fuck authorized him to go. I have seriously wounded men who should have been on that bird."

"Doc Shade let him on the chopper. Besides, we're better off without the dumb sonuvabitch."

Doc Shade was yelling. Lindenmeyer rushed over to find Shade working on Staff Sergeant Miller, who was in great pain and coughing blood from a wound in his left lung. Lindenmeyer rolled the man onto his left side to keep his right lung clear of blood, and Miller shrieked in even greater pain at the move. Doc Shade was a fine corpsman, but he was also close to Miller and was getting frantic, "Give him some morphine. I'm out of it."

Morphine depresses the breathing and is counterindicated for a lung wound, but Lindenmeyer didn't want to contradict Shade in front of Miller or the other grunts within hearing distance. That might adversely affect their confidence in Shade and, since much of their field medicine was psychological, his effectiveness. Lindenmeyer had one Syrette left, but he said, "I'm sorry, I'm out of it too."

Doc Shade had no way of knowing what his partner had or didn't have, but screamed, "You are not! You just hate him!"

Doc Shade was close to Lindenmeyer's feelings about their good but (in Lindenmeyer's view) overly gung ho platoon sergeant. That, however, had nothing to do with his withholding morphine. He couldn't think of anything to say back, so without saying anything he turned and walked back to the casualties in the center of the perimeter. Ten minutes later, Staff Sergeant Miller was dead and Lindenmeyer doubted himself. Maybe he should have given him the morphine to make his last few minutes easier. But, no, he had no right to waste it on a dying man when there was an abundant supply of other Marines in pain whom the morphine might keep alive by keeping them out of shock. Lindenmeyer had never before felt so mixed up, but he was also incredibly lucky: during the afternoon, six of his fellow corpsmen were killed and another six were wounded.

The Marines of Bravo Company (and their attached Alpha platoon) immediately went for the holes upon reaching the Strip. But working parties were needed to get the casualties to the southern side of the six-hundred-meter-wide clearing, so they were up and moving again. It was slow and painstaking. PFC Hendry, for one, started south on his own, but his wounded leg was like a plank. He was getting nowhere before six Marines scooped his naked ass up in a poncho. They trudged their way south, weaving toward any low spots into which they could flatten in case of more incoming, and when they finally bumped into Staff Sergeant Burns in the new, hasty LZ, Hendry grinned at his favorite NCO that this was his ticket home. Hendry rattled on with some other wounded buddies; then his nervous, twisted, and empty guts finally vomited up the warm soda given to him by the Charlie Company grunt.

Captain Radcliffe and Staff Sergeant Burns, meanwhile, got their people spread out to secure the area, and it was then that Major Danielson arrived from Con Thien with his jeep, jeep-ambulance, and six-by truck. Danielson climbed wide-eyed from his jeep. The situation was worse than had been interpreted at the CP. Marines wandered about in shock, wounded men lay in the dirt on the verge of bleeding to death, and everyone, even those up and moving, seemed to have at least one bloody, dirty battle dressing. Major Danielson was ready to help, but his presence was mostly brushed aside by the tatterdamalion Marines rushing about him. His courage became a victim of the attitude expressed by Captain Radcliffe about their less-exposed superiors: *I wasn't disrespectful to him, but I didn't have time to fuck around with him.*

The most seriously wounded were placed aboard the vehicles, but no sooner had that been completed than a pair of CH46 Sea Knights arrived overhead. Major Danielson was surprised to see them for they were, after all, relatively slow-moving helos, and any medevac attempt—considering the potential for enemy artillery on the new landing zone—would put pilots and crews in great jeopardy. The seriously wounded were taken off the vehicles as first one and then the other Sea Knight settled down with lowered back ramps, and in a wind-blasted hustle they were transferred aboard. The process slowed down then as Major Danielson noted:

> The pilots and crew chiefs of the helicopters signaled to me that they were overloaded and would not be able to take off. As a result, I took it upon myself to make instantaneous selections of those Marines, some of whom were in shock I'm sure, who appeared to be the least seriously wounded and order them off the helicopters. Not a pleasant job, but one I thought necessary under the circumstances.

In the heat of the moment, PFC Hendry, who had just been carried from the back of the jeep-ambulance to one of the helicopters (a change he thanked God for) was going crazy. *Playing games,* he thought again, having no understanding why men who'd been carried on were now being carried off. *Wasting time!* He knew that the NVA would take this lingering target under fire, and sure enough, in the four or five agonizing minutes the big Sea Knights sat vibrating on the ground, artillery rounds did begin impacting near the LZ, just a bit off target. When Major Danielson completed his task and so signaled the pilots, the Sea Knights climbed through the artillery fire, taking away to safety PFC Weldon who'd been shot twice (and who was presently staring out a porthole window at the explosions walking in just as they lifted off); PFC Hendry who'd also been shot twice and peppered with shrapnel; PFC Henderson with his five separate wounds; PFC Fields who had two bullet wounds; Corporal Trevino who'd been twice shot, captured and recovered, and then blown off a mined tank; and approximately thirty-five other seriously wounded Marines. First stop for them was Dong Ha. It was about 1600.

★

The only seriously wounded man in the medical bunker, which was cut into the southern slope of the western Con Thien hill (with thirteen layers of sandbags along its three walls, and a roof of twenty-eight layers), was Sergeant Geizer of Alpha Company. He lay on his back on a stretcher across two sawhorses, as the battalion's Navy doctor used long surgical scissors to cut along the seam of his flak jacket's zipper. This done, the doctor peeled off the ragged, bloody body armor to examine Geizer's gut-to-back wound. He had, by then, a stream of blood running down his chest to his crotch from his other wound, the ding in his head, that had congealed into a ridge three-quarters of an inch thick. Because morphine could mask the seriousness of head wounds, the doctor would administer nothing for the pain which was in an ebb-and-flow cycle at this point. And because of the potential of a stomach injury, water was also not allowed. When the doctor moved on, though, Geizer called out for water, and a corpsmen handed him a little in a canteen cup. He dropped the emptied cup under the sawhorse and asked the next corpsman who came by for a drink, pretending never to have gotten the first.

Sergeant Geizer's radioman, PFC Ross, appeared at the bunker entrance, but the corpsmen would not let him in and that was the last they ever saw of each other. A tall, blond lance corporal from the CP did get in. The lance corporal talked to him about how he was doing; then the young man teared up a bit and said he had stood watches with Geizer in the same tent. Geizer recognized the man's face. He had been on the infantry net while Geizer had monitored the artillery net. The lance corporal went on to tell Geizer that he was his role model of what a Marine should be, and that he felt real bad when it came over the radio that he'd been hit.

Geizer was very moved. Shortly thereafter, an officer from the CP entered the bunker to consult with the Navy doctor, "The helicopters don't want to come in. They feel

Con Thien's going to get hit, that we're going to get hit anytime. Can the guys wait?"

The doctor went straight to Geizer and pried open his eyelids—he was, in fact, awake but the doctor didn't ask—then answered the officer, "Yes, I've got one I want to get out of here. The others can wait, but I want this one out of here if possible."

The officer exited the bunker at a fast pace and returned a bit later to report, "Boy, they're really scared to bring choppers in now. They're afraid they're gonna get clobbered. Sure you can't keep him?"

The doctor pressed the issue. "I'd like to get this one out of here." And again the officer departed only to reappear moments later. "Well, I wouldn't do it if I was them, but the crazy sons of bitches are going to come in, so get him and anyone else you got down to the LZ."

Sergeant Geizer's stretcher was lifted from the sawhorses, and up the sandbag steps he went looking at the world from his back. Helicopters dotted the sky, including two Hueys that orbited directly above their knob. One would dart in for him and a couple walking wounded while the other maintained its sky-high watch. When his stretcher carriers crested the hill, Geizer looked down the Strip. He could see vehicles in miniature near the southern edge of the Strip and he could see puffs around them from incoming artillery that looked harmless in the distance.

When the shelling stopped, the rest of the wounded were again placed on the vehicles. Most had been helped aboard when Lance Corporal Cromwell, for one, heard several horrendous explosions and thought for a moment that it was Marine counterbattery fire—until he glanced skyward and saw the rockets coming down right on top of them. Remembering the wounded men who'd been killed in the first LZ, this time the wounded were hustled back off the truck and jeeps and helped to cover. Three times they had to load and unload at the behest of the NVA batteries, and it was during one of the shellings that Bravo Company took its last casualty of the day when one of their lance corporals had three artillery rounds land around him simultaneously. The lance corporal survived and was on his feet, but he was too shell-shocked to function. When a lull finally allowed them to get the vehicles crammed with the casualties once and for all, he was among them.

Major Danielson then ordered Captain Radcliffe and Staff Sergeant Burns to take what remained of Bravo Company back north across the Strip to help those casualties that remained with Delta Three, and to beef up the perimeter there in case of further NVA ground attacks.

"Take a flying fuck at a rolling doughnut!"

The shout had come from one of the bleary-eyed grunts around them, but although Burns had heard it distinctly, Major Danielson either had not or thought it best to ignore it. The order, of course, stood and with that Danielson got back in his jeep and (as Burns put it with anger and some envy) *took off and got the hell outta there.*

The casualty-laden vehicles headed back for Con Thien with Major Danielson, and in the artillery-propelled haste to load them, some wounded men had not been evacuated and some healthy men had taken their places. Thinking the vehicles had also come to evacuate Bravo Company (they had not) Lieutenant Delaney went out this way, Corporal Pitts got the survivors of his squad aboard, and Lance Corporal Cull, looking at the confusion around him, thought it best to jump on the back of the truck. As they started off, the army jeep hit a bump that sent flying the GI manning its .50-caliber machine gun. The GI hurt his leg so badly that he couldn't walk, so Lance Corporal Cromwell "jumped on the gun, threw my radio in the jeep, and rode shotgun on a .50 caliber. I'd never fired a .50 caliber before, but I think I could have done a fairly good job if we would have run into anything."

Stumbling back across the Strip with Radcliffe and Burns's stripped-down, platoon-sized Bravo Company was Herbert's M79-man, face shot and teeth shattered, who had yet to be medevacked. He was shakey. They were all shakey. As the column passed back into Delta Three's perimeter, Doc Lindenmeyer gave an unconcerned glance at a Phantom jet roaring above them—The Sky Is Ours—until he realized it was diving directly at them. He saw two bombs separate, one from each wing, and he fell to the earth, shrieking, *"Innnncominngggg!"*

WOM-W-P-OMP!!! Lindenmeyer kneeled to emerge from the covering of fragmented earth the bombs had showered upon him; then he stood, spitting dirt from his mouth, blowing dirt from his nose, wiping dirt from his eyes and ears. All around him were dirt-shrouded, prostrate human forms, and feeling helplessly alone, he called out, "Is anybody hurt?"

No one answered. Then, all the dirt-covered forms began to move. The Phantom's bombs had exploded in the middle of the perimeter, doing nothing worse than shattering eardrums, nerves, and whatever faith these men still had that this day might actually end.

18

Charlie Company's Turn

★

With the tanks now gone and Charlie Company's rear-guard position reduced to a compact, ragged little circle in the Marketplace, Captain Hutchinson turned to Lieutenant Libutti and instructed him to get their column moving south again. To Libutti, the word from a Captain of Marines was the word from God. So as only a second lieutenant would do, he stood right up to carry out his orders, forgetting about the snipers around them. The company was clustered around him in the elephant grass, all of them prone or kneeling under the occasional fire. Libutti called to them, "Okay, guys, let's go! Get up! We're movin' out!"

No one moved. Libutti crouched back down and changed his tact as he growled at those men within earshot, "Listen, Marines, we're either going to stay here and die or we're going to move out. I tell you to stand up, *stand up*. We're all movin' out of here, goddammit!"

Libutti stood back up, continuing to encourage the

men, and—*thank God,* he thought—everyone got to his feet and formed up on the road. Libutti fell in behind the first three men in line, his radioman a few steps behind him. A hundred meters down the road, AK47 fire suddenly cut down those first three men. Libutti and his radioman instantly hit the deck. Behind them, from the sixth man on back, the column disappeared into the roadside hedges and brush. Libutti crawled forward to where his three point men had rolled on the side of the trail. One man, a big kid, had been shot in the guts and was in bad shape, but the other two, while hurting too bad to pull a trigger, were still coherent. The radioman also crawled up, and as he stripped ammo bandoliers from the most seriously wounded man, Libutti began firing his carbine into the brush ahead to keep their ambushers down, while he figured out how the hell they were going to extricate themselves from this mess.

In short order, Libutti's carbine jammed, and as he was wrapping his hands around an M16 dropped by one of the wounded men, he and his radioman suddenly spotted NVA rushing across the trail ahead of them. The NVA were trying to get into better firing positions, and Libutti and the radioman instantly opened fire on them from the side of the road where they had assumed sitting positions like at the rifle range. They put rounds downrange as hot and heavy as they could, pulling fresh magazines from the pouches of the wounded men beside them, talking to them between bursts, trying to calm them as they reloaded— even as their own sweat poured as they struggled to remain in control. An occasional NVA or two would suddenly appear, darting from one side of the road to the other, trying to find a position from which best to fire into the stranded group.

"Sir, I think I got one!"

The NVA stopped crossing the road. Everything got quiet. Libutti remained in position, the borrowed M16 pointed down the trail; and when he looked over at the big kid who seemed to be in shock, it suddenly hit him. *Holy cow, I got wounded Marines! I gotta do something!*

Libutti unsnapped his field-dressing pouch and tried to wrap the man's gut wound—at least do something to stop the bleeding—as his mind raced. *Okay, we can't stay here, we gotta run outta here or someone's going to come in and shoot us.* He hefted the big kid onto his shoulders, but as soon as he tried to stand up under the near-deadweight, over he went. He settled for dragging the man into the brush along the road. Then he rolled back onto the trail, coming up back to back with his radioman, facing south and the radioman facing north to watch the whole circle around them. They hoped the company would get itself together posthaste and come get them.

There was no time to wait. The first Chicom grenade came over the hedgerow to Libutti's left, and it hit his foot at the same time his radioman yelled a warning. They rolled away, but there was no explosion—a dud—and they wheeled back into their back-to-back position. The next grenade came out of nowhere, hit Libutti in the crotch, and bounced to the ground as they again jumped away and flattened out. Another dud. In the brush to his left, Libutti saw—or afterward he wondered if only his terrified mind's eye saw—an NVA coming through the hedgerow. So with his M16 on automatic, he emptied the magazine into that spot. No more Chicoms. *We have to get out of here, we can't stay in this position!* Libutti had no idea what to do. If they stood they would surely be shot. But they couldn't bring their wounded with them if they crawled.

Actually, help was on the way. One of Libutti's old-timers, Cpl Mike Bradley (who had extended his tour after a full year in the bush), responded to the initial fusillade by moving off Route 561 with his buddy Dick Boni in an effort to outflank the ambushers. Reaching a bamboo tree line, they were halted there by an AK47 burst that kicked eight or so rounds along the top of the earthen embankment. Crouched near a break in the bamboo line, Bradley and Dick were returning fire (they had no idea what was going on, but recoil dust was visible in the brush some fifty to seventy-five meters away) when, to their absolute amazement, the bamboo line twenty meters to their right front suddenly burst into flames. An NVA with a flamethrower came into view then in the open area between the two bamboo lines. M16 to his shoulder, Bradley quickly sighted on the man, who was looking away from him, and squeezed what remained of his magazine into him, about ten rounds, including a tracer that ignited the flame tanks. *Snap, crackle, pop,* Bradley thought, then with a laugh he or Dick said, "I know that prick wasn't trying to light my cigar!"

Back on Route 561, Captain Hutchinson had moved forward, and he shouted at one of their staff sergeants to take some men and recover the stranded point team: "They're wounded or something. Bring 'em in!"

The staff sergeant did not move.

Hutchinson shouted again, until he realized the staff sergeant was frozen with fear. Angry, promising himself that he would court-martial the bastard if they ever got out of this, but with no time to waste on him now, Hutchinson decided to get Libutti himself. Hutchinson signaled two or three men to follow him and called to the rest crouching there in the brush along the sunken road, "Cover me, and put a lot of fire out there—except where I am!"

Libutti had just ceased firing after the second dud grenade, when he looked back, and there was Hutchinson with a handful of Marines. Frustrated, exasperated, gulping air, Libutti greeted Hutchinson with, *"Jesus!* What's going on?" Hutchinson, taking a deep breath as well, listened to Libutti's quick report. And as the rest of the company moved forward to link up with them—the NVA disappearing at their renewed advance—he pulled out a pack of cigarettes. Libutti, normally a nonsmoker, lit one up too.

Back at the Strip, behind the cover of a large, up-turned tree, Lance Corporal Stuckey had just gotten the word that there were NVA running around in USMC uniforms. That's when he saw an Oriental in Marine gear walk up and sit down without a word a few meters away. There were a lot of Marines in the area, and this man didn't seem to be paying much attention to Stuckey's fireteam. But Stuckey wasn't so casual. He had his M16 in his lap, and as unobtrusively as he could, hoping not to startle this potential NVA into action, he eased the M16 in the man's direction and thumbed the safety off. Stuckey watched him like a hawk out of the corner of his eye, ready to blow him away, until another Marine—a round-eye type—walked over, and said to the Oriental, "Hey, Joe, they want us to move up here now."

Lieutenant Libutti was on the left side of Route 561, his view to either side blocked by the hedgerows along the flanks of the road. He sat dead on his ass, his knees drawn up to his chest, and one of the Six's radiomen leaned back on Libutti's knee, equally exhausted. Captain Hutchinson was across from him on the other side of the road with his other radioman, looking around as they got ready to continue south from this spot where the ambush had just fizzled out. The rest of Charlie Company was spread out behind them in as much of a tactical stance as possible, one column facing outboard on either side of the road, squads and platoons intermingled. Marines with bandaged arms and legs were carrying ponchos containing those who were more seriously wounded. They were helped by a squad from Alpha One that had been sent back from the Strip. It was one of these men from Alpha, PFC Horning, watching the road to the south, who first saw the NVA. Two were on the road, and Horning called to the squad radioman, PFC Mesa, "Look at the gooks across the road!"

"Where?"

"There they are!"

Horning and Mesa opened fire. One of the NVA went down and stayed down but the other jumped back up and bounded into the roadside brush.

Almost instantly then, AK47 fire began—from the front, rear, and flanks—and Captain Hutchinson realized that the NVA, who had silently watched Charlie Company's entrance and had probed and harassed their withdrawal, were now massing for the kill. Thinking of Bravo Company, he jumped down beside Libutti, their faces almost in the hedgerow ahead and their feet to the road.

Hutchinson's radiomen had similarly gone to the prone (to his right), and he shouted into his radios, directing an M60 team to fire back down the road the way they'd just come and for everyone else to watch the brush along the road: "Fire low, wait till you got a target and fire low!"

Lieutenant Libutti, down beside the captain, sighted his commandeered M16 first on one NVA he could see darting through the brush and then on another. He couldn't tell if his rounds were striking home. The NVA were trying to get within hand-grenade range. They did. Libutti saw a Chicom land near the CP, and he turned away as the explosion slapped shrapnel into his left shoulder and right knee. It burned terribly, and he cut his pack off to relieve the pressure on his wounded shoulder. But it was also a tremendous catharsis—*Oh shit, that's all there is? Here I've been tensed up all day and now I finally get wounded and it's okay, I'm walkin' and talkin'.*

The NVA had seen the radio antennas marking the CP's hunkered down huddle. More grenades were flipped over the hedgerow at them, when suddenly, like an apparition, an NVA stood up on the trail. *Just appeared,* thought a stunned Hutchinson; this was the first gook he'd seen all goddamn day! The NVA fired his AK47 into the command group, hitting the two radiomen lying between Hutchinson and the NVA, and was himself mowed down in the same instant. Hutchinson saw the NVA spin and crumple on the road, bush hat flying off, his rifle slung around his arm and staying with him during the fall.

"Corrrpsman! Corpsman up!"

One of the radiomen had a sucking chest wound, but the other was awake enough to look at Hutchinson and implore, "Skipper, am I going to die?" His elbow was a mess, red and white and bone shattered, but his flak jacket looked intact, so Hutchinson assured the kid he'd be all right as the corpsman made it up to them. The corpsman, a skinny, mustached kid, sported a number of superficial wounds himself, but he never lost his cool. Moving first to the elbow-shot kid, it turned out the man's flak jacket *had* been riddled. And in minutes both radiomen were dead in the ditch. The corpsman, his face a stoic mask, bounded on as Hutchinson got on the radio again, reporting that he had too many casualties to move and begging for fire support: "Look, you guys got to do something for me!"

"There's another battalion on the way."

But there was no abundance of fire support, and grenades continued to plop down around them. Young Marines, as cool as could be, played tit for tat, lobbing their own grenades a mere five meters into the brush where they could hear the NVA moving. *Oh God,* Hutchinson almost screamed as he watched the first volley of outgoing grenades. *Our own guys are going to blow us up.* But as he ate dirt at the too-close explosions, he could hear the gooks squawling and squawking in pain.

Nearby, PFC Horning was giving his M79 a workout (until almost out of ammunition), and PFC Mesa blasted away with his M16, making sure no NVA got across the road to the south. Mesa, down to two magazines and scared out of his mind, almost shaking, turned his attention away from the road to check on the wounded lieutenant there (he didn't know Libutti) and another anonymous wounded man. Then he glanced back up—right at the sight of a grenade coming directly at his face. Cursing himself for not watching the road better, he sprang away and landed on the other side of the prone and wounded Libutti. He curled up, but his elbows were exposed and when the Chicom exploded, only eight feet away, shrapnel ripped into them. Mesa had been incountry less than three months, but he'd been wounded before. That time he'd screamed a lot, mostly from the fear. Now he just lay there and groaned.

Lieutenant Libutti was moaning a bit too. The grenade had sent slivers and chunks of metal into his right arm and right butt cheek.

It would have gotten worse as dusk slid into night, if not for the arrival of the 3d Battalion, 9th Marines. Everyone's spirits soared as they saw the sky fill with helicopters to the south. They watched them disappear behind the tree lines defining the northern edge of the Strip, then saw green figures emerging in columns from those tree lines headed in their direction. The NVA fire slackened, and when it seemed to have ceased, Charlie Company got to its collective feet, rolled their dead and seriously wounded (about five and twenty-five respectively) into ponchos, and began heading south again. There were dud Chicoms on the road, and as they passed the NVA that had been shot dead on the trail, Hutchinson reached down for the man's AK47 and slung it over his own shoulder.

The hedgerows a bit farther south were broken. It was easier to see into the fields, but the brush was still burning and smoking as it had been on Charlie Company's way in. The smoke hung languidly in the muggy dusk air, and it was here that the NVA lobbed something of a final round on them. It sounded like it came from a captured M79 grenade launcher, and Libutti was hit for the third time (this time the shrapnel lodged in his left hip), so he jumped off the road. He landed on the back of another Marine who'd also sought cover in the roadside depression, realizing the man was actually Captain Hutchinson even before the startled skipper blurted, "What's going on?"

"It's Libutti, sir."

Captain Hutchinson twisted around, then grimaced, "Oh Jesus, are you hit again?"

By the late afternoon of Sunday, 2 July 1967, the leading rumors in the 1st Battalion, 9th Marines, 3d Marine Division, were that they had encountered not NVA, but Red Chinese, and that the battalion had been so shredded as to set in motion their withdrawal to Okinawa, Japan, for complete refitting and recuperation. They nicknamed the battle the Marketplace Massacre.

PART THREE

THE NORTHERN 'EYE' CORPS RESERVE

★

From the "Combat After Action Report (Buffalo), HEADQUARTERS, 1st Battalion, 9th Marines, 3d Marine Division": ". . . 1/9 casualties from 2 July were 51 USMC KIA; 166 USMC WIA; 34 USMC MIA . . ."

From the "Combat After Action Report, Operation Buffalo, 021000H-140900H July 1967, HEADQUARTERS, 3d Battalion, 9th Marines, 3d Marine Division": "Upon notification at approximately 021500 July 1967 of the requirement to reinforce 1st Battalion, 9th Marines elements in heavy contact, Co. K and the Command Group moved to helo-zone, Dong Ha for shuttle helolift to the trace east of Con Thien at YD 130706. Co. L followed being lifted from the field from vicinity YD 213536. Co. I moved by road from vicinity YD 303562 to the helo-zone, Dong Ha to complete the lift . . ."

From the comments of Cpl. Sammie K. Peterson (Weapons Platoon, A/1/9) made during an interview with the 3d Marine Division Historical Section, "The company commander says we're getting a reinforced battalion comin' out, going to help us—it was Three-Nine. Everybody glad to see Three-Nine. You could see 'em—all it is is Hueys, '46s, '34s, they come in waves of six. Good thing to see when you ain't got no water, and your perimeter's about fifty meters around. Start thinking something—there ain't nobody left but you and the gooks. And there's more gooks than there is you."

19

Wall to Wall Trouble

★

0915, 2 July 1967. Dong Ha. As Capt George D. Navadel, S-3 Operations Officer, 3d Battalion, 9th Marines, monitored the increasingly urgent radio traffic from the CP of 1/9 (Con Thien) to the CP of the 9th Marine Regiment (Dong Ha) he *knew*. He knew the terrain in which 1/9 was engaged: 3/9 had spent parts of Operations Hickory and Cimmaron between the Trace (as they called the Strip) and the DMZ. Their last contacts there (three weeks before) were with what was later conjectured to have been the reconnaissance elements of the NVA battalions currently eating 1/9 alive. He knew the game the NVA were playing: 3/9 had encountered these same smothering divide-and-overrun tactics in March when India Company was hit northwest of Cam Lo, and in May when Kilo, Lima, and Mike Companies took separate and equally bloody bashings (not to suggest that the Marines didn't give as good as they got). He knew that the

NVA would only assault Alpha and Bravo 1/9 simultaneously if they enjoyed a substantial numerical superiority.

Captain Navadel also knew that sooner or later the Northern I Corps Reserve would be committed. He wanted it to be sooner, and he wanted it to be when they still had plenty of daylight left, which meant that they would have to begin organizing immediately because, although 3/9 was the designated reaction force (and was therefore not tied to any defensive positions), most of its rifle companies were on patrol and would have to be reigned in. That the area reserve was, in fact, partially committed to the field was another sad comment on the taut-as-a-bowstring manpower situation facing the division. Only H&S Company (2dLt W. C. Helton) and Kitty Kat Kilo (Capt Jerrald E. Giles) were collocated with Maj Willard J. (Woody) Woodring, CO, 3/9, in the tents allocated for them in the interior of the Dong Ha Combat Base.

Indifferent India (Capt Edward H. Coyle) was on a population relocation operation along the Song Thach Han, more than four kilometers southeast of Dong Ha.

Lizard Lima (Capt Troy T. Shirley) was on a routine search-and-destroy sweep approximately four kilometers southwest of Dong Ha.

Mediocre Mike (Capt R. B. Johnson) was opcon to the base commander at Gio Linh for perimeter security and, as a result, was unavailable.

A and B/1/9 still had radio contact when Captain Navadel made the short walk to the 9th Marines CP, a heavily sandbagged bunker between two of the old French barracks that housed the regimental staff. He wanted a look at their intelligence map and operations map, but mostly he wanted to personally emphasize the need to immediately get the ball rolling with the reserve. Navadel shuttled back and forth between Colonel Jerue's people and Woodring, relaying information and making their case with his counterpart at regiment, Maj Billy J. (Bunker) Hill, S-3, 9th Marines. Navadel stressed that the NVA were taking on two companies at the same time, meaning "it's got to be big. Maybe two battalions, two regiments—two *something.* Let's go *now.* Don't wait. Commit us *now."*

The one thing Captain Navadel's eleven months of experience did not tell him about this fight that he was eavesdropping on was just how bad things could get. He was back at the regimental CP when all communications with Bravo Company were lost, and he and the rest listened horrified then to an aerial observer who was over the Marketplace. The pilot saw a group of Marines get up to pull back, and from his perch he could also see the NVA along the route they had chosen. With commo lost, the pilot was really just talking to himself (and the eavesdroppers) as he called out in agony, *"Oh my God! Don't go that way, don't go that way . . . oh no!"*

While the need to reinforce a contact was starkly obvious to those at the platoon or company level, this screaming clarity evaporated by the time the contact became a grease-pencil mark on the acetate-covered map at regiment. A regiment like the 9th Marines on the DMZ, faced with several such map dots a day, could not proceed quickly because the reaction forces did not exist to reinforce each contact. Regiment had to allow time for each contact to develop. If reinforcement proved necessary, that time was wasted. Ideally, an accurate Intelligence picture would have allowed for a rapid assessment of enemy intentions and, thus, a quick response. However, as Brigadier General Metzger, ADC, 3d Marine Division, noted:

> Our Intelligence was limited and all too often slow. It took too long for it to move from III MAF in Da Nang, through division in Phu Bai, to us in Dong Ha. The result was that we had difficulty identifying enemy formations and locations. Too often we were forced to react to enemy actions, rather than anticipate them. In a defensive situation this is frequently the case.

Colonel Jerue, CO, 9th Marines, could not simply order 3/9 to the aid of 1/9 once he appreciated the magnitude of the Marketplace battle. Although 3/9 was organic to Jerue's regiment, once designated as a reserve force, it became beholden to division forward, division rear, and corps. Such an extended accordion of commanders (those making decisions at III MAF in Da Nang were basically on the other side of the world to the Marines on the DMZ) was further indication of the impossibility of the 3d Marine Division's mission (in July 1967 the 9th Marines alone were responsible for 388 square miles); it exaggerated the delay during this particular battle in committing 3/9 where it was needed. Brigadier General Metzger commented that "with hindsight it would have been much better to have the entire division headquarters located in Dong Ha. The DMZ was where the majority of the combat elements were located. The small forward headquarters did not have adequate command- and control-elements for the job at hand."

Division Commander Bruno A. Hochmuth was a tall, rawboned Texan, low-key and matter-of-fact. He was personable and brave, and constantly helo-hopped among his units (his former aide-de-camp, Captain Slater, several times had to organize quick perimeters on patrol because Big Six was dropping in for a look).[1] Perhaps Hochmuth retained his CP in Phu Bai (he had questioned his staff on the validity of such a location upon assuming command) because he trusted Metzger to run their straight-line infantry war on the DMZ; from Phu Bai, Hochmuth could better keep in touch with their other war, the politics at III MAF and with the ARVN. Nevertheless, these inherent command difficulties did exacerbate combat difficulties. In this case, it was not until 1500, 2 July 1967, that Major Woodring and Captain Navadel of the 3d Battalion, 9th Marines, were given the order to commence movement

1. Major General Hochmuth assumed command of the 3d MarDiv on 18 March 1967, and was killed on 14 November 1967 (along with five others) when his Huey helicopter exploded and crashed some eight kilometers northwest of Hue. He was the only Marine general to die in Vietnam.

from Dong Ha to the Trace. By this time, the 1st Battalion, 9th Marines, had been fighting for five hours and forty-five minutes. Bravo Company no longer existed, and Alpha was holding its collective breath.

When the word went out to 3/9's companies in the field (fireteam leader Cpl Bill Collopy of India Company, for one, was informed by his squad leader, "I just talked to one of my friends from Scouts, and he says the AO up by Con Thien reported that they got wall-to-wall gooks in four grid squares"), there issued from the grunts of 3/9 a string of slanders about the abilities of 1/9. They were the Walking Dead, the regiment's Jonah. Their theme song, it was joked, must be "I'm a Believer" by the Monkees ("believer" was the nickname for someone killed in action as in Willy Peter, Make You A Believer),[2] or "Nowhere to Run, Nowhere to Hide" by Martha and the Vandellas.

Such commentary was a product of unit pride, but it ignored 3/9's own recent history in the months before the exceptional Major Woodring came aboard. Posted to Camp Carroll in February 1967 to begin a new war with Nguyen of the North (after much VC chasing in An Hoa and the Arizona Territory and six weeks of refitting on Okinawa), 3/9's first major encounter with this different, unrelenting foe occurred at dusk on 30 March 1967 when India Company separated into several independent ambush positions. The company CP was setting up with their 60mm mortar section and two rifle squads, when the NVA launched a mortar-supported ground assault (simultaneous with holding actions against the other elements of India Company who then tried to maneuver to assist the CP). The company commander, Captain Getlin, although shot and shrapnel mauled, brought in the supporting arms that temporarily halted the main assault. When the reorganized NVA boiled through the CP, Getlin killed six of them with his shotgun; he then hurled back an NVA grenade and was finally killed while trying to snatch up another one. The

2. Willy Peter (or white phosphorus) had much the same effect as napalm on the human body.

weapons-platoon commander, Lieutenant Bobo, had his right leg blown off below the knee by a mortar explosion, and he faced the NVA charge with a web belt tight around his stump. Bobo kept shooting NVA until they swarmed over him. The company top, First Sergeant Rogers, though shot through the thigh, personally killed his share of NVA before organizing the survivors under the cover of the Huey gunship he directed in. The NVA fell back, leaving sixty-seven dead and two prisoners, but India had lost sixteen of its own killed and forty-seven wounded.

Michael Getlin was posthumously awarded the Navy Cross and John Bobo the Congressional Medal of Honor. First Sergeant Rogers lived to receive his Navy Cross, and the Battle of Getlin's Corner became a battalion legend.[3] The next mass contribution to this hall of heroes was provided on 30 April 1967 when Captain Giles's Kilo Company was opcon to 3/3 (after pulling Bravo 1/9 back during the opening stages of the Hill Fights). On this day they assaulted up Hill 881S and, unknowingly, into an expertly constructed maze of NVA entrenchments, which did not come alive with fire until Kilo was strung out along the steep, bomb-denuded slope and hopelessly intermingled with the invisible enemy. It was a hornet's nest of close-in action, made worse by long-range NVA snipers who picked off radiomen and anyone who looked like a leader or who had a map. Two of Kilo's platoon commanders were killed, the third wounded, and Giles was ordered to pull back after seventeen of his men had been killed and fifty-four wounded. The next day, Kilo took 881S. The NVA had pulled out during the night with their casualties and every bit of equipment (*everything,* they even policed up their brass), leaving some of Kilo's KIAs booby trapped with grenades. Other dead Marines were grotesquely spread-

3. The battle also snapped 3/9 into a harsher new mindset; as Cpl David J. Gomez (I/3/9) commented, "When we lost all those people, I seen for the first time NVA troops being pushed out of choppers. I seen 'em tied with wire. I seen 'em beaten. I don't have a problem with that, I really don't—they did it to us, we did it to them."

eagled atop enemy bunkers, on display, with sticks rammed in their mouths and their flies undone, cocks hanging out to mock the Marines that the NVA knew would be coming to recover their dead comrades.

At this time, 3/9 had no confidence in its leaders. Their battalion commander (Woodring's predecessor) was a career-obsessed and image-oriented lieutenant colonel who, concerned only with making no errors that might deny him his eagles, tended to hesitate into inaction. He was known in some quarters as Fertilizer 6. Meanwhile, his glory-chasing XO (known behind his back as Mad Sam) and S-3 (the Golden Greek) formed an unholy alliance to upstage everyone else. They were abrasive, demeaning, and demoralizing, and in combat they were dangerous. On 20 May 1967, Kilo Company was leading a battalion sweep toward Hill 70 in Leatherneck Square. In the late afternoon, Kilo's point platoon encountered an NVA mortar at the base of Hill 70. They killed one or two of the crew while the rest got away, and Captain Giles radioed the CP, "We've just run into an eighty-two mike-mike team. They don't run through the woods alone. They've obviously got a much larger force around here. I recommend that we deploy."

The Golden Greek answered, "Negative on that. Get to the top of the hill and secure it so the battalion can move in for the night."

From atop Hill 70, Giles reported "There's a helluva an amount of NVA footprints up top this hill. It's very, very fresh. I recommend that the battalion deploy immediately. I think we've got lots of company up here."

Again, from the Golden Greek, "I'm tired of you holding back. Your mission is to secure the top of the hill, and you better do it damn quick."

"Roger on that."

While deploying on Hill 70, Kilo Company ran into an equally surprised NVA battalion. The NVA attacked, the Marines went to ground in the old Marine fighting holes dotting the hill; and for the next sixteen hours (while Lima tried hard but unsuccessfully to break through the mortars and machine guns to join them) Giles and Kilo fought a desperate, nightmarish action under the glow of illumination shells and gun-plane tracers. At one point, Captain Giles fired his M16 point-blank into an NVA cresting the hill, and later, he joined three Marines who were unsuccessfully lobbing grenades at an NVA hole forty meters away. Giles made a hole in one, killing both occupants. NVA passed through the Marine line, more in confusion as to where exactly the Marines were than in any final assault, and the battle ended with the NVA's with-sunrise-comes-the-jets retreat.

Giles's position was littered with dead NVA and dead Marines—twenty-five dead Marines—and there were more than fifty wounded Marines. His emotions were a swirl. Anger. Guilt. Revulsion. Depression. And the most intense feeling possible for these Marine grunts around him, a feeling that would take him years to recognize as love. Fertilizer 6 and the Golden Greek marched in then with Lima Company. Coming up the blasted, burned, body-strewn slope of Hill 70, Fertilizer 6 was muttering, "Oh my God, this is awful, this is awful—this may really screw up my career!"

For once, Fertilizer 6 was right. On 29 May 1967, he was relieved of command (Mad Sam and the Golden Greek were also ejected), and Major Woodring was helicoptered up from Phu Bai where he had been serving as the XO and S-3 of 3/26. Woody Woodring was a country boy from the Ozark Mountains of Missouri. He had been a sergeant leading a rifle squad in the 5th Marines from Pusan to Inchon, through the house-to-house in Seoul to the ice-and-fire ordeal of the Chosin Reservoir. Commissioned after promotion to technical sergeant, he was personable, soft-spoken, and down-to-earth, a total pro with a lot of heart. Woodring was the only battalion commander that Giles saw who really got down to talk to his Marines and who did not position himself comfortably to the rear of his fighting elements during contacts. Woodring was also the only battalion commander he saw whose loyalties extended downward, even if that meant being a burr under the saddles of the eagle-wearers who wrote his fitness reports.

During one operation, a water resupply in five-gallon jerry cans was delivered immediately prior to a mount out; after the rationing process, Woodring radioed regiment, "We need to have the water cans picked up before we move out."

Regiment said that no helos were available and to carry the cans on patrol. Woodring replied, "It's going to be like a bunch of cows walking through the woods with cowbells around their necks. We're not going to do it."

Regiment said he had no choice. Unfortunately for regiment, 3/9 was sick of water cans. They were heavy, inefficient, and when delivered by helicopter always resulted in one wet chopper and one wet, unhappy crew chief. Furthermore, 3/9 had previously discovered a super replacement when their supply officer cumshawed a thousand cardboard, plastic-lined milk containers out of Saigon. Though 3/9 wrote numerous reports on these inexpensive, disposable containers, they never reappeared on the battlefield; and told now to carry their antiquated water cans on patrol, Woodring answered, "Well, I'm going to solve the problem. What I'm going to do is take some C4 [plastic explosive] and blow these water cans in place right here."

Regiment suddenly found they had helos for the cans.

The grunts were well served by Major Woodring who was, in turn, well served by his hard-charging S-3, Captain Navadel, who had commanded four rifle companies during his eleven months incountry, and who, as the op officer, retained a fierce devotion to the individual Marine and a realistic idea of what could be expected of rifle companies in terms of distance and movement, etc. In other words, the 3d Battalion, 9th Marines, was as ready as it could be for Operation Buffalo.

On 2 July 1967, Captain Giles's Kilo Company was the battalion's Bald Eagle Company, on standby at Dong Ha to reinforce any battalion in the area in need. Giles was thirty-one, a dark-haired, tall, athletic man who possessed all the technical skills and personal courage, as well as the intelligence and sensitivity, that one could hope to find in a combat Marine officer. He had commanded Kilo Company for eleven solid months, and had been with them at An Hoa, Mai Loc 2, the Old French Fort, Dong Ha, Ba Long Valley, Khe Sanh, Hill 881S, Leatherneck Square, Hill 70, Gio Linh, Charlie One, Charlie Two, and Charlie Three. Giles was a good company commander, but if the truth be known, he was on autopilot by the time of Operation Buffalo. He had become very fatalistic and war weary. The war had actually still been in its adventure phase for him up until Khe Sanh. There, Kilo had just reached the 3/3 CP, below B/1/9's hill. Two corpsmen appeared, running down the hill and dragging a poncho full of gear:

> but as they came by me I realized that what they had by the heels was a dead Marine. I looked down as this Marine came bouncing by, and I almost wanted to reach out and grab these two corpsmen and say, "Hey, take care of this kid, he's a Marine," but then I realized all they were doing is getting the dead off the hill as best they could. And I think at that point in time the Marine Corps hymn stopped playing in my head, and I realized that war was not a game, that war was really a very vulgar and a very final event.

On 2 July, Captain Giles should have been one of the first to get the word that they were Bald Eagling to the Marketplace (Kilo was, after all, the only company in 3/9 on the parade deck at Dong Ha), but he was away from his CP and was, in fact, one of the last. Giles was walking through the battalion (at ease in undershirt, jungle utility trousers, and shower sandals), when he noticed a first sergeant chewing out a man: "If you don't square away, young Marine, I'm going to send you down to Kilo Company and get your ass shot off!"

Man, that sure is true, Giles thought. Good old Killer Kilo. Giles stopped off then at the S-4 tent and sat down with Capt Robert W. Swigart, the battalion logistics officer, who offered a rare beer. Swigart had been monitoring the radio and told Giles of 1/9's contact. They discussed whether or not Kilo Company would be committed. The tent was an oven. Dust blew in from passing helicopters. They talked of the war and the battalion, and Swigart noted that he would be rotating home in a few days. He was not completely pleased about this because, though he was a man who wore the vestments of toughness—the cigar, the hard drinking—Captain Swigart had been the CO of Mike Company relieved of command by Fertilizer 6 for an action on 21 May 1967. Making contact that day, Swigart had been hesitant to close with the enemy (knowing what Kilo had been through on Hill 70 only the previous evening, and knowing he could expect little support from Fertilizer 6) so, instead, he had pulled back to employ supporting arms. Mike Company took casualties, the NVA did not, and a bitter and embarrassed Swigart (failure or scapegoat?) ended up counting C rations and jungle boots in the rear.[4] Swigart and Giles had been talking for more than an hour when Giles, glancing through the tent flap, saw a group of Marines hustling past. Then he realized that one GySgt John C. (Horrible) Hatfield, the gunny of Kilo Company, was off to one side, moving the Marines down the road.

Giles ran out to them, "Hatfield, where in the hell are you going?"

"Well, skipper, we're going to war. Didn't you get the word? They're Bald Eagling our ass up to the DMZ!"

"Holy shit, don't leave without me!"

Captain Giles ran back to his CP tent, kicked off his shower sandals, and stomped into his jungle boots. He didn't even take the time to lace them up—just wrapped the laces around his ankles and made two quick bows. He got his helmet, flak jacket, and M16; threw his pack over his shoulder (realizing then that it was mostly empty except for a couple pairs of socks and a can of C rations); and

4. Swigart's feelings about his relief would impact directly on events during Operation Buffalo.

came out of the tent at a run. He jumped in the company jeep.

Captain Navadel briefed Captain Giles (an old friend) at the Dong Ha helo-zone. Kilo Company was to land at a point on the Trace approximately 1,300 meters northeast of Con Thien and 800 meters southwest of where Route 561 intersected the Trace. From there, Kilo was to push due north some 1,300 meters and effect a link-up with A/1/9. As Navadel understood the situation, A/1/9 had formed a good, tight perimeter but were hopelessly alone. Thus, Kilo's rush to them. The other company in need of salvation, B/1/9, had been hit harder but had already been reached by C/1/9 and was retiring to the Trace. Lima Company, which would be lifted directly from the field, and India Company, presently being returned to Dong Ha by truck, would join 3/D/1/9 on the northern side of the Trace and form a line that Kilo would bring A/1/9 back into. The planned-for helicopter armada did not arrive. What chugged into view instead were three obsolete Sea Horses, straining hard due to the extreme heat. As each pilot landed, he held out a hand from his cockpit window to indicate how many fully loaded combat Marines he could handle. One hand was bad enough, but then only three or four fingers were extended. Navadel and Giles commented to themselves that this wasn't going to be a classic textbook example of a helicopter insertion, but because one had to keep it light, they then laughed, "Here we go, wa-hoo!"

<u>20</u>

Bald Eagling

★

The helo-lift of K Company, 3d Battalion, 9th Marines, from Dong Ha to the Trace (aka the Strip) commenced at 1630, 2 July 1967. Working initially with only those three Sea Horses (which were making round-robin trips), Captain Navadel and Giles re-formed their original squad-sized helo teams into three- and four-man fireteams, machine-gun teams, and rocket teams, so as to maintain some tactical integrity and get the men on the ground in some logical sequence.

After getting about a platoon's worth of men into the Trace, a Sea Knight arrived, which gave Captain Giles the opportunity to gather a dozen members of his company headquarters and get them on the ground simultaneously. To be airborne was to be vulnerable to a mind-bending degree, and when the back ramp sealed shut and the twin-rotored machine began its lift-off, a wordless, here-we-go-again silence engulfed the command group. The ride was short, and as the Sea Knight bounced to a halt on the

Trace, the ramp was already nearly fully open. When it was all the way down the crew chief roared, "Get out, get out!" over the sounds of his helicopter, and down the ramp they went, dry mouthed, into the dust, noise, and confusion. As the Sea Knight struggled to make a rapid getaway, the Marines deposited on the ground could hear artillery shells or rockets exploding off on the right flank. Giles found himself thinking of training exercises at Quantico as he got the first waves of Kilo Company deployed along the bulldozed piles of brush at the northern edge of the Trace. That took about twenty minutes. The rest of Kilo landed thereafter in bits and pieces. And after the usual commotion of finding out where everyone was and getting organized, Kilo Company began their northward, cross-country movement in platoon columns (with 2dLt Jerry Lane, their best platoon commander, on point) heading, finally, toward A Company, 1st Battalion, 9th Marines.

They moved in a loose column toward the sounds and gunpowder smells of the battle. All they could see of the battle, however, was the perpetual dust and smoke over the hedgerows and brush. The closer they got, the more of the NVA fire directed at Alpha Company came their way, high and stray but jolting nonetheless. Every time another round or two would snap by, Giles mused that he could tell the difference between his new Marines and his old Marines: the replacements would hit the deck and try to crawl into their helmets, while his veterans would keep trucking fatalistically along. Giles had to reach down and tap some Marines on the shoulder. "C'mon, get up, keep moving, keep moving, keep moving."

Major Woodring, who, along with his ten-man command group, had landed with the last of Kilo Company and then had moved into Delta Three's position at the mouth of Route 561 (pursuant to Colonel Jerue's orders, he was to take command of all 1/9 elements beyond Con Thien), was, meanwhile, bringing the rest of 3/9 into the Trace. With NVA artillery and mortar rounds landing in the area, and NVA machine gunners and riflemen bringing fire to bear on the LZ from newly assumed positions along the

Trace, each succeeding helicopter wave landed in a different spot along the firebreak to keep the NVA gunners guessing. Each Sea Horse (and they came in one, two, or three at a time) unloaded its handful at maximum speed for minimum exposure. And bit by bit, Captain Shirley's Lizard Lima came in behind Kitty Kat Kilo, followed by the battalion's tail, Captain Coyle's Indifferent India.

Going out on a Bald Eagle into a hot situation—at the DMZ—puts the fear right into you; it's really tough, you really have to psyche yourself up to do the job. So thought Corporal Gomez of India Two, the fourth man to command his squad (and carry the M79 that went with the job) since he had joined it eight months earlier. Gomez was as ready as he could be, thanks in large part to his platoon commander, whom the men knew as Iron Mike. Mike sat near him now in the Sea Horse as they approached the Trace. Iron Mike, a staff-sergeant-turned-lieutenant, had done a lot to keep the platoon tight after the demoralizing loss of Getlin and Bobo and the others at Getlin's Corner. In fact, when he took over the platoon shortly thereafter, he had impressed everyone when he gave each of his squad leaders, Gomez, Black, and O'Conner, an American flag: "If one of us gets wounded and he's out there in the middle of the shit, if you don't come out to get the man at least come out for the flag."

The NVA was a very good soldier and we were afraid of the NVA, thought Gomez. *But by working together as Iron Mike demanded, as Marines, we learned that the NVA died like everybody else.*

Iron Mike was the first man out the door when the Sea Horse made its jolting, rubber-wheeled landing in the chopped-up dirt of the Trace—and over the engines could be heard enemy fire. It came from a group of helmeted and flak-jacketed NVA more than a hundred meters away; Iron Mike's Marines had seen them from the air as the group had rushed across the barren Trace, but had taken them to be their LZ security until, when the Sea Horse was ten feet off the ground, the NVA had begun firing upon it. Iron

Mike directed his people north to the battalion's rallying point of a tree line two hundred meters ahead.

The insertion of India Company continued. When the Sea Knight carrying PFC Roger A. Ford (3.5-inch Rocket Squad, Weapons Platoon) deposited its Marines on the Trace, Ford expected other helos to be landing with them. They did not. *My God, we're all alone!* NVA fire cracked at them, and they took cover in the bulldozed counters of this barren track. Ford was pissed, and he was determined not to die before he could do these gooks some damage. *"Fuck 'em, we gotta get up to the tree line!"*

"What side of the tree line do we go to?"

"We go to the side with the red tracers."

That made sense. The Marines were issued red tracers, the NVA green ones. Ford quickly assembled and loaded his rocket launcher; then, heaped with weapons, ammunition, and equipment, they took off across the pulverized earth of the Trace. It was all brown and barren and stretched for hundreds of meters. They made it to the bulldozed and cratered bramble along the northern rim where Marines from India and Lima companies were visible and where Captain Navadel, the operations officer, was in position, getting each straggling group locked into the big picture.

Captain Slater of Alpha 1/9 was aware of Kilo 3/9's approach through the relatively high ground to their south, and he had Corporal Peterson's 60mm mortar team (the only one left in the company) fire Willy Peter to mark their location. It was twilight by then, and Corporal Power, for one (who knew the NVA would overrun them during the night), looked back again toward the low ridge that defined the southern edge of their perimeter—and he saw fully loaded Marines moving from cover to cover as they crested and started down the slope.

Kilo Company had arrived (it was 1930), and Power greeted the ones moving in to reinforce his side of the perimeter. "Hey, man, my boy! Motherfuckers, are we glad to see you! Whew! Man, you know you got here just in time!"

One Kilo Marine pulled out a canteen for him, but held his hand on it and after Power got a couple swallows, he pulled it away, "All right, all right. I don't know when we're going to get any more."

We could get extincted up here in a jiffy, and they know it too. Power looked at the Kilo Marines. *They're scared shitless.* They were. It was evident to the Kilo Marines that the Alpha Marines had dug in with anything they could dig with—spoons, ammo magazines, bayonets, helmets—and each man had his mags and frags within arm's reach around his position. They also had their K-Bars and bayonets and E-tools ready in the dirt, to be scooped up when their ammunition was gone and the gooks were still coming. Alpha Company had been bracing for annihilation; but now with Kilo Company securing the area (and their own Gunny Hatfield kidding his old comrade, Gunny Santomasso, about "having to pull your sorry ass out of trouble all the time"), Alpha picked up and reclaimed their one area that had been overrun: Lieutenant Muller's 3d Platoon LZ in the westernmost of the three paddy fields.

The paddy was artillery gutted and fire blackened, and it was an unholy mess. Gear was scattered everywhere: packs, helmets, rifles—everything had been looted by the NVA before they had retired. And dead Marines were sprawled about, shot and mangled, some burnt by the fire that had swept through the elephant grass. Several of the immobile wounded had apparently been killed by that fire, but miracles of miracles, PFC Ragland, the machine gunner who had feigned death when the NVA originally overran the LZ, was recovered, alive and well, and he rejoined his squad. Captain Slater was glad about this, but otherwise, he had never felt so wretched, despite the thirty NVA bodies left behind, which meant that many more had been dragged away. Lieutenant Muller, the lawyer-turned-platoon-commander who could have been with regimental legal had Slater not decided to keep him, was dead, and guilt bloomed painfully and permanently inside Slater. There

were equally ugly sights. The LZ perimeter had been so
hastily organized that Slater now came across dead Marines who had been facing the wrong direction—it appeared the NVA had shot them point-blank in the back.
They never had a chance. Another man walking this
parched piece of nothing, Lance Corporal Dishong, came
across one of his buddies who just lay there dead. *Dead.* He
wasn't getting back up—his hair was singed and his eyes
were melted together. Starting back then, Dishong was
overwhelmed by some emotion he could not articulate. He
just went temporarily crazy, falling to the dirt and screaming. Captain Slater said later, "There were a lot of people
crying over Third Platoon. I mean these were their buddies
they had lived with and survived with so long, and they
looked down at their burned, charred bodies, and I mean
they were really uptight. It was a very touching, angry, frustrating moment, because then, to top it off, we never really
did get through to help out Bravo Company. We got it at
both ends."

Corporal Power, who had been separated from his
partner, Lance Corporal Quigley, during the firefight,
found the body of Terry Lynn Quigley during the cleanup.
It was hard to recognize him because his body was swelling
and the sun had already turned him black. Power could not
find the third member of his scout team, Staff Sergeant
Xuan. When he reported this to Captain Slater, they were
both horrified that Xuan might have been captured when
the LZ was overrun. As a former NVA or VC, Xuan would
suffer death by torture from those NVA whose cause he
had deserted. Xuan was well thought of in Lieutenant
Howell's S-2 shop (especially in comparison to their normally lackluster scouts), and Slater got a lot of calls from
battalion. "Is he dead, can you find his body?" They could
not. Power, meanwhile, feeling guilty and depressed over
Quigley and Xuan, salvaged his NVA pack that he'd flung
off during the fight in the LZ. It was burned along one side,
and Power recovered a half-carton of Winstons, his black-

ened July 1967 *Playboy,* and a half-melted canteen that still held some water.

It was at this time that word got around that Kilo Company had policed up a wounded NVA from among the dead ones in and around the LZ. Captain Giles was gravely concerned for the man's safety. The NVA usually fought so ferociously, even when wounded, that the Marines had no option but to kill, and Giles had previously seen only one NVA prisoner in his eleven months incountry. He had sent that wounded man back with two young Marines, who had returned shortly to report that the prisoner had died before the medevacs arrived. Giles was never sure that the two hadn't just been pissed off and killed him. So this time, he called up four of his good NCOs (from Lane's platoon) and told them that their job was to "get him back to the LZ, get him on a helicopter. I want him to arrive alive."

Meanwhile, Corporal Power walked over to the prisoner, who lay on his back nursing a gut wound, his face struggling to remain calm but his young eyes betraying his terror. There were Alpha Marines who would have summarily executed the man.

"Fuckin' dink."

"Zap 'im."

"Blow the motherfucker's brains out."

Power was not surprised. But this time, having seen plenty of atrocities for atrocities, he was finally sick of it. This NVA prisoner looked so tiny, young, and helpless with untended wounds that the corpsmen were too busy to treat, that Power knelt beside him to give him the water that remained in his demolished canteen. Then he lit one of his rescued Winstons and stuck it in the prisoner's mouth. *If I leave this guy, they're going to get him.* He sat down and mumbled thick tongued to the Marines around him, "Leave the motherfucker alone, man, you know, he's just puttin' in a day at the office like you are. Leave him the fuck alone. The man's at work. Shit, he's got his job. You got yours."

The four Kilo NCOs took the NVA in a poncho, and Captain Giles watched them disappear southward into the gathering darkness. The NCOs returned an hour later to report that they had placed the prisoner aboard a medevac, but Giles did not feel certain about the man's safety until several weeks later when Division G-2 provided a copy of their debriefing of the prisoner.[1]

Another medevac came in near the intersection of Route 561 and the northern Strip, and Lance Corporal Herbert of Bravo Two was finally able to pack aboard his wounded A-gunner and his face-shot M79-man. There were other casualties, and Doc Lindenmeyer of Delta Three was still treating them when a Marine from his platoon approached him. "Doc, you remember that corporal who had shell shock? He's come out of it. Now what do we do with him?"

It was best to keep a stunned man busy, so Lindenmeyer answered, "Take off his casualty tag and put him to work digging foxholes for the wounded."

The platoon radioman came by next. He said Delta Three and Bravo Company had been ordered back to Con Thien aboard the four tanks, so Lindenmeyer assigned two Marines (including the walking wounded) to help carry each of his seriously wounded Marines. The two disabled tanks were stacked with dead Marines, while the two functioning tanks (which were towing the former) were loaded with the wounded. The able-bodied Marines of Bravo and Delta then climbed aboard wherever there was space on the decks and something to hang on to. Thinking of the shattered body of the Marine who had held his hand as he died, Lindenmeyer approached an officer. "Sir, there are more bodies out there."

1. According to Gunnery Sergeant Santomasso, a second wounded NVA was recovered, namely (it seemed) the one who had shot him only to be hit by their M60-man: "I figured I had enough casualties, and we were understrength, and the problem that we were in I wasn't about to put up with dragging no prisoner. As it was we had to carry our wounded and dead—I wasn't about to haul no damn prisoner with us, and I'm not going to say anymore what happened to him."

"Doc, I have enough trouble getting *the living* out of here. The rest will just have to stay."

Captain Radcliffe, Lieutenant Howell, and Staff Sergeant Burns climbed onto one of the tanks, and then, from God knows where, a civilian photographer arrived. Burns did not want the families of these dead Marines to open a *Time* or *Life* and see their son or brother hanging stiffly over the end of a tank. So, Burns gave the photog the finger: "No pictures."

The photographer raised his camera anyway, so Burns had an accidental discharge from his shotgun, blasting the dirt about seven feet from the man.

As Captain Navadel worked his way up and down the several hundred meters they occupied at the northern rim of the Trace, two enlisted men moved with him. One was his radio operator, a sharp young black corporal. The other was a white lance corporal (invariably the team was known within the headquarters as Salt 'n' Pepper), assigned as a clerk but adopted by Navadel as his "gun" because, even though Navadel had a WWII Thompson slung across his waist and his radioman had a shoulder-slung M16, they were too busy with the radio to defend themselves. The "gun" was their eyes and ears as they walked and talked, M16 ready in his hands. They were a perfectly synchronized team as they moved, in this case, among the hustle and bustle of the buildup along the Trace. Captain Navadel was concerned with ensuring the continuity of their positions (Lima on the left flank and India on the right) and with getting their attached elements from 1/9 up on the 3/9 radio tac. He was also concerned with the dozen or so casualties from 1/9 still on the ground, and the occasional doses of artillery in the approaching darkness. What he was not aware of was that Bravo Company and Delta Three were packing up:

Here I'm scrambling trying to get defenses organized, and it just happened I was moving to check how we were tied in on the right flank—and all of a sudden the tanks just flat took off. They headed to the west to

Con Thien and—as far as I was concerned—left the wounded with me and our corpsman. I couldn't believe it. I was told that before they took off they had called in for medevac helicopters. These were the same birds, of course, that were bringing us in. Problem was, it was a long Trace. A helicopter would come in, it might land two hundred meters away from you. You simply couldn't pick up four or five wounded people and go running down the Trace with them. I can remember the frustration of seeing a helicopter coming in with Marines and leaving and not being able to put the wounded on it because, of course, the pilot didn't know exactly where we were. He had to get out of there before the artillery came in.

One of the 1/9 WIAs had a stomach wound, always especially painful. Captain Navadel had no idea how close the NVA were to their positions and he did not want this man's screaming to give away their exact location, so he snapped at the kid, "Knock it off. You're a Marine. If you're going to die, die like a man. Stop yelling and screaming 'cause it's not going to help."

At 2015, 2 July 1967, the remnants of B Company, 1st Battalion, 9th Marines, (along with the 3d Platoon of D Company) rode their four tanks back into the Con Thien Combat Base. Captain Radcliffe and Lance Corporal Cromwell were taken to the CP for a debriefing and questions from Lieutenant Colonel Schening and Captain Curd. Lieutenant Howell conducted a quick debriefing of his own with Staff Sergeant Burns. They also put together a list of the able-bodied Marines from Bravo Company. There were Lieutenant Delaney, Staff Sergeant Ritchie, Sergeant Huff, Corporal Pitts, Corporal McGrath, Lance Corporal Cull, Lance Corporal Cromwell, Lance Corporal Francis, Lance Corporal Herbert, PFC Hutchinson, PFC Pigott, PFC Tabor, PFC Watson—approximately twenty-seven survivors in all. Almost all of them were from the 1st Platoon and the 60mm mortar section, for the 2d and 3d

Platoons and the CP of Bravo Company had virtually ceased to exist. In less than seven hours of combat, Bravo Company had lost some sixty men KIA and sixty WIA— the worst single disaster to befall a Marine Corps rifle company during the entire Vietnam war.

Lieutenant Howell felt very badly about what had happened to his old company, but he was all business as he talked with Burns: trying to pinpoint just how many NVA they'd seen, how many they'd killed (approximately eighty), the types of weapons they'd carried, etc. Burns and crew had little relief inside Con Thien, for not only were they to be mortared during the night, but they'd seen so many NVA that they considered an NVA ground assault through the wire to be a distinct possibility. Delta Company held the slit trenches and fighting holes along the northern rim of the CP hill, and in the dark, Burns set his people into the positions on the south side. They sat atop the main bunker there, mute and exhausted in the muggy night air, cleaning their M16s and sharpening their bayonets. Somebody passed by with two cases of beer, which Burns confiscated saying, "I'm Staff Sergeant Burns from Bravo Company, and I got some people that need that worse than you."

21

A World of Hurt

★

It was dark now. With Kilo 3/9 (Captain Giles) providing security and lending a helping hand, the 2d and 3d Platoons of Alpha 1/9 (Captain Slater) had their dead and wounded in ponchos. Gear that was unusable, or which no one had the energy to carry, had been thrown into a pile with dried brush and live ammunition. As Alpha and Kilo started their burdened march south to the Trace, the pile was set afire. They wanted the ammo to be cooking off as they left the area to trick the NVA into believing they were still in position.

Alpha had to carry their sergeant from Texas, the older man who had fought to reenlist in the Marine Corps so as to serve in Vietnam. His hideous, unbelievable laughing was a beacon for the NVA as the column slowly made its way south. Uptight Marines whispered hard at the sun-crazed sergeant, "Hey, man, *keep quiet*—we're gonna get ambushed."

The man just kept howling and laughing.

Corporal Power had one corner of a poncho with a dead Marine in it, an especially heavy load considering the heat and his thirst. And his fear. They were blind. Helpless. The sanctuary of the Strip was a million miles away. They were about halfway back when a Marine who had flipped out, cracked up, or just had a highly developed sense of humor (*some fucking turd up in front somewhere,* as a startled Power put it) suddenly boomed out in a rather good singing voice, "OH, I LOVE A PARADE, IT MAKES ME WANT TO SING AND SHOUT, OH, I LOVE A PARADE—" The singer was quickly censored.

On the left flank, A/1/9 was brought into 3/9's perimeter on the Trace by Kilo Company while, on the right flank, C/1/9 completed its struggle down Route 561 with India Company securing the flanks. Captain Hutchinson, the Charlie Six, came up alongside Lieutenant Libutti, who was a frayed, limping mess—he still had his carbine, but he'd left behind his pack—with shrapnel lodged in his left shoulder, right arm, left hip, right butt cheek, and right knee. Hutchinson assured Libutti that he would be medevacked when they secured on the Strip, but Libutti was a product of the Citadel, "No, sir, I'm not going to be evacuated."

"You're going to be evacuated."

Slowly but surely, though, Libutti was becoming less effective. He had totally lost track of his platoon sergeant, Lefefe, and when they finally stumbled into the Strip perimeter, someone—he didn't know who—took charge of him. He was led to the casualty collection point and told that medevacs were on the way, and there he lay with his back on the ground, aware of little else but the night sky. A reporter appeared from out of nowhere to kneel beside him, hold a microphone to his mouth, and ask him what happened. Libutti answered, "Listen, pal, you ought to be concerned about saving your life and keeping your head down, because this has been a bad day."

When the call had gone out for litter teams, Corporal Collopy of India One had climbed from his fighting hole.

There were KIAs there under ponchos. *Man, I don't want to go near them dead Marines.* Collopy instead put his arm around a bloody, torn-up black Marine, one of the hobbling wounded, and helped him toward the landing zone. "You're gonna be all right, we're getting you on a chopper, you're going to be all right."

The wounded man said nothing. The thumping got closer in the black sky, then, at the last moment, the Sea Horse pilot turned on the nose-mounted spotlight to ensure that he wasn't descending into the trees. *How the hell are they putting that light on—are they nuts—they gotta be drawing fire!* There was no enemy fire. The wounded were quickly helped into the cabin door, and the Sea Horse quickly pulled up and out. Collopy went back to help get another wounded man as another medevac made its approach in the dust and darkness and noise.

One of the three wounded men to be choppered out in the first medevac of the day, PFC Blough of Alpha One woke up many hours later in post-op in Dong Ha. Delta Med (D Company, 3d Medical Battalion, 3d Marine Division) was in business there, and a Navy corpsman told Blough, "You're gonna make it."

"Good."

"I got something I have to tell you—we had to amputate your leg."

"Do I have a knee?"

"Yeah, it's below the knee."

"Well, I'll be able to walk without anybody knowing it."

"Yeah."

"Well, fine, get me the fuck out of Vietnam."

Sergeant Geizer, also of Alpha Company, was also among the early medevacs to Delta Med. Geizer was carried past one general-purpose tent, which was occupied by dead Marines in body bags, and he ended up in another general-purpose tent in which stretchers were supported by two sawhorses apiece. Here, Navy doctors checked and prioritized each casualty. Geizer was lying there waiting his turn when, lo and behold, Doc Woody appeared, the same Doc Woody that Geizer had said good-bye to some twenty-four hours earlier. Woody's reassignment had been to Delta Med, and he quickly checked Geizer's casualty tag and asked him what had happened. He also asked whether his replacement had lived. Geizer said he thought the man had been killed. Woody told him there was a C-130 plane presently on the airstrip, but that they wouldn't be able to get any more in tonight because they were expecting a shelling. He further explained that since Geizer's wounds were not critical, he probably wouldn't go out on that C-130 and would have to wait until the next morning to clear Dong Ha. There were a lot of badly wounded Marines in the tent, and Woody had to get back to them.

Shortly, two men checked Geizer's casualty tag, then proceeded to cart him and his stretcher off the sawhorses and out the tent to a jeep-ambulance. Geizer was surprised. "What're you doin', what're you doin'?"

"We're taking you out to the C-one-thirty."

"Well, I was told I wasn't going on it."

"Hell, we don't know. We were told to pick you up and take you up there."

The C-130 touched down momentarily at the Phu Bai airstrip, then continued south to the main hospital complex at Da Nang. Geizer ended up in a large warehouse-type building—*meathouse,* he thought—filled with Marines dying and screaming under the fluorescent lights. *Legs missing, arms missing, bodies mutilated.* Geizer had never seen so much carnage. He lay untreated and unmedicated on his stretcher, weak from loss of blood as the revolving door of pain and numbness continued. He wanted only to be left alone. He said as much, as politely as he could, to the Catholic chaplain who checked his dog tags, noted the "C" stamped on them, and pronounced that he would "say some appropriate words over you."

The chaplain insisted, and when Geizer asked him again to please pass him by, he turned angry. Geizer finally explained that he was agnostic, that he had had "C" put on his dog tags to ensure a Catholic burial should he be killed to please his grandmother who was like a mother to him. The chaplain, indignant now, barked back that if Geizer would not respect his religion he had better, by God, respect his rank. He tugged on his lapel to show his captain's insignia. Sergeant Geizer wondered what he would have done had he the strength to rise from his stretcher, and then a doctor made his way through the many wounded bodies to Geizer's litter. After a quick check, he and other nonemergency casualties were loaded onto a helicopter for the short hop across the river that ran through Da Nang. Geizer ended up waiting his turn again on a stretcher in the hallway of a Quonset-type medical building. Another doctor examined him and gave instructions to a corpsman to prep him for surgery, and there in the hallway an IV was finally started and anesthesia finally administered. "When I put this mask on, I want you to count backward from one hundred . . ."

When PFC Mesa of Alpha One, who'd passed out upon reaching the Strip, opened his eyes again, he realized he was at Delta Med in Dong Ha. Thank God, thank God. When Mesa had come incountry three months earlier, he'd been convinced that the Marine Corps had given him the best training in the world. His chances for survival thus relatively assured, he'd been impatient to process through to his unit (*hell, I didn't go through all that training just to fill sandbags*) and begin this adventure. When he joined his squad, though, they simply unloaded the radio on him and told him that it would be rough, that there would be times he'd be making love to the ground he'd be so scared. That was all they told him. It was learn on the job or die. The Know-Your-Enemy phase of Mesa's training had included lectures on camouflage, snipers, and booby traps, with a diagram of a VC wearing a straw coolie hat, shorts, sandals, and carrying an AK47 automatic rifle. None of it was relevant to the NVA regulars (*they got short haircuts and all*) that Mesa fought on the DMZ. This was Mesa's second Purple Heart, and according to the Two Forty-Eight-Hour

Hearts rule, he could not be assigned again to a combat rifle company. Thank God, thank God.

Lieutenant Libutti of Charlie Two followed the medevac chain to Phu Bai, home of the 3d Marine Division CP. Someone who was anonymous in the semidarkness of the airstrip was meeting the wounded as their stretchers were lifted off the aircraft, and this man took the time to say hello to Libutti and ask him how he was doing in a very fatherly manner. In clear and straight language, well studded with obscenities, Libutti told this man how screwed up things were. Then he looked again and saw the stars—it was Brigadier General Metzger, ADC, 3d Marine Division.

"Geez, General, I'm sorry."

"That's okay, son, we'll take care of you."[1]

Inside the field hospital were two groups of Marines on sawhorse-supported stretchers. One row was for life-and-death emergencies where teams of doctors and corpsmen were working on each man; the other—to which Libutti was added—was for those who did not need extensive care. There seemed to be about forty Marines on that side of the warehouse. Lying on his back, Libutti was tended by two doctors at once, one working on his left shoulder and right arm, the other on his right knee. Then he was rolled onto his stomach, and one doctor went to work on his right butt cheek, the second on his left hip. In each case, they simply cut the wound open with a scalpel and went in with a pair of metal tongs to pull out the

1. Metzger was, to borrow a phrase, a One-Star Grunt. When the Dong Ha ammo dump was ignited by NVA artillery, he entered the burning depot with three Marines and three Seabees, put out the fire, and saved what ammunition remained. While visiting a field position, he piled into a 60mm mortar pit when he heard an NVA mortar round going down its tube (as the oldest and slowest with a herniated disk and partially paralyzed right leg, he was the last one in); the mortar crew returned the fire while the captain there, noticing the general wore no flak jacket, took his off and placed it over Metzger's back, "Something that I wouldn't do. He got a good bottle of whiskey the next day."

shrapnel. Since the locals hadn't numbed much of anything, Libutti screamed and screamed until he could scream no more. One of the doctors smiled at him. "Why, you're suppose to be a tough Marine—what's wrong with you?"

Libutti laughed. If the doctor was joking, he knew he wasn't going to die. The doctor held up a chunk of shrapnel, clamped in his tongs. "Hey, do you want this?"

"No, I don't want that."

The doctors moved on to the next man, and Libutti spent the night in that area. Coming out of the emotional and physical shock, he thought through all that had happened in the last twelve hours. It had changed him. It had blown away all his young, naive ideas about life. It had sickened him and left him sad. He had not been prepared for such ugliness—and he began to seriously question his original intention of a career in the Marine Corps.[2]

In the CP at Con Thien, Captain Radcliffe passed out during his debriefing. When he woke up several hours later, everything was pitch black, he had no idea where the hell he was, his empty gut ached terribly (he hadn't eaten since breakfast), and there was a terrible taste in his mouth.

When Corporal Collopy of India One got back from his second or third trip to the Strip with the WIAs, he realized there were no more wounded to be helped. But

2. Nevertheless, Libutti's womb was his platoon and after three weeks at Cam Ranh Bay (at which time he was still weak and unable to use his left arm), he hitchhiked without orders or equipment to Camp Carroll, the battalion's new home. Finding the C/1/9 CP tent, he recognized only the first sergeant, who said, "Lieutenant Libutti, is that you—you look like you've aged twenty years." The first sergeant quickly explained that his wounds had been recorded separately; he thus had three Purple Hearts and, according to the rules, no longer had any business in Vietnam. Regardless, Libutti volunteered to rejoin his platoon. The new company commander refused his request: "You're not going on patrol, you draw metal."

the choppers were still coming. They were coming for the KIAs. Collopy had been incountry for more than four months and had lost some friends, but he had missed the Battle of Getlin's Corner because of tonsillitis and had never actually seen a dead Marine. Collopy moved to where the KIAs were. The poncho had been prop washed off one of them. A blond kid. Incredibly young looking. Collopy didn't know what to do, so he reached down and held onto his leg to realize he was really holding a dead brother Marine here. The KIA was hefted in his poncho shroud by Collopy and several other grunts, and that was the last trip Collopy made to the helicopters.

The medevacs were secured as of 2244. All the WIAs were out, and most of the recovered KIAs. At 2300, 2 July 1967, all units under the operational control of Major Woodring, CO, 3d Battalion, 9th Marines, were consolidated in a shallow defense, facing north for approximately five hundred meters, in the first tree line north of the Trace, with Route 561 defining their right flank. At this time, Major Woodring had two complete rifle companies (K and L/3/9) and two-thirds of another (I/3/9) on line (K on the left, L in the middle, and I on the right), and the remnants of a fourth and fifty (A and C/1/9) to the rear with some responsibility on the flanks. The line took advantage of craters and fallen trees, and with no one super-organized, everyone just dug in and hoped for the best. Night defensive fires were established, and throughout the night Marine artillery peppered the area with salvos aimed not at specific targets, but at likely avenues of enemy approach and at nothing at all to keep the enemy off balance and to reassure the weary. Flares popped. The dry flat earth rumbled. In return, NVA mortar crews pumped in quick barrages every now and then, as did (with less frequency) the NVA artillery batteries far to the north. Afraid not to, the survivors of 1/9 dug deep despite their fatigue (catnapping over their shovels and in their holes), while others cursed the powers that be for putting them on the perimeter and making them stand hole watch even though

that whole damn 3/9 was there. Didn't higher-higher understand what had happened to them? They suffered for
other reasons, too, until the resupply of water and rations
that 3/9 had brought them got around in the darkness. The
heat and humidity and paranoia pressed in on them, as did
the god-awful stench of sun-blasted human flesh, which
drifted down the road from the north. Captain Navadel of
3/9, meanwhile, moved back and forth along the line,
checking, conferring, and coordinating, so that he would
later recall, "There was no sleep that night. Things were
pretty wild and the adrenaline was pumping pretty hard.
Your adrenaline's kicking so hard that sleep's not really a
concern."

PART FOUR

LAND THE LANDING FORCE

★

There existed at the time of Operation Buffalo a ready reserve in the form of Special Landing Force A (Col John A. Conway) and Special Landing Force B (Col Harry D. Wortman), of the 9th Marine Amphibious Brigade (BrigGen Jacob E. Glick) on Okinawa. SLF Alpha consisted of Lt Col Peter A. Wickwire's Battalion Landing Team 1/3 (formerly the 1st Battalion, 3d Marines, 3d Marine Division) and LtCol Nick J. Kapetan's HMM-362 (a helicopter squadron, formerly of the 1st Marine Aircraft Wing, equipped with UH34 Sea Horses), and operated from the ships of Task Group 79.4, 7th Fleet. SLF Bravo consisted of Maj Wendell O. Beard's Battalion Landing Team 2/3 (formerly the 2d Battalion, 3d Marines, 3d Marine Division) and LtCol Rodney D. McKitrick's HMM-363 (a helicopter squadron, formerly of the 1st Marine Aircraft Wing, equipped with CH46 Sea Knights), and operated from the ships of Task Group 79.5, 7th Fleet. Rifle battalions were assigned to the 9th MAB on a rotating basis from the 1st and 3d Marine Divisions, arriving at low ebb from the war of attrition Down South (as Vietnam was called on Okinawa) for a month-plus of training on the Rock, as Okinawa was known. The troops were thus rested, reequipped, and brought back to size with replacements. The SLFs then cruised the coast of I Corps, Republic of Vietnam, as quick reaction forces.

22

No Rest For the Weary

★

From the command ship of SLF Alpha, the USS *Okinawa,* Lt Col Peter A. Wickwire, CO, Battalion Landing Team 1/3, could see 1/9 and 3/9's agonies after sundown on 2 July 1967. The *Okinawa* was anchored in the South China Sea at the mouth of the Cua Viet River in preparation for Operation Bear Claw, a proposed landing in eastern Quang Tri Province. However, some thirty kilometers west of this anchorage was the Marketplace, and with the Annamite Mountains forming a backdrop, there commenced a light show of mortar explosions, artillery explosions, and illumination rounds that floated down on their parachutes like distant streetlights.

Whether BLT 1/3 proceeded as planned with Operation Bear Claw or were instead committed to Buffalo, it would be Lieutenant Colonel Wickwire's last go-around. He had only thirteen days remaining on his tour. The battalion was not looking forward to his departure because Pete Wickwire had, in their eyes, the right stuff—*A hell of a man,* in the words of one of his mustang platoon commanders. He was a graduate of the U.S. Naval Academy (Class of 1951), had an extensive background in both infantry and artillery, and was a hard taskmaster: as one of his company commanders put it, *You had better of had your trash together around Wickwire.* He stood about five-eight, hard and athletic on his small frame, and his command presence was tremendous. He was a detail man, down to putting out the word that a Marine who removed his helmet or flak jacket (or his jungle boots after dark) could expect to lose a stripe and up to being a bear about fire control. Always calm, another of his mustang lieutenants reckoned that the only thing that ever really worried Pete Wickwire was the men—*I think he anguished over every casualty.*

Command of the battalion had not demanded the utmost of Wickwire during his first operation with them, Prairie, which from 29 September 1966 to 31 January 1967 saw them in the jungled mountains of Khe Sanh. The paucity of contact was such that C Company, for example, became known as Chickenshit Charlie and the entire battalion could claim only fifteen enemy kills during the four months of Operation Prairie. From 6 February to 10 April 1967, the battalion (rechristened BLT 1/3) trained and refurbished on Okinawa. They returned to Vietnam with SLF Alpha (USS *Okinawa,* USS *Duluth,* and USS *Alamo)* and made their first landing, Operation Beaver Cage, to support the 5th Marines' Operation Union in the Que Son Valley below Da Nang. Operation Beaver Cage (28 April– 12 May 1967) was a complete change from the battalion's Khe Sanh days with 55 USMC KIA, 151 USMC WIA, 181 NVA/VC KIA, and 66 NVA/VC PW. There was no rest for the weary. Operation Beau Charger (15–26 May 1967) placed BLT 1/3 against the Ben Hai River and in heavy contact as part of the 3d and 9th Marines' Operation Hickory. From the DMZ, BLT 1/3 steamed south into the 4th Marines' AO around Camp Evans and the Street Without Joy for Operations Bear Bite (2–5 June 1967), Colgate (7–11 June 1967), Choctaw (12–23 June 1967), and Maryland (23 June–2 July 1967), exhausting but comparatively fallow exercises.

Battalion Landing Team 1/3 had only helicoptered back to their ships on the evening of 2 July when, at 0100, 3 July 1967, Lieutenant Colonel Wickwire was alerted for immediate deployment ashore in the 9th Marines AO. They were to join the light show to the west, and Wickwire passed on the alert to his staff officers and company commanders. Wickwire's XO was Maj Richard W. Goodale, a small, dour, balding, and heartily disliked man who, however, did BLT 1/3 right as an accomplished handler of administrative and logistical matters. Wickwire's S-3 was Maj Richard C. Ossenfort, who was tall, smart, good-natured, and always able to keep a clear picture of the situation no matter how hot the combat. He was so unshakably calm, in fact, that he would have appeared too casually laid back to an outside observer. Internally, though, the wheels were always turning, and when they returned to the ship between operations, he would *just die* (as one company commander put it), he was so in need of sleep.

Wickwire, Goodale, and Ossenfort had a solid group of company commanders. Capt John B. Mack of H&S Company was blond, mustached, and intelligent (reportedly a Yale graduate), and he planned to resign his commission at the conclusion of his obligated service so as to attend Union Theological Seminary.[1] Mack was of a different cut; the BLT's other company commanders (Capt Charles G. Jordan had A Company, Capt Burrell H.

---

1. A junior member of the battalion headquarters commented on an operation near the Street Without Joy in early autumn 1967, "We had found very little but, nonetheless, had taken a couple of casualties from boobytraps, and frustration had mounted. Word was put out to burn all the hootches we found. I thought that this was a stupid order —what better way to turn the locals' sympathies even more towards the VC—but did not say anything. Mack apparently protested the order to Goodale (the CO was scouting ahead in a Huey), who chewed him out. That evening, I heard the XO tell the CO that 'Mack better decide whether he wants to be a Marine or a fucking minister.' "

Landes had B Company, Capt Gerald F. Reczek had C Company, and Capt Edward P. Aldous had D Company) were all career-minded men who were aggressive, brave, and competent.

Lieutenant Colonel Wickwire told his company commanders what he had been told about the battle in the Marketplace, including the misinformation that the NVA had employed tear gas and that English-speaking NVA had been on 1/9's radios. He further informed them that they would probably be landing at dawn to recover those casualties left behind in the Marketplace. As the captains then proceeded to get their own houses in order, the ships became metal-encased beehives. Sgt Kenneth P. Bouchard, Right Guide to Alpha Two, had just gotten to sleep (the enlisted men were housed below deck in multi-tiered bunks that barely allowed enough room to roll over) when the gunny woke him with, "Get the platoon ready. We're going back in."

Bouchard grudgingly opened his eyes. "Jesus, we don't even have our gear. It's all down at the laundry being washed—"

The gunny interrupted him to explain that Bravo 1/9 had just been overrun, and at that point the feet of a suddenly energized Bouchard hit the tile floor. PFC Robert J. Law, the gunner of a 3.5-inch rocket team with Delta Company, was among the last to be returned to ship from their last op. He hadn't even begun the ritual of turning over ammunition, grenades, and other pyrotechnics to supply, or his deuce gear and utilities to the ship laundry. He was, in fact, just filing down the steps to join the other sardines below deck when the word came to saddle up. *Jesus H. Fucking Christ!* Law imploded—*I didn't even get to take the fucking pack off my back!* His reaction was typical, as explained by LCpl Ed Kalwara, a machine-gun team leader assigned to Charlie Two:

> When you come off an operation, the ship is a wonderful sanctuary. As it normally goes, you get anywhere from forty-eight to seventy-two hours free before we go

back out, so you don't rush and a lot of grab-ass goes on. But, in this particular case, we had no idea that seven hours later they were going to be getting us up to prepare for another operation. They sounded the alarm through the ship over the PA system at one o'clock in the morning, and all the lights came on. Since we'd just gotten back most people aren't in bed anyway, they're still up playing cards, they're going to stay up till five o'clock in the morning jawing with each other. We were not prepared for this sudden turn-around. We didn't have our clothes cleaned, we didn't have our mail read—so it just added to the terribleness of what was taking place.

In Officers' Country—that part of each ship where the BLT's officers lived comfortably two or three to a room—each company commander conducted hasty, half-informed briefings with their need-to-know types packed into their quarters. Lieutenants and staff sergeants then passed the word on to the riflemen in platoon meetings held in supply areas or off to the side of the below-deck helicopter hangars. Before, during, and after the meetings, Marines were getting ready. For one thing, ammunition had to be issued. In the case of M16 ammo, it came as loose rounds in cardboard boxes from which magazines were then filled. PFC William V. Taylor of Charlie Two commented on one of these nuts-and-bolts details that made up the big picture:

I took real good care of my stuff, but when everybody came aboard ship all this ammo was taken in—and here I'm getting ammo back from someone who didn't take care of their stuff. It was all tarnished and full of crud. They wanted to use up the old, and it seemed like I was being discriminated against because I was one of the guys who didn't have a lot of time in. Shit rolls downhill. I was really pissed off because I didn't want to put this stuff in my rifle because the M16s jammed as it was, and I remember arguing and telling them I wasn't going to use this—and I wanted extra ammunition on top of it. I made such a big stink out of it that they were going to have me up on office hours because I was disobeying a direct order.

PFC Taylor relented, but it was an embittering reminder of the subtle division between those like himself who had come aboard on Okinawa, or after, and the contemptuous salts who'd been at Khe Sanh. Taylor got around the problem this time through the time-honored Marine Corps tradition of a midnight requisition or, more accurately, a three-in-the-morning requisition. With a buddy as lookout, he stole into the supply area (the bored guard had apparently drifted off) and gathered an arm load of clean, boxed ammunition and—what the hell—sticks of C4 plastic explosives. Not all the new guys were left adrift like this. PFC Billy J. (Rusty) Rusmisell of H&S Company had joined the battalion on the eve of Beau Charger when he was assigned to the Shore Party Team attached to Charlie Company. Now in the early morning prior to Bear Claw/Buffalo, he was switched to fill a radioman vacancy in the 81mm Mortar Platoon, H&S Company:

I got with a staff sergeant named Caballero and a sergeant named Russell, and another PFC named Wolford. I'd never been in eighty-ones before, I'd never called in a fire mission. I was real nervous. They were nervous too, but Caballero and Russell had both been there a long time, they were real professional, they were well liked, well respected. And they helped me out a bunch.

Shortly after first light, Lieutenant Colonel Wickwire departed the USS *Okinawa* by helicopter for the 9th Marines CP at Dong Ha, and from 0730 to 0830, he was briefed by Colonel Jerue's people. Once firmly established ashore, BLT 1/3's operational control would routinely shift from the CO, SLF Alpha, to the CG, III MAF, who in this case intended to transfer control (via the CG, 3d MarDiv) down to the CO, 9th Marines. At this briefing, BLT 1/3's mission and helicopter LZs were announced; they were to commence their helo-lift near the Trace as of 1030, 3 July 1967. With no time to waste, Wickwire climbed back aboard his helicopter. As BLT 1/3's after-action report would later record, "This left the CO, BLT 1/3, two hours in which to return to the ship, estimate the situation, formulate a plan, brief unit commanders who were loaded aboard several different ships, and land the initial assault elements in the LZ. Needless to say this time frame was grossly inadequate."

Aboard ship, as related by Rusmisell of the 81s, preparations continued: "We didn't get any sleep that night. It was real quiet, it was real sober. Everybody that was supposed to have maps got maps and we started pinpointing it in with grease pencil—we were going to land on top of them."

Following breakfast in the ship's mess ("They usually gave us pretty damn good meals when they were sending us out," remembered PFC Taylor. "I mean they gave us like our last meal before we went out"), the various units were called upstairs where they could hear the roar of the helicopters warming up. On the deck of each ship in SLF Alpha, the rifle companies of BLT 1/3 organized into helo teams for their Sea Horses. In the 81mm Mortar Platoon (as PFC Rusmisell recounted) final details were tamped into place:

Staff Sergeant Caballero and Sergeant Russell kept checking to make sure that we all had our equipment, and they were putting us in flights. We had another sergeant they called Sergeant Yaz, and there was another one, Sergeant Balabas, and he checked a lot. Because everyone was real tense, Balabas was coming around, talking to us and telling us it might not be as bad—it wasn't the whole 9th Marines that had been overrun, like we had first heard, it was a company and a half. He was trying to get us calm, make sure we knew what to do, that as soon as we get there we didn't panic, that we started firing just as soon as we got there. They wanted to make sure that the eighty-one rounds were going to be coming just as fast as they could.

Like everyone else, PFC Taylor of Charlie Two was loaded for bear with helmet, flak jacket, automatic rifle, grenades hooked to the ammo pouches of his web belt, pack with attached entrenching tool, and (in his case) stolen ammo, pockets of mess-hall apples and oranges, and his ever-present Kodak camera in hand. The sun was a fierce white glare on the helo deck of the USS *Okinawa*, which reverberated with its locust-like field of Sea Horses. In their turn, Taylor's helo team got the hand signal from the helicopter support team, and they headed for their chopper in a single-file jog, climbing one at a time through the side door. With a ferocious, jolting sound that Taylor hated (for it reminded him of how antiquated their Sea Horses were) the engine revved up to the right pitch, then their stomachs took the plunge as the helo lifted off the deck, leaned forward, and took off right over the front of the ship. Other helicopters followed, and after a circle or two, they began their ship-shrinking, cloud-reaching ascent. Waiting his turn, Charlie Company's CO, Captain Reczek, could look out through the hatch of his helo-team shelter at the U.S. Navy ships firing their smoke-belching six-inch guns toward the DMZ. Reczek thought of how it reminded him of the WWII documentaries he had seen, and it impressed upon him the enormity of this operation by the standards of this war.

PART FIVE

SEMPER FIDELIS

★

From the "Combat After Action Report, Operation 'Buffalo,' 021000H-140900H July 1967, Headquarters, Battalion Landing Team 1/3, 9th Marine Amphibious Brigade": ". . . *Mission.* Commencing at L-Hour on D-Day, land by heliborne assault and move abreast of the 3d Battalion, 9th Marines in support of their efforts to recover casualties previously sustained by the 1st Battalion, 9th Marines . . ."

From the "Combat After Action Report, Operation 'Buffalo,' 021000H-140900H July 1867, HEADQUARTERS, 3d Battalion, 9th Marines, 3d Marine Division": ". . . The NVA forces appear to be fully aware of the Marine tradition to remove all wounded and dead from the battle field. Evacuation efforts were covered by enemy artillery, mortar and small arms-fire . . ."

From the dispatches filed by Tom Buckley of the *New York Times:* "CON THIEN, South Vietnam, July 4— Pledged to recover the bodies of comrades who died in bitter fighting Sunday, two battalions of United States marines pushed forward slowly today against stubborn North Vietnamese resistance less than a mile from the demilitarized zone. 'We don't leave our people,' said First Lieut. Jerry Howell of Alameda, Calif. 'I'm sure they'd do the same thing for me.' . . . the North Vietnamese held on, firing whenever the marines tried to move forward. Tomorrow, said Lieutenant Howell, they would get those bodies. 'We're not going to leave here until we get those people out,' he said, close to tears . . ."

23
Shafted

★

Dawn, Monday, 3 July 1967 Corporal Power (Senior Scout, A/1/9) borrowed the hand set from one of their radiomen. He had to call his boss Lieutenant Howell (S-2 Intelligence Officer, 1/9), up in the CP at Con Thien, and report that his partner Quigley wa dead and that Xuan was missing and presumed dead. *I can't fucking stand to tell him that,* Power thought. *It was a disgrace not to have recovered a comrade's body, and he dreaded Howell's reaction. He never chewed you out, he'd just talk to you calmly and make you feel like a total shithead and leave it at that. We were some cocky motherfuckers, but he could handle us.*

Corporal Power rendered his report. Lieutenan Howell did not reproach him, but only quietly informed him that all their S-2 Scout Marines and Kit Carsons had been killed or wounded. In the span of an afternoon, the scout section had been reduced to Lieutenant Howell Staff Sergeant Waters, their Admin NCO, and, of course

Corporal Power. Something in Power broke as he listened to Howell. Something died. Sixteen months with the Walking Dead and again it seemed that everyone had been rubbed out except him. Why had he been spared? Guilt filled him, as did something akin to self-hatred. He thought of how Garrett had leapt from their crater despite the rain of mortar rounds to help the wounded. Garrett's actions had seemed new-guy dumb at the time, but now Power doubted himself. Was he, in fact, a coward in comparison? Was that why he was alone among the survivors? He looked at the dead Marines awaiting evacuation. He looked at the mounds of helmets collected from the casualties and the piled-up flak jackets, and for the first time he thought, *We have lost this fucking war. This is useless, senseless shit.*

It had taken much to wear Corporal Power down. Under fire for the first time in the Dominican Republic (1965), he had been proud of himself and of the Marine Corps, and appreciative of the accolades showered on them for a job well done. Few such honors were rendered for their efforts in Vietnam. Here, they were ignored (even by the Marine Corps, that was how it sometimes felt) or worse[1] but Power armored himself against the noises of the demonstrators, et al., and soldiered on. When his tour ended, he extended because he was twenty and crazy, but also because he was from Georgia and such was the code of the South—and because he had learned a lot and thought he could keep people alive. He couldn't. No matter what they did, they lost. It was because the NVA were so ruthlessly good, but also because they were forced to fight according to such asinine rules. During Operation Hickory, the first time they had been allowed to cross that imaginary line that demarcated the southern boundary of

---

1. Stories circulated of protesters sending medical supplies to the NVA; conversely, a package was delivered to the Marines at Con Thien from a group at the University of California (Berkeley) which turned out to be a box of dog food on which the students had written, "Eat, Animals, Eat."

the DMZ, he had pissed in the Ben Hai River (Power did like to do everything with a dramatic flourish). But what he really wanted to do was get across into North Vietnam. He wanted to hit them where they lived. He wanted to win. He came to realize, though, that they would never invade North Vietnam. Likewise, he used to ponder a village named Tchepone which was indicated on their tactical maps west of Khe Sanh. He would have loved to have seen Tchepone. It was, after all, a hub of the Ho Chi Minh Trail and a major NVA supply area. But there was a line on their maps between Khe Sanh and Tchepone, indicating that the latter was in Laos and, thus, immune to U.S. ground action. It was ridiculous, maddening, embittering, and on this second morning of Operation Buffalo, Power finally saw the light.

If I die, it won't be for shit. He hated to believe that, because it rendered obscene the memories of those Marines he knew who had died—who had given their all for a lost cause, who had been wasted serving as bait along meaningless map lines. *Such a waste,* he thought. *Such good men. They were some fucking men, buddy. They were for fucking real. It's just a shame that the cause isn't as real as they were.*

On the western flank of the general east-west line held by 3/9 above the Trace, A/1/9 (like C/1/9 on the eastern flank) was in reserve. The Alpha Six, Captain Slater, had been in radio contact with Major Woodring of 3/9 who had explained that because the company was physically and emotionally spent they would not be part of the body-recovery effort. However, if 3/9 bit off more than they could chew when they moved out to recover 1/9's MIAs, Woodring told Slater he expected Alpha to be prepared to reinforce them.

When Slater called up his platoon commanders (Staff Sergeants Leslie and Richardson, and SSgt Freelin Hensley in the late Lieutenant Muller's stead), he indicated that 3/9 might need them. For this reason, they would rehearse navigating forward to their adoptive battalion's positions, even at night. *Shafted again,* thought Gunny Santomasso (who, incidentally, had refused this morning to let their corpsmen write up his Purple Heart so there would be no notification to worry his family), but the platoon commanders did speak up, "The guys are a little bit uptight about still being out here. What they're saying is, 'My God, you know, what do we have to do to get a break? Why can't we just get back, get a shower, and blow it off and drink?' "

Slater, again being blamed for things beyond his control, explained Woodring's position: "We aren't in the thick of it right now, and Three-Nine needs some kind of reserve. The least we can do right now is talk to our people and get their health back and their attitude back, and hold what we've got."

What Captain Slater did not add was that he, in fact, had divided feelings about being pulled out of the line. The one time during his command that Alpha Company had taken a Phu Bai R&R, he felt that between the beer, marijuana, and hell-raising (and the price-gouging, demoralizing Vietnamese merchants) they had lost a lot of ground in terms of combat efficiency. Back in the bush after the R&R, everyone had moved sluggishly, everyone had been more pissed off than usual, and they had had an excessive number of heat casualties. One man from Alpha Company did, however, get out this morning on the Strip. That was the sergeant from Texas who had been driven hysterical during the battle. Now recovered and ready for duty, the sergeant (who had, after all, reupped just for this) was unwillingly directed aboard a resupply helo by Captain Slater. "Thank you very much for your being a patriot and wanting to be with us, but go back to the rear where you can be of benefit."

The saturation air strikes raging across 3/9's front as they saddled up were being directed from Major Woodring's CP with the help of a most unlikely source, namely, a young enlisted man who, as Captain Navadel put it, had gone UA (Unauthorized Absence) in the right direction. The man was with a control-tower detachment of the 1st

Marine Aircraft Wing at Dong Ha, and when he had seen 3/9 Bald Eagling out the day before, he had basically donned the combat gear he had been issued and never used and, without permission from anyone, fell in line with one of the helo teams. Once on the ground, he had tried to join a rifle squad, but had instead been turned over to the battalion CP. Navadel questioned him, and the young man explained, "I came in the Marine Corps to be a grunt, but I had a high GCT and they made an air-traffic controller out of me. I want *this.*"

Major Woodring and Captain Navadel unofficially adopted this UA Marine and turned him over to 3/9's undermanned TACP (Tactical Air Control Party), where he proved invaluable. From his time as an air-traffic controller, he knew the pilots by their voices and they knew him. So, he conducted the battalion's air strikes with an ease and speed unknown to the less-experienced TACP members. ("It's like talking to a friend on the telephone," Navadel explained. "They can say something and it means something to you.") Meanwhile, while the bombs and napalm were bursting, Navadel slung his old-fashioned Thompson and, with Salt 'n' Pepper (his black radioman, and his white clerk riding shotgun), set out to check the lines. After the confusion of the previous evening, he wanted to make sure everyone understood their place in the scheme of things: I/3/9 was astride Route 561 on their right (east) flank, with L and K/3/9 extending the line to the left (west), and A and C/1/9 in reserve on the left and right flanks respectively.

Despite occasional sniping and rocket-propelled grenade fire on the forward companies and intermittent shelling on everyone, almost all hands had their act together. This included, Navadel was pleased to discover, Slater's bedraggled command. *Slater was a solid citizen, ready to fight, ready to do his job.* As far as Navadel was concerned, though, their other attached and shot-up company had some problems. Their CO, Captain Hutchinson, was pleased with the arrival of Major Woodring (whom he considered a "super guy"), but was infuriated by the lack of support he'd been afforded during the battle. Hutchinson's comments then about his own battalion commander were unfair in that Woodring did not have a base to defend and was free to move with his troops, whereas Schening was stuck at Con Thien, but they did reflect the raging emotions of men at war:

Now, with Woodring there, they're lining up the air support, the artillery, and all the things it takes to kill people—which I didn't have. Woodring was on the ground with us, while our battalion commander was back in his bunker. That sonuvabitch. The whole thing was screwed up from the get-go. To get those two companies in a situation like that without a command group was screwed up, and the fact that Schening never came out of the bunker to get out there with his battalion, to do whatever he could, tells me the guy's a goddamned coward. Buffalo is not going to shine in history as one of our most successful operations, that's for damn sure.

Captain Hutchinson was very popular in Charlie Company, but Captain Navadel was outraged:

I was quite upset with him because you simply don't talk down being there when you got to go on to a fight. You build your men up, you don't tear them down. He didn't want to be there. He probably saw some of what happened to Bravo, ". . . and the same thing could happen to us. Let's get out of here. We shouldn't be here. We should move back to Con Thien." I chewed his ass out on the spot in front of his platoon commanders. I made no bones about it because his kind of talk, with his leaders around him—well, that's infectious and everybody's going to feel the same way. I'll have to say he was basically spent. I expressed this to Major Woodring at the time.

Meanwhile, the international press was appearing, drawn by the drama of the Marketplace Massacre. Major

PFC Steve Weldon (foreground) B/1/9 takes a break during a Strip patrol immediately before Operation Buffalo. (Courtesy of D.J. Hendry)

Cpl Charles Sullivan (with hat) and Cpl Dick Boni (second from left) of C/1/9, on the Strip near Con Thien shortly before Operation Buffalo. (Courtesy of M. Bradley)

SSgt Leon R. (Lee) Burns, who won the Navy Cross for taking command of B/1/9 on 2 July 1967. (Courtesy of L.R. Burns)

PFC David J. Hendry (right) of 2d Plt, B/1/9, celebrates his 19th birthday at Khe Sanh. (D.J. Hendry)

Sgt Harvey Geizer, FO, A/1/9, who was shot in the back and head during the rush to rescue B/1/9 on 2 July 1967. (Courtesy of H.N. Geizer)

Best friends LCpl Frank T. Lopinto (with bayonet) and LCpl Harry J. Herbert (with rifle) of 2d Plt, B/1/9. (Courtesy of L.R. Burns)

The Walking Dead: Exhausted Marine LCpl Marshall Belmaine, B/1/9. (Courtesy of D.J. Hendry)

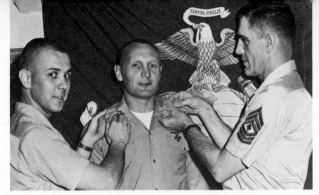

Capt Albert C. Slater, Jr (center), who earned both the nickname Captain Contact and the Navy Cross as CO, A/1/9. (Courtesy of A.C. Slater)

Horrible Hatfield: GySgt John C. Hatfield, who would do anything for the Marines of K/3/9. (Courtesy of J.E. Giles)

An uneven trade: LCpl J. Larry Stuckey of C/1/9, who lost his hand and some of his dreams for the Navy Cross and four Purple Hearts. (Courtesy of J.L. Stuckey)

An Arapaho warrior: PFC David H. Sankey, Asst FO, A/1/9, at ease in Dong Ha. (Courtesy of H.N. Geizer)

Killer Kilo's best platoon leader, 2d Lt Jerry Lane (right) with Sgt Pugh of K/3/9. (Courtesy of J.E. Giles)

War-weary skipper Capt Jerry E. Giles, CO, K/3/9, in his bunker at Ba Long Valley, April 1967. (Courtesy of J.E. Giles)

Capt George D. Navadel, S-3, 3/9 and 1st Sgt Bryce H. Lee, I/3/9, at Cam Lo immediately after Operation Buffalo. (Courtesy of G.D. Navadel)

The underranked hero: PFC James P. Daley, FO, B/1/3, aboard SLF shipping, July 1967. (Courtesy of J.P. Daley)

SSgt Robert L. Morningstar, E/2/3, shortly before an NVA sniper killed him on 5 July 1967. (Courtesy of J.R. Cannon)

Mustang: 2d Lt James R. Cannon, XO, E/2/3, after Operation Buffalo. (Courtesy of J.R. Cannon)

PFC S. John Steiner, C/1/3, after Operation Buffalo. (Courtesy of S.J. Steiner)

Woodring responded thus to a request for a statement from the first dozen or so reporters who arrived: "Well, get out your pencils and paper because I'm going to give you a brief statement. Now, this is my statement. What you're looking at between us is my foxhole, and when the incoming rounds come, if you get in there before I do, I'll blow you out of there. So, my first statement to you is you better dig your own foxholes. It's dangerous out here."

At this time, 3/9 was holding its positions, awaiting the arrival of BLT 1/3 before commencing their joint northward movement, so the reporters could move rather freely along the line. Captain Giles of Kilo Company commented that the journalists in their "dressed-up utilities" were appalled at the shabbiness of his Marines. "Their knees were coming through their utilities. Their boots, which may or may not have fit, looked as if they belonged on some bum off the street. There was a female reporter out there, and I remember her being rather surprised when some Marines came walking by in utilities where the crotch was completely ripped open, and their balls and dicks were hanging out."

The female reporter was Jurate Kazickas, age twenty-four, handsome and tall, an adventurer who'd been swept up by the war during an around-the-world trip. Miss Kazickas was a big hit among the Marines. ("I'd been in Vietnam for a few months, so I don't know how my judgement was," as Corporal Collopy put it. "But she wasn't just Caucasian, this was a very fine-looking lady.") Captain Navadel was impressed that she fixed coffee and cocoa and shared them, plus smiles and conversation, with the obviously enamored grunts around her. Navadel also commented that the NVA artillery began pounding them soon after the reporters' arrival:

They thought they'd be waltzing in there and take some pictures of the dead Marines from Bravo Company —and they ended up *trapped*. No more helicopters were coming up because of the heavy artillery. We ended up with those folks all that night and into the next day, and they never did get their story because when we finally got some helicopters in, they wanted *out*. I can understand it, they weren't fighters. Those reporters never did get to see those bodies, which didn't bother me a bit. I didn't particularly care to see those poor guys flashed around.

They were asking some of the dumbest questions I've ever heard in my life. Corporal Gomez listened with indignation and animosity as the reporters, the woman and two men, talked to his squad in their crater position. What's it like to kill somebody? Have you lost any friends? Do you believe your government's right? *Like I'm really going to stop and think about this shit while I'm getting shot at.* One of Gomez's men finally said, "You guys are here just for a couple hours, then you're gonna be gone, you know. What the *fuck* do you know? What do you care? We're the ones that have to stay here."

24

LZ Hawk

★

Expecting a hostile greeting to include everything from tear gas to artillery, Battalion Landing Team 1/3 commenced its helo-insert as of 1025, 3 July 1967 (aboard the Sea Horses of HMM-362, and four Sea Knights from HMM-164), from the flight decks of SLF Alpha at the mouth of the Cua Viet River. Their destination was an area near the Trace designated as Landing Zone Hawk. The helicopters, making round-robin trips, were to land Alpha (Captain Jordan) and Bravo (Captain Landes) in close proximity, then bring in the Alpha Command Group (Lieutenant Colonel Wickwire, Major Goodale, Major Ossenfort, et al.) as well as Charlie (Captain Reczek) and Delta (Captain Aldous) a bit to their south. The latter elements would advance to link up with their forward companies, and a quick march across the Trace would put them on line with 3/9. Route 561, running north-south, would then be the dividing line (3/9 on the left and BLT 1/3 on the right) as they used the remainder of the day to sweep for 1/9's MIAs.

Events, however, were not shaped exactly by these plans. BLT 1/3 inserted its companies alphabetically into the short, green grass of LZ Hawk, so that by accompanying the third wave, Lieutenant Colonel Wickwire landed with Reczek's Charlie Company. Wickwire, however, could make no correlation between his map and the terrain around him, so grabbing Reczek and a radioman or two, he started north up Route 561 while the rest of the battalion, which would complete its landing at 1400, organized in LZ Hawk. Wickwire's risky little recon had not gone far when Marines emerged from the brush west of the dirt road. These men (who identified themselves as being with a 2/9 platoon dug in as part of their battalion's road-security network) pinpointed their location on Wickwire's map. It turned out that BLT 1/3 had been unloaded not just below the Trace, but in the heart of Leatherneck Square. They were southeast of Con Thien and almost three kilometers south of the Trace. Wickwire and Reczek immediately turned around to return to the accidental LZ Hawk and prepare their companies for a long, hot, hard march up Route 561. The "why" of this gross error was not detailed in BLT 1/3's after-action report, except to comment that having only been briefed by the 9th Marines between 0730–0830 it was unrealistic to expect them to begin their helo-lift at 1030:

> A better solution would have been the issuance of a warning order to the BLT shortly after the alert that would have included the BLT mission and LZ. This would have avoided the cramming of an adequate 9½ hour reaction time into an inadequate two hours. The necessity for adhering to the doctrine of a helicopter reconnaissance of the LZ by the ground unit and helicopter unit commanders prior to landing the lead elements was again made clear when the lead elements were landed 2500 meters south of the designated landing one. This resulted in a considerable delay in the BLT

fixing its location on the ground and moving to its objective.

BLT 1/3 rolled with the punches of this additional problem in large part because of solid company commanders.

Captain Jordan of Alpha Company was a calm, methodical, and self-confident cigar-smoking product of Macon, Georgia, and the U.S. Naval Academy's Class of 1963. He had been in combat with the battalion for almost two years, serving as a platoon commander and company exec before extending his tour to get Alpha Company. He was, in the words of Sgt. Tom Santos, his FO, *fantastic*. He led from the front. When the company had rest stops during sweeps, Jordan would take his XO and conduct reconnaissance forward of the unit; and when VC tunnels were discovered, it was not unknown for Jordan to personally climb in head first with a flashlight and a borrowed .45 pistol. Jordan had become so casual that he continued to wear his sniper-bait rank insignia, and he no longer bothered to clean or carry his own rusty .45 (why bother, as he joked to Sergeant Santos, since he'd only fired it twice in combat—once he'd almost shot his gunnery sergeant, and he couldn't account for the other bullet).

Captain Landes of Bravo Company was small, dark, and intense. He was a former enlisted man, having joined on his seventeenth birthday (he left the Corps long enough after his first hitch to get a college degree), and his initial assignment with the BLT had been as the S-3A. Landes came to Bravo Company after their mauling on Beau Charger and had not yet been seriously tested. He did, however, know how to motivate people—he cared and it showed. And he gave the appearance of a brave, aggressive Captain of Marines who could handle whatever might arise.[1]

1. Writing to a friend three months later, between operations, Landes would speak for most of his fellow officers. "I'm not fighting for any real principles or ideals, and certainly not for the South Vietnamese people. . . . They want to be left alone, and hate both sides equally.

Captain Reczek of Charlie Company was, perhaps, the battalion's most impressive company commander. He was a former Recon Marine, a short, stocky weight lifter (*a little iron man*, thought Landes), and he operated with precision and an air of quiet confidence. He was icy, commented one of his privates, Rusmisell (currently with the 81mm Mortars). *He never changed his expression, but he had a presence —he gave orders and they weren't to be altered.*

Captain Aldous of Delta Company was good, but much more subdued and nondescript than his peers. All in all, a good team (although Delta Company did lose a man on LZ Hawk when a malingerer pounded his kneecap with the butt end of a bayonet), the kind to cause Sergeant Bouchard of Alpha Two (a career Marine) to comment that "every one of us were just at times almost overcome with fear, but they all seemed to be able to tuck their guts in and do the job and whatever it took. It was a terrific battalion. They were tough, field-wise, and the leadership was excellent. Morale was extremely high, and I would not have enjoyed being the enemy running into the 1st Battalion, 3d Marines."

Battalion Landing Team 1/3 marched north from LZ Hawk on Route 561 in a flank-protected double column with Alpha (Jordan) and Bravo (Landes) in the lead, the Alpha Command Group (Wickwire) behind them, and Charlie (Reczek) and Delta (Aldous) to the rear. As BLT 1/3 was thus stretched out like an accordion, Major Woodring, CO, 3/9, passed the word to his company commanders

---

. . . I'm fighting to stay alive and keep my Marines alive; I'm fighting for the Marine Corps, and its proud history of always winning in spite of the odds; and I'm fighting because my country is involved in a war, and I feel I owe my services for all the good things that have happened to me. Sorry my reasons are so shallow, but its a dirty affair. . . . I wouldn't have missed it for anything though. I've learned a lot about myself and about people. I'm proud of myself and many others, although not unashamed of things we have done or been forced to do by the situations we were in. There are no blacks and whites. . . . Its like one continuously grey and cloudy day."

that reinforcements would not be arriving in time to proceed toward the Marketplace. Instead, they were to conduct limited reconnaissance patrols forward of their lines,
while air and arty alternated in the Marketplace for a total
of twelve hours in preparation for what had been resched-
uled as tomorrow's body-recovery sweep.

PFC Taylor of the 2d Platoon of Charlie Company
BLT 1/3 did not, if the truth be known, feel a part of the
Marines in column with him. Taylor was a stocky, strap-
ping, and handsome (in the all-American-boy mold) nine-
teen-year-old from Chicago, a very good kid from a very
bad home, who wanted nothing more than to be a real part
of the platoon. He wanted that so badly that he always
tried too hard—he was constantly trying to be funny. But
Sergeant Jones (his super squad leader) and Corporal
Muller (his bullying fireteam leader), as well as most of the
guys in the squad, had all been with Chickenshit Charlie
since Khe Sanh. They talked endlessly of Khe Sanh, *as if to
rub it in your face,* thought Taylor. *As if to say they were
better than you.*

Taylor humped along now in awe, as always, of these
salts (who, it was easy to forget, were his own age), while
simultaneously resentful of their rejecting cliquishness. *You
had to earn their respect, and you never could. It was going to
take time, and you didn't know if you were going to live
through that time.*

Charlie Two, which was commanded by 2dLt John V.
Francis and Staff Sgt John J. Malloy, was progressing
through this fallow, shell-pocked farmland when Taylor noticed a dead NVA, belly-up in the tall grass. He was just
lying there. Taylor called to the others, "Check this out,
man," as he produced his camera again. The NVA was a
fresh kill, just going a sickly gray, and although he still wore
his boondockers, his headgear, weapon, ammunition, and
equipment were gone. The NVA lay with his fatigue shirt
pulled open, one knee pulled up, a hand on his belly, head
bent back, and face to one side and lost in the overhanging
greenery. He was a big guy, taller and heavier, Taylor real-

ized, than himself, which gave him a bad feeling about
what they were heading into: "Look how big that sonuvabitch is."

"I thought the gooks were like small."

"Are we fighting the Chinese? Who the hell are we
fighting out here—is this like a Chinese Mongol, or what?"

Taylor, who was souvenir crazy as well as a photo
freak, noticed something else. The NVA had a round metal
canteen with a bottle top (the cap was missing) cradled in a
canvas strap. Its green paint was chipping, it was spotted
with dried blood, and Taylor wanted it. They had been
trained not to touch bodies in case of booby traps, but in
another move for which Sergeant Jones was constantly taking bites out of his ass, Taylor scooped up the canteen. He
slung it over his shoulder. They could have stayed with this
novelty for an hour—the NVA, after all, usually evacuated
their dead—but they were causing a commotion in the platoon file and Sergeant Jones barked them along. "Let's go.
Let's move it. Leave it alone."

Captain Jordan of Alpha BLT 1/3 had an unusually full
complement of outstanding lieutenants along with him for
this march from LZ Hawk. They included his exec, 2dLt
Marv Matsumoto, as well as 2dLt Norm Kuhlmann of 1st
Platoon, 2dLt Dennis Kendig of 2d Platoon, and 2dLt
Dave Snyder of 3d Platoon. On their way to the Trace, they
were aware of naval gunfire coming in from the east (its
flat trajectory was easy to distinguish), and as they closed
the gap, they began taking some of the long rounds from
the NVA artillery currently peppering 3/9. Those rounds
were also easy to distinguish by sound, coming down from
on high with a whistling rush, and the column stopped and
started on their cue. The noise was enough to make everyone drop to one knee, but the rounds never hit close
enough to produce a hole-searching scramble.

It was scorching hot and along the way Sergeant
Bouchard (Kendig's Right Guide) noticed another NVA
off to the side, this one decomposing and partially buried.
His comrades had previously laid him in a shallow grave,

but recent vehicle traffic had kicked apart his resting place. Marines passed him with cheerful smiles.

"Good morning, Charlie."

Nearing the Trace, they could occasionally catch the smell of decomposing flesh. It was shocking to realize that fellow Marines, dead Marines, contributed to the foul wind from the Marketplace. The platoon crossed the wide-open expanse of the Trace in a well spread-out rush, and Bouchard, hot and tired as he navigated the chopped-up earth, suddenly tripped over something. He looked down. It was a skull. He gave it an angry, irritated kick that sent it bouncing away, and it wasn't until they stopped on the other side of the Trace that it came to him. *Hey, Ken, that was a human skull that you kicked. Jesus, you've become this hard individual.*

Sergeant Bouchard then noticed the ripped and blood-splattered mounds of helmets, flak jackets, and deuce gear, enough to equip fifty or seventy Marines. *God.* He rose again, as the platoon pressed on, still in the lead. *We are really going to be in some shit here.*

Everything changed for the Marines of BLT 1/3 after they crossed the Trace. Lieutenant Kendig's Alpha Two was directed to effect the linkup with 3/9 along Route 561. And as they moved out, Cpl Stanley A. Witkowski, of the attached rocket team, took note of the blown-to-hell Ontos that sat on a small mound. There were also LAWs lying abandoned in the brush, a Marine helmet that had been blown totally inside out, and another Marine helmet that Witkowski saw in which the NVA had left the previous owner's peeled-away scalp. *Scary,* he thought, an emotion LCpl Steven Lind, a machine gunner also attached to the platoon, would have seconded as he passed the bloody bandages and deuce gear hung up on the hedgerows. The NVA who had done this were still in the area. Only moments before, just before crossing the Trace, an older officer with a Thompson had told Lind to keep the bipod on his M60 folded in to avoid becoming a more desirable target to an NVA marksman.

Lieutenant Kendig's platoon took some fire as they advanced, though the situation was so confused that Kendig wasn't sure the fire was not from 3/9. Perhaps, perhaps not, but it was definitely the NVA who pumped over three dozen mortar rounds and rockets into Alpha Company's advance, and who worked a more general, all-purpose barrage along BLT 1/3's developing line. A few rounds here, a few rounds there, but no casualties, and after effecting the linkup with 3/9 (officially at 1935), BLT 1/3 had (as of 1945) reached its night positions. What was not blown up was actually quite beautiful with its lush green fields, fences, trails, hedgerows, and banana trees. But there was an eerie feel in the hot, still half-light of twilight. *I know there's something bad in there,* thought Cpl Adolphus Stuart, an S-2 Scout. *A haunted place.* A devastated place, mostly. *It's so torn up and destroyed, it's like a black-and-white movie,* thought Lance Corporal Kalwara of the machine-gun team with Charlie Two. *Everything's gray. It's just broken limbs and tree spars splintered and smashed, and the green has just kind of gone out of it.* There was no hope of concealment on a large scale, but there were plenty of things to get down in or behind. As Charlie Two, for example, got into position amid the organic rubble, Corporal Williams, a tall, thin, and very nervous short-timer, remarked with great weight, *"This is the DMZ."*

One of the corporal's squad members, PFC John Steiner, knew exactly what he meant. *We are in as deep as deep can be.* It reminded Steiner of *All Quiet on the Western Front,* where in the distance you can hear the guns all the time. It was like, he thought, they were really *in* the war.

PFC Taylor's adrenaline was racing, and he became even more uptight as he set up for the night. When he went into his pack, which he'd left aboveground while he dropped into an agricultural trench during the brief mortaring, he discovered that it had been peppered with shrapnel. The metal fragments had torn through his C rations and extra socks. To get his mind off all this, Taylor scouted up a nice heavy stick with which he intended to fashion a plug of sorts for his souvenir NVA canteen so that he could use it. He sat down and started whittling with his K-Bar, but the knife was dull and he was reduced to whacking away at the stick. Their platoon sergeant, Staff Sergeant Malloy (whom Taylor considered *tremendous*, though he walked around hunched over and preoccupied, but, in fact, took in everything) called to him, "You better watch out, you're going to hurt yourself."

As if on cue, Taylor missed the stick with the K-Bar and laid open his left hand. There was a gush of blood and a stunned, painless moment. *I can't believe I did this.* The next thing he knew there were four or five Marines there, including a grimacing Staff Sergeant Malloy ("You stupid asshole"), and they wrapped the wound tight. The cut was all the way to the bone in the fleshy part between his thumb and index finger, bad enough for a nonemergency medevac (room would not be made on one for another two nights), but not bad enough for Taylor not to feel like an idiot and maybe a shirker:

> To this day I feel really embarrassed. I think that the Lord looks at this in a strange way. I didn't know what was going to happen the next day. I was scared and maybe deep down in my psyche it was done on purpose. I outwardly in my soul know I didn't do it on purpose, but maybe this is the way that God wanted me to stay alive, and that's why I was medevacked.

At 2045, Bravo Company was in the process of digging in and setting up when NVA were spotted in their interior lines. In moments, one Marine was wounded, one NVA was killed, and one NVA was captured. As he was a highly prized piece of intelligence, he was helicoptered out for interrogation. Officially, this NVA was the operation's second and last prisoner, although Alpha Company did round up another NVA this evening. Perhaps this man was not credited in the official accounts because, although he had the youth and physique of an NVA regular, he was wearing civilian clothes when captured (he was just bopping along a trail, the Marines joked) and his only gear was a walking stick and a pair of Ho Chi Minh sandals. As a patrol escorted the NVA back, he was relieved of the sandals (noted Lance Corporal Lind) by a souvenir-hungry grunt.

With narrow, sunken, north-south Route 561 as the dividing line between 3/9 (Woodring) and BLT 1/3 (Wickwire), both battalions battened down for the evening on an east-west axis. K/3/9 (Giles) was on the extreme western flank, followed west to east by L/3/9 (Shirley) and I/3/9 (Coyle), while the 3/9 CP was in a trench some hundred meters behind the main line, with A/1/9 (Slater) and C/1/9 (Hutchinson) in reserve on the west and east respectively. The line continued directly across Route 561 with, west to east (or left to right), A (Jordan) and B (Landes) on line facing north, and C (Reczek) BLT 1/3 facing a bit north, but mostly east on the far flank. While advancing the several hundred meters north from the Trace, Landes of Bravo Company (who felt very good about being tucked in between pros like Jordan and Reczek) had been able to tie in with Alpha but not with Charlie on the right. A gap of some 200 meters existed between the two companies, so both turned their flanks to face that hole and the 1/3 CP had to deploy additional security, as did D (Aldous) in reserve near the Trace. Meanwhile, from 2320–0300, an emergency helicopter resupply was conducted along the Trace for the rushed-ashore BLT as the NVA fired an occasional artillery or mortar round. NVA scouts also probed along this new Marine line, although they fired not a round. Nervous Marines out on LPs whispered into their radio handsets for permission to throw grenades at things they heard or thought they heard. Illum was also hung in the night sky wherever the LPs reported movement, and mortars placed fire on the spots. Fire discipline was such, though, that Marines did not reveal their positions by firing M16s or M60s even though, noted Corporal Witkowski, there was an English-speaking NVA out there, close enough to be heard as he whispered loudly in an attempt to rattle nerves and to produce a few telltale muzzle flashes, *"Hey, Alpha Company. Alpha Company where are you? Alpha, Alpha . . ."*

25

Killer Kilo

★

"Lordy, Lordy, it's July the Fourth. Here we go again. Hot dog. Hot time in the old town tonight. Bet we make a big contact." So predicted Gunnery Sergeant Hatfield, company gunnery sergeant, to Captain Giles, company commander, as Kilo Company, 3d Battalion, 9th Marines, saddled up on Hill 109, the western anchor of the two-battalion front.

"I'm sure we're going to have an exciting day of fireworks."

"Fuck you, Hatfield, we don't need that."

The guiding philosophy of Captain Giles was that he was there to survive so that he could lead, rather than die needlessly as a special target in the gun sights of an NVA sniper. To that end, he tried to look like just another Marine. Before the Khe Sanh Hill Fights, he had carried an image-enhancing shotgun, but now he had an M16 like everyone else. He wore his binoculars inside his flak jacket and a grunt-style sweat towel around his neck. He did not wear rank insignia, and he pulled his map from the baggy thigh pocket of his jungle utilities only when behind cover.

Giles had been the skipper of Kilo Company for more than eleven months and was profoundly weary, although still confident and ever professional. In fact, even on Hill 109 this morning, his Marines shaved. Where water was scarce, this was achieved by pouring a half cup into an empty C-rations peach can, then dipping in a washcloth and wiping your face as clean as possible. After lathering and scraping, you poured a little water off to rinse your razor, then produced the washcloth again to clean face and hands. Last but not least, your perpetual plastic spoon was rinsed and wiped, so that each morning, each man had had a bath and a shave, and had done his dishes.

Captain Giles insisted on this ritual to remind his grunts that they were still human. That little bit of decency and respect for self made you stand a little taller and prouder. Everybody seemed to care about everybody else in Kilo Company. *There was a lot of love and comradeship and mutual respect,* Giles thought, and the fact that many of their Marines were actually draftees enhanced performance as far as Giles was concerned. The draftees struck him as a little smarter, a little more rebellious, and higher spirited—more independent thinking, which was outstanding when applied to the team effort. When it was not, Giles had no time for the paperwork and record-damaging formalities of office hours or a court-martial. Everything was handled on the spot. Like during their last trip to the DMZ (Operation Cimmaron) when Giles called in his ammunition NCO, "How many rounds of Willy Peter for the sixty-mike-mike mortars do we have?"

"Sir, I don't know. I forgot to count before we left."

"Dammit, we need to know exactly how many we have."

"I really screwed up, sir. I'm really sorry."

"Well, were you acting like a sergeant E-5 ammunition NCO?"

"No, sir, I wasn't."

"What were you acting like?"

"I was acting more like a PFC."

"Fine, give me your E-5 stripes." The man unsnapped the small, metal chevrons from his collar. "Okay, you're now a private in the United States Marine Corps. Pick up your rifle, go down and report to Lieutenant Lane as PFC Barnes. When you feel like you can be an NCO in the Marine Corps, perform like one and do the job required, then come back and let me know."

Captain Giles was ably assisted in maintaining standards by small and wiry Gunny Horrible Hatfield, whose seamed, squeezed-down, perpetually grimacing face spoke of many hard miles in the Old Corps. He had left West Virginia for Parris Island when he was seventeen, and two years later he was with the 5th Marines in Inchon, Seoul, and the Frozen Chosin. With such experience, Hatfield was, in Vietnam, not only the company gunnery sergeant, but also the company executive officer, the company morale man, the company scrounger, the company funny man, the company bad man—the company everything.

To Hatfield everything was "sorry ass," to include the Sorry Ass Marine Corps and this Sorry Ass War, and when he had come aboard during Kilo's An Hoa days it had taken Giles thirty minutes to determine that he would be rid of this madman. He was the most vulgar excuse for a human being that Giles had ever met, a man who made light of everything ("The mosquitoes here in Vietnam are big enough to stand flat-footed in a rice paddy and fuck turkeys") and who was absolutely disrespectful of everything from God and the Commandant on down (he would walk into Giles's tent in the middle of briefings, cut a loud, long fart, and say, "Excuse me, that's just what I needed to do right then"). Within a week or so, though, Captain Giles's feelings had changed:

> He began to grow on me, and I realized that he kept things in a proper perspective. He would do anything, absolutely anything necessary to take care of the young Marines in Kilo Company. I mean he would lie, he would cheat, he would steal, he would barter. I came to

love that man more than anybody in the entire company. They should have made a movie about John C. Hatfield, and the only guy in the world that could possibly have played it would be Steve McQueen. That's the kind of rebel he was. Just horrible, horrible, vulgar, totally out of alignment with the world, but the best man in the world to get the job done.

When Kilo was besieged atop Hill 70 in May '67, Giles had been at the point of their pinned-down column while Hatfield had been about eighty meters down the trail with the wounded and the mortars. The NVA were all around them, and their perimeter was no wider than that trail. But in the middle of it all, Hatfield honked Giles up on the radio to ask, "Skipper, what are you doing up there?"

"Hatfield, we're fighting for our lives."

"Well, I'm back here having just a sorry ass cup of coffee, and I'm really enjoying it."

Of course, he wasn't, but Giles couldn't help but take the bait, "Hatfield, I'm giving you a direct order under combat conditions that you will deliver me a cup of coffee."

"Skipper—stick my fitness report in your eye."

Giles laughed and signed off, but about ten minutes later there Hatfield was, running top speed, sans helmet and flak jacket, with a cup of coffee in his hands. Hatfield hopped in Giles's hole and explained, "Sir, I was really worried about my career. I thought I'd deliver you a hot cup of coffee." He handed it over, spun off another bit of dry sarcasm ("You're doing a great job—stay where you are"), then climbed from the hole and zipped back to his WIAs and 60mm's.

Gunny Hatfield applied a hands-on approach to any malfeasance among the Marines of what he sneeringly called the Pepsi Generation. When a corporal named Saltaformaggio couldn't take it anymore and dipped his canteen into the paddy water they were humping through, which was verboten because of dysentery, Hatfield's voice suddenly boomed out, *"Saltaformaggio,* there's five thousand years of buffalo shit in that rice paddy. You drink that water, the gooks'll be able to follow your trail of shit all the way back to the perimeter!"

When the battalion-level radioman, Charpentier, fell asleep on post one night, Hatfield found him and between the *slaps* and *bams* of flying fists, Charpentier cried out, "Gunny, leave me alone! I'm awake, I'm awake, I'm awake!" And, of course, there was the evening that Hatfield walked into the CP with two M16 rifles. When Giles queried him as to their ownership, he answered, "Well, I just went out and checked on our outposts, and I found our two dipshits out there sitting there eating C rations, weapons off to one side, just totally enjoying life. So I walked out and talked to them for a minute. They apologized for not being alert. I asked them how many grenades they had. They said they had four grenades apiece, and I said, 'Great, you got your radio?' They said, 'Yes, sir,' and I said, 'Fine, we'll see how awake you stay tonight.' "

And Hatfield then walked off with their rifles.

By the time of Hill 109 and Operation Buffalo, the feeling had developed that "as goeth Giles and Hatfield, so goeth Kilo Company." They had been with the company forever, and as far as the grunts were concerned, as long as those two were alive and well the company was going to do okay. Likewise, Giles had the belief that as long as Hatfield was alive and well, he was going to survive. Hatfield had the same belief in reverse. They waited now to push off on this sweep, cigarettes going (as always), and (also, as always whenever they had a moment of spare time) Hatfield pulled a stick of C4 plastic explosives from his pack. He took a pinch of it, laid it on the ground, lit it with a lighter, and within seconds heated up some C-ration coffee. "Hey, skipper, you want a sorry ass cup of coffee?"

"Yup."

"Well, give me your sorry ass cup."

Back in their tent at Dong Ha, Giles had a fine pewter mug (an R&R gift from Hatfield) on which was engraved SORRY ASS CUP/FOR A SORRY ASS SKIPPER/

FROM AN OUTSTANDING GUNNY. In the field, though, Giles's cup was an old C-ration can with a wire handle, which Hatfield presently handed back to him brimming with hot, bitter, black liquid. "Here you go, you sorry ass skipper. Sorry ass war. Sorry ass Marine Corps . . ."

In radio communications with one another, Major Woodring, CO, 3/9, and Lieutenant Colonel Wickwire, CO, BLT 1/3, jumped off in the attack to the north at 0700, Tuesday, 4 July 1967. They advanced with a six-company front, extending from west to east with K (Giles), L (Shirley), and I/3/9 (Coyle), then across Route 561, A (Jordan), B (Landes), and C BLT 1/3 (Reczek). They moved slowly and cautiously, and it was not until 0915 that the battle began with the point of K/3/9 coming under fire from the north.

Well, we've got work to do, thought Captain Giles. At the time, Kilo Company was approximately 600 meters due north of Hill 109 and some 200 meters beyond the trail that ran from west to east into Route 561. They had been advancing in the standard formation of two-up-and-one-back with 2dLt Jerry Lane and 2dLt Clinton H. (Andy) Anderson in command of the lead platoons. Captain Giles's headquarters group followed in the seam between the lead platoons with a two-tank section from C Company, 3d Tank Battalion, while Gunny Hatfield, meanwhile, moved with the 60mm mortar section to the rear.

They were crossing flat, nakedly open, and multicratered farmland where the trees had been shorn of most of their limbs and denuded of most of their leaves. It was parched hedgerow country (*desolate*, Giles thought), and it was in this cover that the NVA had deployed. They were (probably, it was hard to tell) dug in among the bramble of an east-west hedgerow, pouring a hideously loud barrage of AK47s and RPGs into the dirt-eating, pinned-down Marines of Lieutenant Lane's and Anderson's platoons. It was impossible to tell, for the NVA were impossible to see, whether it was a platoon's worth or a company's worth, as was officially estimated. Giles, in radio contact with Lane (who was reporting casualties), instructed the tank lieutenant to follow him with his M48s, then continued forward to make physical contact with either Lane or Anderson.

Radiomen Charpentier and Williams remained steadfastly at Giles's side despite the automatic-weapons fire (long bursts from the fight ahead) beginning to slash the air around them. In fact, they mimicked his every move, sensing in the longevity of his command a specialness that would also keep them alive. If Giles squatted, stood, knelt, ran, or walked, they did likewise, and if he strode into the middle of an open field, they followed without hesitation. It would not have reassured Charpentier and Williams, as they moved to the point of contact, to know that Giles's eleven months in command had so drained and calloused him that he no longer even felt a surge of healthy fear at the high, distinct, bone-chilling crack of the AK47 automatic rifle. He moved forward with absolute fatalism.

Giles, Charpentier, and Williams finally spotted a young Marine lying behind a hedgerow. They ran to and dived down beside him. Giles got his attention, "'Scuse me, Marine, where's your platoon leader?"

"I don't know, sir."

"That's not too good. Where's your squad leader?"

"I have no idea, sir."

"Well, what the hell are you doing out here?"

"I don't know, sir. I'm pinned down."

Oh shit. To the north, across eighty meters or so of dirt, Giles could see the muzzle flashes of AK47s and the dusty back blasts of RPGs along the brushy base of the next hedgerow. It was an old game. The NVA were dug in and camouflaged, and they let the Marines, unaware of their presence, advance so closely that their foe, once ambushed, would be unable to employ supporting arms without risking friendly-fire casualties. As always, the NVA had selected the time and place of the fight, and Giles knew that as soon as the Marines had extracted themselves so as to allow the use of supporting arms, the NVA would withdraw leaving empty spiderholes and hedgerows to take the technological beating.

Giles and radiomen moved back about forty meters, joining other Marines they had seen in the hedge there. It was then that a platoon radioman came up on the net to report that "Kilo Three Actual's a KIA."

Kilo Three Actual was Andy Anderson, who had joined them after Khe Sanh. Listening now to how Lieutenant Anderson had been shot in the head during the initial moments of the ambush, Giles's simple thought was, *well, he's gone.* He had completely shut down about death. He was committed to the team called Kilo Company, but he kept an emotional distance regarding individuals because of the heavy casualties.[1] After Khe Sanh and Hill 70, Giles no longer even referred to his NCOs by their last names, but only as "sergeant," or to his platoon commanders by their first names, now it was simply "lieutenant." *You don't get close to your lieutenants because they're going to die.* Giles could only have hoped that Anderson wouldn't have died as uselessly as he did, standing up to lead his platoon like an officer would at Quantico (everyone else had gone to the prone) and lasting about thirty seconds before an NVA marksman dropped all six-foot-three-inches of him with a head shot. Giles was not surprised. Anderson had always had more faith in the Lord than in cover and concealment. During that night on Hill 70, Anderson had moved around their perimeter without caution, silhouetting himself on the crest, and when Giles had called to him, "Andy, get your ass off the ridge line," Anderson had answered, "Aw skipper, it's okay. God's going to protect me."

The next word (via radio) to Giles was that Whitey,

---

1. Corporal Gomez (I/3/9) concurred, "We showed no emotion over dead Marines. It was just a fact of life, and when you put bodies on helicopters it was just like resupply going the other way—you were just putting something on to be taken out, and you didn't think about that it was a dead friend—a dead brother—because you did not have the time to grieve. Maybe we should have taken the time to grieve because it seems to be catching up with us now."

their point man this morning, was also a KIA. Whitey had been something of a company mascot, a short, little guy with snow white hair and oversized, baggy-assed utilities and boots. Another damn shame, as were the additional KIAs then reported. Looking to his rear through a small opening in the hedgerow, Giles saw his artillery lieutenant kneeling against a small tree directly in front of one of their tanks. He waved at the FO to come forward and turned to face forward again as the man began his race toward him. Just then, there was the crack and back blast of another RPG from the enemy-held hedgerow, and Giles felt the warhead whoosh past his head. Too numb to appreciate how close to death he had come, he merely thought, *wow, that was close, wasn't it?*

The RPG exploded to his rear, the concussion of it sending the artillery spotter sprawling in midrun. He scrambled on up to Giles's position (he had taken a shrapnel wound in the small of his back where his flak jacket had ridden up during his run) and tapped Giles on the shoulder.

Giles turned with a "yeah?"

"I think I owe you a beer."

"Why?"

The FO pointed back across the clearing to the tree that Giles had just called him away from. It was crumpled by the RPG hit. In response, the tanks (as noted in 3/9's after-action report) "fired at the RPG position with canister rounds, and no more RPGs were fired from that position."

While the assault of the 3d Battalion, 9th Marines, west of Route 561, was blunted with the ambush initiated against their K Company at 0915 (and I and L Companies were simultaneously mortared, and two Marines wounded), similarly, Battalion Landing Team 1/3, east of Route 561, began to bog down as of 0930 when their A Company came under heavy rocket and mortar fire.

Captain Jordan's Alpha Company was just moving north at the time, the flatlands ahead of them geysering with the usual arty prep, the usual air strikes, and in this case, long-range naval gunfire. As Jordan was an excellent officer, so were his rifle-platoon commanders in this assault. Lieutenant Kuhlmann of 1st Platoon was, in fact, the best platoon officer Jordan had ever seen. He was a crisp, efficient former gunnery sergeant and drill instructor who knew his craft and never got rattled. Lieutenant Kendig of 2d Platoon was also a former drill instructor, with Korean War service as a BAR man and a previous tour with the Vietnamese Marines to boot. He was, bars or no bars (as far as Jordan was concerned), still a piss-and-vinegar Staff NCO. He came on strong and his Marines worshiped him. Lieutenant Snyder of 3d Platoon was straight out of college (he had been an All-American) and had come aboard only a few days earlier, big, strong, and gung ho. He was the kind of man who when seasoned out would make an excellent leader, but who suffered in comparison with Kuhlmann and Kendig. Thrown into the over-your-head waters of Operation Buffalo, Snyder was floundering badly. He had a good head and a good heart, though, and Jordan was coaching him along.

Alpha advanced with two up (Kuhlmann and Snyder) and one back (Kendig), so that Kendig's platoon was really still in the holes of their night position when the incoming began shrieking in. The barrage caught Kendig and his radioman just after they'd emerged from their old, E-tool-improved shell crater to get the platoon up and following in Kuhlmann and Snyder's path. Everyone naturally made like moles again, so between salvos, Kendig and radioman bounced from hole to hole in a running crouch. It was hard to get people moving when they were taking incoming, but with Kendig making sure they knew where to go and what to do, the line began to emerge again. The platoon sergeant, Reynolds[2] however, was clinging to his practically neck-deep hole. Kendig couldn't blame him since the man was so close to rotating home, but he needed help and, short or not, Staff Sergeant Reynolds was still on the clock.

2. Not his real name.

Kendig stood tall and muscled above Reynolds's hole, made even larger by his helmet and flak jacket (a fellow lieutenant once said that Kendig belonged on the cover of *Leatherneck* magazine), and roared down, "Get on up off your ass and get the people moving! You have to get off your butt every once in a while and take the risks—that's why you get the high pay!"

Staff Sergeant Reynolds got moving. Lieutenant Kendig's élan was due in large part to the fact that he had just taken over the platoon, after initial service as Jordan's executive officer. This was his first combat command, and Buffalo his first operation as a commander. He was *really hot to trot,* so there he was darting to another hole in the jogging crouch, when a mortar round landed to his front just a few feet away. Kendig saw the sudden flash, heard the roar, and then in that same millisecond, he was abruptly on his ass, helmet kicked off and head swimming with the concussion, the front of his flak jacket hanging ripped and torn. Several chunks of red-hot shrapnel were embedded in his upper left arm, and a corpsman was on him almost immediately.

The line was moving now and Kendig, battle dressing in place, protested the corpsman's filling out a medevac tag. "I'm not going."

"The hell you're not. You're getting medevacked."

Kendig finally had to agree; he was getting groggy and because of a cut nerve in his arm, he couldn't move his fingers. So much for a good first outing. Simultaneous with the barrage landing around Alpha BLT 1/3, Bravo BLT 1/3 began coming under sporadic artillery fire. Before long, Captain Landes had nine casualties, including a heat casualty and a bad sprain, and they were moved to the protection of a defilade in a tree line. As they waited for the medevac, one of the wounded, a corpsman with a shrapnel hole in his chest, grinned, stuck a cigarette in his wound, and tried to draw on it. They were such great, brave kids, Landes thought, and when the chopper arrived he was one of four Marines to grab the handles on the corpsman's stretcher. He felt it was the least he could do[3]

At 1030, the NVA's on-again-off-again barrage erupted in the vicinity of the Alpha Command Group BLT 1/3, wounding another Marine. At 1043, another element behind the main battle line, C/1/9, was also hit by rockets. Their CO, Captain Hutchinson, felt the first explosion's punch to his shoulder, even as he was lunging for a hole with the rest. There was no real pain, and after the barrage, as he and a corpsman got his flak jacket off and the bandages tied on, Hutchinson saw that there was not much blood either: a single piece of shrapnel had zipped through the meaty part of his left shoulder, cut across the front of his neck, and kept on going. Hutchinson radioed Major Woodring, "This is Charlie Six Actual. I've been wounded. I'm going out. I'm turning my command over to my First Platoon leader."

Ten other Marines from Charlie Company had been wounded. Their evacuation by helicopter was almost immediate (all medevacs were out by 1050) and as Captain Hutchinson, starting to feel weak, got aboard, the corpsman inside said, "That's a million-dollar wound. It's going to get you out of here, and it won't cause you any problems."

Hutchinson felt great about that. Captain Navadel, S-3, 3/9, was not similarly pleased. He was not sure about Charlie Company, so (already out checking the lines with Salt 'n' Pepper) he hustled over to talk with the lieutenant now in command. The man, however, was obviously a former Staff NCO, and when Navadel asked, "Are you ready to take charge, to take care of things," the lieutenant said, "Don't worry."

---

3. Three months later, Landes would write home to a friend, "I can't say enough about my Marines. They are dedicated, tough and hard. . . . The troops are very aggressive, and once they find out where Charlie is they don't hesitate to move right in on him, regardless of the fire. I have seen men do brave, foolish, and cowardly things over here, and I can't really explain any of them. Sometimes combat is almost a dream world."

Too close to the NVA to employ air or arty, Captain Giles of Kilo Company decided instead to use their two attached M48 tanks, although the tankers did seem rather blind and confused in this hedgerow country, and they were vulnerable to the Soviet-produced RPG-7 which could pierce 9.4 inches of armor[4] Giles, on the radio with the tank lieutenant, pointed out specific spots in one of the hedgerows where he had spotted NVA. The young lieutenant struck him as so new as to be totally disconnected from reality (operating like this was a wargame, as if he did not realize his crews were firing live rounds and people were dying) as Giles directed him. "That's the hedgerow I want you to see. Are you sure you got it in your sights?"

"Yes."

"What I want you to do is sweep that entire hedgerow with .50-caliber machine-gun fire."

The tankers opened fire toward the NVA on Kilo's left flank, and immediately, a voice was shouting over Giles's company-level radio that the .50-caliber fire had just killed a Marine. The tankers had fired into the wrong hedgerow. Giles hollered into the radio to cease fire. Giles might have tried again. If properly brought to bear, the tanks' 90mm main guns and .50-caliber machine guns could be devastating. But cursing the forty-seven-ton beasts as *totally, completely ineffective—blind!*—he did not call on them again for the remainder of the battle.

Captain Giles tried to consolidate Kilo Company in the general vicinity of his command group. However, as Marines and Navy corpsmen moved from their cover to help back the wounded, NVA on the right flank (one sniper, two snipers?) proceeded to knock some of them down. KIA. KIA. KIA. No one could determine where the sniper was firing from. *They were everywhere and nowhere,* Giles thought, *they're all around.* They could not even be sure that the NVA was not popping from a spiderhole

---

4. At 1015, 4 July 1967, one of the tanks supporting L/3/9 was (according to the after-action report) "hit with an RPG round, disabled, and evacuated from the battle area."

within their own lines. The sniper was firing from the right flank, though, so Giles decided to dislodge the NVA by outflanking them on the left of what they'd felt out to be their general line. Maybe they could get in behind them and roll the NVA up west to east. Giles intended to use Lieutenant Lane's platoon (Lane was a former enlisted man, and was in Giles's estimation the best of their bunch —*he seemed to understand what was required better than most),* but first he wanted his 60mm mortar section in position to support.

Gunny Hatfield was with the sixty mike-mikes, so Giles called him up. "Get your mortars and get your ass over here to my position."

"Roger, out."

Two minutes later, Hatfield's radio operator came up on the net. "Gunny Hatfield's been hit, Gunny Hatfield's down!"

Giles had this unspoken pact with Hatfield that *if Hatfield dies, I die.* And now it was coming down, only a week or so before Hatfield had been due to rotate, only six weeks before Giles himself was supposed to go home. So be it. But then, some two minutes after his first call, Hatfield's radio operator was again on the net, this time with screaming enthusiasm. "Hatfield's up. . . . Hatfield's running. . . . Hatfield's gone!"

And, two minutes after that, there came Hatfield, just huffing and puffing and limping, to dive into Giles's position and exclaim, *"Ho-ly Shit!* I thought I was dead!"

"What happened?"

"Well, I was running across this clearing; they opened up on me with a machine gun, and a round hit my foot. I thought it tore my whole leg off. It spun me ass over teakettle."

The bullet had actually torn away the flesh between two of his toes with a terrible sting. Hatfield continued, "I'm layin' out there in the dust, flat on my back, lookin' at the sun, and sayin', 'I'm dyin', I'm dyin', I'm dyin',' and after I lay there for a little bit, I said, 'Hmmmm, that's strange, I'm still breathing.' So I reached down and I touched my leg and I said, 'Oh, my leg's still there, my knee's still there, my calf's still there. Hell, my foot's still there. I'm okay, I'm alive.' Then I said, 'Holy shit, I'm out in the open. Hmmm, I had better get out of here.' "

And so he did. Gunnery Sergeant Hatfield presently turned his attention to getting the 60mm tubes up and ready, while Captain Giles got Lieutenant Lane up on the radio to prepare for their flanking attack. When Lane was ready to go, one of the mortar crews put three WP rounds down their tube so as to provide a smoke screen for the assault, which landed right in Lane's forward positions, wounding a number of Marines. The mortar fire was adjusted, and Lane and platoon moved out against the NVA's left flank. They discovered then that while the main NVA battle line was facing south along an east-west hedgerow, their flank was turned along a north-south hedgerow to face west. It turned again along the next east-west hedgerow in line. *Like a stepladder,* Giles thought (it was now about 1100), as he realized he was running out of tricks.

26

If At First You Don't Succeed

★

By approximately 1115, 4 July 1967, Kilo Company, 3d Battalion, 9th Marines, had taken twelve KIAs and seventeen WIAs without having seen a single North Vietnamese. Kilo's last KIAs had been inflicted by the sniper or snipers on their right flank. He (or they) had administered more head shots as the Marines had gotten up to move back a bit and consolidate, pursuant to Captain Giles's most recent command. With Lieutenant Lane's blunted push or the left flank having revealed the depth of the NVA positions, Giles wanted to put some distance between them so he could safely employ their artillery fire.

Captain Giles was, by now, in a gully behind a hedgerow, personally adding his M16 to the cover fire for those pulling back. With his wounded FO, he started their barrage some hundreds of meters to the north then walked it south through part of the contact area, stopping at a certain point so the most forward Marines would not be endangered. Meanwhile, Major Woodring suggested via radio that Kilo (along with India and Lima) pull back 200 meters to the vicinity of the east-west trail, so that the contact area could be completely saturated with air and arty.

Giles concurred. From his gully position, he had sent everyone back except his company headquarters and one squad (spread out now in the hedge), when one of the "dead" Marines among four or five figures sprawled in the clearing ahead sat up very slowly. Giles watched incredulously and horrified. This Marine had come back to life in an area so vulnerable to the right-flank sniper that Giles had not even considered sending live Marines out there for their dead. The man leaned up against a tree and very slowly reached into his left front pocket. He pulled out a pack of cigarettes, and in slow motion got one to his mouth. He managed to light it.

Captain Giles, waiting for the NVA sniper to finish off this wounded Marine with another head shot, called out, "Hey ——, are you okay?"

"No, sir, I'm just having a cigarette before I die."

"What I want you to do is to roll over on your face and crawl back toward us!"

"No, sir, just leave me alone. Don't come and get me. Leave me alone. I'm dyin', and I just want to have my last cigarette."

Giles looked at the last squad in the hedgerow and gully, then called again, "Lay down on your face, crawl towards us!"

"Leave me alone!"

I can send all of 'em, half of 'em, or one of 'em out there. Giles looked again at the young Marines kneeling with him. *I know if I say, 'Go get him,' they'll go get him. At least they'll make the attempt.* But he felt the young Marine out there was a setup, that the only reason the NVA sniper was letting him live was so Giles would send more Marines out there. Giles sent four more men back, which left five or six, then he called to the wounded man again, who was not really listening.

"Leave me alone, just leave me alone. I'm going to die, and I'm just having my last cigarette."

Giles sent his last Marines toward the rear, then knelt there alone in the gully, looking out at that young Marine whose head was weakly bobbing back and forth. *Do I get him, or do I not?*

If Giles had been young and new, he would have instantly sent someone, or, he liked to believe, he would have done it himself. But now—*I am so tired of this fucking war.* It pissed him off that the kid wouldn't do his part to show some desire to live, and after fifteen indecisive minutes of looking back and forth between this single Marine and the rest of the company setting up several hundred meters to the rear, Giles finally stood up and turned his back on his Marine. *He's not willing to do what he needs to do, and I'm not willing to do what I need to do.* He took off his helmet and pack, slowly stood up, and, slinging his M16 over his shoulder, started back with gear in hand. He walked back across a large open area, disregarding cover in his guilt, daring the sniper to take one last shot. The NVA didn't, and Giles's self-doubt grew: what if the sniper had actually pulled back in anticipation of the Marines' supporting arms, so that the only thing between himself and that wounded kid had been his own weariness and fears? Captain Giles continued trudging rearward.

The withdrawal of 3/9 was completed at 1150, the same time that the CP came under artillery fire. The CP was in an east-west agricultural trench, and as the incoming began, Captain Navadel smiled at Major Woodring and said something about what a fine position he, Navadel, had selected: the north lip of the trench was higher than the south lip, so that the artillery shrapnel (from the north) would carry harmlessly over their heads. It was then that the CP began taking 122mm rockets from the west, and that made a big difference. Again taking advantage of that southern pocket in the Ben Hai that placed them due west (instead of north) of 3/9's current positions less than 7,000 meters from the riverbank, the NVA were firing east now,

instead of south. As such, the NVA were practically looking right down the CP's east-west trench, and Woodring
answered Navadel with a dry, "It isn't all that great a position. We gotta fill up the west end of this trench, so those
flying rockets don't come swooshing right on down the
trench line."

This they accomplished, and once again, this NVA barrage (1150–1225) resulted in no Marine casualties. There
were, as Navadel noted, plenty of ditches, shell holes, and
unused enemy spiderholes for cover:

> And, of course, you improve things awful fast when
> you're inspired. One of the things that really saved us
> from taking a lot of casualties were the agricultural
> trenches. They were very narrow, maybe only a foot
> wide, but we didn't eat that much in those days and we
> fit in them very nicely. We could move around quite well
> using that network of trenches. The trajectory of the
> stuff they were throwing at us was scary as hell, but rela-
> tively ineffective against troopers with good ears and
> their heads down.

Because the Marines had good ears, though, they didn't
always keep their heads down, and Navadel further commented:

> The troopers, the doggone troopers—they're in-
> domitable. Here's all this artillery constantly coming in,
> so they get used to it. You had troopers sitting up on the
> edge of these holes with their helmets off during incom-
> ing, and they'd actually be able to tell by listening how
> close they thought the round was coming, whether or not
> they should put their helmets on or whether or not they
> should climb in a hole. Course I'm having heart palpita-
> tions every time I would see one of those troopers sitting
> up there, yelling and hollering, getting them back in. But
> the indomitable spirit of that Grunt—it was almost like
> they were daring the doggone artillery rounds to come in
> close.

At 1200, 3/9 began calling in air and arty (until 1600) in the area of original contact. The Fire Support Coordinator for 3/9 was not, as was usual, a seasoned artillery first lieutenant, but a newly assigned second lieutenant. Though a conscientious young man, he simply did not have the experience required, and Captain Navadel had to do all the fire-support coordinating. Between that and the operational aspects of his job, he was dead on his feet. Throughout the campaign then, Navadel chided the second lieutenant that he had no problem with the lieutenant drawing his combat pay, but that he, Navadel, was going to get the lieutenant's base pay.

The battalion's direct artillery support during Operation Buffalo came from Whiskey Battery 1/12 (4.2-inch mortars) and E/2/12 (105mm), with general support provided by K/4/12 (155mm), C/1st Eight-Inch Howitzers, and C/1-40 Artillery (105mm), U.S. Army[1] The Marines had more confidence in the army artillery than their own. For one thing, there never seemed to be enough ammunition to fire all the arty they wanted (requests for WP or illumination rounds were routinely cut in half), and for another, word had it that the USMC 105s had been so overused that they were firing smooth-bore. If six tubes were firing, four would be on target, but sure enough, two would not. The Army's Long Toms, on the other hand, put their steel on target and without any apparent ammunition restrictions.

The battalion's fixed-wing air support was provided by the 1st Marine Aircraft Wing and, with some spectacular exceptions, was excellent. This was because the pilots were willing to come in low and take risks in the face of NVA ground fire, and because of the excellent (and wild, highly spirited) Forward Air Controllers assigned to 3/9 from the 1st MAW. Because all Marines were infantrymen, and even the million-dollar pilots had to do grunt duty as FACs and ALOs, the company commanders (who usually had a FAC radioman, but no FAC), had no trouble talking ground lan-

1. During Operation Buffalo, BLT 1/3 received direct artillery support from A/1/12, and 1/9 from D/2/12.

guage to the pilots running their air strikes. There were, however, problems this day, and throughout the campaign, due to the rules that governed the Fire Support Coordinators at regiment (Dong Ha) and division (Phu Bai). Their primary mission was to prevent U.S. aircraft and U.S. artillery rounds from meeting in midair, and the coordinators thus tended to "check fire" (cease) the artillery whenever aircraft entered any part of 3/9's area of operations. Ideally, aircraft would have been directed into flight paths far removed from the trajectory of allied artillery, and the artillery would have only been turned off at those moments when jets were making strikes at the same targets. This, however, was not to be, as Captain Navadel explained:

> We preach and teach coordination of air and artillery, but we had such restrictions placed on us by people on high who were so afraid we might shoot down an airplane with our own artillery. We would have a designated target and have artillery pounding in, and when we wanted to shut off the artillery and bring the air in, they'd let us know they had some air on the way—and all of a sudden the artillery would stop. We might have to wait twenty minutes, a half-hour, for the air to get on station, all the while screaming, "Where's the artillery?!" No answer. People back in Da Nang, or wherever they were, were actually giving a cease-fire to artillery up in the DMZ. The situation was just ridiculous and had us pulling our hair out about people that were back in the rear worrying about the wrong things.

It got to the point during Operation Buffalo that 3/9 became reluctant to request air strikes because, Navadel said, "We couldn't afford the artillery being turned off that long waiting for an air strike. I mean you could be overrun in twenty minutes if you had a big enough force coming at you without artillery to support you."

During this afternoon of air and arty, resupply was received. This was tricky because, as soon as the helos touched down on the Trace, raising a dust storm, everyone knew the NVA artillery would be right behind them. Or it would start pounding even before the helos landed, as the BLT 1/3 after-action report noted, "There were instances of the NVA firing artillery into landing zones as soon as a smoke grenade was used to mark them. This was alleviated by utilizing a survival-type signal mirror." The helicopter pilots became very adept at touching down, discharging their ammo, water, and rations[2] and pulling out in short order. The problem then became how to move this material the hundreds of meters from where it had been dumped off to where it was needed. As Navadel said, "The troops were tired and working parties were tough." In this case, the battalions actually used their good old M274A1 Mechanical Mules (picture a large version of every child's little red wagon, painted olive drab, with an engine mounted under the flatbed), helo-lifting in about four apiece. The field S-4 (supply) of 3/9 was a young, hard charging black corporal. He'd get out there aboard a Mule with a couple white-knuckled Marines and between artillery rounds would go bouncing over the rugged terrain of the Trace, stopping to stack supplies on the Mule, then driving them up to the northern edge of the bulldozed swath. Everyone pitched in. Also in the S-4 shop was an ammunition technician who, along with one of his corporals, would accompany each ammo resupply to the Trace and hop out to make sure it got where it belonged. Captain Navadel remarked, "I'd have to kick him in the rear and make sure he got back on a helicopter, so he could make sure we had the ammo we needed the next day. The troops marched to the sounds of the guns—that's where they felt they should be."

2. The troops subsisted on C rations and the minimum amount of water. From Captain Navadel: "During Operation Buffalo, Brigadier General Metzger helicoptered into the Trace. He was walking along and stopped, and I was right there when he asked a very, very exhausted Marine if he had enough water. That trooper, without getting up, just kind of rolled over and looked him right in the eye and said, 'General, you know we never get enough water.' Metzger said, 'Guess you're right, son.' "

★

Captain Giles of Kilo Company, with helmet and pack in hand and rifle slung over shoulder, kept walking back from the contact area until he found Gunny Hatfield's position. He threw everything into the hole there and sat down.

"Skipper, I think you need a cup of coffee."

Giles told Hatfield about his decision up there with the young, wounded Marine. He tried to justify it in terms of being tired of sending Marines to die, and Hatfield listened, hurting with him and sharing his doubt, but saying little because there was, of course, nothing to say. With coffee and cigarette in hand, Giles directed in most of the arty forward of their new position (now that his FO had been medevacked) and all of their air (the battalion was too short of FACs to have assigned one to his company). He was absolutely nonplussed by the spectacle erupting just *north* of the contact area (where he had called for it on the assumption that the NVA had pulled back to the hedgerows there, and to be on the safe side in case there were any Marines still alive out there). It was just so damn routine; though some excitement did come when a 2000-pound Daisy Cutter bomb exploded with such titanic force as to send shrapnel zinging past the Marines of Kilo Company.

Giles and Hatfield, sitting on the edge of a fighting hole on the hillside into which the shrapnel had just thumped, looked at each other as Hatfield exclaimed, "Holy shit! We don't want to die by our own stuff out here!"

Immediately east of Route 561, Captain Jordan's Alpha Company BLT 1/3 had made heavy contact with entrenched NVA, with Lieutenant Kuhlmann's platoon the most heavily involved. The NVA shelled them as they advanced northward in fits and starts (Kuhlmann had the thought at the time that he was thankful the enemy had no air power), and NVA foot soldiers in superbly placed and camouflaged positions took them under automatic-weapons fire from tree lines one hundred to three hundred meters to their front. *A turkey shoot,* Kuhlmann thought, well aware of what had happened here two days before. The NVA had every nook and cranny zeroed in, and finally, Kuhlmann's advance across this opened, cratered area was brought to a halt some one hundred impassable meters from the Marine bodies they had come to recover.

The NVA fire had grown too intense to keep moving without taking casualties, and from the crater where he'd taken cover, Kuhlmann was on the radio to Jordan, requesting additional fire support to soften up the NVA emplacements. Jordan and his FAC, in turn, requested an air strike from battalion, while Jordan relayed his concern back to Kuhlmann about getting air panels in place well forward of the platoon's lines. Air panels, which were made of silk and measured approximately eighteen inches by three feet, were either hot pink or a fluorescent orange and were highly visible to pilots once laid out and staked down. Calling up his three squad leaders, Kuhlmann instructed each to place two air panels as forward of his squad as a man could move under cover fire, for a total of six air panels across their fifty-meter front.

Once this had been accomplished, the jets flashed past and indicated that they had seen the panels. Jordan and his FAC instructed the pilots to conduct their strikes north of the panels, and the first A4 Skyhawk slashed in, bombs disengaging and diving into the vegetation shielding the NVA positions. Delay-fused bombs were used so the projectiles would smash some five feet into the ground before exploding, the subsurface shock waves thus caving in the NVA bunkers.

Meanwhile, since all the NVA ground fire in the area was coming from the direction of Alpha Company, Captain Landes of Bravo Company had moved with his headquarters element to a piece of high ground on Bravo's left flank and Alpha's right. Landes could see the whole two-company battlefield from this position, and he was concerned about staying tied in with Jordan should the contact turn hotter and heavier. Landes was trying to encourage several traumatized members of Alpha (they were talking of the horrible decomposition of three 1/9 bodies they had found this morning), when he saw a Skyhawk lining up for what would be the second or third pass at the NVA ahead. This one turned in a shallow circle then came in sleek and fast, and much closer than the previous aircraft.

Landes commented to one of the Marines with him, "Holy cow, this guy's off line. I hope he knows where he is."

The Skyhawk was coming in right off the deck (it was now 1415) and Landes watched two 250-pound bombs release from the wing racks. As the jet roared skyward, Landes followed the bombs' forward descent all the way down, right over their heads—and right into Lieutenant Kuhlmann's platoon to the west. One bomb was a dud, but one exploded. Captain Jordan and his FAC quickly called off the remaining Skyhawks[3] Lieutenant Kuhlmann thought it had been an NVA artillery round that landed some ten meters ahead of his crater, between him and his forward positions (he had been expecting a direct hit any minute), the explosion an unbelievably loud shock. He looked up to see earth and rocks soaring skyward from the subsurface explosion. Then they came back to earth in a crashing rain that pummeled his helmet and flak jacket, and dropped a twenty-five-pound chunk on his right ankle from perhaps a hundred feet. Kuhlmann tried to stand but couldn't. He tried to communicate with the semia-

3. Captain Giles (CO, K/3/9) offered a different explanation, "I was informed on the FAC radio that we had some available aircraft on the way and that I could use them on the NVA positions directly to my front. Two aircraft arrived on station and I defined and marked the target for them. After being assured that they had the target in sight, I gave them clearance to make their first run. I noticed the first aircraft lining up differently than others had, more north-south, yet felt the pilot knew where he was heading. To my horror and too late to stop the run, I realized the pilot was lining up on fires burning in the 1/3 area rather than on the white phosphorus markers we had on the targets. I watched the bombs slowly arc right into 1/3's positions, silently praying that they would miss. They didn't."

nonymous faces around him (half his platoon were post-Okinawa replacements) but could not, nor could he understand what they were saying to him. And through the shock, concussion, and confusion, Kuhlmann realized he was completely deaf. His eardrums had been ruptured, and he understood then that he had not actually heard the crashing of the debris but had instead only felt the vibrations of their individual impacts.

In position just west of Route 561, Corporal Collopy of India 3/9 watched the Skyhawk drop its two bombs. First Sergeant Lee was up there with them, and Collopy asked, "Hey, isn't that where that other unit is?"

"Yeah, it sure is."

On the heels of the explosion came the bellows for corpsmen, and Collopy muttered, "I can't believe that shit. Well, I guess I can 'cause it happened. That's enough of this, I'm going back to my hole."

Although deafened and half in shock as blood ran from his ears, Lieutenant Kuhlmann protested the attention his corpsman was giving him in the crater. He mumbled at the man to attend to their other casualties: eight others had been wounded, including bad sprains or broken limbs from the flying rocks. But the corpsman ignored him as he cut the laces to the jungle boot on Kuhlmann's right foot and gingerly removed the boot. The ankle was painfully swollen, and a splint was quickly fashioned from two sticks and some wrap. Kuhlmann ended up between two Marines and was hobbling back in this weakened condition when Captain Jordan passed him on his way up with his company headquarters and additional corpsmen. Jordan instructed his exec, Matsumoto, to take over Kuhlmann's platoon. Then, the ever-calm Jordan continued bringing order to this chaos, but as he moved, talked, and looked, he was seething inside. In less than five hours, he'd lost his two best platoon commanders.

And a Marine's disembodied leg lay in the dirt before him. Its previous owner, PFC Ronald R. Barcalow, was also in the dirt, corpsmen bent over him. Although he would survive the medevac ride (along with his leg which someone had thought to carry to the casualty collection point), Barcalow would die on the hospital ship.

Meanwhile, Staff Sergeant Reynolds's 2d Platoon, at the rear of Alpha Company's two-up-and-one-back formation, was ordered by Captain Jordan to turn around and resecure the night positions they had advanced from that morning. The wounded from the air strikes were to be taken through them to the Trace. Two Sea Horses pulled off with the bloody and the bruised, and upon landing at Dong Ha their stretchers were laid on the runway. As soon as the choppers lifted off again, a group of correspondents appeared from nowhere to bombard the wounded with questions. *Like a bunch of vultures,* thought Lieutenant Kuhlmann. No, they were more like a *covey of quail,* he reconsidered when at that moment an NVA artillery round landed some five hundred meters away on the base, and the correspondents took off running. A few more rounds crashed in, none of them close, but Kuhlmann, who had managed to limp to the entrance of a nearby bunker, was enraged that none of the able-bodied correspondents had taken the time to carry a stretcher into the shelter. *Scared rabbits!* Corpsmen arrived to get the wounded into the aid station, and Kuhlmann was lying on a litter there when more of his men arrived, including his radio operator. They were not wounded, but they had been found in nonfunctioning dazes from the bomb blast.

The damn place sounds like the rifle range at Parris Island, thought Sergeant Bouchard, the Right Guide of Alpha Two, as the exchange of automatic-weapons fire began again up where bombed-out Alpha One was deployed. Bouchard didn't know that his platoon commander, Kendig, had been medevacked, and in fact, he didn't know where the rest of his platoon was. He was with the 3d Squad, which had led the way back to their original holes so as to assist with the movement of Alpha One's casualties to the Trace.

The rest of the platoon had not joined them there. Bouchard crouched with the squad leader and his radioman (mortars were still coming in), as they tried unsuccessfully to raise the rest. Finally, Bouchard decided to send two runners back forward to try to reestablish contact. After a reasonable period of time, twenty minutes or so, the runners came back. They said that after getting the casualties back, the rest of the platoon had been ordered north again, and 3d Squad hadn't gotten the word. They started north. *Hairy,* Bouchard thought. There were places on the trail where the NVA fire was so intense you couldn't raise your head six inches, but amid all the attendant noise and confusion, they rejoined Alpha Two. Informed that Lieutenant Kendig had been medevacked, Bouchard immediately concerned himself with finding Staff Sergeant Reynolds, the next man in the chain of command.

Staff Sergeant Reynolds was in a hole behind the main firing line. He appeared frozen with fear, and Bouchard hollered to him, "Hey, what the hell you doin'? What the hell's going on?"

"Don't panic—the captain will tell us what to do!"

"The captain's too goddamned busy!"

Staff Sergeant Reynolds, his tour almost over, seemed on the verge of hyperventilating, and Bouchard realized that he had to take charge. He did not hesitate; he was, after all, a handsome, cocky career man (age twenty-four) —*a real ball of fire,* in the words of the medevacked Kendig. He called the squad leaders up and they seemed relieved to have someone decisive giving directions. They weren't, however, going anywhere.

27

Try, Try Again

★

From the slope where Kilo 3/9 had settled during the firepower show, their two attached M48 tanks, noted the after-action report, "fired on targets of opportunity accounting for 5 NVA KIA's."

Meanwhile, Mechanical Mules delivered ammunition, water, and rations; plus, coming by foot, arrived none other than Captain Swigart, the S-4 Logistics Officer for 3/9. He was accompanied by a black radio operator from India Company. Captain Giles was absolutely stunned to see Swigart, for he knew Swigart only had about two days left before he was to return to the rear for the three-day out processing. He stood up to greet him with, "Bob, what the fuck are you doing out here?"

Captain Swigart wore a brand-new helmet and helmet cover, brand-new jungle boots, brand-new jungle utilities, and brand-new web gear, and as they sat back down, Giles had to comment, "Bob, you look just like a typical S-four officer. Look at all this nice new shit you're wearing. Look at us here in rags and bags. *What are you doing out here?*"

The answer, of course, was the contact of 21 May 1967 when Swigart, as CO of M Company, had lost Marines while killing no NVA, and had thus been relieved of command and exiled to the S-4 shop. Swigart said as much in answer to Giles, "Well, you know Woody's my buddy, and I really can't go home without at least having led a company in combat successfully, so the other company commander was due to rotate home today, and Woody has allowed me to fly in to take over India Company for the next two days. So, at least when I go home I can say that I served successfully as a company commander."

Swigart got a bit more serious, "So, what have you got scheduled for the rest of the afternoon?"

"Well, Woody and I have been talking on the radio, and in about twenty minutes we're going to jump off once again and try to sweep this area to our front out to about five hundred to eight hundred meters."

"Great, great, sounds like an easy task."

Specifically, Kilo Company was to move forward with their tanks and two India Company platoons and recover the twelve KIAs they had previously left. Giles cautioned Swigart, "No, it's not going to be an easy task. Now what I want you to do since you don't know your platoon leaders, and you don't know your NCOs—you don't know your Marines—what I want you to do is to sit right here in this hole and have a cup of coffee while we do this."

Giles radioed back to Woody Woodring, "Request permission to have elements of India Company attached to Kilo Company during this sweep and have *new* India Six take command after the sweep."

"Roger that. That's a great idea."

Giles liked Swigart and, getting off the radio, turned to him again, "So, you promise me, you're going to sit right here, and you're going to have a cup of coffee, and you're going to watch us go out and do our thing. And then when we come back I'll give your company back to you."

Swigart reluctantly agreed. As Giles stood up to get

into his equipment harness and helmet—it was time to go —Swigart smiled despite his disappointment. "You know, I talked to my wife last night on the MARS station, and she's flying out today from the East Coast to the West Coast. I'm flying home in a few days, and we're going to have an absolute blast there in California. Just my wife and myself."

Moving forward again (as of 1630, 4 July 1967), one of the freely sweating, helmeted and flak jacketed, don't-know-where-I-am-or-what-we're-doing ants in the sweep, Corporal Collopy of India One finally saw a soldier of the North Vietnamese Army. The man was dead. Collopy had been following a tank through bamboo, and there, suddenly visible in the tank's splintered, mashed-down wake, was this NVA, previously shot and killed and now crushed where he had fallen. He had Chicom grenades fixed to his belt, the potato-masher type, one of which had been flattened by the tank. Collopy thought to souvenir one of the grenades but decided to let it go—*nah, this guy's probably booby trapped.*

The NVA had mostly retired from this freshly cratered and napalmed area, leaving behind snipers and RPG teams to harass—to kill—but not to stay and fight. Usually. Corporal Gomez of India Two ended up behind a paddy dike when an NVA machine gunner opened up on his point squad from thirty meters ahead. Pinned down, Gomez could just make out a muzzle flash deep in the brush of a bit of high ground, and shouting, he directed this squad's return fire. But then good buddy Bus Summers, on the left end of the squad line, hollered, "D.J., my rifle's jammed! I don't have a cleaning rod!"

"Well, get one!"

A flattened Marine to Gomez's right hollered that he had one, and Summers shouted, "Bring it down here to me!"

"Fuck you—come down and get it!"

Amid the laughing, the cleaning rod was passed down. Meanwhile, Gomez was on the radio with their company

headquarters (which was under cover in the hedgerows behind them) as they tried to figure out just what the hell to
do. Artillery was suggested, but Gomez responded, "That's
a big negative," explaining that his squad was too close to
the target. Finally, Gomez said that their machine-gun
team would have to be moved forward to provide suppres-
sive fire so that he could maneuver two of his fireteams to
envelop the lone, well-entrenched diehard.

Without exposing his head above the dike, Gomez
continued reloading and blindly raising his M79 in the
NVA's direction. He watched in relief and respect as Corporal Lempa, their machine-gun squad leader, exposed
himself to get two M60 teams set up some sixty meters to
his right rear. *Fantastic,* Gomez thought; *the way those bunkers were situated, they covered each other so another bunker
could have opened up on Lempa's gun teams.* These brave
machine gunners devastated the NVA position with hundreds upon hundreds of rounds (the equally brave NVA
kept firing), covering the one fireteam that pushed off
down the dike to the right and the other crawling low to
the left. After each had gone some thirty meters to the
flanks, they went over the top and into the brush. Working
their way behind the NVA, the fireteams then lobbed hand
grenades from the maximum throwing distance until the
NVA gun finally went silent. At that, the line rose again to
continue forward.

The nickel and diming continued. Corporal Collopy
crouched for a moment near his buddy, PFC Mitchell Frye
(better known as Small Fry because of his slight build),
who did likewise to his right, but behind some brushy
cover. Then Collopy suddenly heard a single round snap
past him. Frye, a much better target with a radio on his
back, dropped with a blurted, *"Oh!"*

Collopy moved to Frye, who'd taken the round
through his radio and flak jacket and into his back. "You'll
be all right, Small Fry."

India One's Right Guide, Sergeant Crosby, checked
Frye's wound, then said to the Marines who were ready to
carry him rearward, "Okay, go ahead back."

Not long afterward, Corporal Collopy passed the latest victim, Sergeant Crosby himself, who sat with a field dressing tied around his arm. The sweep continued, and once again there came the fire of an NVA sniper so close the Marines could hear the report of his rifle and the whip snap of his rounds over their prone bodies though they could not see a muzzle flash or a bush move. PFC Ford sought shelter this time in a shallow gully running along a hedgerow. The sergeant behind him suddenly screamed, *"My God, I'm hit!"* Ford turned, wondering how the sniper had missed him to hit the man to his rear. The sergeant was screaming and clutching his knee. Without hesitating or really comprehending what he was doing, training took over as Ford grabbed the sergeant, ripped open his trouser leg from thigh to ankle (the end of the bullet was visible in the kneecap), and plucked the round out. It was still hot and burned his fingers. Ford threw it aside, tied a battle dressing around the sergeant's knee as other Marines moved to them, and moments after being hit the sergeant was being helped back.

Kilo, on the left flank of India, had advanced some eighty meters when they began taking long-range machine-gun fire. It was obviously a rear-guard action, and not accurate enough to cause the Marines to exert the energy (the heat was terrible) to run to cover. Kilo was still humping along without pause or injury, when the platoon commander running India radioed Giles. "We're taking too many casualties. We're going to pull back."

"How many casualties have you taken?"

India Company had, to that point, suffered one KIA and four WIA, and Giles responded, *"Bullshit.* I'm giving you a direct order under combat conditions to continue to move."

Soon thereafter, Giles's senior radioman, Charpentier, suddenly turned to him. "Sir, India Six is KIA."

"India *Six?* Do you mean the platoon leader?"

"I don't know."

"Well, call back and find out if he's talking about the India Six platoon leader, or new India Six Actual."

A moment on the radio, then Charpentier looked to Giles again, "Sir, new India Six is a KIA."

What the hell? Giles could make no sense of it. He'd left Swigart in the hole where the gunny and he had had cups of coffee for the five hours the air and arty had come in, *and now all of a sudden he's a KIA?* Kilo moved on up into the ambush area, where they found a few bloody NVA pith helmets and some bloody NVA web gear. They also recovered the twelve dead Marines who'd been left behind (including, Giles checked, the man who'd wanted a cigarette who was now crumpled dead beside the tree he'd been leaning against). Napalm runs by Marine Air had started fires that had scorched some of the Marine dead before burning themselves out. *A final indignity,* Giles thought. With shoulders hunched instinctively, drawing downward to present a smaller target, and wincing at every burst of fire and whistling, sailing RPG, the Marines of Kilo Company continued northward. The terrain began to fall off toward the Ben Hai River basin, and at this point Major Woodring gave the word to go ahead and roll back to the battalion's new positions along the east-west trail. This they did at a slow pace, picking up their dead on the way back, with India Company returning in tandem to the east.

By 1830, Kilo Company was back in position, and in the exact same holes they had just left. Gunny Hatfield again had his C rations and a pinch of C4 out, making coffee as Captain Giles sat beside him. There was a dead, poncho-wrapped Marine about eight feet behind their hole. They ignored him. Giles commented then, "I wonder what the hell happened to old Swigart?"

He contacted the radioman who'd been with Swigart before the sweep, "How 'bout reportin' up here?". Then asked him after he walked over, "Where in the hell is Captain Swigart?"

"Sir, he's right behind you."

Giles realized that the dead man behind him (the poncho was not closed securely) was wearing brand-new utilities, brand-new jungle boots. . . . Giles turned away as the radioman explained, "Right after you guys jumped off, and you got down there about a hundred yards, Captain Swigart said, 'Let's go ahead and follow in their trace and see what it's all about.' Sir, we didn't get down there more than fifty, seventy-five yards, and we're standin' there, and all of a sudden I hear a crack of a rifle, and Captain Swigart crumples to the ground. And I knelt down next to him, and he'd been shot just above the eye."

Giles could imagine the obvious target Swigart had presented, standing beside a radioman in his new, bright green gear. He shook his head, his emotional flak jacket momentarily coming apart as he looked at the poncho and those boots and thought of Swigart's wife, still excited from their phone conversation, flying to meet him in California. *She has no idea. She won't even know. They probably won't be able to find her for three or four days. And all because a man was relieved of command. He made a choice to come out here so he could go home with pride—and he paid with his life for it. This war is not worth that man. It's not worth it.*

Then, before turning around to ask Hatfield for another sorry ass cup of coffee and worrying about the immediate, as he had learned to do, Giles took a last look at the dead friend in whose presence he would drink that coffee and eat his C ration. "Goddammit, Bob, I told you to stay fuckin' right here in the hole."

When Captain Swigart had been briefed by Captain Navadel earlier that afternoon, reporters had been present, and one had been especially impressed with the dedication Swigart displayed in returning to the field only days from going home. When word was received at the 3/9 CP that Swigart was KIA, this reporter (whom Navadel considered more knowledgeable of military matters than his fellows) bemoaned the cruelty of such an eleventh-hour death.

Navadel didn't want to hear it. He was thinking of Operation Cimmaron when he had taken over Mike Company following Swigart's relief, and of a young Navy corpsman who had come to the company the same day as he. During Lima and Mike's ferocious fight that day, the corpsman, despite Navadel's previous exhortations to stick with a certain squad leader until he'd learned the ropes, went tearing up there to take care of the wounded. He was killed on the spot. Thinking of that corpsman, but not speaking of him, Navadel spoke coldly to the reporter, "It doesn't make any difference whether you get it the first day or the last. It's all part of the tour."

With Swigart gone, Major Woodring looked at Navadel: he was to take command of India Company. They both knew that India needed a leader, especially with the potential morale dip at the news of a gunned-down company commander. Actually, a lot of the troops didn't know that Swigart had come aboard, and crusty Top Lee passed the word posthumously in terms of "that dumb sonuvabitch captain—I told him not to go up forward." India Company already had a leader in the person of the rangy, tobacco-chewing, and very funny First Sergeant Lee. Lee was another battalion original. In the rear, he was so horseshitty, he made life so miserable, that every screwing-off troop would do anything to get back up front with the company where he belonged. In the field, where Lee spent more time than the average first sergeant, he was a fighter. He was hit twice, once by their own stuff, though he reported neither wound, it being reward enough when the incomparable Major Woodring told him, "You're some kind of goddamn first sergeant."

Presently, Lee looked up at Captain Navadel's arrival, "Well, we were waiting for you to show up. 'Bout time you got here. Have a cup of coffee."

Navadel had left their tall, sharp ALO in charge of the S-3 shop when he went forward to take over as the new, new India Six. This was the fifth time during his tour that Navadel had commanded a rifle company, and after mapping out India's deployment for him, good old Top Lee grinned, "No sweat."

Captain Giles was not feeling similarly sturdy as Kilo Company set in along the new battalion line that was oriented along the west-to-east trail that ran into north-south

Route 561. He had come to Vietnam to experience war and to kill North Vietnamese, not because he ever hated them —in fact, he admired their skill—but because it was part of the chess game. By the time of Operation Buffalo his one and only personal mission was to keep young Marines alive. He had, at least in his own mind, failed at all three objectives, and he felt an awesome sense of guilt over their latest losses. Since returning from Okinawa four months earlier with 5 officers and 213 enlisted men, he'd had 3 lieutenants killed and 2 wounded, along with 78 KIAs and 180 WIAs among his grunts. It was a casualty rate of more than 100 percent, and to what end these Marines had valiantly sacrificed themselves, Giles could not decipher.

Gunny Hatfield was feeling the same way. He had been sorely touched by Lieutenant Anderson's death. *He was the kind of son everybody would like to have.* Giles had never seen this old Marine so frustrated as he talked of the young kids who'd joined the company, and how each had become a casualty and how senseless it was. Hatfield was thinking of his first day in Da Nang when, while processing in, he ran into an old friend and contemporary, a fellow gunnery sergeant, who was rotating out. The poor son of a bitch had looked worn out, and Hatfield had grimaced, "What the hell happened to you?"

"Man, I've been surviving. Let me tell you one goddamned thing. You ain't seen anything like this. Johnson and McNamara and that bunch of assholes. They put you in a no-win situation. Cover your ass. Get in there and forget all this apple-pie horseshit, and try to keep your ass alive and all the troops you possibly can. They've dumped something on us that we don't know what the hell to do with. Cover your fuckin' ass."

Gunny Hatfield realized now that his old friend had been right. It was horseshit, he thought, *real, genuine horseshit.* Bomb the jungle, but don't bomb Hanoi or Haiphong where the goddamned supplies came in. Give the enemy a sanctuary in Laos and above the Ben Hai where they can lick their wounds. Take a hill and give it up, then take it again, *and nobody give a goddamn! Our generals have just rolled over and handed the reins to the politicians.* Didn't any of them have any guts, he wondered. Didn't any of them value their troops' lives over their careers? *Westmoreland— that asshole! Either let us win the fucking war or pull us out!*

The hole in which Giles and Hatfield sat as the darkness gathered around them was not very deep. The ground was hard and they were tired.

PART SIX

CAM LO
SIDESHOW

★

In the main, Operation Buffalo was fought north of the Gio Linh-Con Thien Strip with (under the operational control of Colonel Jerue, CO, 9th Marines) 1/9 (Schening) and 3/9 (Woodring) of the 3d Marine Division, and BLT 1/3 (Wickwire) of SLF Alpha, 9th MAB. However, south of the Strip, 2/9 (LtCol John J. Peeler until 4 July 1967, then LtCol William D. Kent) also played a role, although not one recorded in the official histories. The primary mission of 2/9 at this time was to secure Cam Lo and the Cam Lo Bridge, as well as that section of Route 561 that ran through Leatherneck Square, and to be prepared to provide a counterattack force in case of enemy activity against the Cam Lo Resettlement Area. Operation Buffalo also employed a fifth battalion, namely BLT 2/3 (Maj Wendell O. Beard) of SLF Bravo, 9th MAB. Designated Operation Beaver Track by the SLF (and under the operational control of Colonel Stockman, CO, 3d Marines), BLT 2/3's part in Buffalo was to sweep Leatherneck Square between Cam Lo and Con Thien and provide a screen of sorts for the rear of the battalions doing the hard fighting above the Strip. Unlike 2/9 (which was already in place when Buffalo began), BLT 2/3 was at the time of the Marketplace Massacre south of Da Nang in a place called Pagoda Valley. There, they were wrapping up Operation Beacon Torch for the 1st Marine Division.

28

Moose Beard's Orphans

★

When BLT 2/3 helicoptered into Pagoda Valley on 18 June 1967, their CO, Maj Wendell O. Beard, established his CP near the graffiti-covered walls of a sturdy little stucco-type building in a deserted hamlet. Problems at this time with poorly designed Sea Knight were such that the SLF's eighteen or so helicopters could usually land the first BLT wave without difficulty, but back on ship most would then be "down" with maintenance problems. So when Colonel Wortman, CO of SLF Bravo, arrived in his personal Huey, Major Beard's first question was, "Colonel, how many birds you got flying?"

"Two—and they're both marginal."

Pursuant to Wortman's desires, the BLT had always rendered after-action reports which spoke of flawless operations, each of which had "confirmed the inherent mobility of the Special Landing Force." So now Major Beard got that old mischievous look in his eyes, "Well, Colonel, I guess in your next after-action report you'll have to refer to the inherent *immobility* of the Special Landing Force."

Colonel Wortman was instantly a red-faced, sputtering monument to breached formalities. "Well, I'll see about that! I'll see how many choppers you get!"

No ticket-puncher, Major Beard was instead a huge man who stood six-foot-four and who weighed in around two-thirty (he was known as the Moose), and a natural, unflappable, grunt-oriented commander. Maj John H. Broujos, XO, BLT 2/3, and, like Beard, a decorated Korean veteran, remembered him:

> Beard was very outspoken, and he would let people know exactly what was on his mind, regardless of who it was or what the circumstances were. He had kind of a nonchalant, devil-may-care attitude, but the guy had a heart of gold. I'll never forget standing next to him at memorial service aboard ship when he lost some troops —he had tears streaming down his eyes.

Beard's subordinates, at the receiving end of his high, whiney-voiced, Patton-like tongue lashings were just a bit less enthused. Most would have agreed with Capt Richard O. Culver, CO, H BLT 2/3, when he said, "Moose was a competent sonuvabitch, but he was also the world's most abrasive human being. I could have cheerfully killed him a million times, but you had to love him."

Major Beard, loyal but combative, had been passed over at least once for selection to lieutenant colonel. Nevertheless, he had been given command of a battalion in combat without those prerequisite silver oak leaves. Further, after Beard was evacuated with malaria (on the last day of Operation Beaver Track/Buffalo) and a lieutenant colonel was brought in, the new light colonel lasted less than a month before a still-recuperating Beard was brought back to replace the man. It was a matter of no small aggravation among Beard's officers that, while the Marine Corps was willing to use the Moose as a combat commander (and to recognize him as one so good that they'd rather give the battalion back to him than to all those lieutenant colonels on Okinawa waiting for such a chance), the establishment was not also willing officially to recognize him with a promotion commensurate with his responsibilities. Still, if BLT 2/3 was a reflection of Moose Beard's pugnacious, the-hell-with-the-formalities-let's-do-the-job style (and it was), the fact that Beard was overlooked at the promotion boards was matched by the mood of his Marines that they, too, were orphans, sent into hot spot after hot spot without support, recognition, or respite.

BLT 2/3 had organized on Okinawa fresh from the Battle of 28 February 1967 near Cam Lo in which the 100-plus casualties had included the CO of G (KIA), the battalion sergeant major (KIA), the battalion operations officer (WIA), and the battalion commander (KIA). Joining SLF Bravo, BLT 2/3's first landing was Operation Beacon Star (22 April–12 May 1967) which included several days above Hue along the Street Without Joy (1 USMC KIA, 10 USMC WIA), then a scramble to the Khe Sanh Hill Fights (71 USMC KIA, 349 USMC WIA). Next came Operation Belt Tight/Hickory (20–28 May 1967) in the southern side of the DMZ (17 USMC KIA, 152 USMC WIA), then Operations Prairie IV (28–31 May 1967) and Cimarron (1–10 June 1967) near Cam Lo, and then, of course, Beacon Torch. After fourteen days in and around Pagoda Valley, BLT 2/3 terminated Operation Beacon Torch at 1300, 2 July 1967, having taken 13 USMC KIA in exchange for the claim of 86 NVA kills. The landing had been another sword thrust in the water (even the official history noted it "had no lasting impact, as emphasized by the fact that the departing Marines sighted enemy troops near the beach during the retraction"), and BLT 2/3 retired on the wings of HMM-164 to the sanctuary USS *Tripoli,* USS *Ogden,* USS *Monticello,* and USS *Carol County.* Shortly thereafter, early on 3 July 1967, a message was received from III MAF requesting that SLF Bravo proceed to the vicinity of the Cua Viet River and prepare to support 3d Marine Division units heavily engaged northeast of Con Thien. With tentative planning underway, it was at 0200, 4 July 1967, that the request was received from III MAF to commence landing BLT 2/3 astride Route 561 above Cam Lo as of 0700, 4 July 1967, and then to sweep Leatherneck Square north to Con Thien.

"Tomorrow we land somewhere in the Republic of Vietnam at an unknown time, to meet an unknown NVA force with an unknown amount of support, and I don't know how long it will last."

Capt James P. Sheehan, CO, G BLT 2/3, usually began his on-ship briefings before new operations with a tension-breaking grin for the Marines in a semicircle around him. Given the anxiety of being sent into new, unfamiliar, and, usually, red-hot areas, it was best to keep it light. Especially now, as Sheehan told his men that an entire company of the 9th Marines had been overrun near Con Thien by a large NVA force posing as Marines in captured gear. As they understood it, this company had seen the NVA coming but had hesitated because of the USMC uniforms and had been waiting for confirmation of friendlies in the area when the NVA revealed themselves at close range and overwhelmed them. Now, the Z was swarming with NVA.

Golf Company was ready, in large part because of their absolute faith in Captain Sheehan whom they called Big Jim or Jungle Jim. Having come aboard on Okinawa, the meat-grinder hill assaults at Khe Sanh had been the crucible by which he had become a walking demigod to his young Marines. Sheehan was a ramrod-straight, spit 'n' polish Captain of Marines who also had a ready smile and a good word for these riflemen, many of whom he knew by name. His influence was such that as the men returned to their below-deck, air-conditioned sleeping quarters following the briefing, the rest of their equipment-straightening, prelanding night was nothing like the somber depictions that Cpl Dean A. Caton, a squad leader in the Third Herd, had seen in the movies:

We would spend the evening checking gear and getting psyched up. We would talk big, tell the new guys stories, and joke about who would get hit. We would read fake news stories and sing platoon songs. A coach would be able to compare it to the last practice before a big game, and an outside observer would think us a crazy macho bunch. But it was really a way to hide fear and burn off nervous energy. At least for me.

The Third Herd of Golf Company was a good example of the rough-and-ready Marines in Moose Beard's battalion. Though the platoon commander was on paper one Staff Sergeant Arnold, he was regarded as a scared and confused but likeable old lifer, and their real honcho was Sgt Charles R. McWhorter who had three years in the Corps and was only twenty-one. Before the Corps there had been the Hell's Angels, and this young platoon sergeant's flak jacket was magic-markered like a motorcycle vest to include the trademark skull on the back and the nickname "Morgan" over the left-front pocket. McWhorter was so emulated in the Third Herd that many of his grunts similarly personalized their flak gear. Tough, young, cocky, and brash, McWhorter had decided on a career in olive drab, although he was as intolerant as his troopies of the regulations that ruled their lives. Corporal Caton commented on Sergeant Mac's style:

We came out of the field to a little base camp called Evans. We were in line for our first hot meal in several weeks when a gunnery sergeant, not of our company, told us we couldn't be served because we were out of uniform. We didn't have helmets. Of course we were pissed but we started to leave the front of the line. Mac showed up and told us to stay in line. The gunny went wild. His exact words were, "I'm not used to being talked to like that by a mere sergeant." Mac replied, "Well, you better damn well get used to it if you try to fuck with my people." He also made some references to the easy life of fat rear pogues. Mac got his ass chewed later, but he took care of us and that's why you follow a man when you're scared shitless in a firefight.

At this time, all of Sergeant McWhorter's squad leaders had been with the Third Herd since before the Battle of 28 February 1967. The newest of them was the short, wiry, bespectacled Corporal Caton who had fought hard to get into the Marine Corps despite several medical problems. Nicknamed Dino because of his first name Dean (after the pet dinosaur on the Fred Flintstone cartoon), Caton's squad was known as Dino's Dinosaurs.

Lance Corporal Machado, another squad leader, was a short-timer. He was a stocky Mexican—his squad was nicknamed the Bean Bandits—of a terse, high-strung, and highly competitive nature.

The third squad was led by Corporal Blackman, a big, tall, slow-talking black from Mobile, Alabama, whom everyone called the Bear and whose squad was nicknamed the Cubs. Blackman was something of a legend not only because of his bush smarts and courage (at Khe Sanh he had neglected to report his shrapnel wounds so as to remain with his squad), but also because like many super combat leaders he was a bum in garrison. In fact, during the battalion's month long refitting on Okinawa he simply disappeared and did not return until shortly before they steamed for Vietnam. Brought before the incumbent battalion commander and asked why he shouldn't be court-martialed for his unauthorized vacation, Blackman answered (as the grunts told it), "Because I'm the best squad leader you've got and you can't afford to Go South without me."

Tuesday, 4 July 1967. The flight deck of the USS *Ogden* sizzled as the 3d Platoon of Golf Company, Battalion Landing Team 2/3, waited their turn to be helo-lifted into Operation Beaver Track/Buffalo. Finally, a goggled member of the helicopter support team waved them toward a Sea Knight that had alighted on the deck after ferrying another platoon ashore. Corporal Caton had a lump in his throat as he walked up the back ramp, despite the M79 grenade launcher in his hands (HAVE 79, WILL TRAVEL was emblazoned across the back of his flak jacket) and the bravado-bolstering bull's-eye drawn on his helmet front with the logo DING CHARLIE DING.

"Tight."

"Tight."

The Marines of Third Herd slapped the chest of the guy beside them with the back of their hands as they headed for the chopper, reaffirming their brotherhood with a single word.

"Tight."

Corporal Caton sat down inside the dark, vibrating interior of the Sea Knight. This was the worst part for him. Everyone thought SLF duty was great with its navy mess, air-conditioned living quarters, showers, movies, and all the rest, but they were rarely on ship more than a few days at a time, and when they went back ashore it was usually because someone was in trouble. It was that instant movement from total security to total danger that he found so gut wrenching. The Sea Knight lifted off and swung west, joining three others in a staggered line that closed quickly on the shoreline. Caton said something badass and funny. So did the others, making reference to the real live Fourth of July fireworks they could expect.

The Sea Knights of HMM-164 began the helo-lift at 0640. They took aboard Major Beard, CO, BLT 2/3, and Hotel Company from the command ship USS *Tripoli,* and landed them at Cam Lo at 0705. From Cam Lo, Beard and his Command Group Alpha were ferried by Sea Knight to Landing Zone Canary (an unoccupied clearing astride Route 561, approximately one and a half kilometers northwest of Cam Lo), arriving at 0810.

At 0820, H Company, under Capt Robert O. Culver (a second-generation Marine, a former sergeant, and a hellraiser), completed its lift into LZ Canary from Cam Lo.

At 0950, F Company, under 1st Lt Richard D. Koehler (who was stocky, quiet, and competent), completed its lift into LZ Canary from SLF shipping.

At 1045, E Company, under Capt Robert N. Bogard (a hard-core former sergeant), completed its lift into LZ Canary from SLF shipping.

At 1250, G Company, under Capt James P. Sheehan (rock steady and charismatic), completed its lift into LZ Canary from SLF shipping.

At 1300, Colonel Stockman, CO, 3d Marines, officially took operational control of BLT 2/3 and issued the frag order that outlined their mission. BLT 2/3 was to sweep north of LZ Canary, dig in for the night, and continue their northward attack the next morning on a four-kilometer front to a point just southwest of Con Thien. There the battalion would wheel to the west, advance another three kilometers, then turn south and sweep down to the Cam Lo River on an axis parallel to but west of the original movement north. As it was explained to Major Beard, Major Broujos, and their S-3, Maj D.W. Lemon, units opcon to the 3d Marines had been in the area only two days previously but (as night follows day) reconnaissance elements from the 29th NVA Regiment were slipping back into the area in advance of their parent organization.

At 1330, BLT 2/3 departed LZ Canary. F Company (Koehler) moved to the west then commenced the sweep to the north, which was on three axes once E Company (Bogard) and H Company (Culver) came on line. A platoon of M48 tanks from A Company, 3d Tank Battalion, had arrived from Cam Lo, and E and H Companies were accompanied by two apiece. Meanwhile, G Company (Sheehan) was taxed with security for Beard's CP. As such, they would be the last to leave LZ Canary, and as they waited, Captain Sheehan noticed jeeps and trucks on Route 561 with helmetless, unflak-jacketed Marines aboard. As he later commented, "The impression we had had was we were going into a meat grinder, that the front had fallen up in the Z, but then we were wondering, 'What the hell, our R&R to the Philippines was cancelled for *this?'* "

★

Two hours into the hump out of LZ Canary, 2d Lt James Roscoe Cannon, XO, E BLT 2/3, who was traveling with the rear platoon, received word by radio that they had a heat casualty up ahead. The man, an ammo humper with the attached 81mm mortar team, had passed out, and the corpsman attending him requested a medevac. A boot lieutenant would have let it go at that, but Lieutenant Cannon was a son of the poverty of King George, Virginia, a mustang who had already pulled a tour as a staff sergeant platoon commander with the 3d Marines in 1965. He thought it suspicious that the ammo humper had passed out in the first clearing they had reached that would accommodate a helicopter, so he made his way up the column to where the man lay stripped of his gear.

Cannon knelt beside the ammo humper and, playing a hunch, asked one of the riflemen there for the safety pin holding his bandoliers in place. Cannon explained that he had to pin the unconscious man's tongue to his lip so he wouldn't swallow it. When Cannon attempted this, the man sprang to his feet, and Cannon spoke sharply to the malingerer. "Okay, get on your pack and let's get on with what's going to happen. Move out, Marine."[1]

There existed between Lieutenant Cannon and the Marines of Echo Company a definite love-hate relationship. From Cannon's point of view, there was no doubting the courage of his men. But when it came to such matters as camouflage, digging in, and avoiding the less tiring (but often booby-trapped) avenues like paddy dikes and man-made hedgerow openings, they could be lethally careless. The biggest killer of Marines in Vietnam was not the North Vietnamese Army, Cannon thought, but the Marines' own

---

1. Captain Bogard remembered that it was he who tried the safety-pin trick. Bogard added, "If we evacuated a guy for heat exhaustion, the next thing you'd know we'd have ten cases of heat exhaustion—they'd see that helicopter come in and this guy *leaves* on it, so it's all of a sudden a neat idea to have heat exhaustion. You learn pretty quickly that unless the guy is literally dying, you don't evacuate him because you're going to lose half your damned outfit because they all want to go back to the ship."

willingness to adhere to the by-the-book procedures that made life miserable on a day-to-day basis but increased their chances of surviving in the long run. This seemed especially true at night. They did not lie still in ambush sites. They did not blacken their faces when going out on listening posts. They did not always go where they were told, and on one occasion two nervous LPs pulled back without permission, resulting in one LP mistaking the other for NVA and lobbing a grenade that left one Marine dead and another with one less leg. They did not always stay awake on night watch, something that infuriated Cannon to the point that one night when he crawled out to find an LP asleep at the switch, he pistol-whipped the kid whose turn it was on watch.

The men of Echo Company were least receptive to these methods during Cannon's initial service as the 2d Platoon Commander during the relatively fallow days before Khe Sanh when the lack of contact prevented him from displaying his combat expertise, so that he appeared simply as a cocky bastard. (When the platoon actually nailed two NVA in an ambush, the corpses ended up with ECHO 2 ANIMALS carved across their chests, for which Cannon was rebuked by battalion.) Hard feelings escalated out of control with talk of fragging Cannon, up until the day the newly formed BLT was rushed to Khe Sanh. When, during the battle, the NVA swarmed into Echo's perimeter in a banzai-style night attack, Lieutenant Cannon was an NVA-killing and perimeter-repairing dynamo. His reward was the Silver Star, two Purple Hearts, and the cessation of all behind-the-back threats.

The grunts came to depend on Cannon for their lives, but there was little fondness for this man with his name and a Civil War cannon tattooed on his forearm, whose stated goal was to win the Congressional Medal of Honor. The man never seemed to step off stage. The morning after a grueling night attack, Echo Company rounded up an NVA lieutenant whose jaw had been shot away so that his cheeks hung down, and one could look down his throat. The NVA's arms were tied behind his back for the walk to

the medevac LZ, which the dazed NVA took slowly until
Cannon gave him a shove from behind. "Come on, you
fucker." *Jesus Christ,* thought a watching grunt. *Here's this
guy walking around without a jaw and you're playing fucking
Sergeant Rock!*

, The hump from LZ Canary continued.

Captain Sheehan's Golf Company, along with Major
Beard's CP, were the last to depart the hasty perimeter
alongside Route 561 (and only after medevacking the leg-
shot victim of an accidental discharge) to join the northward sweep. Their movement through the hot, hilly, and
brushy terrain took them through several small, deserted
hamlets where they paused to search without result, so that
by dusk, when each company stopped to dig in independ-
ently, the main topic of conversation was their surprise at
not making contact considering the situation into which
they'd been dropped.

After digging in, the Third Herd of Golf Company
observed their night-time ritual of watching it get dark together, identifying various trees and bamboo thickets that
they knew at night would appear to move. Third Herd's
listening post for the night had gone to LCpl Denny Johnson's fireteam (from Machado's squad), so along with Jake
Livingston Haloo, Tom Huckaba, and Joe Ray Whitted,
they found a spot about 300 meters forward of the platoon.
They divided up the watch time, but when the nervous new
guy Whitted (soon to be an excellent Marine) was up to
bat, he saw things everywhere and made it difficult for everyone else to sleep.

Suddenly, something real: an explosion.

In response, a flare was popped from the platoon line,
and Huckaba looked back from his prone position, wondering what the hell was going on. He could see the silhouette of the perimeter in the eerie flare light.

Johnson got on the radio, but no one at the CP knew
what the explosion had been. They said they would get
back to him. Johnson, Haloo, Huckaba, and Whitted went
to full alert until the CP called back. The only explanation

they could offer was that the explosion had been an outgoing grenade. The entire company was now on alert, and the LP was returned to the perimeter. Nothing further developed, and in the morning an explanation made its way through the enlisted ranks after one Lance Corporal Albright from 2d Platoon confessed to a couple friends that he'd thrown the grenade because, as he put it, somebody had to say Happy Fourth of July.

29

Ghosts

★

On Wednesday, 5 July 1967, 1/3 and 3/9 got 1/9's bodies back. Specifically, at 0450, the guns began booming again against the front occupied by 3/9 (Major Woodring) and BLT 1/3 (Lieutenant Colonel Wickwire) above the Trace. The weight of the NVA barrage was on the BLT. Approximately one hundred 60mm and 82mm mortar rounds landed on A Company (Jordan) wounding five men, and another hundred fell on B Company (Landes) wounding one. At 0545, outgoing mixed with incoming as Marine artillery was initiated in preparation for the upcoming body-recovery sweep. The arty prep was lifted at 0635, and next, from 0700 to 0730, air strikes were employed.

Meanwhile, at 0715, Woodring jumped off in the attack with I (Navadel), K (Giles), and L/3/9 (Shirley) west of Route 561. Wickwire followed suit east of the road with A (Jordan) and B (Landes) BLT 1/3, accompanied by a section of tanks from A/3d Tank Battalion, which had arrived only twenty-five minutes earlier. These five companies stepped slowly through this desolate, pulverized terrain, but (as noted in the 3/9 after-action report) they encountered only signs of an NVA withdrawal:

> At 050856, both Companies I and K reached the LOA. 050919 Co L reported finding 15 of 1/9 MIA's halfway to the LOA (YD 135725). Within the next hour Co L uncovered a minefield with 20 assorted mines, 1-250# bomb, and 2-500# bombs all set for electrical detonation. All ordnance was blown in place with C-4. At 051000 Co I set out OP's approximately 75 meters from their position. Negative contact resulted. S-2 captured one crypto authentication table at an 81mm position. 051030 Co L captured 43 rounds of 82mm with a large amount of increments and cleaning gear at YD 131723. 051121 Co. I captured a 60mm mortar complete with base plate and bipod assembly at YD 130726.

The after-action report of BLT 1/3 likewise reflected burned-once-twice-shy caution, but little contact and steady progress:

> 050910   Co A, Co K and Co L at LOA, Co B had
>   contact with Co A and is moving up.
> 050920   Co's A and B advised to advance forward of
>   LOA with Co's K and L.
> 051028   149727 Co B spotted 15 VC, Arty fired,
>   results unknown. Co A reports 8 USMC KIA
>   from 1/9 to direct front.
> 051115   Co A sent 1/9 KIA's to rear on tanks.

The NVA had presumably retired during the night, and the day's task then became to recover the thirty-one MIAs from the Marketplace. Elements of 3/9 pushed north to secure the area, while elements from BLT 1/3 actually bagged and tagged the dead. The NVA had littered the area where the bodies lay with propaganda leaflets, whose photos of deserters and flag-burning demonstrators only made worse what was, in the understated words of Maj John C. Studt, XO, 3/9, who was sent forward to supervise, "a grisly task."

Captain Bogard, the CO of Echo BLT 2/3, could tell that the lieutenant from A Company, 3d Tank Battalion, whose two-tank section had joined him the day before, was an up-from-the-ranks pro. Nevertheless, as Echo Company stepped off at 0700, 5 July 1967 (along with the rest of BLT 2/3), to complete their Cam Lo-to-Con Thien sweep, the inherent problems of the lieutenant's beasts made Bogard increasingly intolerant of their presence. The occasional steepness of the hilly terrain through which they moved (north) limited the tanks' mobility and channelized the entire column through exposed areas that Bogard would otherwise have avoided. Even when they cleared the hills, the tank picture did not improve as providing them with flank security upset the established pattern. The tanks were a noisy anachronism, Bogard thought, that let everyone know they were coming.

By 1500, Echo Company had progressed to the vicinity of Thon Tan Hoa, some three kilometers almost due south of Con Thien. Captain Bogard called a break so they could get their bearings. As Lieutenant Cannon walked up from the rear of the column, he barked at various Marines who, instead of being in an alert posture, had taken advantage of this momentary pause to rest their weary bones. Cannon was joined by SSgt Robert Lee Morningstar, one of his old 2d Platoon favorites, a shotgun-toting, chain-smoking Indian who talked abusively of everyone, but who was actually a loyal, dedicated Marine NCO with a heart of gold.

Lieutenant Cannon and Staff Sergeant Morningstar stood shoulder to shoulder with Captain Bogard near one of the halted, engine-roaring tanks. Bogard had his map out for them.

Suddenly, a shot. Before his eyes, Bogard saw Morningstar instantly drop as the round smashed into one side of his chin. Hitting the deck, Bogard already knew what had happened. He had recognized the report of the shot as that of an SKS carbine, and he could picture a scope-equipped NVA sniper being drawn to their aerial-marked huddle. The sniper had skipped over him because he was younger looking than Morningstar and prudently wore his binoculars and shoulder-holstered .45 under his flak jacket. So the sniper had settled his cross hairs instead on the head of Morningstar who carried a shotgun, typically a company commander trademark.

While Cannon, also at the prone, requested an emergency medevac and Morningstar pointed weakly to the hole in his face, Bogard jumped to his feet and turned toward the tanks. He shouted at the tank lieutenant to lay fléchette rounds into those desicated tree lines where the shot might have come from—he was at least sure where it *hadn't* originated—but between the noise of the tank engines and the general confusion of the situation, it took several minutes for Bogard to get his instructions across. The tanks did open fire, but by this time, Bogard knew the NVA were long gone.

And Staff Sergeant Morningstar was dead, the face shot having ricocheted internally to blast out his chest. In moments, a helicopter arrived to medevac Morningstar's body and a wounded man. Major Beard contacted Captain Bogard by radio, "I heard you lost your sergeant."

"Yes, he was like the Morning Star."

They spoke cryptically because the rules did not allow for using names over the radio. Still, to the XO Broujos at Beard's side there was something about the tone in which Morningstar's death was reported that made him consider it the most respectful tribute to a dead Marine he'd ever heard. The incident closed with an infuriated Bogard calling Beard about the tanks ("I don't want these damn things, do something with 'em!"), and a squad patrol being organized to escort the two tanks to join the two presently with Hotel Company.

During the morning of 5 July 1967, F/2/9 (2dLt Frank B. Westerfield), which was securing a stream crossing on Route 561 several hundred meters above Phu An, was hit

by an NVA mortar team from the vicinity of the old blue
Catholic church to the west. When it was reported on the
battalion net that Foxtrot had taken casualties, the CO of
Hotel Company (Capt Frank L. Southard) had a sudden
premonition about Lieutenant Westerfield—*I bet that guy
got killed.* Only the evening before, Southard had been
Westerfield's guest at the stream outpost. Southard's Hotel
Company had left Cam Lo by truck only that afternoon (4
July 1967) and had bivouacked for the night in a joint perimeter with Westerfield's Foxtrot. This had only been
Southard's first operation, but Foxtrot seemed overly relaxed. The troops had been wandering around without helmets, flak jackets, or shirts. *Loose as a goose,* he had
thought (an opinion ultimately shared by others closer to
the outfit in question), and he had alluded to his concerns
during his meeting with Westerfield that night.

Lieutenant Westerfield was a good, old mustang officer, but he was also a saltier-than-shit short-timer. He had
answered with, "Well, don't worry about us. Nobody
messes with crazy people."

That was the kind of overconfidence that killed, and
sure enough, that evening an NVA probe had gotten within
hand-grenade range and one of Southard's Marines had
been wounded. Hotel's gunnery sergeant, Gunny Evans,
had supervised the night medevac, and the next morning (5
July 1967) Southard had bid Foxtrot good-bye to continue
north along Route 561 per instructions. His premonition
was soon confirmed: it had been Lieutenant Westerfield
killed in the mortar attack. Battalion commander Kent reported that "the NVA got in very close with a couple of
60mm mortars without base plates and hit Westerfield's
position with several rounds propelled only by their igni-
tion cartridges. The time in flight is very short that way,
and the NVA got away clean that morning."

On that sunken, hedgerow-lined section of Route 561
running through the Marketplace, the recovery of the bodies continued all afternoon. For those involved, it was emotionally devastating work that was carried out (after don-

ning gas masks against the unreal smell) in a quiet, let's-get-this-over-with manner. With security deployed along the flanks from 3/9, working parties from BLT 1/3 entered the road itself to gather equipment, remove grenades and other pyrotechnics (to prevent accidents when this gear was loaded on helicopters), to collect personal effects in upturned helmets, and then to carry the corpses themselves to the tanks.

Captain Jordan (A BLT 1/3) originally sent one platoon forward, but when he saw several of his men vomiting as they came back with the first few body-bagged remains, he reconsidered. *This isn't the kind of thing that you can assign to somebody.* Jordan moved up then with part of his company headquarters and personally helped his grunts load the body bags. *Nauseating,* he thought. *One of the worst experiences I've ever been in.* Horror compounded horror. PFC Law (D BLT 1/3) came upon a scene in a dry gulch off Route 561:

> The bodies were of white Marines but the sun had turned their bodies charcoal black. Maggots had infested them and you could see them crawling through eye sockets and mouths. They were bloated, with the skin very taut, and one had popped open and spewed its contents from its midsection. One Marine had his genitals cut out and sewn to his face, with a picture of his girlfriend stabbed into his chest. Though I knew there were more live Marines from my own outfit with me, I felt as though I was the only one alive.

Although one MIA was never accounted for (LCpl Wayne V. Wilson of B/1/9 was eventually declared Presumed Dead), it was obvious that the NVA were not taking prisoners. Corporal Gomez (I/3/9) was so sickened and infuriated by the scene (*I'll never forget those faces, I can't imagine the horror they must have gone through*) that when the time came, he extended his tour for six months in search of payback. *It didn't matter why we were in Vietnam,* he thought (he'd long given up on this "stupid, self-defeat-ing war"). *All that mattered was that Marines died, and somebody's going to have to pay:*

> I remember seeing bodies that had superficial wounds—and bullet holes in the head, back of their heads blown off. I remember some of the bodies being mutilated, genitals cut off and put in the mouth. The gooks like to do things like that to play psychological games—to scare the fuck out of you—but I don't think that worked because I remember being very pissed. Very angry. I have never seen so many people pissed off. I have never seen so many people ready to kick somebody's ass. We wanted to fight. We wanted to even the score. We wanted to prove to the NVA that you just can't do this and fucking walk away. I cannot believe that human beings would do that to other human beings, and I can't believe—though I did it—how much of an animal you can become once you've seen something like that, once you've seen what they've done to your brothers. That anger becomes the determination to become the best combat Marine there was, and when you get the chance you do the same fucking thing to them that they did to you. Fuck Vietnam and their democracy. Fuck Vietnam and their civil war. There were no more rules. Now it got to be revenge. The new guys became vets, the vets became hard—there was just a brand-new meaning to the war.

Cpl Larry Miller and his radioman LCpl Jim Groeger (NGL BLT 1/3) hefted another body into a Sea Horse on the Trace, but the helo was overloaded, and the door gunner casually kicked the corpse back out. In an instant, Miller had his .45 cocked in the door gunner's face, and he stared with hatred at this nice, clean, uncomprehending aviator type. The door gunner apologized with his eyes, and Miller slowly dropped the hammer and reholstered the weapon. There were other ways to honor these fallen men. Corporal Collopy (I/3/9) noticed as they recovered Bravo's gear, including that which had been stripped from the bodies by the NVA and discarded off the road after they had taken what they wanted, that many Marines who already had bayonets in their scabbards were fixing the dead Marines' bayonets to their rifles.

There was reverence this day, and irreverence. Lt Lester L. Westling, Chaplains Corp, U.S. Navy, of 3/9, was saying final prayers over one of the bodies brought back to the Trace, when he looked up into the "eyes and ears of the world, and CBS thrust a microphone in my face and said, 'Would you say that a little louder please, padre, so the people back home can hear?' And what I said in the microphone, the people back home undoubtedly were not allowed to hear."

Chaplain Westling and his super grunt-turned-assistant, Cpl John Ray Phillips, tended each of the dead Marines brought to the Trace. While last rites were given to each by Westling, Phillips would check wallets or dog tags and following the prayers, he or Westling would use a grease pencil to write the dead man's name and service number on his chest. They would then bag (or rebag) the body and go on to the next. They had to conduct much of their business under the tanks parked there, because whenever the helicopters came in for the dead or with resupply, so did the NVA rockets and artillery. During one of the first doses of incoming, Westling had rolled under a tank and shouted over to Phillips, "Are you safe, are you down far enough?"

Corporal Phillips's answer had been in the best grunt tradition, "It's good for your career, Chaplain, it's good for your career!"

As the horrible afternoon wore on, however, Phillips's spirits wore down. *Some of the things we saw were pretty upsetting.* Finally, during another shelling, Westling saw Phillips sitting apathetically on a tree stump, and he had to literally grab Phillips and drag him under a tank. Captain Giles (K/3/9) was another horrified eyewitness:

I remember seeing the tanks coming back and the tanks were loaded, I mean loaded to the top of the turret with bodies. The bodies were bloated, rigor mortis had set in—the grotesque positions and the stench, the absolute stench was just awesome. And as the tanks came rumbling by us on back to the rear, again the thought came—this war has nothing to do with winning, man, the only thing it has to do with is survival. And the stupidity of it all came to me because this was the same area that Woody and the battalion and Giles and Kilo Company had been through so many times.

In this case there was nothing to do but put the best face possible on the disaster. One way was to inflate the enemy body count. Captain Navadel, temporarily in command of India Company (a Capt. William A. Conger would replace him later in the day) looked over his Marines' latest finds, including an NVA 7.62mm machine gun, fifteen yet-to-be-buried antitank mines, forty-three 82mm mortar rounds attached to poles for carrying, and an NVA notebook and Laotian currency. They also found five dead NVA in individual shallow graves, the victims, Navadel surmised when they were unearthed, of napalm. Navadel remembered, "Those were the only bodies I physically saw. I feel certain we got a lot with artillery and air (at least I hope we did), but we never got to see any bodies. There were enough live ones to carry away their dead. I think they listed about 1,200 NVA killed on Operation Buffalo. If they did, I sure didn't see it, and no one else did. The 1,200 NVA body count was run up to offset the number of U.S. casualties."

By 1300, 5 July 1967, the thirty bodies in the Marketplace had been loaded on the tanks. And at 1445, Major Woodring ordered I, K, and L/3/9 to fall back to the main battalion line, an order echoed by Lieutenant Colonel Wickwire to A and B BLT 1/3. At 1500, as this was being accomplished, Landes's Bravo Company spotted numerous pieces of U.S. equipment forward of their lines near Hill 57. But a patrol received heavy sniper fire, and the decision was made at battalion not to press the issue. NVA followed the Marines back, and it was at 2145, as everyone battened down for the night, that Jordan's Alpha Company reported 35–40 NVA to their direct front.

At this time, as Jordan got his mortar section firing, Alpha's outposts were withdrawn. One of the two-man LPs had just started back from their hole when an NVA rocket landed in their vacated position. Corporal Miller watched the two complete their run back into the lines, when one of them, unnerved by having missed death by only ten paces and a few seconds, threw his M16 to the ground and declared, "I ain't doin' shit, I ain't goin' back out there no more!"

A sergeant asked the man if he understood what he was doing, and when the man said he did, the sergeant said, "Okay, asshole, start picking up C-ration cans."

The man kept his mouth shut and policed up old, rusty debris until he was directed back toward a resupply helicopter. Next stop (presumably) was the Da Nang brig, which he found preferable to the Dead Marine Zone. Meanwhile, Jordan brought in the artillery (until 2220) then dispatched a patrol that returned (at 2310) to report one USMC WIA, eight NVA KIA, and fifteen NVA KIA probables. Jordan had a tank attached to him for the night and as Lance Corporal Lind noted, it "sat behind us with motors running and loaded with canister rounds, and if they yelled, 'Beehive!' we were to drop into our holes."

30

The Four Gates to Hell

★

At 0535 on Thursday, 6 July 1967, an NVA platoon of some twenty-five men walked right into Echo Company BLT 2/3.

At the time, Echo was dug in near a bushy hillock in the dry rice paddies immediately south of the hamlet of Thon Tan Hoa: 200 meters east of where Staff Sergeant Morningstar had been shot during the afternoon; less than three kilometers southwest of Con Thien; and one kilometer west of an old Catholic cathedral known as the Four Gates to Hell Church. The routine between company commander Bogard and executive officer Cannon was that Cannon would catch his sleep where he could during the day, then give Bogard a break by handling the night activities. So it was that after having been resupplied by helicopter in the spot of Morningstar's death, and after Bogard had decided it best to move east (it was dark now, and NVA scouts had last seen them setting up in the resupply area), Cannon had personally conducted the reconnaissance of the new area. Cannon had then set Echo Company in the dry paddy with 1st Platoon assuming the curve of the circle from twelve to four, 2d Platoon from four to eight, and 3d Platoon from eight to twelve.

Lieutenant Cannon had figured that if the NVA were to come during the night, they would come from the thick woods at eleven o'clock, to about where 1st and 3d Platoons were tied in. Therefore, he had removed a slice from the company pie at that spot so that if the NVA attempted to take advantage of that dense terrain, they would be caught in the crossfire of the platoon on either side. He had also had the 1st Platoon, to the right of that missing wedge, deploy a machine-gun team to cover a north-south dirt trail that cut through the perimeter.

The NVA came from just where Cannon had predicted. When it started, he was sitting up against a tree in the CP area west of the trail, monitoring the radios with one or two radiomen who were also awake while Bogard took his turn sleeping. The 3d Platoon Commander, 2dLt John Eller (a mustang), radioed Cannon to report that his LP at twelve o'clock had movement in that wooded area that he was going to take under fire. Cannon rogered that, and the Marines commenced firing.

The NVA's return fire was immediate.

Awakened by the shooting, Captain Bogard called to Lieutenant Cannon, "Jim, tell them goddamn idiots to quit shooting at each other."

"Well, skipper, did you issue either of the platoons green tracers?"

The night was alive with green AK47 tracers, and seeing no red M16 tracers in return, Cannon's initial thought was, *My God, we must be catchin' hell!* But neither the 1st nor 3d Platoon Commanders reported any casualties, and the absence of red tracers was the result of fire discipline: so as not to reveal their positions, the Marines were throwing grenades into the woods and only firing when they had a clear target. The NVA were caught in a cross fire that Bogard and Cannon added to with their 60mm mortar teams and their attached 81mm mortar section. Their LPs maintained their positions and requested their preplotted artillery concentrations to be fired wherever they had movement in those areas. *Easy,* Cannon thought.[1] The platoon commanders had everything under control, and the M60 team covering the trail to the north was barking out a stream of thirty- to forty-round bursts. Echo Company finally did take one casualty. Apparently, several NVA made it up to the fighting hole of a Marine, who then beat a retreat toward the center of the perimeter, where a mortar man with the 81mm section mistook him for an NVA in the flare-splashed night and took him out with an M79 grenade launcher. When the confusion was sorted out, it turned out that the Marine had only been wounded.

The firefight eventually petered out as the NVA thought it prudent to disappear before daybreak. Even before the platoon commanders got their reports in, Captain Bogard hustled to the woods where the NVA had gotten chopped up, then called back, "Hey, Jim, come here quick! Oh my God! Look at this, Jim!"

Cannon ran up to Bogard to see several dead North Vietnamese sprawled in the shrapnel-gutted vegetation. Altogether, fourteen NVA bodies were found along with miscellaneous gear, web belts, medical bags, ammunition pouches, sixteen grenades, twenty clips of ammunition, and two SKS Chinese carbines, as well as enough bloody bandages and drag imprints to justify the claim of an additional nineteen probable kills. The latter figure was highly unlikely—it would have meant the Marines had killed more NVA than they had probably been fighting.

★

1. Captain Bogard thought that the NVA (having seen the resupply helos land in one spot) had, in fact, been surprised to encounter the Marines in another spot, "The bad guys literally walked into us—I mean like in a formation. They were in what we would call in the Marine Corps an 'approach march' to an objective area—it was dark, they were trying to stay together, so they would normally do that if they didn't think we were around—and they actually ran into us because we'd moved into their path after dark. It was a total slaughter."

Simultaneous with the assault on Echo Company,
Command Group Alpha (Beard) and Golf Company
(Sheehan) were mortared by the NVA atop their rocky
hillside near Thon Bai An, five klicks southwest of Con
Thien. It was a good, solid forty-round barrage that killed
one Marine, seriously wounded four, and left fourteen others with wounds that could be treated in the field. The
NVA mortar went silent in the face of Marine counterbattery fire, but then an NVA sniper opened up from the twilight gloom, snapping two dozen shots into the hill in the
next five to ten minutes. Meanwhile, come daylight on 6
July 1967, patrols were mounted from each of BLT 2/3's
four independent company positions, and for Hotel Company (Culver), their particular concern was the Four Gates
to Hell Church on the eastern fringe of Thon Tan Hoa.

Captain Culver was convinced that the NVA were using the large, impressive stone cathedral as an observation
platform (priests and parishioners had, of course, long
since been evacuated), so keeping the two-tank section under the mustang lieutenant at his hillock-top CP, he dispatched his other two-tank section with one of his platoons. The platoon moved north and was just nearing the
Four Gates to Hell Church when, at 0800, they came under
AK47 automatic-weapons and 60mm mortar fire. One
Marine was killed and six wounded. SSgt Max Fallagan's
two tanks added their .50-caliber machine guns and 90mm
main guns to 2dLt Carl Zander's M16s, M60s, and M79s.
Fallagan then maneuvered forward when, according to
Culver, who was still at the CP but plugged into eyewitness
Zander by radio:

Fallagan was hit with three RPGs just as he had
gone up, and was teetering between going down a rice-
paddy dike or a hummock of some kind. One hit the
bogey wheel down in the suspension. One hit the driver's
hatch, which was opened (it was so goddamned hot that
everybody was driving unbuttoned) and knocked the
driver out—he subsequently died—and it knocked out
all the electrical systems in the tank. The third one rico-

cheted off the turret, knocked a chunk out of the turret, and blew old Max—who was sitting up there with his sunshades on—out of the turret as he was about half-climbing out to see what had happened. Well, Max got a little on the bent-out-of-shape side, don't you see. He climbs back aboard the tank, hand-traversed the turret, and they fired something like fifty-seven rounds of cannister in there. I don't recall specifically whether they ran out of ammunition first, or the gun jammed, but I mean this is no mean feat when you got no electricity in that thing.

Artillery was also called in, 156 rounds that sent the NVA packing and allowed medevacs to flap in. At 1030, the contact heated up again, and again, Staff Sergeant Fallagan (whom Culver had known as a take-nothing-seriously jokester during their Marine Corps Rifle and Pistol Team days) proved that he was "an animal of sorts" when it came to shooting for real. Based on Zander's radio reports, Culver's narration continued:

Old Fallagan carried with him a sawed-off Mossberg bolt-action shotgun, and he had an old seven-sixty-two bandolier left over from the M14 days filled full of fléchette. So he climbs out of the tank after its obviously of no more service, and fired all of his rounds at the various NVA that he could find. Then he borrows a rifle from one of my rocket gunners—shoots an NVA out of the church steeple. In the meantime, the other two tanks —hell, we hear what's going on and we send the cavalry to them—these other two tanks show up on the scene. One of them was a Zippo—a flame tank—and when that flame started around, these little suckers were just running into each other trying to get out of the way. In the meantime, our relief force headed down—I was with them—but the tanks, of course, got down there first. By the time I got there, those guys had left because of that flame tank—boy, they packed their shit and left—so there wasn't much left except debris when we got down there.

That debris included (according to the BLT 2/3 after-action report) sixteen NVA dead, and whatever evidence was needed to claim ten additional probable kills. The tank lieutenant approached Captain Culver then to hand him a slip of paper on which he had written his name, service number, and organization, and said "If you feel that we should get some awards, my name is . . ."

Nonplussed by this self-promotion, Culver's only recommendation was a Silver Star for Fallagan, which to his knowledge was never approved. Once Hotel Company and their tankers had cleared the NVA foot soldiers from the church area, NVA mortar men began (at 1530) to place preregistered 60mm fire on them. Counterbattery fire (mortars and artillery) quieted the barrage, but not before fifteen rounds had wounded thirteen Marines. During all this, Culver noted, "Old Max Fallagan stands there—sunshades still intact—and directs one of the other tanks that hasn't been injured to come back, hook onto his tank, and we towed it back up to the position."[2]

In Hotel Company's original perimeter in the hills south of the contact area, Culver pointed Fallagan back toward the Four Gates to Hell. "Max, how come that damn church steeple is still there—I mean, they obviously use it for an FO?"

"Well, skipper, it's a national landmark. The Area Commander won't let us touch it."

"Hmmm, Max, let me ask you a question. Am I, as a member of the SLF, currently working directly for the Area Commander?"

2. Meanwhile, at 0930, the NVA detonated a claymore mine on an F Company patrol (3 USMC KIA, 1 USMC WIA); at 1000, the NVA detonated two claymore mines on a G Company patrol (no recorded casualties); and from 1222–1417, an E Company platoon pursuing the NVA into Thon Tan Hoa engaged a bunker complex (2 USMC WIA) until retiring to turn on their air and arty.

"Well, no."

"And since you're attached to me, are you basically working for me?"

"Well, yes, sir."

"If I gave you the order to blow that sonuvabitch away, would you do it?"

"Why, you bet your sweet ass I would."

With that, Culver rang up Major Beard (currently in position with Golf Company) for permission to open fire on the cathedral. He did not expect to be denied (after all, "Old Moose was a fairly understanding sort," and he was already not a little upset about various other firepower restrictions), but Culver thought it best not to specifically identify the target over the radio for the whole world to hear. "Look, we got an obstacle down here that they're using for an FO position on a regular, consistent basis, and have been for years. I intend to reduce it to rubble. Do you have any objections?"

"Well, I reckon not."

Culver then ran a patrol back to the Four Gates to Hell Church to evacuate by helicopter all the crucifixes, vestments, statues of the Virgin Mary, etc., at which time a Mexican Marine from East L.A. asked Culver to ship all these items to his neighborhood church. Patrol back, Culver turned to Fallagan, "Okay, Max, he's all yours." The tankers worked their way down the stone steeple with HE rounds, then Culver's FO called in some eight-inch fire. When the artillerymen reported that they were beginning to bottom out on ammunition, Culver requested an air strike through battalion, which was delivered so that he could later report that "when we left, that sucker was about two feet high."

As the sun went down, Golf Company's patrols were ordered back to the hilltop where they had spent the previous night, a maneuver that drew mixed response from the grunts. The idea of offering themselves up as sitting ducks to NVA mortar men whose aim had drawn blood at dawn drew mutterings about suicide, but drained by the sun, they were also glad they would not have to dig new holes. Their supply helos alighted on the hill, and in the middle of this hustle and bustle, Captain Sheehan passed the word to saddle up. This took everyone by surprise, but the idea was deception. They knew the NVA had observed them moving onto this hill and had observed them receiving resupply, which generally meant that a unit was there to stay. But if they could surreptitiously march off this hill in the twilight gray, perhaps they could trick the NVA into mortaring an empty hill, while they settled in for a peaceful night on another hillock.

Good enough, except that the resupply had deposited lots of stuff on their hill, so, humping unopened cases of C rations, ammunition crates, and five-gallon water cans down tangly jungle trails, Golf Company moved out. The grunts considered the whole exercise a waste of time, but were joking nonetheless and hoping it would work. It didn't. No sooner had the last Marine humped up their new hill than they could hear the thumping of an enemy mortar tube.

This time they didn't have any holes.

As Corporal Caton clawed into the elephant grass— everyone scattered at the first *thunk,* looking for cover among the trees—he could hear Captain Sheehan calling out in a calm voice, "Stay down, lads, that's incoming!"

The skipper's just too cool, Caton thought, as Sheehan remained standing, radio in hand to direct counter artillery on the enemy. Caton fully expected Sheehan to be the commandant of the Marine Corps someday. The mortar raid was short and produced no casualties. And when it was over, the irrepressible Sergeant McWhorter and Peter Kluchnik—a hell of a field Marine and a hell of a bitcher— began singing, "You Made Me Leave My Happy Home."

The NVA pecked at BLT 2/3 during the night. They mortared Sheehan's Golf and Culver's Hotel, producing no casualties, though Culver's counterbattery fire resulted in two secondary explosions in the dark. The silhouette of an NVA scout was spotted in front of Hotel's holes (an M79 was fired at the man, and a blood-soaked U.S. M14 ammu-

nition pouch and magazine were found at dawn), and an
LP from Bogard's Echo reported movement west of their
perimeter. An experienced FO would have responded with
a few rounds, but the barrage that Echo's new artillery
lieutenant delivered seemed endless. Bogard mused that
he would probably be reprimanded for expending this
much ordnance on what was probably a few water buffalos.
As he got the reports from the LP that had started the
whole thing, he was even less enthused. The Marines out
there had heard voices, and Bogard doubted the NVA
would be that sloppy, considering this was Echo's second
night in the same place. He wondered if they were actually
shelling villagers who, by the rules, shouldn't have been in
this free-fire zone but who were known to return in small
groups to their ancestral homes. Maybe so, maybe not. Officially, Echo was placing steel on Communists: their twilight sweep of the impact area discovered enough blood-
stained bandages and drag imprints to come up with the
claim of eight probable NVA kills.

PART SEVEN

NIGHT MOVES

★

During the body evacuation on the Trace on 5 July 1967, helicopters arrived not only for the casualties, but also with the resupply due 3/9 and BLT 1/3. It did not all arrive intact. Survival in the face of the NVA artillery demanded the helicopter crews minimize their exposure time in the preregistered Trace; as such, slingloaded nets full of plastic water bladders were sometimes unhooked in midair (as pilots pulled up in the face of incoming), and five-gallon water cans went out the door at a hundred feet. The result was bursting plastic bladders, split-open water cans, and dehydrated and hungry riflemen. In the case of one of the nine rifle companies above the Trace, Landes's B BLT 1/3, all his Marines had from 5 July into the afternoon of 6 July 1967 was a cup of water apiece and however many cans of salty Vienna sausages they could stomach (cases of this type of ration and only this type of ration had been kicked out in abundance). The situation was such that Marines were getting sunstroke just sitting in their holes (Landes had to evacuate two heat casualties during the day), but sometime after noon battalion commander Wickwire arrived with several Mechanical Mules loaded with water cans. Landes told Wickwire how greatly relieved he was, but it was not until several hours later that Landes realized what a godsend the water had been. It was then that the 90th NVA Regiment came, in the assault, trying to push the entire two-battalion line back into the Trace. Landes's swollen-tongued, cracked-lipped Marines had been so weak from the sun that without that water resupply, he later surmised that most of them would have died in their holes, unable to resist.

31

A Piece of Cake

★

"**M**ajor Woodring!" Having been pointed in the right direction, 1st Lt Stephen M. Hartnett, Platoon Commander, Third Force Reconnaissance Company (attached to the 3d Reconnaissance Battalion, 3d Marine Division), walked toward the CP of the 3d Battalion, 9th Marines, 3d Marine Division. Hartnett and platoon had just hiked across the Trace from Con Thien, having detrucked there after riding the convoy circuit from Dong Ha. At the time, Major Woodring was improving his bamboo-parapeted foxhole. He had a good six-foot hole going for himself, and he looked up with, "My God—Hartnett!"

Lieutenant Hartnett, who hadn't seen Woodring since he was his CO at the Basic School two years earlier, was surprised that the good major remembered him. Woodring next remarked, "Well, what in the hell are you doing here, Hartnett?"

Because of the NVA artillery occasionally impacting in

the area, Hartnett briefed Woodring on his mission from the prone position beside the major's hole. Hartnett took his orders from Brigadier General Metzger, ADC, 3d Marine Division, who, as he now explained to Woodring, wanted confirmation of the NVA units north of the Trace between Gio Linh and Con Thien; additionally, Hartnett was to pinpoint the infiltration routes the NVA had used (and would surely use again) across the Ben Hai River to access this area. To accomplish this, he had a reinforced platoon with four four-man teams (as opposed to the normal three), plus a corpsman and additional radio operators. Hartnett showed Woodring which route he intended to take toward the DMZ, and they decided it would be best if his platoon moved out with a regular rifle company so the maneuver would look to NVA scouts like a routine sweep. As Hartnett explained, he had a counterpart from Force Recon presently joining BLT 1/3 to the east where the decision would also be made to camouflage their movement with a rifle company.

At about 0700 on Thursday, 6 July 1967, as Marine artillery prepped forward of their lines, Captain Slater, CO of the recently combined Alpha-Charlie Company, 1st Battalion, 9th Marines, 3d Marine Division, listened to the operations orders from Major Woodring, CO, 3/9, with something akin to incredulity. As Major Woodring explained, with their original body-recovery mission successfully completed, division now taxed them with an additional reconnaissance mission. Having benefited from three full days in battalion reserve (albeit under occasional shell fire), Slater's Alpha-Charlie Company was to establish a patrol base some 1,200 meters forward of the battalion line, due north of Hill 109, in the deserted hamlet of Thon Phuong Xuan. From this patrol base, Woodring continued, a recon platoon would slip further north (the southern edge of the DMZ was only 1,500 meters from the proposed patrol base, the Ben Hai River only another 2,500); recon would then roll back to the patrol base, and the whole show would return to the battalion line.

Captain Slater was exactly four days from giving his company up in preparation for rotating home, and he had to admit the mission order left him *a little bit spooked.* He answered Woodring, "Be glad to do it, but you gotta understand—my people are scared. Tired. What if we run into a massive enemy out there. You know, I don't think we could sustain ourselves. Even with Charlie Company adding to Alpha Company we still don't have that big a strength."

"Well, we have some sections of tanks. What we'll do is we'll send 'em up to you, and they'll help you out of whatever you're in."

"I gotta have some artillery support—that's our bread and butter."

"You'll get everything you need."

It was comforting to Slater to have the 3d Tank Battalion on his side, as well as the long-range support of the 12th Marines and even the 40th Artillery Regiment, U.S. Army, if needed. It was time to get Alpha-Charlie Company back in the saddle before their battle shock became permanent, and Woodring patted Slater on the back, "Okay, go ahead. Get out there."

Captain Slater then hooked up with Lieutenant Hartnett (who immediately impressed him as a real good hard charger) and his twenty-man platoon. He was also awarded the battalion's handful of attached combat engineers. With recon types and engineers in tow, he briefed Lieutenant Telep of Charlie Company, plus Staff Sergeants Leslie, Richardson, and Hensley, the platoon commanders in Alpha Company. From there, word went out to the troops. If Slater's response to this mission had been trepidation, their's was absolute outrage. *Put us here, put us there—it's more or less just like torturing us,* thought Lance Corporal Dishong of Alpha Company who, after the events of 2 July, didn't have time for any worthless explanations about how they'd had three days to recuperate. *Here's all of Three-Nine, and there's One-Three, a whole battalion, full strong, about two hundred men to a company—and here we are, chewed up, tired, beat, morale as low as you name it, short everything. And they're keeping us out here!*

Lance Corporal Dishong, who had started this operation as a rocket man, was now carrying over his shoulder the machine gun recovered from Jack Rush's overrun position. There was no gun team, just him with the M60 and his squad leader, Corporal Yandola, who didn't know much about machine guns anyway, tagging along as ammo humper as they started north. Every squad in the company was similarly undermanned. Not only were they so skeletonized that most of the men had expected a rotation to Okinawa for a complete refitting, but they were also hurting for resupply and replacement of the equipment lost on 2 July. There were virtually no LAWs or M79s left, little ammunition for the remaining grenade launchers, and they were even short of gun oil for their prone-to-jam M16 rifles. *Mass confusion,* Dishong's internal rebellion continued in step with the plodding northward movement of gaunt, dust-caked Marines in tatterdemalion utilities and sun-bleached helmets and flak jackets. *They don't know what the hell they're doing with us. This is pretty stupid.*[1]

Moving on north through the east-west tree line defining the edge of the battalion line, Lance Corporal Stuckey of Charlie Company, to the rear of the column, took one last look at the M48 tanks parked there. *Are the tanks going to move with us, or what?* he thought with some hope—their firepower would have been a tremendous security blanket. Tanks, however, were noisy, let everyone know you were coming, were prone to break down, and had no place on this get-in-get-out mission. Alpha-Charlie Company, in fact, carried little in the way of water, rations, or overnight gear. Lance Corporal Stuckey could only hope that Captain Slater had been right when he had briefed them full of confidence, the NVA had probably pulled out of the area

---

1. Gunnery Sergeant Santomasso put it this way: "We were so under T.O. we had C Company with us; they weren't much but one lieutenant and a couple of half-ass platoons and I still don't think I had 140 men on paper."

and promised tank support if needed. "Hey, this is going to be a piece of cake—we're just going to get out there, make the recon, and get back."

While A-C/1/9 established their patrol base north of 3/9, Major Woodring had his other opcon company, Captain Southard's Hotel Company, 2d Battalion, 9th Marines, 3d Marine Division, in a less vulnerable patrol base south of 3/9. Southard was set up several hundred meters south of the Trace and had, upon establishing this position the day before, run a squad across the Trace to make physical contact with Woodring's CP. That morning a helicopter dropped a two-man sniper team into Hotel's position as the day's patrols began.

Captain Southard briefed the scope-equipped sniper and his observer (who carried a commercial handgun, a .38 Smith & Wesson), and they hoped to find a good observation point in which to set up. They requested a fireteam for security, so a four-man fireteam was provided and the party moved out. They hadn't been gone thirty minutes when Southard was alerted that they were on their way back: apparently, while moving through some thick brush, they'd had a "meeting engagement" with a couple of NVA also blindly moving through the brush. An NVA with an AK47 had drilled the sniper through the shoulder, but the observer (according to the story Southard got) had then dropped that NVA with his .38, and both sides had decided to scoot for home.

With the wounded sniper still on his feet, the six-man team walked back into Hotel's perimeter, and a medevac was requested. Shortly thereafter, another of Southard's patrols, a squad-sized one, also returned after a "meeting engagement" of sorts. These Vietnamese, a half-dozen of them, were unarmed and included an old man and a pair of very young teenagers. They carried water buckets and told Southard's interpreter (a sharp young Marine corporal from S-2) that they had been out looking for water. A ridiculous story, Southard thought—this was a free-fire zone from which all inhabitants had been previously evacuated.

This was only Southard's first operation, but his training and common sense told him that these "civilians," either voluntarily or through coercion, were working with the NVA. They were probably scouting for the NVA, and even if detected (as they were), their appearance on the battlefield would force a Marine patrol to expose itself and take on a burden.

Southard requested a helicopter evacuation for them.[2] Meanwhile, though, he noticed a corporal from the squad that had brought them in wearing a half-assed smile as he talked among his buddies about "wasting" these "gooks." Southard took the man aside to tell him to cease and desist. The other Marines hadn't reached the corporal's level of cold-blooded murder, but their hostility toward these Vietnamese was also palpable. Southard felt compelled to call up his platoon commanders—sharp lieutenants all, but young enough perhaps to be influenced by the lethal anger of some of their men—and set it straight that there would be "absolutely no 'wasting' of Viet Cong suspects or prisoners. This crap just isn't going to happen."

With the prisoners along for the ride (the S-2 corporal stayed with them), Hotel Company moved north several hundred meters to a low hummock in the bulldozed earth of the Trace, just above the southern edge. The position was too small to accommodate a rifle company (their new perimeter was rather compact) but it was loaded with old fighting holes and rain-eroded fissures and gullys. That was fortuitous because in the summertime, digging into this sunbaked, claylike earth was like digging into concrete: not impossible, but you'd wear yourself out. Like most areas in the Trace and above, there was plenty of individual cover, but the unit as a whole was very much in the open. Southard had selected this position, nonetheless, because it af-

2. Southard would later learn through his lieutenants and Staff NCOs that this corporal had executed an NVA/VC suspect several weeks prior to Southard's arrival, and Southard concluded that "the corporal was a killer, you could tell looking at his eyes—kind of a dead, lifeless look, as though he had absolutely no emotion."

forded them clear fields of unobstructed fire in case of a ground assault. What had happened to Bravo 1/9 dictated a whole new set of possibilities to every company commander involved in Operation Buffalo.

Captain Slater of Alpha-Charlie 1/9, who, of all people, was especially attuned to the lessons of Bravo Company's disaster, was lucky enough to discover an even better patrol base, no thanks, though (as might have been expected), to Lieutenant Hartnett's recon platoon. Slater had wanted recon on point, but Hartnett had declined, thinking of Suicide 1/9's shaky reputation. *Bullshit, we're not getting out in front of you guys and have you hose us down.* Instead, the remnants of Alpha were in the lead, followed by Slater's headquarters and the engineer and recon teams, with thinned-out Charlie coming last. They moved the 1,200 meters north to Thon Phuong Xuan in a spread-out, staggered column with point team and flankers well out. Approaching a low hill that, on their topo maps, looked like the outline of two shelled peanuts, on a north-south axis, 200 meters end to end, Slater told his new artillery spotter, PFC Sankey, to call in a marking round ahead of them. The first smoke round burst directly over the unnamed, peanut-shaped hill, which reassured Slater that his coordinates were right.

Things got better from there. Moving up the gentle rise of high ground, the Marines found themselves in a temporarily unoccupied NVA bunker-and-trench complex that had been invisible during their approach because of the elephant grass and banana trees in which it sat. The place was a splintered, napalmed, shell-pocked mess and 3/9 had blown all the individual NVA positions with C-4 the last time they had been through, during Operation Cimmaron. But half demolished or not, it still provided fantastic cover and concealment. *My God, we couldn't have asked for anything better,* Slater thought. The enemy bunkers had been constructed flush to the ground, their tops reinforced with logs three to six inches in diameter and with one to two inches of hard clay. There were also three circular positions four feet deep and eight feet in diameter, previously used by NVA mortar and antiaircraft crews. More than two hundred 12.7mm shells were found in one, and slit trenches interconnected most of the bunkers and dugouts. *Fields of fire are beautiful,* Slater thought as he inspected the area. *The camouflage is great, and it has deep, deep pits that we could get into without having to do a lot of digging. Everything's perfect!*

Captain Slater ordered his Marines into a three-sixty perimeter in the southern half of the two-peanut hill (it was now 0840), and the grunts gladly moved into the torn-open NVA dugouts; as Corporal Peterson thought, *gooks make an outstanding position.* Slater established his CP in the center of the circle with Gunny Santomasso and had FO Sankey fire smoke rounds into the area to ensure that the on-call concentrations from their supporting artillery were precisely locked down. Lieutenant Hartnett, meanwhile, established his CP's antenna farm in a crater near Slater, with his radio operators, corpsman, and one recon man, while his four teams prepared to move out. These Super Grunts (as the regular, dirt-eating riflemen called them) had the bush hats, the camouflage paint in greens, browns, and black—the whole nine yards—and Hartnett dispatched the four teams separately to the north. As Hartnett later commented:

The NVA going across the Ben Hai might cross in squad or platoon size units, and then, of course, they had assembly areas on the southern side of the DMZ. Their support people would go in first, lay in all the supplies and ammo, and mark the route. These guys would take a C-ration can, cut it and fold it like an arrow, and mark their unit on it. They'd tack them up to trees and that gave them directions. My patrols started reporting that they were finding numerous ammo and supply caches, and the standard guide points for assembly areas. I recall them mentioning the Chinese and Russian ammo was all new and shiny. Additionally, they found some medical supplies—gifts from the Friends Society of Pennsylvania.

There were also medical-supply gifts from the University of Michigan, and they found some whole-blood units with French description and some morphine Syrettes.

With recon out doing their thing, Slater left his CP to walk his entire three-sixty. By this time he didn't have a lot of confidence in the security measures of his Marines and felt the need to oversupervise—still haunted by the image from 2 July of dead Marines found facing the wrong way in the overrun LZ. So, Slater went totally around the perimeter, meeting with all individually, putting them into positions, letting them know who was to their left and right, giving them specific fields of fire, and if they were just sitting around when he showed up, then having them (if necessary) drag logs over their holes in the elephant grass or use machetes to improve fields of fire. Slater noticed, though, that his was a completely different company in terms of sloppiness. Because of the hard slap of 2 July and because of the isolated vulnerability of their patrol base they didn't cut corners anymore. As Corporal Power put it, "We were some paranoid motherfuckers at that position."

While A-C/1/9 (Slater) and H/2/9 (Southard) established their patrol bases, the remainder of 3/9 (Woodring) remained in position with I/3/9 (Conger), K/3/9 (Giles), and L/3/9 (Shirley) on line west of Route 561. On the east side of Route 561, BLT 1/3 (Wickwire) similarly maintained their east-west line with A (Jordan) and B (Landes), with C (Reczek) turning their flank to face east. Meanwhile, following arty prep fires in the area (from 0700–0745, 6 July 1967), D BLT 1/3 (Aldous) left their position as the battalion reserve to provide a second Force Recon platoon with a patrol base to the north. Like A-C/1/9, D BLT 1/3 moved through terrain that, until the day before, had been heavily defended. Neither company now drew a single round of enemy fire. It appeared that the NVA battalions had indeed retired back across the Ben Hai River into the sanctuary of North Vietnam.

32

The Best Staff NCO in the Marine Corps

★

The NVA had indeed vanished on the morning of 6 July 1967 except, that is, on the extreme eastern corner of the two-battalion front. There, the North Vietnamese held their ground against Lieutenant Francis's 2d Platoon, Charlie Company, Battalion Landing Team 1/3, Special Landing Force Alpha, 9th Marine Amphibious Brigade.

Lieutenant Francis had been with Charlie Two since Operation Beaver Cage, and he was, in the estimation of company commander Reczek, a good, brave young officer, but one typically handicapped by his relative inexperience and one whose aggressiveness bordered on recklessness. From the bottom up, Francis was most unpopular. *A hot dog,* some said—*a phony.* And few combat-seasoned grunts were inspired by his banal, come-on-folks-we-have-a-war-to-fight pep talks. Charlie Two took their cues instead from their platoon sergeant, for they had never seen anyone as combat-smart, anyone as tough, nor anyone who stood up for them as much as the Jockey-short, whippet-thin, hunch-shouldered Staff Sergeant Malloy. *A salty, intelligent, assertive, earthy guy who spoke his mind,* thought PFC Steiner, a brave, sensitive troop who put no stock in the usual Marine Corps swaggering. *Malloy was genuine.* Malloy, originally from Massachusetts, had fought in Korea and had served as a Parris Island DI before joining the BLT during their post-Khe Sanh rotation to Okinawa. Malloy was aggressive, but no glory chaser. Recalled PFC Wayne Pilgreen, a tough, brave, and wild Alabama shitbird:

> I seen Malloy stand up to Lieutenant Francis, that was back before Operation Buffalo. We had some planes flyin' over and they said we was a little ol' bitty company and we was fixin' to get involved with a couple battalions. Lieutenant Francis got wounded in the arm, and he was laying on the ground and still trying to get people killed, trying to tell 'em to go in. Malloy come up, grabbed the radio out of his hand, and says, "Hell no. I'm in charge. This is Staff Sergeant Malloy, and we're pullin' our asses *out.*" Francis said something to him—I can guarantee it was some cusswords—but he told us, "Let's go," and you can guarantee your ass when Malloy said something, we did it. He saved our ass then.

A journalist who interviewed members of Charlie Two wrote that when it came to Staff Sergeant Malloy

> they would remember his fairness above all else, which even extended to the way he opened cases of C rations. A case contained twelve meals, each labeled on the top. Most platoon sergeants opened the top of the box and gave the officers first choice. Malloy opened the box upside down, so no one knew which meal they were choosing and a private had as much chance of getting something good, like beef slices, as a lieutenant; when people began to figure out where the best meals were positioned in each case, Malloy went so far as to switch them around.

Rounding out the platoon command group was the radioman, LCpl John K. Cravens, who was short, athletic, and looked like he belonged in a prep school. He was a quoter of F. Scott Fitzgerald, and PFC Steiner, no dummy himself, couldn't imagine what Cravens was doing in the Marine Corps. Cravens probably wondered himself what had possessed him to enlist, and he was very sardonic when talking about things military. He could also get arrogant with his less educated compadres, although he was usually pretty friendly, and he tended not to take Lieutenant Francis seriously. Only Staff Sergeant Malloy could put Cravens in his place. Such was Malloy's warrior status that he was idolized by nonconformist smart asses like Cravens, good old boy rebels like Pilgreen, middle-class kids like Taylor and Steiner, and even a mean-tempered badass like PFC Cooper, who felt compelled to write on the back of a photograph of Malloy, ". . . Best staff NCO in the Marine Corps."

During the night of 5–6 July 1967, Captain Reczek could hear, from the thicketed rise where his CP trench was dug, a large number of NVA moving across the company's front to the east. Brush crunched, equipment clicked together (the NVA seemed to be moving northeast), and Reczek radioed Major Ossenfort, the S-3, to bring their artillery to bear. Reczek also instructed Lieutenant Francis to get a squad-sized patrol forward of their lines to help adjust the arty. This hairy task fell to a Sergeant Wiley who, come daylight on 6 July 1967, found himself observed by the NVA and then taken under considerable fire, to include 12.7mm machine guns. Reczek immediately ordered Lieutenant Francis and Staff Sergeant Malloy to advance on those NVA positions. With their packs left in their fighting holes and agricultural trenches, Charlie Two advanced quickly from their wood line to the next one. They then continued down a gradual slope into dense woods that tapered off into a sunbaked clearing some fifty to seventy-five meters across. The NVA were dug into the wood line on the other side, and hunkered down among the trees, both sides sustained a monstrously loud exchange of fire. The NVA had a 57mm recoilless rifle, about which PFC Pilgreen said:

> We was up against the shore 'nuff regulars, and we was getting our ass stomped. We were having heavy recoilless-rifle fire. Every time somebody would move or do anything, you'd hear that *wrrrr* of an incoming round. Every time you turned around they was hollering for a corpsman. There was a bunker they kept throwing fire at, which had the recoilless rifle in it. You couldn't get close enough to throw a grenade. You could shoot it with a grenade launcher, but every time you do anything to it, automatic-rifle fire—anything—a few minutes later it'd fire right back.

The recoilless rifle's dusty back blast provided the Marines a firm target, and perhaps they were killing a succession of gunners; but the recoilless rifle itself remained in working order. Between it and the rain of machine-gun and automatic-weapons fire, Charlie Two took two KIAs and three WIAs by 1000. It was maddening, and Staff Sergeant Malloy moved out then, with Sgt Donald C. Pike, to take out that murderous recoilless rifle. PFC Pilgreen opined:

> Malloy just had all he could stand—he didn't really break, but then again be did. He did something he shouldn't ought to, he had better sense than to do. He figured he could sneak down there to the recoilless-rifle bunker and grenade it—but it didn't work out. He almost got there, but he was hit dead-face with a recoilless rifle—just blowed away.

Staff Sergeant Malloy was hit in the left side of his chest by a 57mm shell that knocked him six feet in the air, spun him head over heels, and slammed him back to earth shattered and limp. It was incomprehensible to Charlie Two that Malloy, who was super, super people, had been killed at all—and Sergeant Pike too was cut down—even worse, though, that his body was in the open and unreachable. As Lance Corporal Kalwara, whose machine-gun team was attached to Charlie Two, explained it:

> We needed to find this man; we needed to make sure that this man came out unmutilated. That's what the enemy did with our Marines, they mutilated them. The most important thing was to find this great Marine and to bring him home to the U.S.A.

PFC Steiner, who had held his fire at first rather than fire over the heads of other Marines, had worked his way to the fringes of their tree line; from there, he emptied magazine after magazine into the NVA tree line, although he could not see a single one of them. He *never* saw one of them. Steiner shouted something to Jim Rose, who humped the radio for Sergeant Roberson, but the concussion of a recoilless-rifle shell or of one of the mortar rounds that were beginning to fall, had deafened him. *"I can't hear!"* Steiner helped Rose get the radio off, and on his own volition, he slipped his own arms through the shoulder harness. He had picked up enough radioese, he was proud to discover, to handle the new job, and he set off through the noise, commotion, smoke, and danger of the tree line to find Sergeant Roberson. Word came that reinforcements were on the way with tanks. Steiner was elated at the news, until he overheard Sergeant Roberson comment to another Marine, "We're not out yet. They have to bring in a chopper for the bodies, and they'll never get one in."

From his hilltop CP trench, Captain Reczek and his sharp XO, 1st Lt William H. Neuss, had been bringing in the artillery fire for Lieutenant Francis. The nut would not crack, however (as Francis kept reporting, "We just can't get anything going on this . . ."); and with Charlie Two hung up to the east, Captain Reczek, Charlie Six, radioed Captain Landes, Bravo Six, to send reinforcements from the west. Captain Landes was presently back up the slender tree that marked the tall-grassed hillock where his CP was dug in. The tree was only about twelve inches in diameter and Landes had his legs and one arm locked tight around the trunk just below where the branches and leaves sprouted, with his radio handset in his free hand, the cord stretched up as far as it would go. His radioman stood at the base of the tree, arms aching as he held his twenty-five-pound radio as high as he could over his head. Landes made sure to stay on the side opposite Charlie Company's fight (he could not see any individuals from his perch, but he could see smoke rising through the treetops) as he spoke with a Bronco-riding Tactical Air Controller Airborne. The TACA had a flight of fighter jets coming on station.

Captain Landes, controlling the air strike through the TACA, said, "Let's make a couple of dummy passes before we make any strafing and bomb runs in there to make sure we know what we're after."

The dummy runs resulted in one of the jets being enveloped in a hail of NVA tracers as the pilot pulled out—successfully—and Landes blurted to the TACA, "Hey, that's good enough for me—those are bad guys!"

Having clearly determined which tree line the NVA were in, the jets screamed in to expend their ordnance, but the NVA fire on Charlie Company sustained its withering pace. It was then that Captain Reczek radioed Captain Landes. Reczek explained that he had taken four KIAs, but only two had been recovered and he was hesitant to commit his other platoons to this action or he would have no line at all. He therefore requested that Landes send him one of his platoons and the three tanks presently in Bravo Company's perimeter.[1] Landes, an old friend of Reczek's,

1. A five-tank platoon from C Company, 3d Tank Battalion (1stLt Wayne M. Hayes) had arrived the day before, and when Lieutenant Colonel Wickwire had asked who wanted them, Landes (a rare infantry commander who liked tanks) had spoken up. He was given three of the five (along with Hayes), and when Reczek called, the three tanks were presently deployed behind B Company's defensive line, ready to be shifted where needed.

rogered that, then gave the word to 2dLt George C. Norris to pull his platoon out of their position on the company's west flank where they were tied in with Alpha Company along a vulnerable north-south dry canal and move east to reinforce Charlie Company. Lieutenant Norris, a colorful character and an outstanding platoon commander, moved out posthaste, despite the intermittent, and wound-producing mortar fire beginning to land now along the entire battalion line, while other squads from Bravo Company were shifted to reoccupy their vacated fighting positions. Lieutenant Hayes and his three M48 tanks accompanied Norris; and PFC Steiner of Charlie Two, who had no idea who these reinforcements were or where they'd come from, described their entrance into the fray:

I heard the tanks a long time before I saw them, and when one did appear it ploughed right through the trees like a bulldozer and came right on line with us. I'd seen war movies and things, but I'd never seen a real tank in real combat, so I was fascinated by that and just awe-struck at the power of it. I still can't imagine the North Vietnamese standing there with that tank approaching, and I don't know what I would do if a tank approached me. There was a guy sitting out of the turret when the tank came up, but there was a lot of fire so he pulled down inside the tank. I was looking right across into where the recoilless rifle was, and the tank swiveled its turret and aimed its gun point-blank at where the recoilless rifle had been firing from—and it fired, blammo, right into there. It was right on target—exactly on target—so they must have had radio contact with someone that was directing them.

The 90mm main gun firing into the NVA recoilless rifle was Lieutenant Hayes's own. His first direct hit was followed by several more from the long, ominous main gun, and the NVA position fell silent. Perhaps again the recoilless crew had been killed or wounded, but the area's agricultural trenches allowed for replacements to be fed quickly and surreptitiously to the main firing line. What happened next, after the victorious pause following the tank's last round, was just as astounding, unfathomable, and demoralizing as Staff Sergeant Malloy's death had been. As PFC Steiner continued his narration, they were again all witnesses to the impossible:

There was sporadic fire throughout and I was keeping low, but I didn't feel too fearful after the tank had fired. The fury of the tank just seemed incredible, the damage, the intensity of that tank—I couldn't imagine anything holding up to it—but then the recoilless rifle knocked out the tank with a dead hit. I don't know how it survived but it knocked out the tank. The recoilless rifle was not audible because of all the commotion and the tank engine, but I did see the direct hit on the tank. I was twenty, thirty feet from the tank. I was staring at it when it happened, and the tank caught on fire instantly, internally and externally.

A single 57mm round penetrated Lieutenant Hayes's tank where the turret met the deck. Hatches popped open with smoke pouring out, and flak-jacketed crewmen scrambled out—*like cats out of water,* thought Lance Corporal Kalwara—bringing out with them Lieutenant Hayes, who had a sucking chest wound. They dragged him behind the tank. A hospital corpsman from Lieutenant Norris's Bravo Three performed an emergency tracheotomy under fire to keep Hayes alive (Captain Landes subsequently recommended the young corpsman for a Bronze Star); the tank-platoon commander was too far gone, though, to survive his medevac ride. It was now about 1210, and the only firefight along the two-battalion front had bogged down intolerably. PFC Steiner, for one, simply rolled back into his prone firing position, reshouldered his M16, and resumed firing into the smoke-obscured NVA tree line. Not that he really felt he was doing any good. He was working on automatic, his mind basically shut off to the spectacle around him. "The adrenaline was at such a high level and the excitement was so intense and everything that had happened was so awesome that one more awesome event didn't affect me that much. I was at fever pitch, and my senses had been overloading for days—it wasn't that big a deal anymore. The tank just sat there and burned and burned and burned. It turned into a black hulk."

33

The Assault Barrage

★

Captain Giles of Kilo Company, 3d Battalion, 9th Marines, had accepted the initial NVA artillery fire of 6 July 1967 with numbed fatalism. He and Gunny Hatfield were sitting by their hole in the CP area, each with a sorry ass cup of coffee and Giles with another Marlboro, when the NVA artillery began firing from above the Ben Hai River. Its first shells were far off, and Hatfield turned to Giles. "Whoops, looks like a zone sweep."

"Yep, sure is."

They continued to sit and drink their coffee until the artillery crews, traversing their fire in seventy-five-meter increments, placed rounds only seventy-five meters from their position. "Well, next one's on us."

"Yep."

Giles and Hatfield dropped into their holes then several rounds crashed into the vicinity. Then the zone sweep traversed another seventy-five meters, and they popped from their hole, dusted themselves off, and resumed their coffee. As Hatfield remarked, "Well, another sorry ass day, another sorry ass dollar."

The day was actually just beginning. The helos that delivered Kilo's resupply also returned to them one Cpl Charles Saltaformaggio, a twenty-year-old solid Marine, a former high-school discipline problem from New Orleans who dropped out of school to join the Marines and had been on incountry R&R at China Beach. The reason for his vacation was that three weeks earlier, when Killer Kilo had run out of water and Saltaformaggio had used his K-Bar knife to get at the water in some bamboo, he had sliced right through a stalk and into his left arm. The wound was incredibly painful, but the company was too shorthanded to medevac him. So he humped along for the next few weeks even though he could not hold anything in his left hand and could touch a cigarette to the arm and not feel it. When the company pulled back to Dong Ha, Saltaformaggio was sent to China Beach to recuperate; then came Operation Buffalo and it was back to the bush. "That's the breaks of the game, but in those days you really didn't want to look like a candyass, you know, and say, 'I can't take it anymore, I got to go back to the rear.' My hand ached constantly, but I didn't mention too much about it—that was just part of being there."

Corporal Saltaformaggio, just off the resupply helo, hunted up Lieutenant Lane, his platoon commander, who told him about their Fourth of July casualties, then added, "Well, you've got it—you're now platoon sergeant."

It was getting late, and Lane and Saltaformaggio walked over to Captain Giles for the evening briefing. Giles and Navadel, the S-3, were standing and talking when there was a sudden, synchronized drumroll of NVA artillery being fired from the north, so many pieces that the sky literally exploded with their combined roars—and then the air was alive with the freight-train rush of incoming rounds. Navadel dropped to his gut, as did Giles. And looking at each other, they simultaneously exclaimed, "Holy shit—see ya later!"

Navadel took off for the battalion trench on his belly, while Lane and Saltaformaggio made a straight line for a bomb crater, which, in their panic, they didn't realize was actually forward of their lines. They tumbled in, Lane without a weapon (it was back at the platoon command post) and Saltaformaggio somehow losing his .45 (he realized his holster was empty about the same time they realized they were on the wrong side of the perimeter). Their unspoken thought was *is this the day we're going to die?* When Saltaformaggio wrote home five days later, he tried to make light of the terror of that moment. "We had a snake in it too, so while they hit us we were throwing mud clogs at the snake. Gave us something to do. All you could do was sit tight and hope the rounds don't land in the hole with you because they sure can mess up a good foxhole."

As for the previously fatalistic Captain Giles, the sudden, unbelievable fury of the barrage sent him scrambling for the nearest hole. There was already a Marine filling it, so Giles pulled his dive short and, playing the brave captain as opposed to a scared, scrambling grunt, he smiled down at the Marine. "How ya doin'?" Giles then turned around, walked away a few steps and, once out of that Marine's view, threw himself to the ground moments before the next salvo roared in. After the explosions, he took off for the next hole he could see, and there inside was another Marine smiling up at him. So, said Giles again as he stood tall, "How ya doin'?" And then he sprinted away, desperately seeking cover. He finally found it with Gunny Hatfield in their original position. The word among the Kilo grunts afterward was how goddamned cool their skipper had been during the barrage, going from hole to hole to check on them. But when Giles told Navadel the reality of the situation, Navadel commented that "we laughed about that good and hard for a long time."

This search-and-traverse barrage, which encompassed the entire line held by 3/9 and BLT 1/3, was initiated by three simultaneously firing NVA artillery batteries (mostly 100mm) and one NVA rocket battery (122mm and 140mm) above the Ben Hai River and was augmented by the usual, fleet-footed NVA mortar crews (60mm) already in the area. The barrage began at precisely 1645, 6 July 1967; it was at 1644 that Captain Landes, CO, B BLT 1/3 (who was still up in his tree) was contacted again by the TACA orbiting the battlefield in his Bronco. "Lease Breaker Bravo Six, this is Dream Hour. Over."

"Roger, Dream Hour. Go ahead."

"Bravo Six, this is Dream Hour. There are a large number of Vietnamese soldiers headed toward your position, crossing the Ben Hai River."

This startling message was delivered in a very calm, very routine voice. (They always tried to maintain a laconic exterior that was helped, Landes figured, by the fact that they were usually bone tired.) Landes responded, despite the sudden acceleration in his pulse, with an equally cool, "Roger, Dream Hour. Can you give me any idea how many?"

"Bravo Six, I really hate to tell ya. There's just a mess of 'em coming. I don't even want to tell you how many—"

It was exactly at that moment, even before the aerial observer could finish his report, that NVA artillery commanders dropped their arms and the sudden kettledrumming of the barrage began. *Unbelievable,* Landes thought, all hell really was breaking loose. And he slid down that tree so fast he skinned his nuts. He hit the base. His radio operator, who'd been holding the radio above his head, was already running. Landes was instantly scrambling after the radioman for the L-shaped trench the CP group had dug in the deep elephant grass of their hillock. The L-shape was so that Landes could keep a radioman in each wing, and be assured of good comm even in the case of a direct hit on one of the wings. The radioman got there first, and Landes did a racing dive into the trench right after him. He landed squarely atop the radioman, just smashing him down to the bottom of the slit trench. The radioman, a goofy kid who was not really bright enough for the job, started yelling, "What are you diving on me for, you know I could of gotten hurt!"

Captain Landes stared at the kid for a second as the whole world roared and shook around them, and almost laughed at the irony of this Marine being worried about a few bruises—*when, in fact, we're all going to die anyway.*

When the shells began roaring in, Corporal Miller of the Naval Gunfire Liaison Team BLT 1/3 was out on an OP several hundred meters north of their line with Moose Moyer, one of his primary radiomen. They had reached the area via the agricultural trenches and had set their OP in an old crater, around which they found NVA backpacks, cooking utensils, and rice. Miller, disgusted, had said, "Moose, shit, we're stopped right in their CP area. This is stupid, they know exactly where we're at. I'm sure they seen us move in here, as close as they are. They know exactly where the helicopters lit, they know exactly on the map so all they have to do is crank their guns up for that exact coordinate."

When that sudden, overwhelming roar began, Moose Moyer looked up with, "No, those are outgoing."

"Bullshit, they're incoming!"

Miller and Moyer charged back into their lines and jumped down into the agricultural trench where their team had their packs stashed. There was an NVA-dug spiderhole on the floor of the trench, and they squeezed into it. They had to wrap their arms around each other to fit, and Miller, holding Moyer tight, could hear him muttering, *"Oh God, oh God, oh God,"* against the roar enveloping them and the fragmented earth showering them. The trench, their sanctuary, was, however, alive with spiders and other jungle insects, and every time there was a pause in the drumroll, Miller and Moyer would scramble out to brush themselves off before diving back in.

At this time, Corporal Miller's other primary radioman, Lance Corporal Groeger, was at Con Thien, having jeeped up as Lieutenant Colonel Wickwire's temporary radio operator for an operations conference in the 1/9 CP. Con Thien became a target itself, mostly of mortar fire, and Groeger, waiting outside the command bunker, dropped in a hole—at least long enough to notice a Mechanical Mule nearby stacked with mermite cans of hot food. Groeger, who hadn't had a square meal since the operation began, jumped aboard, opened the cans, and stuck his hands in to scoop up fistfuls of mashed potatoes and beef. As he wolfed down the chow, he simultaneously kept an eye on his hole fifteen feet away and on how closely the mortar rounds were landing.

When one exploded some twenty meters away, Groeger made his run and was just jumping for the hole when the next round must have landed six feet behind him, because the next thing he knew, his legs were in the hole but he was sprawled facedown on the opposite side. He pulled his concussion-battered self down into the hole and realized then that the antenna from the radio on his back had been snipped off at neck level by shrapnel.

Lieutenant Colonel Wickwire appeared with his escorting riflemen. Their little detail was getting back to the battalion, and they roared away from Con Thien in their jeep and truck. They were let off near the northern edge of the Trace, and they immediately took off running north as the next artillery salvos roared in. Several rounds impacted directly behind them, the direction of fire propelling most of the shrapnel southward and thus sparing them, but the concussion was still powerful enough to blow them off their feet in midstride. They never stopped running, landing, sliding, crawling to stand back up—when it happened again. Once back in their lines, Groeger continued his sprint toward the agricultural trench where he'd left team members Miller and Moyer that morning.

Miller and Moyer were tucked down in their cover when there came Groeger from out of nowhere, crawling up the trench toward them. Groeger was a big guy, six-foot-five and heavy, and in Miller's opinion, a real smart ass. (Miller was always on this new guy for his casual, comic attitude toward everything. "Hey, Groeger, this ain't no joke.") But now he was pale white, his eyes were like saucers, and he was mumbling, "Miller, I know what you were talking about."

"Yeah, now you know it's no joke."

"Have they hit so close that you can't hear 'em go off?"

"No," Miller answered, and right on cue, all they could hear was this *pinggg, pinggg, pinggg.* It felt like their eardrums were going to burst. Dust and smoke clouded their sky, and Niagaras of exploded earth carpeted them in their trench. Jesus! The air stunk of cordite, and Miller looked at Groeger like he was bad luck incarnate and began screaming, "Groeger, get the fuck out of the area! Get the hell away from me!"

Captain Slater was well satisfied with the patrol base that Alpha-Charlie, 1st Battalion, 9th Marines, had established on the peanut-shaped hill in Thon Phuong Xuan. They were isolated, yes, but they were well situated and well camouflaged with Staff Sergeant Leslie (Alpha One) from twelve to five (they had a tall, old tree to the north and called that twelve o'clock), Lieutenant Telep (Charlie Six) from five to nine with Staff Sergeant Hensley (Alpha Three), and Staff Sergeant Richardson (Alpha Two) from nine to twelve. Additionally, Slater's FO, PFC Sankey, had their artillery support preregistered and on call, and neither their LPs nor Lieutenant Hartnett's recon teams had spotted any NVA in their area. It appeared to Slater that they had been able to establish this patrol base in no-man's-land without detection, a fact confirmed to him when (at 1645) the barrage began on the main line twelve hundred meters to the rear. It sounded like a dozen freight trains were rushing over their heads at the same time, volley after volley,[1] but not a single round fell on their patrol base. The area, as a former NVA position, would have been preregistered with NVA fire (as all good soldiers did),

1. Captain Landes (CO, B BLT 1/3) stated, "I talked to a pilot later on who was flying over our position at the time, and he said he didn't know how anybody survived. He said it looked like the moon, just constant eruptions and craters everywhere, and he said it just looked like an absolute wasteland."

and Slater was elated now at not being part of the NVA game plan. He knew his Marines were uptight, though, so he put out the word via his platoon commanders. "Hey, that's reassurance that they don't know where we are."

At 1700, the entire picture changed. Slater had previously been monitoring the aerial-observer net and had heard their reports of an estimated four hundred NVA crossing the Ben Hai River, north to south, but it seemed that was taking place far from his patrol base. Fifteen minutes after the barrage began, however, one of Hartnett's recon teams came up on the radio, "Here they come. Boy, there's just a huge number of them in route march."

Route march. That meant the NVA were moving at almost a jogging pace and would be on the patrol base (the recon team reported that was precisely the direction they were headed) in short order. Slater turned to the recon lieutenant. "Hartnett, get those guys back. We gotta get out of here; we can't stand up against these guys."

Hartnett radioed his four team leaders to "get back here as soon as possible," while Slater passed the word to his platoon commanders. "Just as soon as they get to us, we're going to all pick up and go back. Have all your gear together and just stand by to pick up and go if you get the word from me. Be alert, look around. Be very, very cautious."

Captain Slater did not tell his battle-rattled troops that a force outnumbering them four to one was bearing down on them. But he did, of course, alert Major Woodring. At this time, all USMC artillery units along the strongpoint system were fully engaged in placing counterbattery fire on the NVA artillery emplacements above the Ben Hai River. Woodring, however, had his battalion 81mm mortar section, his companies' 60mm mortar sections, and the 90mm-equipped M48 tanks along his line, as well as the closest 4.2-inch howtar detachment in the area all begin lobbing indirect fire into the path that the recon people reported the NVA were taking. At this point, all Captain Slater could do was hope that the recon teams got to their patrol base before the NVA did.

★

Lying with his radio operators in their L-shaped trench, Captain Landes, the Bravo Six of BLT 1/3, had his helpless feelings suddenly replaced by a picture that formed in his mind's eye of one of his Basic School instructors standing on a lecture stage. The instructor, a captain who had never seen combat (this was, after all, 1961), was describing the characteristics of an Assault Barrage (in other words, artillery fire under whose cover assaulting infantrymen move); he said that even though Marines were trained to keep their heads up, their first instinct would be to drop to the bottom of their fighting holes and pray. The instructor stressed how important it was for a commander to insure that his men were heads-up, because the enemy would come running in through their own barrage (accepting those friendly fire casualties) and be in your holes before you saw them. This classroom lecture was suddenly vivid in Landes's mind after having lain dormant for six years, and he blurted out, *"Damn,* that's an Assault Barrage!"

Captain Landes told his two radiomen to stay in the trench; then, he climbed out himself into the hellfire (give a man responsibility for the lives of other men, Landes mused, and all concerns for his personal safety instantly evaporate). He ran forward the hundred meters or so between his CP and Bravo Company's main line, then ran the length of it, moving along behind the holes and pausing beside every second or third one to talk with his kids. "Keep your heads up! It's an Assault Barrage! They'll be coming in under it! Keep your heads up!"

"Hey, don't worry, skipper, we got it!"

"You shouldn't be out here, sir!"

"Get down!"

"Be careful!"

Landes, under heavy fire for the first time, moved west to where Bravo was tied in with Alpha Company, then retraced his steps east to where Bravo was tied in with Charlie Company. Captain Jordan, the Alpha Six of BLT 1/3, was doing the exact same thing. Neither Landes's nor Jordan's hole-to-hole scramble spotted any approaching NVA (yet), but they did discover that casualties were almost nonexistent (thanks to fighting holes and those agricultural trenches), despite the rumbling and thundering, the showers of dirt clods, and the severed, spinning tree limbs. The Assault Barrage was, thus far, not lethal, merely nerve-rattling. Corporal Stuart of the S-2 Scouts remembered:

> As we were moving through Bravo Company's sector, we got hit. . . . Jesus Christ, it rained artillery. I was scared to death. I was praying some serious prayers. We had to get up and move when the North Vietnamese were reloading their guns. . . . I was running and jumped in what appeared to be a tiny Vietnamese-built fighting hole—two feet by two feet. And this huge Hawaiian gunnery sergeant Kikohana, says, "Get out of that hole, Stuart. That's mine." He's standing up to direct traffic as these fucking artillery explosions are going on all around us. And he's telling me, "Go find your own hole, goddamn it, that's mine." I had to make a mad dash to another position while hearing the pop of artillery coming in. It's, "Oh no, in a few seconds they'll be here." And the closer they came, the louder the sound—you can hear them whistling right in on you. It didn't help my sanity.

When the barrage began, Captain Aldous, the Delta Six of BLT 1/3, was forward of the battalion line with a Force Recon platoon. Delta and Recon were immediately ordered back into their reserve position near the BLT 1/3 CP, and PFC Law picked up the account there:

> We started digging in for a big assault. The other two guys I was with started saying the Rosary, droaning on, "Hail Mary, full of grace . . ." This was a bit much for me—I decided if I was going to get it, it was going to be fighting and not by some gook emptying his AK47 magazine in my back while I whimpered in some hole. I decided to get out of the hole with my .45 drawn and be

ready. Here was all kinds of bombs going off, the stuff whizzing past me as I ran around, jumping in and out of craters, looking for gooks to kill.

Captain Reczek, the Charlie Six of BLT 1/3, was in his CP trench under NVA artillery fire so accurate that he reached up to pull down a poncho rigged overhead: he thought the NVA might be using it as an aiming point. Major Ossenfort, the S-3, radioed him to prepare for an NVA ground assault and to get his people (Lieutenant Francis's Charlie Two and Lieutenant Norris's Bravo Three) back in the battalion line. Ossenfort prudently indicated that if any Marine bodies had to be left behind at this point, so be it, and Reczek relayed this withdrawal order to Francis. Their Marines, however, were still under considerable automatic-weapons, recoilless-rifle, and mortar fire (a brushfire had also ignited in the bone-dry woods), and there was a lot of smoke and confusion, and very little unit integrity. PFC Steiner, for one, had just sucked into the ground as low as he could get as the woods filled with smoke and dust from the pistonlike pounding of the mortars, and as steel filled the air, oscillating past with a thick *fff-fff-fff!* Steiner couldn't see anyone else when he did raise his head, and finally he realized that the platoon was pulling back and that if he did not get up he would be left behind. He started back, seeing no one except his good buddy Mel Sands, an unlettered farmboy and one of the few grunts who Steiner really thought knew what he was doing in the bush. Steiner and Sands ended up shoulder to shoulder (Steiner with his radio aerial waving above him) as they backpedaled up the footpath leading to the company perimeter. Both walked backward and fired their M16s into the smokey woods to keep down the heads of NVA they could not see but who they were sure were following them. It seemed they were the last ones out.

Cpl Michael Brugh, a machine gunner with Delta Company, had not made it back into battalion lines with the rest. Throwing himself flat when the barrage had begun, he had lost visual contact with everyone else, and pinned to this one spot, belly down under his helmet, flak jacket, and ammunition bandoliers, he had occupied his frightened mind by counting the incoming rounds. He was up to 155 when the next round landed five feet to his left, the direction in which he was already looking. And after witnessing this sudden, dirt-showering explosion, to his amazement he was still alive. He felt no pain, but he realized he couldn't get up. That's all he knew, he had to get out of there, but he couldn't stand.

Brugh anxiously looked down and there was a softball-sized hunk of flesh and muscle hanging by the barest strands to the calf of his left leg. Both trouser legs were ripped and bloody, and he hollered for a corpsman. One appeared, accompanied by a Marine—neither of whom Brugh recognized. They explained they were with Alpha Company and administered a Syrette of morphine. Another salvo was whistling in, and with that, the corpsman and Marine picked up Brugh's M60 machine gun and took off for their holes.

Brugh was alone again.

Well, they'll get to me as soon as they can, he thought, still feeling no pain and imagining how busy the corpsmen must be. Brugh suddenly realized that there were NVA visible about three hundred meters to the north. They were moving in banzai style, and with a hundred uncrossable meters between himself and the battalion line to the south, he figured it was all over. He unholstered his .45, chambered the first round, and prepared himself. He knew what the NVA did to wounded Marines. *I'll do my own shit in before I let them kill me.*

Running back, PFC King and PFC Pilgreen of Charlie BLT 1/3 were suddenly hurled off their feet by the concussion of an artillery round exploding behind them. Up in the air, Pilgreen felt his M16 buck in his hands meaning he had involuntarily squeezed the trigger. At the same time he saw King, in his peripheral vision, turn in midair right where the barrel had been pointed. King crash-landed in the dirt.

Pilgreen, horrified that he had just accidentally shot his buddy (and pissed that his safety had been off despite his usual safety-conscious standards), jumped atop King to check him.

King jerked around, unhurt and uncomprehending of Pilgreen's attention. "What the hell you doin'?"

"You all right?"

"Yeah!"

"Let's get the hell outta here!"

They ran near one of the similarly retreating tanks. Pilgreen, thinking of that blown-away tank they had just left behind, shouted to King, "We're going to be a damn fool to stay by this goddamned tank! We can just get the hell away from here!"

The grassy clearing through which the Marines were running was situated between the fire-swept tree line to the east and the supposed sanctuary of their agricultural trenches to the west. Immediately prior to the barrage, the clearing had been used as a hasty LZ for the Sea Horses delivering an emergency ammunition resupply for the firefight to the east. One of the helping hands in that exercise had been LCpl Mark Chartier, a radioman with the Tactical Air Control Party assigned to Charlie Company. Chartier had leaned his M16 against a tree to one side of the LZ as he had used his radio and hand signals to bring the Sea Horses in and then to help unload them. Now the barrage had sealed him against the earth before he had had a chance to retrieve his weapon.

Marines were rushing past in the elephant grass, and Chartier could hear AK47 fire. And then, suddenly—Chartier couldn't believe it—there were North Vietnamese coming through the trees at a run right into the LZ. They had palm leaves and banana leaves all over their headgear and equipment harnesses.[2] Chartier, covered by upturned

2. It was subsequently theorized that the NVA on the east flank planned to launch their attack simultaneously with the arrival of the columns presently approaching from the north. However, C BLT 1/3's patrol action triggered a premature NVA assault on the east flank.

earth, jumped up and took a couple steps toward where he'd left his M16. But it was fifty meters away and he couldn't see it anymore, and he'd never been so scared. This was coming out of nowhere. So, crawling and running, he joined the retreat, feeling worthless without his rifle. Everyone was moving back (there was no reason to make a stand in a clearing), some of them firing and running, then spinning to fire again. Others dropped to one knee to place careful shots into the charging NVA. And Chartier saw—or his adrenaline-charged mind's eye told him he saw—some of those running bushes abruptly skid face first into the elephant grass.

Lance Corporal Kalwara scrambled out of the clearing and over an embankment with his gun team; his gunner threw the M60 back atop the berm and opened fire. Kalwara screamed to the other Marines there, *"Give me your grenades, give me your grenades!"*

Fragmentation grenades were piled up; then, Kalwara grabbed the Marine to his right. "You start throwing grenades. The rest of us will keep shooting and try to pick 'em off as they come through the smoke, but all your job to do is just pull these pins and throw 'em. Pull these pins and throw 'em, just keep throwin' 'em."

Kalwara threw his M16 to his shoulder.

Corporal Chartier made it back to this hasty firing line, then went down into an old, deep crater. He went all the way to the bottom, unarmed, terrified, and just knowing the NVA (whose shouts he could hear) would overrun him, kill him, blow him away. There was another Marine in the crater, a lieutenant he did not know who had his act together and his .45 ready. Chartier looked up toward the rim of the crater, waiting for an NVA with a blazing AK47 to charge over. With no obvious options in response, he crammed his face into the loose dirt of the crater. He

---

Lance Corporal Kalwara said, "They were very lightly equipped so they were swift, they were fleet. They were really hot, they were moving, they were firing and screaming and yelling like they were crazy, like they were unorganized and just crazy, like, 'We're gonna kill ya and here we come!' "

didn't want to see the guy who was going to shoot him. He looked back up. Nothing. He looked back down, then up again.

There was nothing to see because finally presented with targets to square their sights on, Lieutenant Francis's Charlie Two stopped the NVA cold. With Captain Reczek and Lieutenant Neuss pouring the artillery on with the lance corporal who served as their FO, the NVA were forced back to covered positions. The cacophony continued but the pressure was easing, and though still under the Assault Barrage, Lieutenant Norris was able to move Bravo Three back into their original positions along the north-south canal between Alpha and Bravo Companies. A magnificent performance, thought Captain Landes, although Norris did lose the tanks moving back with him. "They got as far as our lines; then, instead of going back into position—and we needed them—the tanks kept right on going. Never did figure that out, what the problem was, whether they were totally unnerved or out of ammunition. George Norris got out in front of them, tired to stop them, and damned near got run over. The tanks disappeared from the battlefield."

34

Let's Kill the Sons of Bitches

★

Shortly after Captain Slater passed the word to be on the lookout for the returning recon teams (at 1700, 6 July 1967), LCpl Charles L. Olson of the 1st Platoon, Alpha Company, 1st Battalion, 9th Marines, detected an element approaching their patrol base in Thon Phuong Xuan. Olson, with radioman and riflemen, was in the hideaway of an OP situated at about two o'clock on the perimeter circle. The figures he saw were moving in from the north or northeast, generally approaching the tall tree north of the patrol base that had been designated as twelve o'clock. Olson counted the single-file figures, made indistinct due to the distance and the elephant grass and denuded trees through which they moved—one, two, three, four, and on up to ten—and then he saw twenty more figures behind the first file, and he knew it wasn't recon. The four recon teams combined had numbered sixteen men. Olson was not the type to see things that weren't there (this was his fifteenth month incountry, and his first tour had included Operations Starlite and Harvest Moon, bad ones both), and he immediately radioed the company headquarters that NVA were approaching their lines in column.

Captain Slater realized that Hartnett's recon teams were not going to reach the patrol base before the NVA, but also that the 400 approaching NVA seemed unaware of his 100-plus Marines in Thon Phuong Xuan. The enemy columns were not fanning out for an attack, but were continuing their route march straight for their predug bunker complex, presumably to get out from under the mortar, howtar, and tank fire currently being directed on them and to use the peanut-shaped hill as a rallying point before pressing on with their attack against the main Marine line. About the time of Olson's OP report, NVA bugles sounded to the north. Corporal Fazio of Alpha One (near the twelve o'clock position), looking around incredulously like everyone else, saw Staff Sergeant Leslie, his platoon commander, tearing across a field as fast as he could while shouting, *"The gooks are coming! There's a whole regiment out there!"*

Fazio looked at the M79 grenadier sharing his hole and muttered in here-we-go-again resignation, "I don't believe it."

"I don't either—but just get down."

Corporal Fazio waited and watched, and then, a hundred or so meters off through the cratered clearings, he could see bush hats bobbing in the elephant grass. Dozens of hats coming straight toward them. The closer they got the more focused they became, and Fazio was amazed at the fast, steady pace these NVA columns were keeping. They were just bouncing along in cadence like a centipede, like they were walking on air despite the packs on their backs, the ammo vests on their chests, and the AK47s or SKSs in their hands, or the RPGs over their shoulders. To his left, he could see two NVA dragging along a large, two-wheeled 12.7mm machine gun like it was a toy, just bouncing it along behind them. There were also NVA without weapons, each of whom had a dozen 60mm mortar rounds secured to both ends of a bamboo pole and balanced over his shoulder. Fazio reckoned they'd come all the way from Hanoi humping those rounds, and they looked like they could keep up this brisk pace all day. *Very enthusiastic,* he thought—*very aggressive.*

And very unlucky. The NVA point element was closing with the Marines at twelve o'clock—fifty meters, forty meters, thirty meters—when one of the attached engineers announced their presence by opening fire. Captain Slater knew it was an engineer because they were the only ones who still carried M14s. Concerned that one of his extra, noninfantry bodies had panicked, he shouted, "What the hell you shooting at?"

"Hey, they're NVA!"

"There's a whole column of NVA right in front of us!"

There were about thirty NVA immediately visible to Alpha One, and that engineer's shot set off a spontaneous chain reaction from the log-covered holes of the Marines nearby. The first long bursts sent most of these NVA sprawling before they even knew what hit them, most of them the victims of an M60 gunner who would afterward report that several females (presumably field medics) were among those he could see dropping over the recoiling concussion of his weapon. The stunned NVA survivors scurried in a dozen different directions, they and the next targets in line mostly heading, though, for a particular crater as the Marines continued to pour the fire in.

Dropping like flies, Fazio thought as his foxhole partner with the M79 slammed rounds right in among them. Even Gunny Santomasso got in on it with the AK47 he had retrieved from their previously overrun LZ to replace his jammed M16. Santomasso squeezed a burst into an NVA just coming into view through the trees about forty meters away, then decided not to fire again. He was concerned that the distinctive sound of his captured AK might draw Marine fire or rattle the troops. (And, in fact, a couple of grunts did get on him afterward, "Boy, we heard that AK of yours poppin' off and we thought the gooks overran the CP!")

Captain Slater had also come forward to see that only a few NVA, dripping with leaves for camouflage, were returning fire. The rest had been mowed down or scattered, and an NVA bugle was being frantically sounded. *A turkey shoot,* Slater thought with elated relief, running back to his CP to tell his FO, "Okay, Sankey, bring in the artillery . . ." With the arty beginning to hammer in, the OPs around the patrol base made it back in, as did two of the reconnaissance teams. However, one to the north and a second one to the northeast did not. Between them and the patrol base were 400 (minus thirty) stirred-up NVA and a circle of shoot-anything-that-moves Marines. Slater told recon commander Hartnett to pass the word to his two stranded teams: "Don't come back. Find a place to hide. If you come in here right now, you're going to get killed."

When Lance Corporal Stuckey of Charlie Two originally set in at about nine o'clock on the patrol-base circle (along with fireteam comrades Smith and Smitty), he had not taken the exercise as seriously as he should have. It had really appeared that the NVA were good and gone, so they had just sort of half dug in near an old crater, which they avoided as shelter in case the NVA had booby trapped such a handy piece of cover. They had been sitting casually about, packs and gear unshouldered, eating C rations, when the firing suddenly erupted from the positions at twelve o'clock. They had no idea what was coming off, but their automatic response was to drop their rations, scoop up their helmets and, each with an M16 in one hand and about half his previously unslung ammunition bandoliers in the other, sprint for that potentially dangerous but deep crater.

The crater appeared suddenly inviting in comparison to their half-scratched holes. When Stuckey jumped in he prayed in that midair second, *please, don't let this crater be mined or booby trapped!* And when his feet hit good, solid, unexploding earth, he'd never been so relieved.

Stuckey, Smith, and Smitty had left their packs, canteens, and a lot of ammo down by their fighting holes in their hasty scramble for cover. Any ideas they had about rushing back to retrieve this gear evaporated when, almost immediately, a radioman and a couple other Marines ran past them, falling back to the center of the perimeter.

The NVA were right behind them. They were weaving through the trees to the west, avoiding the firing at twelve o'clock, and probing, trying to determine the extent of the Marine perimeter and how to get past it or into it. From their crater, Stuckey, Smith, and Smitty delivered a fully automatic M16 surprise into them, throwing the NVA into a where-is-it-coming-from state of confusion. For a moment, the fear washed away, and the Marines were almost like excited kids at a shooting gallery.

"I got him! I got him!"

"That's one!"

Another burst, another shout, "That's two!"

Stuckey and crew counted up to eight before the NVA got their act together. It had been a *game,* it had been *fun,* and Larry Stuckey, a good, solid, sensitive kid, was suddenly ashamed at how subhuman those North Vietnamese soldiers in his rifle sights had seemed at that moment.

The patrol base occupied by A-C/1/9 opened fire on the NVA sometime between 1705 and 1715, 6 July 1967, at which time 3/9 (1,200 meters to the southeast) was readying itself to meet additional NVA columns coming across the Ben Hai and bypassing the blazing patrol base. Major Woodring and Captain Navadel had (at 1320) moved their CP just northeast of Hill 109, some 150 meters to the rear of their forward companies. The Assault Barrage was still raining in[1] as Major Woodring briefed Captains Conger (India), Giles (Kilo), and Shirley (Lima) about the ap-

---

1. The NVA placed 500–600 artillery rounds on 3/9 between 1645–1735, 6 July 1967 (the NVA then shifted the preponderance of their fires on BLT 1/3), without inflicting a single recorded casualty. Major Woodring himself, however, would be hit at dusk (shrapnel in the left calf which the battalion's senior corpsman would treat on the spot); he would hesitate in reporting the wound lest regiment overreact and transplant him from his battalion to a hospital ship.

proaching NVA infantrymen. He said to be prepared for anything from NVA attempting to infiltrate their lines in USMC gear to Soviet PT76 tanks, which had reportedly been spotted by aerial observers.

Major Woodring's operational plans were always to the point, and he turned first to Captain Giles. "Kitty Kat, have you got plenty of LAWs?"

"Yep."

"You got your gas masks? We may have to gas this whole area."

"Yep."

"You got plenty of ammunition?"

"Yep."

"Thank you."

Woodring asked the same of Indifferent India and Lizard Lima, then concluded, "Okay, you guys, everybody's all ready for tonight. Okay, here's my operations order: let's kill the sons of bitches."

The company commanders just kind of looked at their battalion commander, and Woodring responded, "Ain't much else to say, but just kill the sons of bitches if they show up."

"Yes, sir."

Back in position with Gunny Hatfield, Captain Giles felt a different, new fear in his heart. Giles couldn't help but reflect on how casual their VC-killing days at An Hoa now seemed, and he commented to Hatfield, "Man, this war had changed. You know, we used to set anyplace, we'd go out and run and chase and hope to make a contact. And now, all of a sudden, these guys are crossing the river, they're coming with tanks[2] and they're shooting with artillery. I mean they have upped the game. They obviously figure they're ready to face us head on."

PFC Ford of India Company was dug in with his rocket team in an agricultural trench, the hedgerow behind

---

2. As it developed, no enemy tanks made an appearance (the aerial observers had probably spotted trucks bringing ammunition to the NVA artillery batteries along the Ben Hai River).

them shielding a tank whose 90mm main gun pointed toward where the Nguyens of the North were supposed to be coming. Ford had the greatest respect for those sons of bitches (they were not merely Charlie, they were Mr. Charles), and he had his 3.5-inch rocket launcher assembled and the ammunition ready. He laid his .45 in the dirt before him, along with two ammunition magazines and the grenades off his flak jacket. Then he unsheathed his K-Bar fighting knife and slid its blade into the dirt—ready and waiting, just in case. Ford was scared—*a human wave attack? This is it, this is the last few minutes of my life.* It was incomprehensible (he was only nineteen, he was supposed to live forever), indescribable, inevitable—horrible, horrible. And yet Ford also felt another indescribable emotion. It was pride. His fellow Marines were hunkering down around him, preparing to fight to their last breaths. Ford once saw a Marine with a single .45 round tucked in the elastic band of his helmet, above which he'd written on the helmet cover THIS ONE'S FOR ME—in other words he'd kill himself before he'd allow himself to be captured. That was how Ford saw it. These were American fighting men. And when the chips are down, and there's no food and there's no water, and they know the odds are against them —*they manage to reach down inside themselves and fight back!* Just like their grandfathers in WWI and their fathers in WWII or Korea. Just like he had seen during the Battle of Getlin's Corner. *This is it, I'm going to take as many of those little bastards with me as I possibly can!*

The 3d Battalion, 9th Marines, which had been placing 60mm and 81mm fire on the NVA since about 1700, commenced fire at 1715 with M16s, M60s, and M79s as the NVA became visible to the north, coming south. The NVA assault seemed to fizzle out then and there in the elephant grass (perhaps they were a diversionary force for the efforts against A-C/1/9 and BLT 1/3), and their return fire consisted mostly of RPGs sizzling toward the tanks on the battalion line. They scored no hits, and the long 90mm main guns of each M48 tank sent HE and Beehive rounds in thunderous return.

And my fuckin' ears were ringing, thought Corporal Gomez of India Two. The incoming had caught him before he'd dug in. Lying on top of the ground with his gear around him, he had his squad radio to his ear. He exulted at the reports of approaching NVA, thinking of yesterday's body-recovery mission. *Now they're going to fight, now the shit starts, and we're going to kick their fuckin' ass!* No targets, however, loomed into view, and though the expectant tension was terrible, Corporal Collopy, for one, found that with his M16 not needed, his mind was reawakening to his almost unbearable thirst. Their gunnery sergeant, Gunny Smith, was trooping their agricultural trench at this point, and a Marine of the same mind as Collopy called out, "Hey, gunny, where's the water?"

Now, Gunny Smith always talked like he had marbles in his mouth, and he answered with, "The gookfs blew upf the water. They rocketed the LZ, and they blew upf the water."

"Hey, *fuck you, gunny!* We don't want to hear that bullshit, we want our fucking water! We don't need your fucking excuses; we need some fucking water!"

"You better watch it, I'll haff your aff court-marfalled!"

"Fuck you, gunny!"

A few more "fuck you, gunny"'s (the men considered him a benign idiot, and First Sergeant Lee would soon relieve him for not fighting hard enough to get his people what they needed) and the steam had been blown off. Hearing that they weren't going to get their water resupply, Corporal Collopy poured a packet of orange Kool Aid into his mouth in an attempt to activate his salivary glands. No way. It was like chewing orange-flavored ash, and Collopy smiled weakly to himself that this hint-from-the-field wasn't going to net him twenty-five dollars from the "If I Were Commandant" feature in *Leatherneck* magazine.

★

From his hummock-top patrol base on the southern side of the Trace, Captain Southard (CO,H/2/9) watched the Assault Barrage traverse back and forth, and up and down. The artillery eventually rolled south across the Trace itself, and he dropped into an old, shallow fighting hole that didn't allow him to get his head completely down. Gunny Evans bellowed at him from the hole into which he'd moved to "get your head down, skipper." Then emphasized the point with a shouted story of an FAC the gunny said he had seen decapitated in similar circumstances. Nearby, Southard could see the Vietnamese-speaking corporal from S-2 making sure that the prisoners they had rounded up that morning (the ones the other corporal had gleefully talked about wasting) found holes for cover. He even pulled two of them down in his own hole (they were eventually evacuated by helicopter), but luckily the barrage stopped a hundred meters short of their patrol base before rolling north again. This happened several more times—the barrage would be within a hundred meters of raining death and maiming on them, and then it would reverse directions.

Captain Southard was amazed and thankful. The NVA barrage was obviously intended to include them, but he could only deduce that they had the patrol base's coordinates wrong on their maps. Southard was instructed by 3/9 (to whom H/2/9 was opcon) to move across the Trace and link up with their CP. This was accomplished by platoon rushes, the company headquarters behind the lead platoon. Despite the artillery fire, it didn't take as long to cross the open ground as Southard had anticipated, and, miracle of miracles, they didn't suffer a single casualty during the run. Southard spoke with Major Woodring who directed him to deploy Hotel Company between the 3/9 CP and the Trace. They were to stand by in reserve. It was a brief meeting, but Southard left it confident in the coolness and abilities of his new commander. Southard was also impressed by the major's concern for his men, having heard Woodring comment that he had seen enough of the killing of young Marines in Korea to be profoundly disgusted with this situation.

The NVA response to the surprise sprung on them in Thon Phuong Xuan by Alpha-Charlie 1/9 was, in a word (provided by Captain Slater), *magnificent*. Almost immediately, they brought their 60mm mortars into action, and where they had identified Alpha One's twelve o'clock position on the patrol-base circle, they quickly brought two captured M60s forward. Under this cover fire, the NVA closed bush by bush with the Marine fighting holes. Finally, the M79-man sharing Corporal Fazio's position counted his ammunition and said, "I only got about ten rocks left. Let's get the hell outta here. I'm not going to stay here and get my ass blown apart. Let's just pull back maybe twenty feet."

Fazio was praying the whole time as they jumped from their hole and, under fire from the two captured machine guns, ran back toward a grove of banana trees. They made it. Fazio went to the prone behind one of the trees; the NVA were now throwing Chicom grenades at them. As he frantically looked around, he saw an NVA pop his head up from a spiderhole. The NVA saw him too—and smiled (?!) —as Fazio, on his belly and tangled up in the tall, sharp grass, tried to get his M16 pointed in that direction. He got off three or four quick shots; then, he heard a hiss-pop noise and a thump—and there was a Chicom beside him. If he moved away from the grenade, he figured he'd be seen and shot, so he lay where he was, covered his head, and waited an eternity for the explosion. When it came, it rolled Fazio over in the grass and blew the M79-man's helmet off, but neither got a scratch. Fazio hollered, "Let's pull back to the next crater! They're coming all around us!"

All around the patrol base, the NVA pressed in like the mean, motivated sons of bitches they were. They lobbed Chicom after Chicom at those Marine positions they had identified. They moved in close to fire AK47s at almost point-blank range. They expertly expanded the fan of their mortar barrage to include each new part of the line they discovered. To determine just how many Marines they were dealing with and where exactly they were dug in, they tried to draw fire by shaking trees and shouting in Vietnamese. The Marines responded with grenades (it sounded like they were getting more than a few of the NVA), and Corporal Peterson, for one, heard an NVA begin yelling in English. He shouted at the Marines to fall back. He hollered for a corpsman. He shouted a taunt. "Are you in One-Nine?"

A grunt sent an M16 burst in the caller's direction, followed by a defiant, "Yeah, I'm in One-Nine!"

As the platoon commanders relayed these movement reports to Captain Slater, he and PFC Sankey shifted the arty onto them. Slater knew the NVA's game plan. They were trying to surround his patrol base, and his guidance in return to his platoon commanders by radio was, "Okay, you don't shoot these guys until they're coming in our perimeter. Also, try to pick on somebody from the flank. Don't shoot the guy right in front of you. Have somebody off to the left or right pick him off with maybe just one round, but don't disclose your positions."

35

The Assault

★

As soon as SSgt William H. Head, of the 3d Platoon of Bravo BLT 1/3, saw the latest salvo land within their lines, he knew it was something different: a thin white mist rose from the impact area.

"Gas!"

"Gas . . . Gas . . . !"

Staff Sergeant Head, already down in a hole in their secondary positions, quickly donned his never-before-used gas mask, even as he saw one of his unmasked Marines, running for his hole, go down and gag. The gas, however, was not deadly. Nor did it linger, and Marines began removing their rubberized, claustrophobic masks. It had probably been tear gas, though Captain Landes had his doubts when Head's platoon commander, Norris, reported it as such via radio. The muggy, dusk air was already heavy with a sharp, acrid cordite smell from the artillery, and Landes thought his people were mistaking this eye-irritating residue for tear gas.

Officially, Lieutenant Norris and Staff Sergeant Head's platoon was teargassed, which made everyone a little more paranoid as word got around the battalion line. If the NVA did, in fact, have a supply of mortar-propelled tear-gas cannisters, it would make sense that they would expend them on Bravo Three's positions. They covered the deep, vulnerable north-south dry canal that divided Alpha and Bravo Companies' east-west line. Coming in under the on-again-off-again Assault Barrage, it was this canal the NVA were drawn to, hoping to use it as a covered approach to get between and behind their foe's main line. As the NVA artillery dribbled off in the area, the NVA point squads hurled fused blocks of TNT ahead of them to simulate the crash of incoming and keep the Marines' heads down. Other NVA attempted to jam Marine communications with captured radios. These khaki-clad, pith-helmeted, rice-powered, and well-equipped soldiers had come across the Ben Hai River to win, and the BLT 1/3 after-action report recorded the following:

Specific information obtained from captured documents revealed that the 7th or 8th Battalion of the 90th Regiment [324B NVA Division] had a mission to defend the area of Long Son and that the overall mission of the 90th Regiment was to 'Defeat the American troops.' American phrases were passed to NVA troops such as 'Surrender,' 'Put the gun down,' 'Put the hands up,' 'Sit down,' 'Go to the hospital,' and 'Follow me.'

These NVA were approaching Marines who also intended to win. Captain Landes had placed Bravo Three at the line's weakest point precisely because Lieutenant Norris was his finest platoon commander. He was a six-foot-four, handlebar-mustached former Shakespearean actor; a cool head as the grunts would put it. They loved him for his skills, his friendliness, and even for his showing off—if there was a grenade to be thrown by the platoon, he threw it because he knew how photogenic it looked. Norris gave his squads masculine Shakespearean names as radio call signs (King Lear, Richard the Third, Othello), and their LPs feminine names; so that when the squads conducted minipatrols to place one of their fireteams into an LP position (called "Laying the LP"), he could then report to the Six, "The listening post's call sign is Queen Anne, and King Lear has just completed laying Queen Anne."

A shithot platoon commander, Staff Sergeant Head thought again as Lieutenant Norris ran down the line to ensure their people were not fooled by the TNT charges. They needed to keep their heads up and be alert. Marine air and arty were already tearing up the fields ahead of Bravo Three's line.

On BLT 1/3's left flank (held by Lieutenant Matsumoto's Alpha One), a Marine paused beside the three-man hole where Lance Corporal Lind had his M60 set up. He told them they were under strict orders not to fire until they were attacked, especially the M60; then, he rushed on to relay this don't-reveal-your-position order to the next holeful of tensed, waiting Marines. Things were deadly quiet in this area as Lind and his buddies looked down from their meager high ground across a hundred open feet to the next tree line, and three NVA in green utilities suddenly walked out into the open with neither headgear nor web gear and weapons. They simply stood there looking around, close enough for the dug-in, vegetation-shrouded Marines to see their faces. These NVA were probably bait (and probably stoned, Lind thought) to tempt Marines to give away their individual positions by firing, or perhaps, by coming forth weaponless they wanted the Marines to attempt a capture and thus enter an ambush. No one responded and the three NVA finally turned to reenter the woods. The Marine beside Lind couldn't resist firing his M16, dropping one NVA (he got him in the back) while the other two scrambled behind trees. Lind could still see one who was on his knees. It would have been a perfect, clean head shot, but he didn't want to risk exposing his M60's position. No one would hand Lind their M16 either, arguing that they were not supposed to fire at all, until finally, the NVA disappeared altogether. They waited again, and when the AK47s and Chicoms did come, they were down the line to the east. Away from them.

It's like the 200 yard line rapid-fire on the rifle range when all the targets go up. Staff Sergeant Head of Bravo Three (who was on the second of three combat tours) thumped a fresh magazine into his M16 and rose again from his hole, shouldering the rifle as he swung it back toward the tree line some 150 meters north. The NVA wave had reached it and was preparing to cross that last open area between them and the Marines. *They're all over the place—there's no way you can miss!* The muzzle flashes of AK47s blinked in the wood line, as several assault squads of NVA made their rush down at least one agricultural trench. Some were outfitted as Marines down to the jungle boots (one NVA packed a captured M79 grenade launcher), others were normally—and expertly—camouflaged with elephant grass and banana leaves. Mostly unseen, they got in amid the brush where Norris's machinegun team leader, LCpl Duane J. Dull (a draftee), had his M60 gunner returning fire. Dull could hear Marines shouting, *"Where are they coming from?"* Then suddenly, to his right and left, he saw Marines scrambling backward out of their fighting holes. In the cacophony, he had heard no order to pull back, but behind him he saw Lieutenant Norris holding up five fingers to indicate how many meters to fall back (fifty). Dull's team joined the retreat to their secondary positions in the next hedgerow back. They were running. The Marine behind Dull was hit. Dull turned to help, and there were the NVA, throwing grenades then rushing into those cleared spots. Two Marines to Dull's left rushed back for the wounded man, and when they all piled into the agricultural trench in the next hedgerow, Dull's heart was pounding with relief. *Thank God, thank God!*

Lying in his shallow hole near Lieutenant Norris's CP, PFC James P. Daley, the company's lacking-the-rank-but-not-the-skills artillery spotter, couldn't break in on the radio traffic already on the artillery net. He could hear his counterpart FOs with Alpha and Charlie Companies requesting fire, and their direct support artillery responding that they had split the battery so as to fire both missions simultaneously.[1] Frustrated, Daley and his radioman, Corporal Eberly, ran to an unmanned (and, presumably, ammo-exhausted) tank behind them, and Daley climbed on the back deck to get a good look around.

He couldn't believe the view. There were NVA coming across the clearing to the left, near the canal. He could actually see them rushing out of the tree line there. He could see the pith helmets and curved banana clips, he could see gold and silver belt buckles flashing on those NVA he assumed were the officers, and there were others fluttering with leafy camouflage as they ran. Then something suddenly exploded near the tank, and the next thing Daley knew, Eberly was dragging him back toward their holes, as he came awake, mumbling, "Well, what—how did I get here?"

Eberly got him in the hole, then commented that he "should do something about that," and Daley suddenly realized that he'd been peppered with tiny pieces of shrapnel in his face.

No matter. Daley and Eberly ran forward past the wounded who were limping back and ended up in what they took to be an old, thousand-pound-bomb crater. At this point Daley finally made contact with an artillery unit. It was a U.S. Army 175mm self-propelled battery and when Daley requested a fire mission, they asked him for the "danger close factor." Daley had never heard the term before, and putting it in other words, they asked him how close the intended target was to his position. He answered approximately 100 meters, and the battery commander

1. Captain Landes routinely placed his FO at their most vulnerable position, because in PFC Daley (a twenty-year-old from Wisconsin, the son of a WWII vet), Landes knew he had a smart, sharp kid who could be counted on to deliver their artillery trump card where it was needed most. Thus, Daley was not in the L-shaped CP trench but was just east of their weak link of a canal.

then came on the line to refuse the mission. He explained that his directives would not allow him to place 175mm fire within 800 meters of friendly troops. Daley began screaming, and in vulgar language he advised the battery commander that he could either fire and take a chance of maybe killing them, or he could hold his fire, and the NVA certainly would kill them.

"Well, how close are the North Vietnamese?"

Daley keyed the handset and held it up from his crater, so the battery commander could hear the din of automatic-weapons fire. He got back on shouting, "Is that close enough?"

There was a moment of silence. Then the battery commander returned to say that they were going to fire the mission, but that Daley would have to take the responsibility for any friendly casualties.

"Go ahead!"

The 175mm redlegs fired one tube as Daley had requested, and he shifted this fire along the tree lines to their front where the NVA had been coming out, then along the north-south canal where it entered their lines. The Army, hesitant enough to fire, was accurate when it did, and the result was a considerable pause in the amount of NVA fire coming from their front. Mortars and other artillery were also called, and Staff Sergeant Head, for one, was overjoyed to see the WP on target and then the VT rounds fired for effect, achieving airbursts directly above the tree line full of NVA. To his rear, Head could see an equally ecstatic Captain Landes (back up in his tree) as he whooped out, "A dead gook is better than sex!"[2]

Amid the continuing Assault Barrage, the 81mm Mortar Platoon of H&S Company BLT 1/3 placed fire on the NVA from their vulnerable positions along the dike of a dry rice paddy. So much for being part of what the grunts

2. "All emotions are manifested to the fullest; you laugh uproariously, though the humor is often sick." Captain Landes wrote to a friend between operations; "All in all, a good firefight is rather exhilarating."

called the Hide and Skate Company. Their fire-control party was dug in atop a hummock behind them: Staff Sergeant Caballero and Sergeant Russell were in a two-man hole, and their radioman, PFC Rusmisell, was about two feet away in a one-man hole with his PRC25 placed aboveground between the two holes, close enough to pass the handset to Russell if necessary.

Rusmisell was down in his hole, radio handset to one ear and hand to the other one to muffle the noise around him, as he worked with Sergeant Santos, the artillery spotter with Alpha Company. Santos was reporting NVA ground movement and screaming coordinates, which Rusmisell was shouting over to Russell to be fed to the gun crews and—CRASH! The air above Rusmisell suddenly flashed yellow, and the radio at his ear went dead in the same millisecond that the concussion and roar of the NVA artillery round enveloped him. He knew instantly that Caballero and Russell were dead as a section of their sunshade poncho flapped across his peripheral vision—and then (everything was happening at the same time) all was black. He was buried. His legs were free of the embrace, though, so clutching the handset the whole time, he began frantically kicking and pushing his way out.

"Sergeant Russell? Sergeant Russell?"

Still partially buried (only seconds had passed), Rusmisell could hear fellow radioman Wolford hollering from his nearby hole. There was no answer. Wolford's shout grew desperate, *"Sergeant Russell, Sergeant Russell!"*

A hand latched onto Rusmisell's flak jacket and yanked him up from his demolished hole. At the same time, Wolford scrambled up on his hands and knees to the adjoining hole. He looked in and became totally hysterical, screaming and screaming and screaming, and Rusmisell looked in too. Sergeant Russell was dead. He was half out of the hole, arms outstretched (guys were wondering if maybe he'd heard the whistling descent of the shell that got him and had tried to scramble out), but part of his head was blown away and his legs were gone. Staff Sergeant Caballero was also dead, smashed and pulpy at the bottom

of the hole, though most of his head was still recognizable
—and Rusmisell suddenly realized there were little pieces
of both men splattered all about on the ground.[3] Wolford
was still screaming, and a first sergeant pulled him to the
ground and held him down, while another sergeant asked
who had been in the other hole. Rusmisell was pointed out,
and the sergeant talked with him and asked if he was okay.

Rusmisell was standing in a semidaze, still clutching
his radio handset with about eighteen inches of severed
cord. His head was roaring; he could only hear out of one
ear.

"Yeah, I'm all right, I'll be all right."

Sergeant Balabas and the buck sergeant nicknamed
Yaz got everyone organized again. As their 81mm mortars
resumed firing, Rusmisell helped get the bodies out. They
had to use E-tools, and they got the pieces on two ponchos
that had been laid out and—Jesus Christ, he couldn't believe this shit—Caballero's head kept falling out when they
picked up his poncho. Rusmisell was sick—sick to his stomach from the smell around him, and sick knowing that Russell had only a week or two to go before returning home,
and how Caballero had spoken of his pregnant wife. They
had been such good NCOs, and he suddenly felt so, so
tired. Tired and empty. There were other responses. During the hole check during the next lull ("you okay, you
okay, you okay?" then, "yeah, okay," "okay," "okay!"),
Corporal Miller of NGL BLT 1/3 commented, "There was
no holler from that hole. Word came down they took a
direct hit. There was an E-5 in there. I didn't like the guy, I
didn't like him a lot. It sounds sadistic but we started
laughing almost when he got it. He was smart-assey, he was
all order bullshit and all that stuff. I said, 'The hell with
him. Glad it was him.' "

★

3. The NVA placed one thousand artillery rounds on BLT 1/3 between
1645–1900, 6 July 1967, resulting in the deaths of SSgt Gilberto Caballero and Sgt Randal K. Russell of H&S Company, and PFC Verne M.
Greeley of B Company.

For PFC Brugh, the machine gunner with Delta Company who had been left stranded forward of their lines with his shrapnel-crippled legs, salvation had come (just before the NVA had) in the form of four Alpha Company Marines who rushed out to him with a nylon-strap stretcher.

Just as they were hustling into their lines, another artillery salvo screeched in, and they slid Brugh into a shallow slit trench before jumping into their own holes. Afterward, a big Marine reached into the trench and hauled Brugh out by the corner of his flak jacket, banging his legs against the dirt: *pain!* He realized he was hurt a lot worse than he had thought (the fibula between his left knee and ankle was, in fact, shattered and most of his right kneecap was gone), and though not screaming, he was conscious of nothing anymore but that pain as the Alpha Marines got him back in the nylon-handled stretcher. Then from out of nowhere, like manna from heaven, appeared his old buddy, Raymond Kelley. *A crazy fucker,* Brugh thought, just the kind of Marine he wanted at a time like this. *You could count on him, his word was gold.*

Lance Corporal Kelley just happened to be passing with LCpl Ronald L. Fox. When they saw that it was Brugh in the poncho-type stretcher (there was so much clotted blood inside that it looked to Kelley like dark red jello), Kelley went into an excited, shouting overdrive and really lit a fire under the Alpha Marines who had previously been moving at a worn-out half-speed. With Kelley and Fox grabbing a strap apiece and two Alpha Marines on the other two, they ran with Brugh all the way back to the Trace, huffing and cursing and moving as fast as they could as AK47 rounds occasionally snapped past. Bouncing along, jolting with pain, Brugh prayed. He had to make it. He was only three days short of rotating home.

They reached the casualty collection point about the same time that two casualty-loaded Sea Horses lifted off. Another Sea Horse landed, and into its cabin went three dead Marines, then the wounded. A Marine who'd been wandering around the LZ with no visible wounds but with a crazed look on his face started to step into the last place in the cabin, but Kelley shoved him away. "You're going on the *next* fucking ride, you son of a bitch!"—then grabbed a strap of Brugh's litter. Thanking God he was finally on his way out, Brugh shared the ride to Phu Bai with the unbagged and horribly smelling dead; then, upon landing he was on a jeep-borne stretcher. The pain was becoming intolerable again, and it really pissed him off that the doctor's initial check of him in the aid station resulted in a casualty tag tied to his toe. He'd only seen tags on the toes of their dead.

A Navy chaplain stayed with Brugh, and because he'd lost a lot of blood and because the doctors were presently too busy to treat these shattered legs, he thought it best to administer last rites.

The motherfucker's putting oil on me! Brugh protested, "There's no fucking reason for this. I'm not dyin', I'm fine."

"Well, sometimes we don't know."

"Your ass we don't know!" Brugh answered, and with that kind of never-say-die attitude he was halfway home.

Meanwhile, Lance Corporals Fox and Kelley ran back to Delta Company's positions behind the main battalion line. Dropping back into his hole with his M79, Kelley heard the corpsman in the next hole calling to him for help. He said he'd been shot in the foot, which seemed inconceivable—he was in a *hole*—unless it had been the corpsman's own .45 and not the NVA that had done the damage. Kelley was so convinced that the corpsman had shot himself that when he called again for Kelley to drag him to the LZ, he shouted back that he wouldn't. It was left for a Hispanic kid nicknamed Poncho to pull the doc back, and for Kelley to think with irony that *Poncho probably doesn't think I have any balls.* Kelley had his doubts about a lot of the guys himself. They had too many replacements in Delta Company, and so many Marines were helmets-down in their holes that Kelley bellowed at them, "Look it, we're gonna get hit—the fucking gooks, they're going to come in after the artillery! You've got to get your head up! You got to get your shit together. They're going

to hit us, don't you understand! You're going to be fucking
dead!"

Hearing the automatic-weapons fire from the forward
line, Corporal Miller and Moose Moyer (Naval Gunfire
Liaison Team BLT 1/3) quickly filled their north-south slit
trench with dirt in the direction the NVA would be coming
from. Moose had only his .45, and Miller's M16 was the
same one that had seized up on him two nights ago. He'd
since obtained a cleaning kit, though, and he broke out the
cleaning rod, screwed it together, and stuck it in the dirt
alongside the ammo magazines he had laid out: "Moyer,
when they come down that trench, we're just going to kill
all we can, you know. If it jams up, I'm going to open it up
and you jam the rod down the bore to knock it out—and
we'll just keep going, you know."[4]

Someone was running toward them from the front.

Corporal Miller had his M16 to his shoulder, and then
the figure rolled into the trench in front of their little
earthen blockade, and Miller almost squeezed a burst into
him in the second before he realized it was a Marine. Bullets had been snapping at the man as he'd jumped down,
and now he scrambled past Miller and Moyer, continuing
his retreat.

Miller could see movement ahead in the bushes then
—quick flashes of NVA with banana leaves on and all that
crap—who put AK47 fire in their direction. Miller bobbed
up with his M16. It was the same old story—two or three
shots, then she'd jam, whip out the cleaning rod, two or
three, then she'd jam . . . Miller couldn't tell if he was
hitting a thing.

★

4. Lance Corporal Groeger (NGL BLT 1/3) stated, "They told us to fix
bayonets because they were going to be on us in like three or four
minutes, and I don't think I'll ever forget the sound of like 300 bayonets simultaneously coming out of their scabbards. A bayonet rings
when it comes out, and all you could hear was *shring, shring, shring,
shring, shring.*"

From the hilltop CP of Alpha BLT 1/3, Captain Jordan kept in radio contact with his platoon commanders (Matsumoto, Bouchard, and Snyder) and told them to keep in touch with all their holes, to make sure that no one ended up unaccounted for during the NVA rushes. Toward dusk, one of his platoons reported that they were no longer getting answers back from the last hole on the right flank, where they tied in with Bravo Company. Jordan radioed Landes, Bravo Six, who said that he too had lost contact with his people in the holes along the fire-swept canal. It appeared they might have a break in their lines, and Jordan called the battalion command post to suggest they send up Delta Company from their reserve position.

While waiting, Captain Jordan called up Sergeant Bouchard of Alpha Two. "I need you to go down off to the right flank here. The enemy has punched a hole in the lines, and we need to tie into Bravo Company."

Sergeant Bouchard moved his people downhill into a washed-out streambed near the canal. As far as he could tell, this was where Jordan wanted him. They began hollering for Bravo Company. Bouchard then placed his men into position, and they were digging in as he rushed back down into the streambed with his radiomen to make contact with Jordan and Landes. He was on the radio when one of his squad leaders began shouting from a little knoll overlooking the streambed. They had NVA in Marine gear moving in on them from the cover of a tree line. Bouchard called back with his Massachusetts accent, "Are you shore?"

"Yeah!"

"Well, hold your fire! We gotta make shore!"

Bouchard, with no time to rush up to see for himself, relayed the squad leader's observations to Jordan. The location of those men seemed to be behind the part of the line that Jordan still had commo with, so he told Bouchard he would get back to him after checking with Snyder and Matsumoto. The squad leader was still bellowing, "Sarge, I can nail 'em from here!"

"Are you *shore* they're not Marines?"

"Yeah!"

Bouchard tried unsuccessfully to get back in contact with Jordan, then finally shouted to the squad leader to take those figures under fire. He trusted this fine squad leader not to panic and see NVA in the bushes when they were really Marines, but it was a terribly confusing situation of explosions, smoke, shouting, and firing—and suddenly, of NVA popping up in some bomb craters right in front of Bouchard's platoon. The Marines lobbed their frags right in on them.

Captain Reczek of Charlie BLT 1/3 was still bringing in the arty on the blunted NVA attack to the east, when AK47 fire suddenly snapped over their heads from the north. Reczek took the handset plugging him into Major Ossenfort. "There's enemy inside our position, because I'm taking shots across my trenches here." Ossenfort wanted to know if NVA had followed his engaged platoon back into their holes, but Reczek (on the horn to his platoon commanders with the handset against his other ear) replied, "No, I don't think they came through my position because my people said no, they didn't." Ossenfort then informed Reczek that Delta Company had been set in motion with the mission to sweep up to the Alpha-Bravo-Charlie line and eliminate any NVA on the wrong side of their fighting holes. As Delta started forward, Reczek could see Marines from Alpha and Bravo being led through Charlie's interior lines on the way to the Trace LZ, coming through wide-eyed and bewildered. Shell shock. Reczek's lance corporal of an FO then got off the arty net to report, "Captain, the battery's callin' and they want to know if they can slow down. Their guns are gettin' too hot." To which Reczek reluctantly replied, "Just a little bit."

While Sergeant Bouchard of Alpha Two moved toward the north-south canal from the west, Staff Sergeant Head of Bravo Three likewise moved in from the east per instructions from Lieutenant Norris after contact had been lost with their squad there. Slung with extra ammo, Head took his Right Guide, a Hawaiian, and an M79-man, and firing and maneuvering, running and ducking, they made it into a large bomb crater near the canal. About forty meters ahead they could see two Marines, including the platoon's Indian, popping up to fire from their hole. They were apparently the only Marines still in the area, and Head shouted to them, though they could not hear him in the din.

There were three NVA in a crater, throwing grenades and firing on that last two-man position (it looked to Head like the Indian was snatching the Chicoms and flinging them away), but they hadn't noticed Head's team. As Head and his M79-man rose from the slope of their crater to fire on them, the tree line far to their north abruptly exploded with AK47 fire, so that Head saw a burst of green tracers crisscross right past his face. Undeterred, the M79-man tried again and dropped a shell right on target. With that crater silenced, Head, his corporal, and his grenadier crawled up to their two survivors. Their area was littered with dud Chicoms and both Marines, down to their last magazines of M16 ammunition, had fixed bayonets. Nevertheless, Head was shocked to realize, the Indian retained his expressionless mask at the arrival of his rescuers. He was as calm as could be.

Staff Sergeant Head radioed Lieutenant Norris to confirm that the NVA had punched through their lines and to report that he couldn't see any link between their platoon and Alpha Company on their left.

Meanwhile, Lieutenant Norris appeared at the edge of the thousand-pound-bomb crater where PFC Daley and Corporal Eberly were set up.[5] Norris was calling for his squad leaders to rally to him (they had to get organized to

5. Daley and Eberly had just returned to the crater, having been previously ordered by Norris to run to the CP for M60 ammunition. This they had accomplished in a hunched-over jog to avoid all the steel in the air. Each had been handed two 400-round boxes by their short, greasegun-toting gunnery sergeant who, relatively new, was now proving highly visible and effective under fire.

plug the gap), as he himself stood tall for the whole world to see. *That's dumb, that's absolutely dumb,* Daley thought. But that was Norris, playing the fearless leader for his men. Norris called to Daley, "Get outta that hole, get up here. We gotta talk about the situation."

"Is our LP/OP in?"

"Yeah, they're in."

"Well, who's that then?"

Daley pointed to a spot of brush less than a hundred meters away where a man wearing a pith helmet was situated. He could just see the pith helmet moving right and left as the owner looked around, but the situation was confused enough that Daley couldn't just start blasting with his M14 rifle. Norris seemed nonplussed as he took a look. "I don't know who that is. Now get out of the hole."

If he's not worried about it, why should I be worried about it. It seemed to Daley that all of them were operating a bit sluggishly by this point, because there he was, against all better instincts, climbing out of his protective crater. Norris had his map out for the six or seven of them—and then an AK47 opened fire from those bushes, the firecrackers of its rounds hitting the dirt between at least one Marine's feet. Daley ended up at the bottom of the monkey pile at the bottom of the crater. No one had been hit, and they finished their meeting under cover.

It seemed to Captain Landes (Bravo Six) that Daley's artillery had snipped off the NVA attack; perhaps several squads of NVA had darted through their lines, but the reinforcements following the first waves had been blown apart, disorganized, or otherwise sent packing by the artillery. At this time, Landes received a call from Captain Jordan (Alpha Six) regarding Delta Company, which Lieutenant Colonel Wickwire had sent to reinforce them. Jordan commented that, given the distances involved (a few hundred meters), Delta Company should have already reached them. He could only conclude that they were lost or didn't know exactly where they were going. Jordan and Landes both let the other know that they had no company reserve to seal the hole the initial NVA assault had punched at the north-south canal. Jordan then suggested they both personally move with their company headquarters to that point and reestablish the line themselves. Landes agreed. It was now starting to get dark.

36

Castaways

★

This shit's going to go on forever. Here I am again. Custer's Last Stand and I ain't a fucking Indian again. Down in his hole, Corporal Power, S-2 Scout with Alpha Company, 1st Battalion, 9th Marines, was raging. What was happening was a realization of the worst fears they had had when originally briefed on the patrol to Thon Phuong Xuan. *These motherfuckers keep hanging our asses out here, dangling us out on the fucking line like bait—and when the fish bite, they just let them eat the bait.* Power knew they could not pull back nor could reinforcements reach them until morning. *Shit, this is over, this is it.*

LCpl Lee Strausbaugh of Charlie Company, 1st Battalion, 9th Marines, had the NVA in the sights of his M60 machine gun. There were ten to fifteen that he could see, moving single file at the edge of the trees, brush, and bamboo that sprang up about forty meters from his hole. They were moving across his front, unaware that their squad column was passing the five o'clock position of the patrol base they were probing and surrounding. With his assistant gunner, Humphries, at his side, Strausbaugh abruptly sprayed the NVA from front to back, getting off almost a hundred-round burst before the surprised NVA (those still alive) managed to disappear behind cover.

Strausbaugh and Humphries turned their M60 on new targets. Twenty meters to their right, one of their new guys fired his M16 from his hole. Twenty more meters to the right, Strausbaugh's good buddy and fellow Southerner, LCpl Larry Bennett, brought his M79 into the action. Bennett couldn't see a single NVA through the brush line, and apparently they could not see his hole, because very little of their return fire cracked his way. But Strausbaugh and Humphries hollered directions at him in reference to a big tree out there: "To the left of the tree!"

Thunk-Boom! Reload.

"To the right, to the right!"

Thunk-Boom! Thunk-Boom! Bennett fired his first few shells almost straight up, trying to use his experience to drop them on target. He was firing blind, and after Strausbaugh and Humphries raised hell with him for missing (the NVA were too close for high-angle firing), he started pumping direct, from-the-shoulder fire into the brushy tree line.

The M79 grenade launcher was a single-shot weapon. After each shot, Bennett crouched in his shallow hole (he could barely get the top of his helmet level with the ground) to break open the breechloader and fit in another plump 40mm shell. He had almost a hundred, and was too flush with adrenaline to feel the kick that propelled each one-pound projectile as he fired them by the dozen. Meanwhile, Strausbaugh's M60 ate ammo by the hundreds of rounds, but the new kid between them probably didn't get off more than one magazine during the entire two hours the NVA came at them. His M16 kept jamming. Each time, he broke his weapon down and Bennett tossed him the extra can of gun oil that he always carried. They must have thrown it back and forth a dozen times.

Then the M60 jammed. Apparently the bolt was chipped, and with no replacement parts they were reduced to firing a few shots, clearing the jam, firing a few shots . . . and Strausbaugh and Humphries were clearing it again when a single brave NVA soldier rushed them. He made it within twenty-five meters before Humphries got his M16 to his shoulder and—*bap-bap-bap-bap-bap*—squeezed most of the magazine into the man's chest and stomach. Sprawled out, the NVA tried to get a grenade loose so that Humphries had to shoot him two or three times in the head to get him stopped. Bennett, firing and reloading, firing and reloading, hadn't seen any of this.

Thunk-Boom! Thunk-Boom! Eventually, the NVA were able to surround A-C/1/9 completely. *A vise,* thought Captain Slater, and as the NVA tried to isolate individual Marine positions and thus overrun the perimeter piece-meal, he poured the artillery on—twenty-five hundred rounds' worth during the evening. Because Slater was a true believer in supporting arms, he'd ensured that they'd had on-call fire, thus accounting for its swift, accurate delivery now; but because Slater had to leave the CP to check the lines (leaving Gunny Santomasso at the con), he let PFC Sankey run most of the firepower show. This Sankey did with calm precision, responding to screaming radio messages from various points on the line: "Hey, they're really forming here, they're ready to overrun us!"

Sankey would shift the artillery to that sector and walk it in until the Marines in need, with the NVA suddenly off their backs, then shouted, "Hey, stop the artillery! You're only fifty yards from where we are—you can't get it any closer."

The NVA kept trying, and it was becoming painfully clear to Captain Slater as the sun went down that this fight was going to drag on all night. The tension was such that he radioed Major Woodring and (knowing what he was asking for was stupid even as he asked) requested that their promised tank support now be dispatched. There was no way the tanks could reach them through the NVA-swarming no-man's-land, and Woodring of course refused the request. Slater signed off for the moment with, "They're all around us, and they're big. We've done very, very well, but I don't know how long we can hold out. Give me some air support. Give us a solid committal of artillery. Give us as many batteries as you can get. If you can do that for us, then we'll see you in the morning."

While tucked down in the thousand-pound crater, PFC Daley, FO of Bravo BLT 1/3, heard a thud a few feet from the edge of the crater. He stuck his head up and instantly thought, *now this is stupid,* when he saw the NVA grenade lying in the dirt in front of his face. Daley had no time to drop back down before it exploded, but in that millisecond he recognized the grenade as a stick-handled Chicom with a potato-masher head—and he recognized that he'd probably survive. The potato mashers tended to break into two big chunks along the seam around the explosive head, and if those two pieces missed you, you were generally all right except for minute fragments (as opposed to the pineapple type, which produced more fragments). Sure enough, when Daley dusted himself off after the explosion, he was still okay. In addition to the shrapnel that had already peppered his face, though, he now had another smattering of flesh wounds in his chest where his flak jacket hung open (the zipper didn't work) and where the fiberglass plates on the second-hand vest were missing—*the shit we're issued.*

The Assault Barrage was petering out along BLT 1/3's line (and the sun was orangey on the horizon) as Captain Jordan (Alpha Six) and Captain Landes (Bravo Six) began moving with their command groups to seal the break along the north-south canal. In Landes's case, he called Lieutenant Norris (Bravo Three) up to his L-shaped trench and told him to take command of the company, while he, Landes, and his greasegun-toting gunnery sergeant rounded up seven or eight bodies and headed west to ren-

dezvous with Jordan, who was presently heading east along
a tree line with only a few men himself. Captain Landes's
group ended up on the southern side of a hillock near the
canal. Landes really couldn't tell where he was, so he
crawled up behind a slender tree at the top that offered
much psychological comfort if not physical cover.

Landes looked about (quickly because of all the firing
in the area), and there was the canal's berm. No one
seemed to be near it—but then, suddenly, an NVA became
visible in an adjacent crater. He was maybe only fifty meters away. He wore a net-covered pith helmet. Landes
could see his face. Landes had his .45 out, which he'd never
done anything with but clean, so he motioned or called for
an M16 from the Marines below him on the hillside. One
was passed up, and Landes rolled from the cover of the
tree and squeezed a shot at the NVA. The man did not go
down, but Landes's heart was pounding too furiously for
him to be aware whether the NVA realized he'd been shot
at or whether he was returning fire. He was shut down to
all sensations but locking that NVA in his sights and killing
him, as he rolled away from his cover for the eternity of
lining up a second shot. And then a third.

The NVA dropped abruptly at the third shot.

Landes moved back to his group, and they made it to a
large crater. Jordan was a voice in his ear over the radio.
He said the NVA had penetrated fifty meters into his perimeter, but they had been sealed off. This made sense to
Landes, because his group was about fifty meters behind
the main line, and he was pretty sure no NVA had gotten
past them. They kept moving hole to hole, grenading them
as a precaution before moving to them, and before long,
Captain Landes made physical contact with Captain Jordan. It was now about 2015, and with Major Ossenfort, the
S-3, on the radio to promise them that Delta Company
would be reaching them soon, they prepared to reestablish
their lines. The NVA, it seemed, were pulling out. At least
in this area.

★

The NVA were massing once more against Captain Slater's patrol base, now near the nine o'clock position where Charlie Company tied in with Staff Sergeant Richardson's Alpha Two—and this time the line cracked. The NVA 60mm fire was continuing to rain right along the Marine line when Lance Corporal Dishong, for one, realized there were NVA a mere twenty feet from the hole he shared with Corporal Yandola and their M60, close enough to hear their singsong jabber talk. *So close,* Dishong thought with horror, *you could spit on them.* He turned to Yandola: "What the heck, you know, we gotta pull back!"

They were in one of Alpha Two's forward positions, so they started working their way back to the main trench. They'd made it to a large tree before the NVA spotted them, and with a torrent of fire suddenly coming their way, they disappeared into two holes that appeared in the elephant grass. There they sat out the storm.

"Everybody get back!"

Captain Slater could hear the panicked shouting from Alpha Two's nine-to-twelve-o'clock sector of the circle, and he was raging: *Where's this coming from? I can't believe this!* He couldn't get Staff Sergeant Richardson on the radio—he couldn't get anyone there on the radio—and he ran over to his FO, Sankey, to get him to shift their arty to that area. Marines were pulling back under heavy fire, and over the radio Slater could hear other Marines discussing one NVA who had followed them into the interior of their patrol base and jumped in a hole.

"Okay, somebody's in."

"There he is, over there."

"Okay, I got him."

Scratch one more NVA, but there was also a friendly KIA report over the radio. Apparently, the last man pulling back from Alpha Two's forward positions, Lance Corporal Saunders, had been shot in the cross fire, and Slater wasn't sure that he hadn't been killed accidentally by other Marines. It seemed the NVA had opened a door between nine and ten o'clock, and Slater ran to the area, pushing people forward here, there, and everywhere to close the gap. He finally got hold of Staff Sergeant Richardson, who was new to the outfit and appeared scared now to the point of losing control of his platoon. Slater snapped at him, "Everything that has happened in your sector has been unsat, you've got to take charge of that unit." Then he said to the platoon radioman, who seemed to be doing more than anybody else to keep the show together: "Keep it up."

In the crater at the patrol base's nine o'clock position, Lance Corporal Stuckey of Charlie Two could hear the NVA calling to one another as they closed in, bush to bush and hole to hole. When he raised his helmet on a stick to see how close they'd gotten, they obliged him by shooting the steel pot from a distance of only thirty meters. No idea what was going on, Stuckey called to the only Marines he was in contact with besides teammates Smith and Smitty, those to his right. They were under a poncho rigged over a trench. When Stuckey had shouted to them before to see whether they were all right, a disembodied voice had answered.

This time there was no answer. Stuckey had no idea whether they'd been hit or had pulled back. He had no idea whether they were alone or still part of the line. Dust and debris splashed them from AK47 bursts along the crater's rim as Stuckey, Smith, and Smitty popped up to fire quick bursts into brush that moved here, there, and (it seemed to their adrenaline-charged minds) everywhere. They were running out of ammunition. Stuckey shouted to go to semiautomatic, then finally to fire only single shots at precise targets. Smitty volunteered during a lull to go back for the ammo they'd left lying beside their original fighting holes, but Stuckey refused. They were going to stay together in the crater, he told them, until nightfall (it wouldn't be long), and then under the cover of darkness they would make their way back.

"Chicom!"

The NVA had made it within hand-grenade range, and their stick-handled Chicoms tumbled end over end through the air. Stuckey, Smith, and Smitty had six grenades among them; and since Stuckey was the biggest guy there (who, incidentally, had had pneumonia during hand-grenade instruction and had never actually thrown one) at six-foot-one, he scooped them up. "Give me the grenades—I can throw one farther!"

Inevitably, a Chicom finally bounced into the crater. In a reflexive lunge, Stuckey grabbed it—he knew the NVA wanted to make them duck so they could banzai the crater on the heels of the explosion—and instantly flung it back out, even as he screamed desperately at Smith and Smitty to get back up. Another grenade. It exploded inside the crater, the concussion rattling their brains, but they were instantly back at the crater's rim (they had curled up when grenades landed) as low as they could get while still able to see any NVA that might rush them. They couldn't see anybody. The bushes and elephant grass had turned gray in the twilight. Another grenade tumbled through the air from nowhere, and as soon as it hit, Stuckey had it in hand and threw it back out.

Another grenade. There it was.

Lance Corporal Stuckey reached for it, had just gotten his hand around the stick handle—and it went off right in his face.

Everything went black for what seemed a second; then, as Stuckey's senses unfogged, he realized he was lying back against the slope of the crater. He'd been blown backward, his glasses were gone, his ears were ringing terribly. He lifted his right hand to check for wounds and suddenly realized his hand was grotesquely stripped of all flesh. His wrist was broken, and the bloodless, skeletal remnants of his hand hung straight down. He let his hand drop onto his stomach, but the bone painfully scratched against his flesh. Infuriated, he lifted his bad arm with his good arm and stumbled to his feet, squinting without his glasses for his rifle. His M16 had been wasted by the grenade blast. Stuckey's adrenaline was out of control. *We're going to die, no doubt about it.*

Smith had been hit also—he was bleeding badly from shrapnel in his ribs—and when he saw Stuckey's demolished hand, he started shrieking. Stuckey screamed back before the man totally lost control, *"Don't look at it! Don't look at it!"*

Only Smitty was still firing. Smitty was a dark-haired kid, a real baby face who was incredibly cool under fire. Stuckey moved to him and tried to convince his friend to take hold of Smith and pull back. "Get out of here. Give me the weapon and you get on out of here. I'm done for."

Smitty told Stuckey to shut up or he'd shoot him himself (the man was so brave it was *unreal,* Stuckey thought), then added, "Just take it easy. We're going to stay right here. We're going to stay here together."

Lieutenant Hartnett of the Third Force Reconnaissance Company deployed the two four-man teams that had made it back as security around his antenna farm, while simultaneously maintaining radio commo with the two teams stranded north and northeast of the patrol base. As far as he could tell, both teams had found good cover where they had assumed the Wagon Wheel, on their stomachs and facing outboard with their heels touching *(probably as tight as a sphincter muscle will draw you in,* as Hartnett later put it). Hartnett's main concern was that between all the artillery he, Slater, and Sankey were calling in, he might whack his own people out there. The artillery was doing a good job, though, in terms of accuracy; and the two stranded and puckered team leaders did a good job of remaining calm as they shifted the arty onto the NVA reinforcements moving past them, "The enemy's all around us . . . the enemy's scared and confused, and they're screaming—you've got the artillery right on top of them . . . you're killing 'em, keep it up, keep it up."

The NVA melted away from the wood line covered by Lance Corporal Strausbaugh's M60 and Lance Corporal Bennett's M79 sometime before dark. The darkness was interrupted in steady intervals by swaying, parachute-borne illumination rounds that cast a carnival of shadows through the forest, and by the high-explosive rounds that crashed in more steadily. Bennett was down to three rounds for his M79 and three mags for his .45, and Strausbaugh and Humphries sat with their malfunctioning M60, reinforced by the AK47 that Strausbaugh had rushed out to take off the closest dead NVA. Between their two positions, the new kid whom Bennett had finally told to keep his can of gun oil was practically defenseless with an M16 guaranteed to jam. He was so scared that two or three times during the long night, Bennett could hear him crying. He whispered encouragement and also told him he needed to knock off the noise. Bennett himself was parched after the adrenaline overload, but because this was supposed to have been a short patrol he did not have his usual four canteens. He had only one, half full. He drank little of it, though, instead filling his mouth and then spitting it back.

After Captain Jordan, the Alpha Six of BLT 1/3, and Captain Landes, the Bravo Six of BLT 1/3, rendezvoused at the canal, they separated so as to push forward the fifty meters between themselves and their forward holes that had gone silent early in the assault. It was all dark and noisy as Jordan worked his way within sight of that last empty fighting hole on his right flank. They got a flare up, and a bomb crater became visible beside the fighting hole. Jordan could see heads bobbing up to look around from that crater. They were probably NVA stragglers (the NVA in the area were still throwing a lot of grenades, but they seemed only to be covering their retreat), and the command group took them under fire. They also attempted to lob grenades into the hole, and when one of them finally made it, Jordan and crew could see (under the flare light) the NVA scramble out of it. They headed north, back the way they'd come when the sun was still up.

Like Captain Jordan, Captain Landes reorganized his lines against crumbling enemy resistance. They had moved north about twenty-five of those fifty meters when a platoon from Delta Company, whose commander Landes had been in contact with as they moved up from behind, finally reached them. They were disorganized, but Landes got them together with his company headquarters and they made it to the bomb crater where Landes had previously shot at the solitary NVA with the pith helmet. A fire had been flickering from inside the crater as they'd approached, and it turned out that the uniform of the dead NVA was partially on fire. Landes jumped into the crater and rolled the body onto its back. There was a bullet wound in the NVA's neck. At that moment, a shadow that Landes knew was a Marine from Delta Company grabbed the AK47 beside the dead man. The man started out of the crater, but when Landes called to him to stop, he took off running. In a burst of anger that Landes later considered ridiculous, he bolted after the souvenir hunter. He tackled the man (losing his helmet in the dark in the process), took the AK47 away from him, and told him to kill a Vietnamese of his own if he wanted a Communist rifle.

Landes placed Marines from Delta Company into Bravo Three's overrun positions until they got to the most forward holes, and one of Bravo's Marines was still out there. Landes recognized the grunt as he climbed from his hole—it was one of his better guys—and besides being overjoyed to see him, it was in that moment that Landes was most proud of the Marine Corps. As a company commander, Landes knew he could influence things only where he was physically, and that the rest depended on the training, loyalty, and dedication of those scared-to-death young Marines out there. *You can't say enough about the kids and how they hung in and did things.* Landes and the lone diehard greeted each other like long-lost brothers. "*Jesus, Captain, am I glad to see you! You told us never to bolt, and to hold out at all costs and, goddammit, we did.*"

I'm going to die here tonight, and where the hell are those tanks? Lance Corporal Stuckey sat in his crater, remembering the tanks they'd passed that morning on their way out. There were no tanks, and although he could see the blinking lights of aerial observers and helicopter gunships and fighter aircraft, none were headed in his direction. He was again struck at the lethal isolation of this crater. They had no radio. No one seemed aware that they'd been cut off out here, or that despite all their technological might, the only thing between him and the shadows in the forest was Smitty and his M16.

What the hell are those spotter planes doing over there? Why aren't there any air strikes here?

Abandoned and forgotten, it was time to die. Or time to run like hell. Smith, holding his shrapnel-splattered ribs, had previously been helped to a little opening that the NVA had carved in the back end of this crater so that they could use it in case of Marine attack without exposing themselves. Stuckey crawled over to Smith. "When I tell you to go, you take off and you get back to wherever—get out of here!"

When an artillery round exploded between their crater and the NVA, producing a smoke screen of dust and debris, Stuckey shouted to Smith, *"Take off!"*

Smith disappeared into the night.

Stuckey, half blind without his glasses, with neither rifle nor grenades, and holding his unwrapped, skeletonized hand, decided to go next as Smitty covered him. Stuckey came out of the crater in a running crouch and made it five or six steps before he caught an AK47 round in his left thigh that knocked him off his feet. The pain was terrible, worse than his hand, and it took him a few seconds to register what had happened—that he'd been *shot*—and then he could simply lie flat in the little gully into which he'd rolled as the NVA fired several more bursts over his head.

Moments later a grenade exploded with a terrific blast inside the crater, and everything went deathly quiet. It was dark, Stuckey's ears were still ringing from the grenade that had removed his hand, and lying in the furrow, facing toward the now-silent crater, he called out for Smitty.

No answer. Nothing.

Stuckey knew that Smitty was dead, Smitty who could have saved himself. Wasted. Stuckey lay there bleeding and sick, and then he heard *something* move in the crater. There was an unfamiliar noise from the hole like the opening of a pop-top on a soda can. A second later he saw an object sail from the crater, land in front of him, and roll to his face—*and it's a grenade!* Stuckey let out a scream when he realized what it was, and he swatted at it with his good hand, sending it bouncing down the furrow toward his feet a second before it exploded. The shrapnel tore into his rear and the concussion tossed his legs over a foot to the right— and then, seconds later, he heard another pop from the crater.

Oh my God! This time he knew what the sound was (a Chicom being fused), and he saw or sensed this grenade go over his head and land six feet behind him, overthrown. He survived the explosion, but the concussion rattled him again and he decided to just lie still and play dead for the NVA in the crater. No more grenades.

The right side of his face was to the ground and he continued to lie perfectly still, squinting with his right eye. There was nothing to see, nothing to hear through the ringing in his head. The crater was again silent. He wondered who had won, he literally wondered who was going to come for him. The way it looked, he expected an NVA to walk up any moment and put a bullet in his head. He had no weapon, and in the meantime, as the dark, buzzing, light-splashed hours dragged by, he had enough to worry about with blood leaking from the softball-sized hole in his thigh. He began to pass out from loss of blood, but then came awake, then started to fade again—he knew he was dying— but again he came out of it. This time he was angry. If he was going to die, he wanted to get it over with. There was no reason to pray for himself, he was beyond hope, but he asked God to take care of his mother, because he knew that when she received the notification of his death *she would die.* He hated himself for that.

37

Flying Telephone Poles

★

Marine Air was operating full steam now in the flare-dappled darkness, and from their hummock-top command post, Captain Giles and Gunnery Sergeant Hatfield of Kilo 3/9 were among the spectators. Jets came in from the south in pairs, heading north toward the NVA artillery positions. One jet would break left and the other right after releasing their bombs, and a moment later the skyline would flash as the ordnance landed.

The next pair were making their approach when Hatfield suddenly exclaimed, "Oh my God, there go some SAM missiles!"

"Where?"

"Look, right over there!"

There on the horizon, coming out of North Vietnam, were two surface-to-air missiles, known as Flying Telephone Poles because of their length. It was like slow motion as Giles watched, the two jets seeming never to waver from their course and the two SAMs coming, coming, com-

ing, locked on target by radar. Right before the rear aircraft would have been hit, it broke hard and fast to the
right to confuse the radar, and the SAM arched on south to
self-destruct. Giles watched the lead jet in absolute horror
and fascination as, like its wingman, it held a steady course
until the last moment. Then it too broke right a moment
before connection with the SAM, and at that instant the
Flying Telephone Pole exploded. Giles and Hatfield, along
with scores of others across the battlefield, watched the
stricken jet spiraling down in the darkness until it disappeared behind a ridge line in North Vietnam. Then came
the explosion.

"Oh Christ, we just saw a pilot buy the farm."

The aircraft in question during this SAM launch were
a pair of one-seater A4 Skyhawks piloted by Maj Ralph E.
Brubaker and Capt Harl J. Miller, Operations Officer and
Maintenance Officer, respectively, of Marine Attack
Squadron 311, Marine Aircraft Group 11, 1st Marine Air-
craft Wing.

Brubaker and wingman Miller had launched after dark
from Chu Lai with the specific mission of eliminating the
SA-2 SAM site in the DMZ. They homed in on the signal
emitted by the site's radar as it scanned the night sky for
targets. The SAM itself (all 35 feet and 5,000 pounds of it,
up to and including its 286-pound warhead) was dependent
on its mobile, van-mounted radar crew. The SAM was a
fast, maneuverable, and (for a blind piece of technology) a
very personal killer. So were the Shrike AGMs (air-to-
ground missiles) that Brubaker and Miller carried under
the wings of their Skyhawks, two apiece. They were two of
only six pilots in the group qualified to fire the Shrike, and
they carried no other ordnance on this mission. The Shrike
was a miniaturized SAM in reverse, designed so that once
the pilot locked the missile's guidance system on the radar
beam emanating from the SAM site, the Shrike would follow the beam all the way down to the rice paddy or hilltop
where the SAM crew had deployed—the cover of darkness
or camouflage be damned.

Flying in the black void at 26,000 feet, Brubaker and Miller began their independent descents toward the SAM site, which was "visible" to them only as a certain radio frequency pitch on their headphones caused by the SAM radar unit. Brubaker, in the lead, followed his instrumentation until he was below 20,000 feet and had the pitch in his headphones that indicated his Shrikes had locked on target. The two Shrikes under his wings could be fired singly or together, and Brubaker elected to fire his as a pair.

The Shrikes flashed toward the ground, and almost at the same moment the SAM radar search signal in Brubaker's ears changed (there was a simultaneous flash below) to the high-pitched tone that indicated the SAM had been fired and its radar was now in the guidance mode. There was, hard on the heels of the first flash, a second flash.

"SAMs launching."

Brubaker and Miller warned each other at the same time. Unless SAMs were fired from a distance that would allow the pilot to dive instantly to the deck and avoid them altogether (with the enormous thrust that a SAM required to gain altitude and speed, it could not easily reverse its upward course), the trick was to let them get very close—but not within their two-hundred-foot killing radius—before taking evasive action. A rapid, high-speed turn could leave a SAM sputtering in confusion, as the missile needed five seconds to compute its target's course changes.

Miller thus got away, Shrikes unfired.

Brubaker broke away hard from the first SAM—and flew right into the range of the second SAM, which self-destructed directly beneath his Skyhawk in an engulfing flash.

Captain Landes of Bravo BLT 1/3 had just been able to make out the two ascending SAMs by the faint glow of their booster rockets, and after the explosion he followed the one Skyhawk's plummet into North Vietnam. He called battalion to render an approximate location of where it appeared to have crashed. It was relatively quiet in his area at this time, but he wasn't sure they weren't going to be hit again. To see that jet go down gave him a sensation of utter insignificance. Landes felt like an *ant,* he felt as if *the cosmos were just swallowing them up.*

Major Brubaker was not dead. The SAM explosion had rendered useless and lightless all the instrumentation in his cockpit, and he had no control over his Skyhawk as the aircraft responded to the shrapnel damage to its underside by buffeting wildly. His immediate thought was to get out. Just as the good book said, he straightened his back, put his feet on the rudder pedals, and reached over his head in the dark to pull down the ejection face curtain. In response, the canopy disappeared in the jetstream. Brubaker was awash in adrenaline and wind as the seat fired, and he was soaring, jolted out into the night sky as the parachute automatically deployed above him.

Brubaker couldn't see a thing, but as luck would have it, his parachute deposited him in the short grass of a relatively clear, open area. He disentangled himself from his parachute harness and went to stand up—but couldn't. He realized then that he couldn't feel his right leg. He reached for it in the dark and instead of being stretched out where he thought it was, it turned out he was sitting on it. The knee had been completely dislocated, and Brubaker imagined that the wind power he'd collided with during his high-speed ejection had done the damage. He removed his survival vest and G-suit to get more comfortable (covering this gear and his parachute with brush) and sized up the situation. He had conveniently landed not only in a clearing but also in a small, house-sized one that was depressed two or three feet below ground level. He was thus not readily visible to any NVA out looking for him. There was, however, a bunker entrance in one corner of the submerged clearing, and he expected an NVA to enter or exit it at any time.

Brubaker tried to make contact via his emergency survival radio. No one answered, and to save the batteries he turned it off.

Brubaker's knee was beginning to hurt to the point

that he decided to administer morphine. He moved back to where he had covered his G-suit (the morphine was kept in a pocket on the right leg), but the entire pocket had been ripped away. The wind stream could not have done that, and he understood then that he'd actually injured his leg inside the cockpit while ejecting. The pain was tolerable, but his condition was such that he elected not to draw his .38 revolver or to touch the half-dozen hand grenades hooked to his survival vest. He decided to sit quietly, one eye on that damned bunker entrance. If the NVA stumbled upon him, so be it; he would then be on his way to the Hanoi Hilton. The NVA were definitely in the area—there was an enemy rocket position in the wood line immediately south of his clearing. Brubaker could hear the rocket crews talking, he could hear their fire commands, and he could see their rockets shrieking out of the trees toward his infantry counterparts on the other side of the Ben Hai River.

Captain Slater was back in the crater CP of Alpha-Charlie 1/9 as the NVA pressure on his patrol base finally began to relent, and as jets roared in to drop their bombs in the flare-illuminated fields across which the NVA presently retreated. Streams of green tracers went up from NVA antiaircraft guns. *Holy cow,* Slater thought, *we've never seen anything like that.* As one of the invisible jets pulled out, Slater saw a SAM launch in a flash from the blackness of the hills of North Vietnam. The SAM roared heavenward in a frightening display of sparks, but having missed its target, the missile self-destructed in the night sky.

"Aw, that's a jet with his afterburner on."

Slater felt no need to correct the nearby Marine who'd made that incorrect comment. Everyone was uptight enough as it was, and between the incoming and outgoing there were shouts in the darkness: "I need more grenades!"

"I'm running out of M-16 ammo!"

"What do we do, what do we do?"

Three or four hours after midnight, the last of the

NVA around them pulled back under the cover of a two-tube 60mm mortar barrage.[1] The fire came from due north of the patrol base and was abbreviated at about the fortieth round when Captain Slater called his premier M79-man to his CP. Slater pointed to the mortar tubes flashing several hundred meters away, and since there were no trees around the CP, the M79-man could do some high-angle firing. Once again his rounds were right on target, and the mortars fell silent. Fantastic, Slater thought with a certain how-does-he-do-it wonderment. At this point, he radioed his platoon commanders, "Stay where you are. Just stay awake, seventy-five percent alert. Make sure at least one man at a time gets his sleep 'cause he'll need it. We don't know what's going to come off. At first light we're going to pack up and move. We'll see recon back at the Trace."

The only time during the night that Major Brubaker thought the NVA were actually coming was when he heard a small bell approaching. Dragging his injured leg, he crawled up just high enough to see over the edge of his sunken clearing—and there was a big black water buffalo, so close that he could see the bell secured around its neck by a red ribbon. Sometime later during this sleepless, mosquito-plagued, and pain-wracked night, about three or four in the morning, Brubaker decided to try again with his survival radio.

This time someone answered. His blind broadcast had coincided with the return of a USMC A6 Intruder from a strike up north, and the pilot then used his aircraft instrumentation to fix Brubaker's approximate position by homing in on his transmitted signal.

After the Intruder departed, Brubaker was again without radio contact with anyone, but at first light the cavalry

1. The NVA ground action of 6 July 1967 consisted of an 0900-1700 (all times approximate) contact with C BLT 1/3 and C/3d Tanks (5 USMC KIA); a 1705-2200 assault on A-C/1/9 (3 USMC KIA); a 1715-2130 assault on 3/9 (no recorded casualties); and an 1830-2100 assault on BLT 1/3 (3 USMC KIA). Sporadic contact and enemy mortaring/rocketing continued through the night.

arrived in the guise of the 3d Aerospace Rescue and Recovery Group, U.S. Air Force. The sky filled with aircraft whose orbit of Brubaker's position drew 12.7mm fire every time they passed over the wood line to the south, so that their Skyraiders and Skyhawks had to dive in to place bombs and napalm, and automatic-cannon fire, on the NVA antiaircraft crews. Through this cover fire, approaching from the east, came two HH3E Jolly Green Giant helicopters. The lead aircraft's approach was a bit off and it continued past Brubaker, its flight path uncorrected despite his radio call; but the second Jolly Green Giant was right behind the first and perfectly on target. When the helicopter was close enough that it could land well in advance of any NVA who might rush the position Brubaker was about to expose, Brubaker popped a smoke grenade. A young para-rescueman exited the helicopter as soon as it landed to sprint to the clearing, hoist the injured Brubaker onto his back, and rush back aboard—at which time the pilot immediately pulled out of the wildly flapping, prop-blasted elephant grass.

The NVA directed more 12.7mm fire at the Jolly Green Giant from the wood line, which was returned by the door gunner's electronically powered, 6,000-rounds-a-minute minigun, so that for Major Brubaker it was a joyous and noisy ride to safety.

38

Indomitable

★

These guys are all something special, thought Captain Slater of Alpha-Charlie Company, 1st Battalion, 9th Marines, 3d Marine Division, as the first light of Friday, 7 July 1967, spread over his patrol base in Thon Phuong Xuan. They had held, they had performed as Marines in the highest tradition. Not only did Slater come to appreciate the Marine Corps this morning as he'd never before understood that he should, but the night-long action had cleansed by fire whatever acrimony still lingered in his mind toward his troops. He remembered the anger with which he'd initially viewed his unmotivated, throw-away-the-book Marines. That anger had been tempered a bit at the Second Battle of Phu An, but the company's morale, discipline, and performance had always lagged behind Slater's expectations—until this hellnight. *In the little firefights they looked terrible,* he thought, *but when their back is to the wall and it's a life-or-death firefight, that's when the American spirit comes through. These guys are great.*

Everyone involved appreciated the tenacity of their showing. They considered it payback, a real turning of the tables from 2 July. Victorious though they were, it was time to get out. They were out of food and water, and having gone in with an inadequate resupply of hand grenades, M79 rounds, LAWs, and 60mm shells, they were now almost completely out of ammunition of all types. *We got a lot of gooks by being set in,* thought PFC Ragland in a voice that reflected the general bitterness at the situation, *but we could have got a lot more if we'd had the right equipment.* As Slater's platoon commanders reestablished their lines and accounted for those Marines with whom commo had been lost during the night—at this point Slater had no idea what his casualties were—Lieutenant Hartnett contacted his two stranded recon teams. Although the NVA had ceased firing two hours before dawn, Hartnett had elected to leave the recon teams where they were. He reasoned that if they moved toward the patrol base, they would probably encounter NVA recovering their casualties under the cover of darkness. Hartnett now instructed them to work their way back to 3/9 on their own, heading west and then south to avoid the patrol base altogether.

Slater meanwhile reorganized his fireteam and squad pockets. "All right, get out of your holes. Be careful. One man at a time, keeping low, come over to the big trench line over here."

One of those pulled back as the perimeter shrank in on itself was Larry Stuckey. Lying abandoned in his little furrow, facing east, it was almost as if a voice said to him that he was going to survive when he saw the horizon begin to lighten. Squinting without his glasses then, he tried to discern the figures coming toward him on the footpath. It was two Marines and a Navy corpsman coming straight for him—apparently Smith, who had made it back, had told the platoon about their crater—and the first thing Stuckey said was, *"Get down,* there's gooks all over the place!"

The three grunts got down beside Stuckey, and the corpsman administered morphine as he asked, "Where's your other man?"

Smitty. "He's in the hole. He's dead."

The two Marines went down into the crater, then one shouted back, "He's not dead. He's all right!"

Stuckey was absolutely elated. More Marines came on the scene and (before he could actually see Smitty)[1] six or seven of them lifted Stuckey into a poncho and carried him back to where Slater was organizing their withdrawal. One of their best squad leaders had been brought back with a bullet in his head, along with two other dead and twenty-one wounded[2] and it was great for everyone now to see the indomitable Stuckey, who, smashed hand and all, was joking with the guys. They were ready to go. Many Marines were slung with AK47s, and each of the company's 60mm mortar crews had saved two rounds (on Slater's orders during the night) in case of ambush on their return trip to the Strip. Captain Slater addressed them: "Okay, we're going to head back in column. It's going to be an aggressive column. If we hit anybody on the way back, we're not going to stop and dig in. We're going to fight our way through or go around them."

At 0545, 7 July 1967, the NVA began placing 60mm mortar fire on A and B BLT 1/3. Bravo had four wounded, three of whom required evacuation, and Bravo also again reported the suspected use of enemy tear gas. At 0610, Alpha reported an estimated thirty NVA several hundred meters north of the east-to-west footpath that ran into Route 561 in the Marketplace. The NVA, who appeared to be in a northward retreat, were brought under artillery fire.

1. In conversations aboard the USS *Sanctuary,* Smitty described to Stuckey how he'd been knocked unconscious by the grenade in the crater. When he awoke, he feigned death because an NVA, having already relieved him of his rifle, was presently searching him. This NVA, the only enemy soldier to get in the crater, then tossed the grenades that further wounded Stuckey. The NVA then ran back toward his unit, leaving Smitty to think that Stuckey was dead, just as Stuckey had spent the night thinking Smitty was dead.
2. The KIAs were Sgt Frank I. Riviere, Lance Cpl Charles E. Manns, and Lance Cpl Darryl E. Saunders.

While air support was requested, the line companies were advised by Lieutenant Colonel Wickwire (according to the after-action report) "to send out patrols as feelers covered by fire not to exceed three hundred meters."

The lead elements of A-C/1/9 started south at about 0530, 7 July 1967, while Captain Slater remained with the rear platoon to insure that no equipment or casualties were inadvertently left behind. When Slater and the last platoon finally pushed off (at about 0620), they had moved only about twenty-five meters when they heard the bass drums to the north indicating the firing of NVA artillery, a barrage whose whistling descent indicated seconds later that it was headed directly toward them. Slater, absolutely scared to death, automatically hit the deck, as did everyone else in the last platoon. The first salvo landed in their vacated patrol base and Slater sprang instantly to his feet, shouting, "GET UP, GET OUT!"

As these Marines sprinted away through the elephant grass, the NVA placed a twenty-minute artillery barrage directly on the patrol base that had tormented them during the night. They saturated the complex, never having to adjust one round, Slater realized as he looked back. Such accuracy was testimony to the skill of the NVA artillerymen even when they weren't relying on their forward observers. This was obviously unobserved fire, or else their forward observers would have adjusted the barrage onto the withdrawing Marine column. Slater could only be glad that the NVA had waited so long to commence fire. Perhaps they had been awaiting resupply of the tons of ordnance they had expended during yesterday's Assault Barrage.

Alpha-Charlie Company took no more enemy fire during the 1,200-meter march back to 3/9's lines. Lance Corporal Stuckey, for one, was so grateful to be alive that he talked the heads off the Marines carrying him in a poncho. He went on a mile a minute about how he wasn't going to forget 1/9, said he was going to send goodie boxes to the guys (a promise he would keep), and didn't stop jawing until they laid him down on the safe side of the battalion line. There, Sergeant Lefefe took his good hand and squeezed it. "Stuckey, you did a damn good job out there."

Stuckey smiled back, unable to say a word.

Pulling rear drag for the column were Lieutenant Hartnett's two recon teams. Hartnett had again declined the offer to walk point but maintained radio commo with his other two teams. The two stranded teams had joined together and while moving south had reported a unit moving north through nearby brush—NVA stragglers or rear guard. When Hartnett's group crossed the west-to-east trail immediately north of 3/9's lines, his stranded teams reported that they had seen the movement. They had also seen A-C/1/9's movement across the trail, but Hartnett had instructed them to remain under cover, lest a grunt mistake them for NVA and shoot first and ask questions later. Hartnett now talked the two teams out of the bushes (via radio), and finally getting back together, he thought, *there was some boys that want to do some huggin' and kissin'— they'd been through it.*

Captain Navadel, the S-3 of 3/9, greeted Captain Slater as he came in the lines. Navadel had been concerned about what kind of shape Alpha-Charlie Company would be in[3] and he was also anxious to debrief Slater to obtain the type of detail crucial to the Navy Cross recommendation he and Woodring planned to write for Slater. As they talked, Stuckey was carried past in his poncho, and Slater related the tremendous job this young lance corporal had done out there. In fact, he intended to recommend James Larry Stuckey for the Congressional Medal of Honor.

---

3. As well he should. Corporal Fazio (A/1/9) commented soon thereafter to the 3d Marine Division Historical Section, "There was guys walking around staring like they were on their last legs. . . . Guys were really getting mad, I mean they were just getting depressed. A lot of them just turned around and just gave up. . . . Everybody was just saying to each other, 'We've gone through so much the past week . . . that it's pathetic, and they're still going to keep us out here.' Clothes torn, just scummy, just didn't know what was coming up. Didn't even know what day it was really."

From Navadel to Slater came the all-important post-battle question, "How many did you kill?"

"I wasn't about to stop and count. We saw a lot of enemy dead, but I just don't know."

"Well, give me an approximate."

"Geez, how can I do that?"

Slater called up his platoon commanders and Hartnett, and they came up with 300 to 400 kills. Slater, downscaling that estimate to 200 to counterbalance the exaggeration factor, reported this body count to Navadel. He cautioned, however, that he "would like to have some kind of substantiation," and aerial observers did overfly the patrol base and report numerous bodies. Slater's command was credited in the subsequent official histories with a realistic 150 NVA kills, but in the heat of the moment when careers hinged on good body counts, the 3/9 after-action report recorded an absurdly precise 394 confirmed enemy kills from the patrol base action.

At this point, Captain Slater was directed to move his company into battalion reserve, where they were resupplied with C rations and water. The troops were so dehydrated that Slater made them drink their water ration slowly to keep from getting sick.[4] The dead and wounded, meanwhile, were carried or helped to the casualty collection point on the northern edge of the Strip. It appeared to Lance Corporal Stuckey that he was the only wounded man on his back, as the rest were sitting or standing (but he still couldn't see Smitty). It was he whom Chaplain West-

---

4. The post-battle resupply resulted in an incident that Corporal Gomez (I/3/9) would always be ashamed of. "After splitting up the cans of juice between my fireteams and radioman, we had one can left over which I was going to divy out later on. I was taught the squad comes first, but I drank from that can and I did not share it. One of my riflemen walked up to my hole to ask me something and he saw me drinking that extra juice. He and I were real close, and we continued to be real close after that. He said something to the effect that he thought I was one of the few NCOs that was a good guy who took care of his people, and he was real surprised to see me do some shit like that."

ling of 3/9 approached. He offered words of encouragement, as well as a cigarette—*which was just great*—as Stuckey, growing apprehensive, rattled on again, *"Where are those choppers, where are those choppers?"*

The wait for the medevac was interrupted by incoming artillery in the general vicinity, and several Marines dragged logs around Stuckey as cover. Finally, a Sea Knight landed in the Strip. The only man being carried among twenty or so walking wounded, Stuckey was worried to death that since he'd survived the impossible, he was sure to die on the routine helicopter evacuation. *Just let me make one more chopper ride.* The Sea Knight made it to a medical station, presumably Dong Ha. Stuckey had no idea where he was or where he was examined. He was terribly thirsty and kept asking for water, but all they could do, in case he had a stomach wound, was place a water-soaked cotton ball in his mouth. Then he was tagged and placed aboard a Sea Horse. Smitty was also on board. Finally together again, they talked a blue streak during the flight to the USS *Sanctuary*. There, Stuckey ended up in preop on a gurney, where a needle was applied and he drifted off into the numb void. When he awoke from surgery the next morning, he was in a rack in the ship's hospital ward. He raised his right arm to examine the wound and was shocked to see that the hand had been amputated, the stump bandaged. He turned his head to the right where no one could see him and cried for about half a minute, "and then I was okay."

While the NVA lobbed 60mm mortar fire among BLT 1/3's positions, without producing casualties ("They appear to be registering," it was noted in the battalion journal), the reconnaissance patrols from Captain Landes's Bravo Company came back bearing AK47s and 12.7mm belted ammunition, plus enemy pith helmets, canteens, medical supplies, web gear, and the like. They also told of dozens upon dozens of dead NVA, and even the official history reported that "the grisly carnage was beyond description. Hundreds of bodies covered the scarred battlefield, some half buried, others in pieces, all surrounded by a carpet of battered equipment and ammunition. Counting enemy canteens was one method used to try to establish realistic figures."[5]

The NVA had been slaughtered during their assault, but they did not slow down. At 0915, 7 July 1967, the NVA placed fifty artillery rounds on Captain Shirley's Lima 3/9 (wounding four men), which was dug in along a ridge that afforded them excellent observation into North Vietnam. They could not actually see the Ben Hai River for the tree lines along its banks, but they could see dust rising from the woods just north of the river in an area indicated on Shirley's map as a road. This sighting (at 1030) was confirmed by an AO as NVA troops moving along with a truck convoy, east to west, and Marine artillery was followed by jets and gunships, which were followed by more artillery.

Captain Navadel had moved by then to Shirley's CP. He was a happy participating director of and witness to the turkey shoot (resulting in twenty confirmed kills and fifty probables), but he found the sight of the NVA convoy's rising ribbons of dust nothing short of eerie. The NVA almost always trucked the ammunition resupply to their forward rocket and artillery positions under the cover of darkness. Risking a move like this in broad daylight indicated the importance the NVA were placing on this campaign. *They just keep bringing in more artillery pieces and bringing in more ammunition,* Navadel thought. He imagined the damage their USMC firepower had wrought during yesterday's battle and continued even now, as the NVA attempted to replace those losses. *These NVA, they're indomitable also.*

---

5. An obviously exaggerated total of 490 confirmed and probable kills was claimed by BLT 1/3, and 681 by 3/9, during Operation Buffalo, most from the Battle of 6–7 July 1967 (which cost the lives of 11 Marines).

PART EIGHT

THE HILL OF ANGELS

★

Once, in peacetime—nearly thirty years earlier—the cratered knoll rising only about five hundred feet . . . had been known to local missionaries as 'The Hill of Angels,' " wrote the combat photographer David Douglas Duncan (chronicler of the Marines in the Pacific and Korea) after his visit with the next generation of Marines atop Con Thien in the fall of 1967. "It was those few hundred feet of red-clay elevation—lifting it that much closer to heaven in missionary eyes—which gave the hillock a special tactical value to the entrenched commanders facing each other across the DMZ. Con Thien was the greatest natural observation post along the entire battleline between South and North Viet-Nam . . . Saigon and Hanoi considered the place priceless. . . . Marines viewed it through rather different eyes."

Following the Marketplace Massacre of 2 July 1967, the sole responsibility of Lieutenant Colonel Schening, CO, 1/9, was the security of the Con Thien Combat Base. With A and C Companies opcon to 3/9, Schening thus had

B Company deployed along the southern half of the perimeter and D Company along the more exposed northern. The Marines did not leave the wire during the remainder of Buffalo, and the NVA initiated no ground action. The NVA instead pounded Con Thien with 60mm and 82mm mortars, 122mm rockets, and 85mm, 100mm, 122mm, 130mm, and 152mm artillery pieces. During the course of Operation Buffalo (2–14 July 1967) H&S, B, and D/1/9 lost 26 KIA and at least 70 WIA atop Con Thien.

"That cratered knoll, Con Thien—'The Hill of Angels' to the Vietnamese, 'The Graveyard' to the Marines—was a place of no special law except mutual support," wrote Duncan. "Men there shared everything. They alone seemed to be proof that the hill's Vietnamese name was the right one."

39

Direct Hits

★

During the afternoon of 6 July 1967, Captain Radcliffe of Bravo Company contacted his old friend, Captain Sasek of Delta Company, over the landline that connected the various positions of good old Con T. "Hey, Sas, I got to write some guys up for that action on the second of July, but I don't have any perspective. You know, that was my first day."

Captain Sasek knew all about Radcliffe's first battle. Radcliffe had been too busy the day after to talk about it, but the next day it had welled up in him. Sasek, with the common sense of a country boy from Topeka, Kansas, and of a combat officer whose tour was winding down, had offered Radcliffe an unmaudlin way to let him get it off his chest: "I'll come over and shoot the shit with you."

Now, Sasek answered Radcliffe's latest call. "Well, come on over. I'm writing you up."

"Oh, bullshit."

"Yeah, you ought to get the Medal or a Navy Cross out of this. Now come on over here."

That did not sound inviting. Sasek's side of Con Thien faced the DMZ and Radcliffe answered, "You gotta be kidding me. You get your ass over here, you dumbshit. We'll sit down by *my* hootch and talk about these things."

Radcliffe and Sasek never spoke again. On his way to the 1/9 CP, Radcliffe heard shouts that the Delta Six had been hit, and rushing up the hill he was greeted by the sight of a row of poncho-wrapped bodies. They had been put outside the entranceway of the command bunker, along the footpath that led downhill to the perimeter entrenchments. Under those ponchos were the mortal remains of Capt Richard J. Sasek, 1stSgt Jettie Rivers, Cpl Joseph W. Barillo, LCpl Edward M. Brady, HM2 Christopher J. Maguire, and HM3 Michael R. Dotson. As it was pieced together, they had been standing atop the Delta CP bunker, watching the Assault Barrage presently pounding those battalions above the Strip, when (at 1930) the NVA unexpectedly shifted a salvo toward Con Thien. One round scored a direct hit on the company command bunker.

When Doc Lindenmeyer of the Third Herd of Dying Delta got the word, his first reaction was, *well, what the hell were they all doing standing around together out in the open presenting a target?* Lindenmeyer finally dismissed the latest casualties as stupid sightseers and put them in the category *gone.* It was a neutral slot his mind had created in which dropped all the faces that were no longer a part of his world, whether the man was wounded, dead, or had rotated home. *Gone.* They were simply, painlessly gone *(and gone was good because gone wasn't here and here was hell),* and Lindenmeyer's attention turned to a certain personal benefit of the disaster. With two of the company's corpsmen thus erased, including the senior one, all the remaining corpsmen would receive a promotion of sorts when new corpsmen arrived. Lindenmeyer savored the relief of knowing he would now be bumped up to the mortar section, which always stayed with the company commander.

Well, at last, I'm not going to have to go out on ambushes anymore and I won't have to walk as far.

Delta Company, as a whole, was devastated by the annihilation of their company headquarters. Captain Sasek, besides being tactically competent and personally courageous, had enjoyed an unusual affinity with his troops. He cared about them and they knew it, and even a cynic like Doc Lindenmeyer had to acknowledge that "Captain Sasek was the finest kind. He didn't waste men. He knew what the hell he was about, he devised tactical approaches to the situation as we met it in the field instead of going necessarily by the book."

One of the platoon commanders, Lieutenant Snyder, took over as the Delta Six (and was wounded by shell fragments two days later) until a new officer, Capt Francis L. Shafer, joined them at Con Thien three days later. Shafer, a brave, taciturn, and super-aggressive commander, quickly became one of the most unpopular officers in the battalion. His grunts despised him and thought he was using them as career stepping stones. *The guy wanted a Navy Cross,* thought a fellow company commander, *and he didn't care how he did it—nobody wanted to go to war with him.* Even Captain Radcliffe had to wonder which guided Captain Shafer more, a glory wish or a death wish. Shafer did, however, offer the battalion a sense of continuity by eschewing reassignment off the line after his six months of command time, and he was a favorite of each of his battalion commanders.[1]

Delta Company also mourned the loss of First Sergeant Rivers, their calm, soft-spoken, and young-for-his-rank black topkick from Tennessee. Old-timers in the company remembered how when Rivers came aboard (around

1. Captain Shafer died just like his predecessor (on 30 March 1968 during the Siege of Khe Sanh), at which time most of the Con Thien Marines had rotated or been medevacked to be replaced by men who viewed the skipper through eyes unprejudiced by the beloved Sasek. The Khe Sanh Marines deeply mourned Shafer's death, and the battalion commander was devastated by it.

January 1967) a lot of the blacks talked of how they'd be catching some slack now that a black top had arrived. Rivers, however, had called a company formation to introduce himself. "See what color you're wearing? It's Marine Corps green, and that's the way you're going to be treated—as Marines." Rivers routinely accompanied the point platoon, and he became legend in May of '67 during the latest battle of Phu An. Despite being wounded in the ambush that fragmented the company, First Sergeant Rivers ranged across the battlefield with utter abandon, doing whatever needed to be done at the moment (positioning troops, recovering wounded men, distributing ammunition, leading fireteam-sized rushes against NVA probes and assaults) until a relief force arrived the next morning. For this, Rivers won the Navy Cross, awarded posthumously. One of his grunts remarked that Rivers was "the most respected man in the company, and he gave the enlisted men someone we could really brag about to the snuffies in the other companies."

First Sergeant Rivers was also posthumously awarded a battlefield commission to second lieutenant, reportedly the first black to receive such a commission in the Vietnam War, so his successor, like Shafer, was being taxed to fill a giant's jungle boots. As one rifleman said, he was rejected by the body known as Delta Company. "The new first sergeant was a sniveling coward hated by officers and enlisted alike. He was an embarrassment to the company, and there were plenty of fantasies about stuffing a frag up his ass or putting a .45-caliber round in his brain-housing-group."

While Delta Company was being demoralized amid the shell fire of Con Thien, Bravo Company was being rebuilt in the days following the Marketplace Massacre. *These guys don't know me from Adam,* Captain Radcliffe thought the morning after they had stumbled back to Con Thien, so he met with each of them. Likewise, he greeted each of the replacements who arrived by helicopter or truck to flesh out Bravo Company, at least until 10 July 1967, when a new officer, Capt R. C. Wells, took over and

Radcliffe became the S-3. Some were fed in via the normal replacement system, and some, like Corporal Montgomery, were old-timers coming back from R&R who were just now getting the story. In Montgomery's case, he was at the Da Nang PX when a Marine from Bravo, who also had been out of the field on the fateful day, recognized him and suddenly gave him a bear hug.

"What's the matter?"

"Man, we got wiped out up at Con Thien, and I thought for sure you were with them! Just about the whole platoon got it."

"No, you're kidding me!" Montgomery replied, remembering all the body bags that Bravo Company had already filled at Khe Sanh.

Many of the replacements, however, were from perimeter guard detachments and such in sanctuaries like Da Nang and Chu Lai. *The cooks, bakers, and candlestick makers,* Radcliffe mused, as they arrived a dozen or so a day. One of them was a pugnacious, tattoo-covered sergeant named Zeeb, who told Radcliffe, when asked, that he had been running a mess hall with Marine Aircraft Group 11, but that "I volunteered to come up here."

Radcliffe questioned another Marine who said he'd been with the 1st Military Police Battalion, but "we heard about Bravo One-Nine gettin' it, so I caught a helicopter up and jumped on a convoy."

At the same time, those Bravo grunts who'd been medevacked with superficial wounds were coming back to Con Thien. They, like the Marines who had willingly given up their safe, rear-echelon tours, practically made the hair on Radcliffe's neck stand up. *These guys didn't have to come back so soon, but they did.*[2] Staff Sergeant Burns initially

2. Not all the replacements arrived eagerly. For example, 1stLt Bill Masciangelo (I/3/3) was instructed to select eight to ten of his platoon members for transfer to the 9th Marines, based on the time remaining on their tours. "It didn't give you a hell of a lot of choice, and it was a very painful thing to have to tell them. I can remember the reaction of people saying, 'Oh my God!' You really felt like you were sending people to their deaths, because of the reputation the 9th Marines had.

viewed his pogues as the bottom of the barrel, but after he started working these people in, running road sweeps and patrols, he appraised the reconstituted Bravo Company: "Most of my platoon were *interesting* people. I had some good field Marines. In garrison none of us would have probably been any good, but in the field I had one hell of a platoon."

The 1/9 CP bunker was the best bunker at Con Thien, and at 1345, 7 July 1967, a single NVA 152mm shell with a delay-fuse scored a direct hit that blew it apart. The round smashed through the sandbag wall protecting the entranceway at one end of the rectangular-shaped bunker. Like a guided missile, it went right through the doorway to explode against one of the vertical timbers holding up the crossbeams and their five-foot layer of sandbags. The round thus detonated inside the bunker with an underground sound, a vibrating *whump!* When these circumstances were pieced together as the bodies were carried away, Captain Radcliffe would think with helpless rage, *if the NVA fired the rest of this goddamn century, they couldn't do that again!*

Captain Radcliffe had just missed being one of those casualties. Shortly before the direct hit, when the incoming was fast and furious, Lieutenant Colonel Schening had summoned Radcliffe by radio from his B/1/9 CP with the message, "I've got somebody up here who wants to see you." That somebody was Radcliffe's Camp Pendleton compadre, Capt. Robert T. Bruner, who had just heloed into Con Thien an hour before. Bruner was a caustic, broad-shouldered, narrow-hipped Texan with a big mustache and an omnipresent cigar. He was also a hell of a character, and would prove a hell of a fighter when (after Wells was hit, like three of the four captains before him) he took command of Bravo Company. He gave it up only after

---

It appeared from the propaganda leaflets that we picked up operating in that area that the North Vietnamese had, in fact, targeted 1/9 or the 9th Marines for destruction."

receiving his third and fourth Purple Hearts on the same day during the Siege of Khe Sanh. Radcliffe greeted Bruner now in the CP with an enthusiastic, "What the hell you doin' here?"

"Well, I had to come bail you out. See what happens—you've already been in trouble!"

Lieutenant Colonel Schening introduced another brand-new officer, 2dLt J. M. George, and after Radcliffe got his daily orders he was instructed to escort George to his platoon. They stopped on the sandbag steps leading up and around the CP entranceway. The battalion sergeant major was sitting, as usual, ten meters away under his lean-to, armed with a pair of binoculars and a radio with which he brought artillery to bear on any NVA patrols he spotted. Radcliffe turned to the boot brown-bar. "Hey, George, I'm not any old hand here, but let me tell you something, son. When we walk out of here, if you hear any incoming—even if you *think* it's incoming—hit the deck. Don't worry about being embarrassed. Don't worry about 'lieutenant's pride' and all that bullshit. Just hit the deck."

Radcliffe and George were no more than ten paces beyond the hunting sergeant major when they heard another artillery round rumbling through the sky in a descent that seemed to have their names on it. They threw themselves down, and the explosion sent hurling past them a piece of what Radcliffe took to be the sergeant major's shelter. It wasn't. It was a piece of the instantaneously demolished CP bunker. Not knowing this, Radcliffe and George continued their dash over the crest of this most-exposed hill. They separated ("George, your platoon's right over there!"), then Radcliffe rushed on to his company headquarters, where a Marine immediately exclaimed, "Skipper, the CP's been hit!"

"Awww, *shit!*"

"We thought you were up there. We thought you'd got hit, Skipper!"

"Nah, I just left."

1stLt Charles Budinger of the Communications Platoon had also narrowly escaped. He'd just left the CP to establish a secondary/alternate CP in the adjacent H&S bunker. Now, thinking, *oh, it couldn't be, it couldn't be,* he rushed to the H&S bunker entrance. The CP bunker was buried under smoke and dust. Budinger rushed back to his two alternate radios and radiomen, instructing one to inform regiment of the disaster and the other to raise their direct-support artillery. He knew a ground attack would be the NVA's next move, and he got the artillerymen to get a precautionary barrage pumping north of their wire.

Lieutenant Budinger returned to the doorway of the H&S bunker. He could see a figure emerge from the smoke-belching hole at the collapsed end of the rectangular CP bunker. He appeared to be the first man out. It was Capt Chris DeFries, their Air Liaison Officer, and despite being stunned and battered and having dirt in his eyes, he recovered quickly upon reaching Budinger. DeFries, in fact, became the eye of the recovery effort, ripping open sandbags to smother the fires in the bunker, putting out the word for fire extinguishers, directing men where to dig, running back to the radios to check on the medevacs. . . . Men joined DeFries from all directions as the call echoed across the hilltop, which was now silent, as the NVA had ceased firing.

Lieutenant Dixon, the CO of H&S Company, had been inside the CP when the killer had roared in. At that moment, Dixon had been walking toward Lieutenant Howell's S-2 desk. Considering himself an old salt, Dixon had not worn his helmet for the battalion briefing, but Lieutenant Colonel Schening had sent him out to get his steel pot and Dixon had just come back with it on. There was a sudden, blinding flash that seemed to erupt where Howell was sitting near the hatchway. In that instant, the lights in the bunker burst—Dixon could feel the shattered glass stinging his ears and scalp—and a support beam caved in atop his head, his freshly donned helmet saving him from a split skull as everything went black. Dixon, concussed and bleeding, came to moments later to smoky darkness and mass pandemonium. Everything was a blur.

He could see light filtering in from a hole in the bunker corner previously occupied by his friend Howell, and as he began crawling toward it, strong arms latched onto him. Dixon was pulled to safety through that hole.

At the other end of the bunker, Captain Bruner, having been hurled through the plywood wall divider of the battalion commander's personal area, came awake under the colonel's cot. Fires dotted the bunker's long tunnel of claustrophobic darkness, and some hand grenades and ammo magazines cooked off in quick flashes as Bruner struggled with his helmet, which had been smashed down against his nose. He could feel wetness splashed across him and thought that he'd been hit bad, but the only wounds he could find were from the porcupine-like mass of splinters along his back. Most were embedded in the plates of his flak jacket, but some had gotten him in the ass and where his flak jacket had pulled up along his waist. The ooze on him was the remains of the shattered dead. Bruner hollered in the dark when he heard digging from topside. Together with an anonymous shape, the only man apparently on his feet at this end, Bruner started pulling and clawing at the ceiling. They made an opening, and with the Marines on the outside pulling away sandbags and using their hands and entrenching tools to enlarge the hole, Bruner and his companion came out, hands first.

LCpl Robert Gossen of the Communications Platoon sprinted up to the CP with his buddy Macon. Kicking away the debris blocking the bunker entranceway, the first man they saw was staggering toward the opening with his chest ripped open. Gossen thought he could see the man's beating heart—he couldn't understand how he could stand—and he and Macon got this shell-shocked survivor up and out of there. They laid him on the footpath other rescuers were rushing up along, then spun back to help clear the sandbags and smashed timbers from the entranceway. They climbed through, barely able to see in the dark, smoky, gutted interior. Bodies here, bodies there—it appeared that all the radiomen who'd been at field desks along one of the bunker's map-covered interior walls had been killed.

Gossen and Macon went to those who were still moving. The wounded were gotten out. The smoke was clearing. Gossen went back in and saw a pair of jungle boots sticking from the dirt wall at the collapsed end. The feet were still inside; they were attached to someone. As helmets and shovels were brought into frantic play, a double-rack emerged in the dirt wall. A dead Marine—it was Glenn Ogburn, the colonel's driver—lay atop an air mattress on the rack, on his back, hands folded on his chest as he'd been sleeping.

Nearby, two other members of the Communications Platoon, Cpl Brian Tuohy and LCpl Robert Burkhardt, were struggling with a Marine who, it seemed, had been impaled through the chest by a support beam. "Hey, Brian, ain't no way we're gettin' this guy out unless we cut *him* up!"

1stLt Gatlin J. Howell was KIA.
MSgt Robert C. Dambeck was KIA.
SSgt Glendon L. Waters was KIA.
Cpl Kenneth B. Kooser was KIA.
Cpl Peter Moskos was KIA.
Cpl Glenn R. Ogburn was KIA.
Cpl Michael B. Smith was KIA.
Lance Cpl Richard R. Davis was KIA.
Lance Cpl John H. Ferril was KIA.
Lance Cpl Richard H. Lopez was KIA.
Lance Cpl Andrew C. Rabaiotti was KIA.
Lance Cpl Joseph R. Riebli was KIA.
PFC William W. Davis was KIA.
PFC Thomas R. Walsh was KIA.

Lieutenant Colonel Schening had survived because his personal area where he had his cot and footlocker was at the end of the bunker opposite the entranceway. He'd been protected by a vertical timber at that end, but he had been slammed into it by the concussion and knocked unconscious. He now stood above ground, concussed, bruised, deafened, and bleeding from the nose and ears. With hands on hips, Spike Schening tried to buck up, shaking his head and standing tall. To his Old Corps way of thinking, a medevac for himself was completely out of the question.

Lieutenant Shaw, battalion artillery liaison officer, emerged from the bunker with raw, gaping wounds and burnt, blackened skin. He was a grizzled old mustang and wouldn't let anyone help him. Staff Sergeant Howard, with battalion supply, was a burnt version of the good-looking blond guy he'd been a few minutes earlier. He was on his feet and his utilities had shielded him from the flashburns, but where his sleeves were rolled up and on his face and neck his skin hung in burnt strips. Staff Sergeant Cooper, with battalion communications, helped with the wounded despite the fact that he had to use one hand to hold in the intestines slipping from the wound in his stomach. *Just amazing,* Lieutenant Budinger thought, as he finally got Cooper to slow down long enough for a corpsman to bandage him: "Hey, you need to go get on a helicopter, because you could go into shock at any time."

"Aw no, I'm fine."

The whole event was crazy and the procession of wounded was endless: Captain Curd; Staff Sergeant Dunlap; Corporals Clarke, Jones, Menadue, Taylor, and Wheeler; Lance Corporals Logsdon and Palmieri; Privates First Class Bell, Bergeen, Blunt, Carter, Conant, Hare, Hedeen, Hixson, Horton, McMurrey, and Tull; Private Morris; and Hospital Corpsman Kersey.[3] Surprisingly, one

---

3. On 9 September 1967, Lieutenant Colonel Schening was transferred. This departure was over three months shy of the usual six-month command tour, and a rumor considered credible by much of 1/9 was that Schening had been relieved of command for the excessive casualties of 2 and 7 July 1967. Untrue, Major Danielson (XO, 1/9) stated. "Fifteen years earlier, while he was recovering from wounds in Korea, he was assigned as an adviser to the Korean Marine Corps (KMC), where he typically did an outstanding job and became close friends with a KMC battalion commander. In September 1967, that KMC officer—by then a general—arrived in Vietnam in charge of a KMC brigade. The general made a personal request that his old friend, Spike Schening, be assigned as the USMC liaison officer to the KMC brigade. Schening's strong objections to leaving 1/9 were overruled."

of the wounded, Captain Bruner, was also one of the rescuers, going back in with a flashlight in one hand and his other hand gripping a line of commo wire so he could find his way out. He knew where the men inside had been standing when it happened. After Bruner's second trip, there were no more survivors to be found—Marines were coming out with body parts now. It was then that the battalion chaplain noticed what Bruner had not: Bruner had a long splinter, the width of pencil lead, sticking out both sides of his neck. The chaplain wrapped a towel around Bruner's neck, and the battalion surgeon, who had his people up at the bunker, grabbed one end with a pair of wire cutters, pulled it out, and got two Band-Aids in place.

A Mechanical Mule arrived, its engine so loud that its driver would have been unable to hear the next salvo had the NVA fired it (which for some reason they did not); but he didn't care, he had buddies to take care of. A half dozen at a time, the seriously wounded were taken aboard the Mule for the jolting downhill ride to the helo-zone. Craters there provided cover until the medevacs arrived. Meanwhile, Corporal Power, who had just helicoptered up to help organize a new scout section, sifted through the debris where he had last seen Lieutenant Howell. He gathered into a poncho the dismembered remains that he took to be Howell. With his mind completely zoning out, he folded the poncho, threw it over his shoulder, and began walking listlessly to the landing zone. There was no one left, he thought over and over. Power, battle-rattled and alone, was now the S-2 section.

Lieutenant Fagan, late of Alpha Company and on R&R when Operation Buffalo began, talked with their acting first sergeant in the company tent at Dong Ha. Not only had his worst fears about what had happened to the company been realized (he had seen the action on television in Hawaii), but the battalion rear was also buzzing with talk of the Con Thien CP's having just been wiped out. Fagan, with his .45 reissued by the first sergeant, crossed the road to Major Danielson's tent. "How bad is it?"

Major Danielson told him what he knew (he would shortly be Con T-bound himself). Then Fagan, with more than six months in the bush, offered, "If you got something for me to do on the battalion staff, I'm ready to give up my platoon."

"Okay, we need an S-two."

Lieutenant Fagan was on the next chopper to Con Thien. It was still chaotic, they were still evacuating casualties, and he noticed Lieutenant Colonel Schening, sitting off on a rock still recovering from his concussion. It was then that a helicopter set down with a dozen-man army of camera-wielding, microphone-thrusting, and wire-trailing reporters. Fagan, doing what he could here and there as a new CP was hastily established, ended up in charge of the reporters. He approached Schening, shouting into his deafened ears, "Colonel, the press is here, they want to talk to you!"

"You take care of it."

The correspondents all wanted to talk with the colonel and see the bunker, but Fagan informed them as he led them up from the LZ, "You can't talk to Schening. I'll take care of you guys."

Twenty meters from the demolished CP, a single NVA round splashed on target. When Fagan picked himself back up, he tried to coax the press out of the small, pitch-black bunker into which they'd disappeared after running around like madmen during the whistling warning. "C'mon, listen, in the last *hour* that's the only round that's come in. Let's get this over with."

They would not budge, and the conversation suddenly turned to LBJ and the uncrossable DMZ. Fagan responded with a few acidic comments about the frustration of being in a seemingly endless combat situation, and when the reporters finally emerged to take his photograph, he realized they had a tape recorder running. "What're you guys doing?"

"We got our interview. Your colonel wouldn't talk to us, we'll use you."

Thanks to Lieutenant Budinger's people, who recov-

ered what radios they could from the old CP and relaid the
wire, by the evening of the seventh Lieutenant Colonel
Schening and his new S-3, Captain Radcliffe, had a hasty
CP made operational in the adjacent H&S bunker.[4] Come
8 July 1967, though, Schening, Danielson, Radcliffe, and
Budinger decided it would be wise to relocate the CP to
the less-exposed south side of the hill. As Budinger got
busy turning the small bunker they had selected into a
command post,[5] one of his men arrived from Dong Ha,
where he had been relatively safe with a job in the battalion communications center. The Marine, LCpl Donald H.
Kito, had volunteered for the more dangerous duty at Con
Thien. Kito had, in fact, demanded it, as Budinger's first
sergeant, Top Cavalier, had made clear via radio during the
last couple of days. "Kito's driving me nuts back here. He
really wants to get up there and see what's going on."

"Well, if he insists, we'll talk about it tomorrow. I
mean, I could use him."

Kito did insist, and on the morning of the eighth a
chopper delivered him from Dong Ha. He was an unlikely-
looking volunteer, with his slight build and the perfect skin
of a teenage girl (he was half-Hawaiian, half-Eskimo). And
he was *just the most cheerful little goddamn puppy-type dude,*
as his buddy Corporal Power put it. *Everybody just loved*

4. A quarter of a century later, Schening would angrily refuse an interview for this book ("just so that you and others can make a buck!"),
leaving Fagan to comment, "I loved Schening. I can remember the
change-of-command ceremony, and he regretted leaving very, very
much. So it must have been a terrible period in his life to take command of this battalion, and see it almost destroyed, and not be around
to see it resurrected."

5. Colonel Jerue, CO, 9th Marines, was also blown out of his CP.
Their old French barracks were undoubtedly prominent features on
NVA artillery maps; and after their own direct hit on 6 July 1967,
Major Hill (S-3) commented: "That location was right under my chair
in the CP, and it made me heartily second Jerue's motion to move the
CP out of Dong Ha." Reestablished in Cam Lo, Hill continued: "Our
living conditions became more primitive, but we were able to operate
more or less unhampered. In fact, I don't remember us being shot at
after moving to Cam Lo."

him. Regardless, as Power thought, *the dude had made it through Parris Island and he was a fucking Marine.* Kito reported in to Budinger in the new, almost-finished CP, and Budinger decided to show him how authentication sheets worked. "Listen, Kito, go and get me these authentication sheets."

When Kito took too long in getting back from the H&S bunker (and present CP), Budinger went out to look for him—and was no more than fifty feet away when he had to drop flat at the sound of an incoming shell. It exploded in or near the new CP, and Budinger rushed back to find that Kito must have made it back just after he'd left, only to be killed instantly. Kito was dead in the hole, part of his shoulder blown off.

Kito's death was a morale-crusher, but Lieutenant Budinger's platoon had to zip two more comrades into body bags before the afternoon waned. A working party consisting of Barnes, Burkhardt, Jones, and Tuohy was transferring sandbags atop a Mechanical Mule from the north side of the hill to their new positions on the southern side. The incoming shell landed behind Burkhardt. He blacked out, flung crashing into the open-topped bunker they'd been cleaning out. He came to almost immediately and realized that blood was gushing over the edge of the bunker and down its earthen wall. It was from Jonesy, who'd been ripped in his middle. LCpl Perry K. Jones, an inner-city black from Philly, died there in the dirt as Burkhardt held onto him. Tuohy emerged unscathed from the hole he'd been blasted into, and he and Burkhardt rushed to the Mule on which Barnes had been sitting. LCpl Jimmy O. Barnes, a kid from Minnesota, had half his head blown away.

The accuracy of the NVA artillery was uncanny, and thoughts turned to the Nung troops who had recently shared the Con Thien hills with them. Speculation was that their ranks had been riddled with VC. There even was talk that one of their Green Beret captains had had his throat slit *inside* the wire. It also was said that on those occasions when one or two Nungs had entered the Marine positions, they not only had stolen watches and radios (the Marines had beaten those they had caught), but also had paced off all the important positions. *If I set it up, they blow it up,* Lieutenant Budinger thought with frustration as he scouted for a better CP position. The new CP he was working on had proved too small, so the decision was made to transfer the radios to a larger H&S supply bunker in defilade on the south side of the hill. Three direct hits in three days had him worried—*where are they watching from?*—and he cautioned his men to be discreet as they set up the new CP. "If you walk in with a phone, you better make sure it's under your jacket."

Two months later, after the Walking Dead had left the Hill of Angels for Camp J. J. Carroll, Corporal Power lay on a folding cot in a troop tent around which a waist-high sandbag wall had been layered. It was nighttime. The monsoon season was just beginning, and a cold, misty rain breezed in where the tarp had been rolled up. The floor of packed earth was soggy and turning to mud. Power stared straight up in the darkness toward the top of the tent as he shivered in the cold. A blanket lay on the empty cot beside him. *If I got that fucking blanket off that cot over there, it probably wouldn't be so goddamn cold.* This thought congealed very slowly in his head, as did most thoughts since Con Thien, and as did the realization that the legs at the head of his cot were gradually sinking into the muddy floor. *If I turn around and put my head down at that end, I probably wouldn't feel so fucking weird.* Power did not reach for the blanket. He did not switch positions on the cot. He did not move.

PART NINE

SANDCASTLES

★

From the U.S. Marine Corps Vietnam Operational History Series: "The latest enemy offensive had failed. Con Thien had held and at least one firstline enemy regiment was in shambles. The Buffalo victory did not breed overconfidence, but the body-strewn wasteland along the DMZ proved mute evidence of the effectiveness of III MAF's defenses."

Operation Buffalo had developed from a two-company sweep into a five-battalion campaign as dictated by the NVA. When Colonel Jerue (CO, 9th Marines) and those above him were given their first breathing space, following the decimation of the 90th NVA Regiment on 6–7 July 1967, they immediately began to fold up the operation. On 8 July 1967, 3/9 and BLT 1/3 were ordered back across the Trace into Leatherneck Square, where 1/9, 2/9, and BLT 2/3 already were. On 9 July 1967, 3/9 headed for Cam Lo, replaced on the line by 2/9 and followed (on 11 July 1967) by BLT 2/3. On 13 July 1967, 1/9 departed Con Thien for Camp J. J. Carroll (relieved by 3/4); and at 0900,

14 July 1967, Operation Buffalo was officially terminated. At 1000 that same day, Operation Hickory II began, sweeping with sufficient forces (1/4, BLT 1/3, and the 1st Amphibian Tractor Battalion, with 2/9, 3/9, and BLT 2/3 in reserve) back across the Trace and toward the Ben Hai River.

From *Payback* by Joe Klein: "New troops would come with resupply, filling the gaps left by the dead and wounded. There would be more paddies to cross and—inevitably—another tree line. They would assault other village complexes, then leave them to be assaulted, pacified, blown up or burned down by other grunts. There would be more medevacs, and then more fresh troops . . . but never any clear-cut resolutions. Only the land would remain."

40

Six Has Been Hit

★

As of 1030, Saturday, 8 July 1967, Captain Sheehan, CO, Golf Company BLT 2/3, could hear the furious popping of automatic-weapons fire from the point of his two-platoon patrol. He could see nothing. Literally blind in the thick underbrush and bamboo under a double canopy of trees, they had been pushing themselves up another one of the foothills four kilometers southwest of Con Thien. The NVA, however, could see them. 1stLt Peter N. Hesser, the very sharp point platoon commander, reported that he had casualties. The NVA seemed to be in spiderholes near the hill's crest, and Sheehan instructed Hesser to halt and bring in the artillery.

Problem Number One: Hesser couldn't control the arty because his radio signals were being blocked by the foothills around them. Sheehan's radio operators still had contact with the outside world, so Sheehan told Hesser to adjust the mission through him.

Problem Number Two: Hesser couldn't tell exactly

where all his platoon elements were under the canopy. Sheehan started firing long and blind, working it back and adjusting roughly. "Did you hear that?"

"Yes."

"Where was it?"

Sheehan and Hesser managed to get the arty right on the entrenched NVA, and Hesser started his casualties back as Sheehan advanced to the point of contact with his company headquarters.

Problem Number Three: A hand grenade was bouncing in Sheehan's direction. The grenade had apparently been thrown by a Marine, but it had hit the bamboo around his NVA target. Thus repelled, it came rolling back downhill. Sheehan, hearing the warning shouts, looked to see it coming right at him; but instead of hitting the deck, Sheehan (one of the few unscathed heroes of Khe Sanh) remained standing as if he were invincible. He pointed to a nearby Marine and shouted at the kid to get down.

The grenade was ten feet away, rolling closer— BOOM! Spun around and dropped on his ass, Sheehan's first coherent thought was that he was pissed. *How dare they hit me!* His left trigger finger had been torn and the bone broken, and a corpsman was beside him quickly to splint the finger and wrap it. Sheehan refused morphine, despite the terrible pain, for fear it would fog his thinking.

When the 1st and 2d Platoons of Golf Company had departed that morning, while leaving 3d Platoon to secure their hill, Tom Huckaba of the Third Herd was most relieved. He had been feeling shaky. The day before, in fact, sitting on this hill after a day of patrolling, he had jumped in his hole at the first sound of outgoing Marine artillery. His good buddy, Chuck Graf, had looked at him and asked if he were shell-shocked.

"I don't think so."

"Well, I think you're getting shell-shocked, because that's friendly fire and you're shaking like a leaf."

Huckaba had gotten out of his hole then, realizing that no matter how much he hated the whining, rushing sound

of artillery and its frightening, tremorous impacts, he had
better calm down. He had no choice but to control himself
if he wanted to survive the remaining ten months on his
tour.

Or, in fact, July 8, because Captain Sheehan presently
ordered the Third Herd to join the fray now audible in the
distance. They were told to move fast, even to leave their
packs. It was a real hurry-up affair and the men went about
it with tight guts, because Sergeant McWhorter had gotten
off the radio to inform them that Captain Sheehan had
been hit. They didn't know how badly, or whether he was
alive or dead. Sheehan was their security blanket—he was
Captain Invincible to them—and as the word passed like
wildfire from man to man ("Six has been hit"), it thor-
oughly demoralized them.

The word to saddle up had caught Corporal Caton
wearing only his trousers, with both his .45 pistol and M79
grenade launcher taken apart for cleaning. Caton had not
been a superstitious person before the war, but in 'Nam
everything had to be done precisely according to a ritual:
New Testament in the left pocket of his jungle jacket, St.
Christopher medal around his neck, belt buckle aligned a
certain way, and so on. It bothered him greatly that he had
time only to slap his M79 together and throw on his helmet
and flak jacket—no time to pull on his shirt with the Bible
in the pocket—and that he was moving out down the trail
with the platoon even as he tried to reassemble the pistol.
The .45 was a tricky weapon to get together under normal
circumstances, let alone at a fast walk with nervous, shaky
hands, and Doc Holt, who was walking beside Caton, gave
him some shit about being all messed up. Caton responded
that it just wasn't his day and to remember C-7781, his
medevac number. He added that if he made it through this
day he was home free for the rest of his tour, because there
was no way he could ever be less prepared.

As they rushed down the trail, Lance Corporal Huckaba was near their radioman. En route, he heard a voice
using Sheehan's call sign telling the platoon where to go
upon arrival. *The captain must still be alive!* He was further

bolstered when another voice came over the radio, this one from Major Beard's CP, asking Sheehan whether he wanted to pull back. The answer was, "No, this is no big deal. I'm going to go right through this."[1]

Huckaba prayed it would be over before they got there. No chance. Nearing the hill, the platoon passed the scene of a recent air strike—fresh craters and burnt-out splashings of napalm that still filled the hot air with an unforgettable, nauseatingly sweet smell. Automatic-weapons fire came at them from the hill—most of it well over their heads, probably stray bursts from the fight on the hill. They used the rent earth for cover as they continued forward, discovering then that a dead NVA lay charred, bloated, and reeking against the side of one crater. The heat and smell and anxiety were too much, and several Marines turned their heads to vomit on the move. The firing from ahead grew louder, more intense, more personal as their single-file column rushed through the sandy, tree-dotted approach to the hill. Word was passed that after air and arty were laid on the hill, they would make an on-line assault, but first they were to get belly down to wait out the prep fires.

The artillery roared in first, and Huckaba, already down, could only press deeper when he realized that the whining rush in the air was coming directly for them. The roar and concussion of the impact was unreal. Huckaba knew another salvo was on the way, and in the middle of this he noticed Chuck Graf out the corner of his eye. Niceguy Chuck Graf, who had been with him all the way from day one at Parris Island to the Third Herd; Chuck Graf, who had gotten a DEATH BEFORE DISHONOR skull

1. Captain Culver's H BLT 2/3 was directed to move into a blocking position west of the NVA-occupied hill to interdict any withdrawal in the face of G BLT 2/3's assault. At this time, H BLT 2/3 had just medevacked 8 USMC WIA from a booby trap tripped while collecting and destroying NVA equipment found around a crashed and stripped Sea Horse. H BLT 2/3's subsequent sweep to the hill fight came under sniper and mortar fire, then tripped a bouncing betty mine, resulting in 2 USMC KIA and 1 USMC WIA.

tattoo—a real gungy item—one night at Oceanside, California, on the way to Vietnam, and who had egged Huckaba into getting a USMC scroll on his right biceps. Chuck Graf was looking back at Tom Huckaba as their own Made-in-the-USA 155mm artillery rounds screamed down onto them, and they both rolled their eyes and shared a grimace that said *this is it.*

Staff Sergeant Arnold, their nominal platoon commander, was trying to reach the artillery so as to bring a cease-fire. The staff sergeant usually kept his frightened and confused self out of the way, but every now and then—as at this moment—he tried to rise to the occasion. He was usually ignored, as Corporal Caton recalled. "At the start of most firefights Arnold would tell someone to do something and we would hear a loud 'Fuck you, Arnold' or 'Shut up, Arnold.' It was a rare lance corporal or above who hadn't told Staff Sergeant Arnold to get fucked at least once."

Now a fellow NCO was going to relay that message. Sergeant McWhorter, their young Hells-Angel-turned-outstanding-platoon-sergeant, screamed at Staff Sergeant Arnold to get the artillery turned off. Arnold, looking up from his radio, screamed back, "I'm doing all I can!"

"It's not enough!"

Sergeant McWhorter ran down the trail toward Arnold—Mac was the only man in the platoon not at the prone—and as he passed the shrunken figures of Huckaba and Graf, he shouted on the run, "Don't worry, I'll get this off of you! I'll get this incompetent sonuvabitch to get this artillery off of us!"

McWhorter grabbed the handset from Arnold, and in the heated exchange, Mac barked, "If you can't get this stuff off of us, I'll do it for you!"

The artillery was thus adjusted onto the NVA hill, and McWhorter called out, "Is anybody hit?"

Caton answered, "I think I'm bleeding."

Corporal Caton really wasn't sure. He'd been up and moving when the first salvo had fallen short. He had heard the incoming whistle, but instead of dropping instantly—as he knew he should have—he turned to make a dive for a barely noticeable depression he had just passed. Instead of reaching this cover, he had gotten caught up in some underbrush. But the explosions did not kill him, and he tore loose and rolled away, thanking God and the trees around him that seemed to have absorbed most of the shrapnel. Then he noticed blood on his right leg, and not being in any pain, he thought it might be someone else's. Sergeant McWhorter knelt beside him to slit open Caton's trouser leg, then examined the shrapnel wound on the shin and stated matter-of-factly, "Yeah, you're hit."

Meanwhile, north of the Trace: Charlie BLT 1/3 (Reczek) controlled a reconnaissance patrol that at 0700 slipped into the tree line, where two days earlier a tank had been reduced to a burnt shell and abandoned, along with the bodies of two Marines. The recon confirmed the location of the bodies, then moved back as Reczek prepped the area with air and arty and briefed Charlie Two's Lieutenant Francis on their body-recovery mission. The platoon moved out at 1200, and Lance Corporal Kalwara and another Marine rushed to Staff Sergeant Malloy's body. The second man hefted it over his shoulder, (Kalwara saw a leg flopping as if hanging by just a remaining shred of muscle), then turned to sprint back as Kalwara ran backward behind him, firing his M16 just in case. Kalwara and his buddy laid Malloy down among the trees, as the other dead Marine was similarly retrieved.

Exposed as they were, the Marines moved quickly to roll their dead into ponchos, but not so quickly that PFC Steiner, for one, did not get a close look at the corpse. Malloy's body was covered with flies, which the Marines brushed away with only momentary success, and his skin had gone taut. Steiner hated what he was seeing, hated that Malloy—whom he considered such a noble warrior—had been changed into something so repulsive.

Steiner didn't know what to feel for the second man whose body he and six or seven other Marines lugged back in a poncho. Like almost all their casualties, this second man was a stranger to him. None of the books like *Battle Cry* had prepared him for the DMZ, where the faces changed so quickly that he could police up the body of a platoon member whose name he didn't know, killed by an enemy he had never seen, in a tree line they would cede back to the enemy as soon as their tail-chasing operations took them elsewhere.

At 1300, 8 July 1967, following arty and air prep, Captain Sheehan led the Marines of Golf Company BLT 2/3 back up the unnamed, enemy-occupied hill. There was no hornet's nest of NVA fire this time, but a number of AK47s did open up; and the Marines, with horrible flashbacks to Khe Sanh, took on the bunkers one at a time. They methodically hammered each with rifles, machine guns, and grenade launchers, then rushed in to finish the job with grenades. It soon became apparent, though, that those shots received as they had come sweating uphill had been the last covering bursts of the enemy's rearguard as their main body crested the hill and withdrew down the other side.

Golf Company consolidated atop the hill and requested medevacs. Corporal Caton, who'd made the assault with a stinging, bandaged shin, was lifted onto the back of Corporal Blackman, who was acting more like a mother hen at the moment than the legendary Bear, and carried back down the hill. Caton then walked to the medevac assembly area, where Doc Holt said he should be medevacked to have the wound cleaned out in case there were fragments against the bone. As Doc Holt filled out a medevac card for Caton, he asked what his medevac number was, then caught himself. "That's right, I'm supposed to remember it."

Sea Knights landed for the dead and most seriously wounded (that hill had cost Golf Company 2 USMC KIA, 21 USMC WIAE, and 8 USMC WIANE),[2] and Captain

2. Lieutenant Koehler's F BLT 2/3 had deployed in blocking positions southwest of Golf's hill in anticipation of an NVA withdrawal. At

Sheehan finally asked his corpsman for a Syrette of morphine. The pain of his wounded hand had become so bad that he did not think the drug could fog his brain any more than the pain already had. Walking back down the hill, Sheehan saw the hangdog looks of his Marines, and trying to buck them up, he spoke jovially of having ice cream when he got back to the ship. Grunts looked back at him as though he were a little goofy, and he wasn't sure just how coherent his head and tongue really were from the morphine.

Captain Sheehan, due to be medevacked with the last of his casualties, spoke with Capt. Joseph J. O'Brien, the S-3A. Sheehan did not feel that his XO was equipped to take command of the company, so he put it to J.J. that he wanted him to skipper Golf in his stead. Major Beard agreed, and with Captain O'Brien in command (as of 1630), Golf Company got moving again to pursue and maintain contact. They did not catch up with the NVA and finally humped on up a hill to dig in for the night. As they crested the hill, a soft-spoken black Marine from Mississippi began shaking and muttering, "Aw, man, I just can't take it, man, I just can't take it anymore." As other Marines tried to console him, he suddenly fired his M16 toward the base of the hill, shouting that he saw NVA there. He was crying. This man was a vet of Khe Sanh and no one thought he was malingering, so Sergeant McWhorter led him up to the CP and told him he would be medevacked.

1430, 8 July 1967, they collided with a terrible intensity that resulted in an official accounting of 1 USMC KIA, 21 USMC WIAE, and 20 USMC WIANE, to 73 NVA kills. A Navy Cross was won this day by LCpl Merritt T. Cousins, an artillery radioman with Foxtrot. "He was wounded by shrapnel, and he and four comrades were cut off forward of their unit and completely surrounded by the enemy. . . . He called artillery in so close that shrapnel was hitting their position. As the artillery fire rocked the enemy position, they made an assault. . . . Hand-to-hand combat ensued, and Lance Corporal Cousins was wounded a second time . . . he refused to leave his radio and continued to adjust artillery fire upon the enemy and relay their situation until he succumbed to his wounds with his radio handset in his hands."

The exhausted veteran sat crying at the CP until the helo arrived.

Soon thereafter, Sergeant McWhorter led a squad-sized patrol to recon the area. Not far from the hill, they happened upon what appeared to be a graveyard. Mac told Huckaba to dig up one of the mounds to see what they could find, and when he swung his shovel into the freshly turned earth, a spurt of blood shot up onto his face and flak jacket. Encouraged that they might actually have some kills here to make up for the wilting fear of the hill assault, Huckaba kept digging until he'd uncovered a dead NVA in khaki fatigues, wrapped in a poncho. That first shovel blow had split open the stomach of this fresh corpse. Other Marines digging on the hill were finding more poncho-wrapped bodies; altogether, from body scraps on the assaulted hill and from this hasty burial site Golf would claim thirty-five confirmed kills and twenty probables. Sergeant McWhorter radioed in their find with unabashed glee. Payback. Everyone felt great.

41

Not Exactly the Sands of Iwo Jima

★

While BLT 2/3 fought Operation Buffalo's last-pitched battle in the hills between Con Thien and Cam Lo on 8 July 1967, Major Woodring, CO, 3/9, was contacted at 1330 by the CP of the 9th Marines and ordered to withdraw immediately south across the Trace. Woodring's CP alerted Lieutenant Colonel Wickwire, CO, BLT 1/3, of this sudden changing of directions, and Wickwire's CP radioed regiment to authenticate the directive. It was something of a bombshell, as neither battalion was presently under any pressure. They were, in fact, still counting coup from their recent slaughtering of the 90th NVA Regiment; and with patrol activity all along the front, neither battalion was in a position to disengage as rapidly as regiment desired.

The word to withdraw must have been cherished by Staff Sergeant Reynolds, the increasingly nervous short-timer nominally in command (after Lieutenant Kendig's medevac) of Alpha Two BLT 1/3. Corporal Witkowski of the rocket section, for one, realized that Reynolds was wrapped too tight when he commented with what seemed like panic in his voice about a 3.5-inch round hanging from Witkowski's unshouldered pack. The round had a shrapnel nick in it. Reynolds was afraid it would explode.

"Don't worry about it."

Staff Sergeant Reynolds then commented about the warning stamped on the round that it was to be kept out of direct sunlight. "It could explode. Why don't you put it in some water, cool it down."

"Dump it in *water?*" Witkowski gave Reynolds a strange look, wondering how he could have forgotten about the electrical components in a 3.5 round. Later, Reynolds held a meeting around his hole to the rear of the platoon line, along with Sergeant Bouchard, who was really running the platoon. Reynolds told them to fill their holes back in and be ready to move in thirty minutes. The word had come down that the whole battalion was pulling back across the Trace so that B52s could "bomb the shit out of the place."

At that moment, the NVA artillery to the north commenced firing. When it was finally over, Witkowski raised his head from his hole to see that there were packs in the trees, gear was scattered everywhere, and the six-inch-thick trees in front of his hole were now gone. Of the equipment he had laid out before his hole for easy reach in case of another ground attack, he found one of his .45 magazines with the metal peeled back by shrapnel. There was also laughter, for the lifting of the barrage found Sergeant Bouchard, who had not been able to make it to his forward hole before the first shells hit, sprawled in the dirt and holding over his head the only cover within reach—a piece of C-ration cardboard. Everyone found this highly amusing, "What's a piece of cardboard going to stop?"

Sergeant Bouchard didn't think it was too damn funny at first, but then he too had to laugh. Staff Sergeant Reynolds, however, could no longer shrug off with such bravado what the NVA were throwing at them, so he simply left. The circumstances of this retreat were unclear, whether

the company gunny perhaps saw the devastated look in
Reynold's eyes and ordered him out on the resupply helicopters presently landing, or whether Reynolds's departure
was simple desertion. One story was that a corpsman tried
to push the unwounded Reynolds out of the helicopter before it took off, but that he relented when he realized this
career Marine had simply cracked up as any man might
have.

Staff Sergeant Reynolds's departure aboard one of the
resupply birds corresponded with Lieutenant Kendig's arrival aboard another one. Kendig of the Old Corps had
been trying to get back to his platoon since having his arm
stitched up aboard ship on July 4. He had caught a resupply bird into Dong Ha only to be interdicted by Lieutenant
Colonel Wickwire, who ripped him up one side and down
the other about being a show-off. Figuring the colonel had
since cooled down (and sick of the artillery pounding Dong
Ha), Kendig had hitched a ride aboard another 1/3-bound
resupply helo this morning. He hopped off in the Trace just
as Wickwire and his sergeant major were approaching on a
footpath. Wickwire lit into Kendig again about being in the
field with stitches, but then laughed it off and pointed toward their lines. "You know, if you're that anxious, get the
hell outta here."

Lieutenant Kendig had no sooner hooked back up
with Sergeant Bouchard when he got the word that they
were immediately withdrawing. So there was Kendig
backpedaling again, carrying two full water cans (the
resupply had just been distributed to the companies), while
Bouchard had his hands full with ten or fifteen recently
arrived gas masks. The rest scooped up the remainder of
the ammunition, rations, gas masks, water cans, and sundry
packages stacked there in this hurry-up-and-go affair. The
scene was the same all along the line, and Captain Landes
of Bravo Company, for one, was appalled. It was as if the
powers that be had blinked in the face of what the NVA
had been throwing at them, forgetting that the NVA had
been decimated during their recent night attack. *We had
'em, we owned 'em, we were the king of the heap*—and then

suddenly arrives this panicky, knee-jerk order to abandon the field. *Chicken,* Landes thought. Lieutenant Colonel Wickwire was not pleased either that the 9th Marines demanded they execute the withdrawal order immediately, although as noted in BLT 1/3's after-action report, "A daylight withdrawal by itself requires careful and detailed planning." The situation was made "extremely perilous," the report continued, because

> the battalion was required to cross 600 meters of open ground that provided the enemy excellent observation, . . . two crippled tanks had to be extracted, and . . . the battalion had just received its resupply and had no organic transportation to move it to its new location. . . . It is believed that a careful analysis should be made of a unit's situation before directing a daylight withdrawal.

For their part, the grunts were just glad to be departing this hairy area. PFC Law of Delta Company watched one Marine celebrate by detonating C4 plastic explosives under a dead NVA in a bomb crater. ("Body parts went everywhere, and I remember we chuckled about it.") Within thirty minutes (at 1400) the lead elements were starting south. The retreat was so hasty that wild rumors spread about aerial observers having spotted hundreds upon hundreds of NVA crossing the Ben Hai River and bearing straight toward them, reminiscent of 6 July. It was easy to believe, because an incredible amount of air and arty was being placed forward of their lines. This was being orchestrated by Lieutenant Colonel Wickwire, not against observed targets but to cover their exposed rushes across the Trace. Also, as the lead elements, C and D Companies, moved out they could hear NVA artillery and mortar rounds beginning to land amid A and B Companies' positions. The shelling was most intense between 1425 and 1430, and it increased again at 1545 as Wickwire's Alpha Command Group also started back. By 1615, the command group, plus C and D Companies, had all completed their

platoon-by-platoon sprints across the Trace and immediately began digging in as A and B Companies followed in
their wake.

The NVA came out of the woodwork to bid them
good-bye with sniper fire, and by 1700, when A and B
Companies had worked their way back to the northern
edge of the Trace, Captain Landes of Bravo had taken a
casualty. He requested a medevac, which was, of course,
refused. So he had the wounded man and a heat casualty
loaded on one of the tanks with them as he continued to
coordinate with Jordan on his left flank. At this point,
Landes lost all radio communications, so he personally
moved over to the left to ensure that he and Jordan would
pull across the Trace in flank-protecting tandem. No one,
however, appeared where Alpha Company was supposed
to be. Landes, trying not to panic, rushed back and got
Bravo Company moving across the Trace before the NVA
could take advantage of his exposed flank. This they did,
only to discover that Alpha Company was actually still in
position above the Trace. Alpha backed out then with both
flanks uncovered. They were the last Marines out of the
area, and the only consolation for the haste, confusion, and
demoralization of their retreat (though the individual platoons maintained good order during the maneuver) was
that despite their exposure on the Trace, Bravo's single
casualty was the battalion's total.

On the left flank, Major Woodring, CO, 3/9, had
recrossed the Trace (with Captain Southard's H/2/9 on
point) by 1655 without casualty. As the battalion spread
out in preparation for consolidating with BLT 1/3 on their
right flank (which completed its movement by 1800), Captain Conger's I/3/9 and Captain Giles's K/3/9 both came
upon signs of NVA units surprised by their sudden arrival.
India had fresh tracks from a wheel-mounted machine gun
in a deserted ville and Kilo had, even better, an NVA
bivouac site that had been vacated so quickly the rice was
still steaming in its bowls. Gear and bloody bandages littered the ground. The NVA infantry never left stuff behind

like this, and Giles requested that an aerial observer be made available to lead their pursuit of what he conjectured to be a panicked NVA headquarters element. Battalion responded that regiment would not authorize pursuit on the grounds that 3/9 had been scheduled to return to Dong Ha the next day. Giles exploded. For once they had caught these sons of bitches with their pants down, he thought, but regiment had picked this point to terminate the operation —and it wouldn't fit into their goddamn paperwork to extend the operation!

The 9th Marines ordered 3/9 and BLT 1/3 to deploy amid the cover of east-west wood lines and prepare to direct supporting arms on any NVA that followed them across the Trace. This was accomplished by 2000, and as both battalions then commenced with their night activities, Captain Jordan of Alpha BLT 1/3 also had to conduct a medevac for a Marine who'd been shot through the hand. The Marine in question, a tall, lanky private whom Jordan recognized as one of his poorer troops, claimed that an NVA sniper had nailed him. He stuck to his story as Jordan questioned him (despite the corpsman's report that there were powder burns around the back-of-hand-to-palm hole, indicating the shot had been fired at close range), and Jordan elected not to bring the man up on charges. *If he wants to get out that bad,* Jordan thought (coming to the conclusion himself at this point that he'd rather choose another profession than endure another Buffalo-like operation) *well, I know what's going through his mind.*

LCpl Jim Mason of Echo BLT 2/3 had just gotten off watch on his three-man LP when the radio hissed with the voice of Cpl Richard Backus, who had the LP to his right. Both were deployed in a hedgerow, on the other side of which were terraced rice paddies, each level dropping away another ten feet from the relative high ground that Echo Company occupied. Backus was reporting movement and he requested permission to throw a grenade. Lieutenant Cannon rogered that, and one frag was tossed out into the black.

There were two explosions.

Mason was brought completely awake by that. The secondary explosion meant something really was out there, and he could hear Backus shouting, *"We're coming in, we're coming in!"*

Mason could hear them running in the dark. At the same time, he could hear his LP partners, Buckum (an unmotivated Marine he did not really trust) and Loerzel (a new Marine he did not really know), rustling in their position. Then they were suddenly gone, making an unnerved run back for their lines with such haste that Buckum left the radio and his .45 and Loerzel even forgot his M16. *Assholes!* Mason was tempted to follow them in, but that field suddenly looked long and open. With the nearly full moon *it would be like walking under a streetlight,* he thought —a fine target to the NVA, who must have zeroed in on all their noise.

Instead, Mason policed up the abandoned pistol, rifle, and radio, as well as their poncho and his own weapon and gear, and jumped down into an unoccupied NVA spiderhole in the hedgerow. On the other side of the brush, the terraced paddies seemed to come alive with NVA on the move. He could hear the clank of their equipment. He could hear the water in their canteens. Scared to death, Mason sat scrunched in his hole with the radio handset pressed tight against his ear to muffle any sound as he waited for Lieutenant Cannon to call him. It didn't take long. Cannon wanted to know what had happened and why he hadn't come back like everyone else. Then he released his transmit key and sent a static burp through Mason's handset that sounded as if it was over loudspeakers despite Mason's efforts to muffle it. Mason dared not answer. A whisper would bring the shadowy enemy.

Catching on, Cannon called again. "Do you have enemy contact? Key your handset once for yes, twice for no."

Mason gave it one good, scared squeeze.

Cannon played the key-your-handset game with Mason then, asking next which direction the NVA were from his hole and going through the choices one at a time until

Mason gave a one-squeeze response. Cannon asked Mason if he wanted artillery. One squeeze. Cannon switched radios to bring in the first spotter round, then Mason adjusted with the handset method, walking it pretty close to his hole. When the arty lifted, there were no more NVA sounds, and Cannon instructed Mason to return to the perimeter.

With the weapons and gear of three men slung over his shoulder and in both hands, Mason made a flat-out, heart-in-his-throat run across that open, moonlit field that was now deathly quiet. He happened to run right toward the fighting hole of his squad leader, Corporal Boyer, who'd been alerted he was coming in but who was paranoid, nonetheless, after four consecutive nights of contact. Boyer shouted, *"Stop!* Stop, who goes there?"

"It's Mason, it's Mason!"

"Well, hold on!"

"Fuck you!" Mason shouted as he hurtled over Boyer's hole.

Lieutenant Cannon called Mason and Backus, his two LP leaders, up to his poncho hootch. One of Cannon's cardinal rules was that no matter what happens, LPs were too important as the company's eyes and ears to pull back —even in the case of an NVA ground attack—and he told Mason and Backus to reestablish their LPs. Backus, a good, solid squad leader, replied that he did not feel comfortable doing that, because their original positions had been compromised and the NVA could watch them set up new ones in the moonlight. Without raising his voice, Cannon insisted, "Now get your ass out there."

"Okay."

Mason, of course, also agreed. He played the game all the way, down to burning his letters from home after reading them.

Mason rounded up Buckum and Loerzel, and barked at them a bit. "What the hell you doin' leavin' your weapons out there for? That was a real horseshit thing to run in there and leave me out there with everything." Backus similarly gathered his people, but prior to leaving the lines, he approached Mason. "We're not going out."

"Well, what are we going to do?"

Backus's let's-don't-but-say-we-did plan was the one they followed. ("We'll just call in our spot reps like we're supposed to, but we'll do it from the perimeter.") Lieutenant Cannon never had reason to suspect.

As of 0700, 9 July 1967, BLT 1/3 (Wickwire) began running air strikes on the vacated two-battalion line above the Trace, on the likely presumption that the NVA would be foraging their fighting positions. Meanwhile, 3/9 (Woodring), on the left flank, saddled up to return to Cam Lo. They were to be replaced by 2/9 (Kent) out of Cam Lo. At this point, H/2/9 (Southard) and A-C/1/9 (Slater) were chopped opcon from 3/9 to 2/9 (Slater and Woodring's parting words naturally concerned that hell-night: "everything fell into place"); and A-C/1/9 got the word to move out for their home port of Con Thien.

Starting south, Slater passed through Southard's position, and Southard was struck by the look in their eyes as they trudged through with their AK47s and thousand-yard stares. He spoke briefly with Slater, who said not a word about the battle but instead spoke quietly about being short and on orders for Quantico. Slater moved on then to bivouac with a shadow-spooked, grenade-happy Marine unit of unknown origin. In the morning, 10 July 1967, he completed the march to Con Thien. Because there was no safe room within the perimeter, he settled Alpha-Charlie 1/9 into a position south of the wire, then hiked up to the CP to report to Lieutenant Colonel Schening. This was only their second or third face-to-face, and Spike Schening, ever the rough-cob, cut Slater to the quick when he asked, "Why couldn't you have joined with Bravo and saved them? Couldn't you have done it better than you did?"

Slater was already hurting over the events of 2 July and was horrified to realize that since being opcon to 3/9, Schening apparently had the impression he'd sat out the rest of the operation in reserve. The whole conversation was a bitter anticlimax to the campaign. Slater finally wound up his defense with, "I did my best," and left the CP thinking his career was in a shambles. *They're writing my fitness reports and they probably think I'm a complete failure!* Slater's tour was over at this point, and he walked his replacement, Capt J. P. Ryan, around the company perimeter, introducing him to the weathered grunts and exclaiming, "These guys are great!" He recommended the company be pulled off the line to rest (they weren't) and the next thing Slater knew, he was on the convoy to Dong Ha, regretting that he would never be able to show the Marines of Alpha A Go-Go the new appreciation he had for them. To them he would always be Captain Contact.

Although an after-dark reconnaissance patrol run back across the Trace on 10 July 1967 by BLT 1/3 had confirmed that NVA had moved into the battalion's former CP position, no NVA had yet been foolish enough to cross the Trace and expose himself to the bamboo-and-banana-leaf camouflaged positions of 2/9 and BLT 1/3's east-west line. On the afternoon of 11 July 1967, B BLT 1/3 (Landes) was directed to dispatch a reinforced squad (a Sergeant King got the mission) across the Trace to see what effect their continuous air and arty bombardments were having. Captain Landes assigned his stalwart artillery observer, PFC Daley, to accompany Sergeant King but when Daley asked for one of his two radiomen, who were both corporals, to saddle up, they basically told him to take his single stripe and shove it. The two had long felt aggrieved that as artillerymen they had ended up in an infantry outfit: "We weren't assigned to do that, what're you, nuts?"

Daley couldn't believe what he was hearing. He had established a good working relationship with Captain Landes and the NCOs of Bravo Company by having his artillery team up front where they were needed, instead of back with the company headquarters. Daley told the two corporals, who technically outranked him, that King was going out with only a six-man squad, a corpsman, and a machine gunner, and he needed not only the firepower they could summon but also their extra rifles. "This is what we have to do."

"That's what *you* got to do maybe, but it ain't what *we're* going to do."

"Aw, he's a fuckin' lifer."

Hoping finally to shame one of them into going, Daley barked, "Okay, give me the radio. I'll take it."

"Fine with me."

Ignoring them now (and too embarrassed about the refusal to report it to King or Landes), Daley shouldered one of the radios himself and tagged along with King's squad across the Trace. Moving inland, the point man had not taken them far before he silently motioned for King. Ahead in the thick vegetation, they could hear NVA walking and talking, apparently at ease in a bivouac area, and between a few whispers and hand signals King got his squad turned around and headed south.

That's when an AK47 burst, directed at the rear of their southbound column, came out of nowhere, clipping the bushes behind which the Marines instantly went flat. The bush came alive then with the sound of scrambling NVA. Blindly scything the vegetation with M16s and their M60, plus Daley's M14, the patrol got back to the southern edge of their tree line. Before them was a hundred meters of open ground to the next tree line, and after that the Trace. Daley requested a WP marking round to start the artillery show. He called to King that they had a round on the way, and everyone kept their ears cocked. In that thickly vegetated area they probably wouldn't see the WP's detonation, but they could hear its impact and adjust from there. Daley heard the explosion, but was at a loss regarding direction and distance, until King thumped his shoulder and said with a sarcastic grin that he had called in a pretty good grid. He pointed, and Daley saw the white phosphorus roiling up thirty meters to their rear in the clearing.

Daley then requested a One-by-One Zone and Sweep from the firing battery, with that WP round to be the center of a barrage that would place one round every twenty-five meters in a one-hundred-by-one-hundred-meter box.

"Fire for effect."

With the rounds on the way, King got his squad to their feet—their area was part of the impact zone—and they really hoofed it back across the clearing and the Trace as the arty covered them.

Daley had nothing of substance to say ever again to his two reluctant corporals. Courage and cowardice, however, are quicksilver elements. When a squad-sized OP was over-run during their next operation (Cochise), Daley simultaneously covered their retreat with grenades and helped with the wounded. He and four other Marines then charged back up the hill in an NVA-shooting fury and retook the position. Again carrying Daley's radio, one of the previously reluctant corporals had been one of those courageous five.

It was on 12 July 1967, after 3/9 had settled into Cam Lo (and after a new officer, Capt R. L. Close, had come aboard), that Major Woodring called Captain Giles into his CP tent, "Giles, we got a new captain in today, and he wants to be a company commander. You're due to go home in six weeks, and I'll give you the choice. You can either keep Kilo Company for the next six weeks, or we can assign a new company commander today. Which do you want to do?"

"Woody, I'll tell you real honestly, I'm real tired of this war. I'm tired of taking Marines out and having them killed. And with my current attitude I'll probably get more Marines killed than I'll ever do killing NVA, because I really don't care if I live anymore. And if I don't care, then somebody else is going to die around me. I don't want that to happen, so with your permission I ask to be relieved of command."

Woodring looked at him, then cracked a small, commiserating grin. "You know, I totally agree. I'm tired of this war too, so we'll assign Captain Close to take over Kilo Company as soon as possible."

42

Déjà Vu

★

October 1967. They were back in the Marketplace and there it was in the dirt for the present members of Bravo Company, 1st Battalion, 9th Marines to see: the shrapnel-shredded flak jackets, the helmets shot full of holes, the blotchy battlefield dressings, the rusting ammunition magazines, the broken pieces of M16 rifles. There were even bone fragments, noted PFC John Flores, another sun-beaten grunt in this sweep. He had joined Bravo One ten days after the Marketplace Massacre. He had heard the stories. He knew what had happened here, and he could not suppress the shivers running up his baking back. There was not the slightest stirring of a breeze here, nor, Flores realized, were there any of the animals or birds they usually noticed on patrol. It was like walking through a cemetery. No one in the sweep stopped, no one said a word.

★

The two weeks of Operation Buffalo, conducted in the twenty-eighth month of the initial 3d Marine Division deployment to Vietnam and thirteen months after the beginning of their war on the DMZ, consumed 1,066 tons of ordnance as delivered by Marine Air, 40,000 rounds of Marine and Army artillery, and 1,500 rounds of Naval gunfire; and (officially) the lives of 159 Marines and Navy corpsmen, the wounding of another 345, and the lives of 1,290 North Vietnamese soldiers. The 3d Marine Division's defense of the DMZ continued, after Buffalo, with Operations Hickory II, Kingfisher (which included the September–October 1967 Siege of Con Thien), Fortress Sentry, Osceola, Kentucky, Fortress Ridge, Lancaster, Ardmore, Napoleon, Scotland (which included the January–April 1968 Siege of Khe Sanh), Saline, Pegasus, Scotland II, Dawson River, Badger Catch, Fortress Attack, Proud Hunter, Swift Pursuit, Dewey Canyon, Purple Martin, Maine Crag, Montana Muler, Virginia Ridge, Herkimer Mountain, Cameron Falls, Utah Mesa, and Idaho Canyon. Between July and November 1969, the 3d Marine Division withdrew from Vietnam as part of President Nixon's Vietnamization, followed between October 1970 and May 1971 by the 1st Marine Division. Marine casualties in Vietnam (compared to 86,940 in WWII and 30,544 in Korea) were 103,324, of whom 14,691 were killed.

Brigadier General Metzger (ADC, 3d Marine Division) received the Legion of Merit and Bronze Star as a battalion commander in WWII and Korea, and the Distinguished Service Medal and Bronze Star in Vietnam as well as the RVN National Order of Merit and Cross of Gallantry. He retired as a lieutenant general with his wife to La Jolla, California.

Major Brubaker (S-3, VMA-311) was grounded for two years due to the injuries sustained supporting Operation Buffalo, then served a second tour over Vietnam as an A6 squadron commander aboard the USS *Coral Sea,* 1970–71, retiring as a lieutenant colonel with three Distinguished Flying Crosses, the Bronze Star, numerous Air Medals, and two Purple Hearts. Married and the father of three, he now makes his home in Alexandria, Virginia. Lieutenant Hartnett (Third Force Reconnaissance Company) wound up his 1967–68 tour as CO, C/3d Recon, then served a 1971–72 tour as a Vietnamese Marine adviser, earning three Bronze Stars, three Navy Commendation Medals, and two Purple Hearts. Retired a major, he is now an ordnance consultant, living with his wife (he is the father of three and thrice a grandfather) in Dunedin, Florida. Lieutenant Coan (A/3d Tank Battalion) left the service with captain's bars and a Con Thien Purple Heart. Now married and a father, he is a licensed clinical social worker, living in Stockton, California.

Lieutenant Colonel Schening (CO, 1/9) retired a colonel and is now a grandfather and an active member of the retired military community in Springfield, Virginia. Major Danielson (XO, 1/9) received the Silver Star for Operation Buffalo and an end-of-tour Bronze Star. He retired as a lieutenant colonel to become an attorney in Alexandria, Virginia. Lieutenant Howell (S-2, 1/9) was posthumously awarded the Navy Cross and Purple Heart for Operation Buffalo. Captain Radcliffe (S-3A, 1/9) won the Silver Star for Operation Buffalo. He took over A/1/9 in October 1967 when their CO was KIA and led them through the sieges of Con Thien and Khe Sanh (picking up another Silver Star, plus a Bronze Star and Navy Commendation Medal) before finishing his tour as aide-de-camp to the division commander. Married afterward and now the father of two, he retired as a colonel to become a training manager with a luxury-cruise company in Emerald Isle, North Carolina. Captain Bruner (H&S/ 1/9) retired as a lieutenant colonel with the Bronze Star, two Navy Commendation Medals, and four Purple Hearts. Married and the father of two, he is now the director of solid disposal for Corpus Christi, Texas. Lieutenant Dixon (CO, H&S/1/9) received a Bronze Star and Purple Heart during his six months as a platoon commander in C/1/9, and a second Purple Heart during Operation Buffalo, which ended his tour. Married, with two children, he is now a federal magistrate in Raleigh,

North Carolina. Lieutenant Budinger (H&S/1/9) won a Bronze Star and Purple Heart at Con Thien and is presently a lieutenant colonel in the Marine Reserve. The father of two, now divorced, he is a supervisor in the state insurance office and lives in Springfield, Illinois. Corporal Tuohy (H&S/1/9) is now married, with two children, and works as a fireman in Milton, Massachusetts. Lance Corporal Burkhardt (H&S/1/9) also is the father of two and is a welder in Edison, New Jersey. Lance Corporal Gossen (H&S/1/9) is married, has a daughter, and is currently a master sergeant.

Captain Slater (CO, A/1/9) earned thirteen Air Medals for his AO duties, a Purple Heart and RVN Cross of Gallantry for the Second Battle of Phu An, and the Navy Cross for Operation Buffalo, plus a Navy Commendation Medal for a much quieter Vietnam tour (1970–71) as a company commander with the 1st Marine Division in the Da Nang-Que Son area. He retired a lieutenant colonel—and not without some of the nightmares and difficulties affecting the younger veterans. Together with his wife, he owns a printing shop and lives in Encinitas, California. Captain Ryan (CO, A/1/9) was mortally wounded at Con Thien by NVA artillery on 12 October 1967. Lieutenant Fagan (A/1/9) decided against going career and left the Corps a captain with the Bronze Star, two Purple Hearts, and the RVN Cross of Gallantry. Now married, with two children, he manages a stock-brokerage office and lives in Sudbury, Massachusetts. Gunnery Sergeant Santomasso (A/1/9) retired shortly after his Vietnam tour with neither the Bronze Star he'd been recommended for in Korea, nor the Navy Cross he was informed he'd been recommended for after Operation Buffalo (which always bothered him), and he had declined a Purple Heart. He became a custom picture framer and now lives with his wife in Concord, North Carolina. Sergeant Geizer (FO, A/1/9) received no personal decorations for his bravery during sixteen months in Vietnam and only one Purple Heart for his four separate wounds (all in keeping with normal treatment of enlisted men vis-à-vis the awards system). Discharge in 1967 was followed by several years of just getting his head on straight, then marriage, two children, a degree in architectural design, the nearing of completion of a master's in geology, and current employment as a geologist in Tulsa, Oklahoma. Private First Class Sankey (FO, A/1/9) survived an extended tour unscathed, but he was medically retired for injuries suffered during training at Camp Pendleton and thereafter slid into alcoholism, depression, and menial labor. A redeeming moment came in 1979 when Lieutenant Colonel Slater pinned on his long-overdue Silver Star for Operation Buffalo in a ceremony that involved a Marine Corps guard and traditional Arapaho warriors. Sankey told Slater then that the medal meant he could rest in peace, that he had done his WWII Marine father proud; and he died shortly thereafter of cirrhosis of the liver at the Oklahoma Arapaho Reservation. Corporal Power (A/1/9) left Vietnam three months after Operation Buffalo with a bone infection from his foot wound of July 2. Still on crutches, he was assigned to Camp Lejeune as a squad leader in the 2d Marine Division (a real paper tiger, its manpower gutted for Vietnam), where he drank cough syrup until he had to wear sunglasses indoors, hoped not to become a casualty of the increasing on-base racial violence, and was busted to Private First Class, thanks to his new, casual attitude. Following discharge, Power entered law school on a waiver, earned a doctor of jurisprudence degree, passed the bar, and practiced law in Georgia for several years before the depression, alcoholism, and nightmares caught up with him. His ex-wife obtained custody of their two children when they were divorced; and Power, with a 100 percent disability for wounds and post-traumatic stress disorder (PTSD), now lives alone in Clearwater, Florida. Corporal Toy (A/1/9) spent fifteen years as a laborer and/or forklift operator. He went through three marriages before a nervous collapse that rated him 100 percent disabled for PTSD and consigned him (thus far) to life as a semirecluse in his home in Milwaukee, Wisconsin. Private First Class Blough (A/1/9) was medically discharged with one leg and corporal chevrons to begin almost twenty years of drinking, drugging, and roaming. Clean and sober thanks to group counseling at a Vet Center, he is now supervisor of the telemarketing department of a children's book company and lives in Milwaukee.

Captain Coates (CO, B/1/9) and Lieutenant King (B/1/9) both posthumously received a Bronze Star and Purple Heart for Operation Buffalo. Staff Sergeant Burns (B/1/9) won a Bronze Star for the Khe Sanh Hill Fights, plus the Navy Cross and a meritorious promotion to gunnery sergeant for Operation Buffalo. Married before the war, he is now the father of two sons and is a scheduler/field supervisor with a security-guard company, living in La Puente, California. Corporal Montgomery (B/1/9) was discharged with a Purple Heart from the Khe Sanh Hill Fights and now is a family man in Sandusky, Ohio. Private First Class Hendry (B/1/9) received two Purple Hearts and a lifetime of nightmares, depression, and alcoholism from his sixteen weeks in the field (which also resulted in a first-person account of Operation Buffalo in *True* magazine in 1968 that gained fame among battalion vets). Twice divorced and the father of two, he is now a postal employee in Medford, Oregon. Private First Class Weldon (B/1/9) was discharged a corporal with a 30 percent disability for wounds. Now married and the father of two, he is nighttime supervisor in a cheese plant in Auburn, New York.

Captain Hutchinson (CO, C/1/9) received the Silver Star and Purple Heart for Operation Buffalo, and remaining a bachelor, retired as a major to a farm in Tiline, Kentucky. Lieutenant Libutti (C/1/9) won the Silver Star and three Purple Hearts for Operation Buffalo, and he served a 1972–73 tour with an amphibious squadron off the coast of South Vietnam. Divorced from the woman he married before his first tour, he is now remarried; and now a colonel, he recently commanded the 11th Marine Expeditionary Unit, one of whose components was 1/9. Corporal Bradley (C/1/9) won a saving-the-wounded Bronze Star and a booby-trap Purple Heart during his eighteen-month tour. Married, with three children, he is presently director of a prison for the state department of youth services and lives

in Worcester, Massachusetts. Lance Corporal Bennett
(C/1/9) rotated with two Purple Hearts and a bust to Private First Class for his short-timer's shakiness and several
run-ins with a boot lieutenant in the field. Now married
and the father of two (and a PTSD sufferer), he is a postal
employee in Parkersburg, West Virginia. Lance Corporal
Stuckey (C/1/9), after spending six months in various hospi-
tals to heal his amputated hand and other wounds, was
discharged a corporal with the Navy Cross and four Purple
Hearts. He immediately entered junior college (during
which time he married), then went on to a university to
earn his degree in criminology. During his employment as
a social worker and then as a juvenile-delinquent coun-
selor, it didn't take long for the work-related stress (every
issue seemed life-and-death) to conjure up flashbacks so
intense that Stuckey twice required hospitalization. He finally resigned in 1973 to become a househusband for his
wife (who stuck with him and went on to become an ele-
mentary school principal) and their two children in Semi-
nole, Florida.

Sergeant McGuigan (D/1/9) retired as a sergeant major. He is presently in his third marriage, is the father of
five and the grandfather of four, and is working on his
associate degree while living in Stafford, Virginia. HM3
Lindenmeyer (D/1/9) received the Purple Heart for a two-
stitch shrapnel wound received at Con Thien during Operation Buffalo. He went on to earn his biology degree and
now, married for the second time, with a daughter, is an
ecologist for a regional park district, living in Castro Valley,
California. HM3 Shade (D/1/9) was killed along with two
others on 13 October 1967 when a misguided night air
strike dropped three 250-pound bombs inside the wire at
Con Thien.

Captain Southard (CO, H/2/9) was severely wounded
in the left leg in September 1967 at Con Thien by a 122mm
rocket; he was medically retired as a major and (several
years later) the leg had to be amputated below the knee.
Married, with two children, he is now a manufacturer's rep

for industrial material-handling equipment and lives in Yorktown, Virginia.

Major Woodring (CO, 3/9) received the Navy Commendation Medal in Korea, as well as the Silver Star and Purple Heart for Operation Buffalo and two Legions of Merit and the RVN Cross of Gallantry for the remainder of his Vietnam duty. Married and the father of two, he retired a colonel to become a farmer (he is also associated with a construction management firm) in Fallbrook, California. Captain Navadel (S-3, 3/9) won a Silver and a Bronze Star, then served a 1971–72 tour on a classified assignment with Special Operations Group. Retiring as a colonel, he is married, the father of five, and is a general manager of a diversified management and technical services company, living in Vista, California. Lieutenant Westling (chaplain, 3/9) received the Navy Commendation Medal and Purple Heart, plus a Bronze Star for his second tour (Naval Support Activity, Saigon, 1969–70) as a circuit-riding chaplain with the amphibious craft in the Mekong Delta. He retired as a Navy captain to become rector of All Saints' Episcopal Church in Redding, California. First Sergeant Lee (I/3/9) retired two years after Vietnam and became a tool sharpener in a GE factory. After they raised three children, his wife passed away; and, retired from his second job, he now spends his days fishing and hunting in Schenectady, New York.

Corporal Collopy (I/3/9) received the Purple Heart, and was discharged a sergeant only to reenlist (after earning his degree) in 1972 and receive an OCS commission. Joining the Marine Reserve after release from active duty (he is currently a lieutenant colonel), he is now a banker, the father of three, and a resident of Houston, Texas. Corporal Gomez (I/3/9) served a full infantry tour, 1966–67; then a six-month extension with division recon, 1967–68; and finally an easy sea tour, 1969, with the Marine detachment aboard an aircraft carrier off North Vietnam. There he was busted from sergeant to lance corporal for dereliction of duty and an unauthorized absence. Now married and the father of six, he suffers from PTSD and bone cancer; presently unemployed (though a guest lecturer on Vietnam at the local college, and a youth athletic coach), he lives in Sioux City, Iowa. Private First Class Ford (I/3/9) received two Purple Hearts during the Siege of Con Thien, extended his tour six months to serve in a combined-action platoon, and was discharged a sergeant. Divorced, with three children, he is now a lieutenant in the state police, living in Everett, Massachusetts.

Captain Giles (CO, K/3/9) won a Navy Commendation Medal for his first trip to Vietnam (six weeks in 1961 conducting beach surveys for 3d Recon), plus the Bronze Star for Hill 70, the Silver Star for Operation Buffalo, and another Navy Commendation Medal for his final Vietnam stop, a 1970–71 tour as a liaison officer between the Vietnamese Joint General Staff and MACV. His first wife left him after his 1966–67 tour due to his excessive drinking. He married again after his final tour and had two children before that union also ended, in an amiable, non-alcohol-related divorce. Retired as a lieutenant colonel, Giles has totally separated himself from his former military persona and is presently a counselor/instructor with a personal-growth seminar company, living in Novato, California. Gunnery Sergeant Hatfield (K/3/9) won the Silver Star and Purple Heart for his twilight tour in Vietnam, and retiring then, he was also divorced soon thereafter. He currently makes his home in Crystal River, Florida. Corporal Saltaformaggio (K/3/9) was discharged a sergeant. Now married with two children, he is a lieutenant in the state police, living in Metairie, Louisiana.

Lieutenant Colonel Wickwire (CO, BLT 1/3) retired as a colonel to Beaufort, South Carolina. Corporal Miller (NGL 1/3) was discharged with a Purple Heart, immediately went through a whirlwind marriage and divorce, and now, married again and the father of three, owns a roofing business in Rice Lake, Wisconsin. Lance Corporal Groeger (NGL 1/3) went on to earn his master's degree and, still a bachelor, is a contractor living in Chicago, Illinois. PFC Rusmisell (H&S 1/3) rotated with a Purple Heart and an RVN Cross of Gallantry and with a personality transformation. From an average, hardworking North Carolina boy, he became someone cold and angry who drank his way through his final year in uniform, lost a stripe, and did thirty days in corrective custody for an unauthorized absence. Rusmisell then plunged into chronic PTSD and unemployment (he was a licensed electrician), and—after two sons—a failed marriage. A nervous breakdown in 1986 resulted in three years in a VA hospital, and he is now living in Newport News, Virginia.

Captain Jordan (CO, A 1/3) received the Bronze Star and RVN Cross of Gallantry for Operation Beau Charger; then during Operation Cochise in August 1967 a booby trap exploded in the VC tunnel into which he'd climbed and he was rendered unconscious by the residue fumes and lack of oxygen. Sergeant Bouchard entered the tunnel to loop a rope around Jordan, and a corpsman managed to get his heart and breathing started again. He finished his tour on the battalion staff, resigning his commission shortly thereafter to become a lawyer. Now married, with two children, he is director of public affairs of the water department in Denver, Colorado. Sergeant Santos (FO, A 1/3) received a commission and retired as a major to become a high-school teacher, living now with his wife and children in Renton, Washington. Lieutenant Kuhlmann (A 1/3) won the Bronze Star and two Purple Hearts. Resisting any effort to retire him medically (he was one of the few active-duty officers to wear a hearing aid), he went on to retire as a major. Married, with three children, he is now the plant operations superintendent for an asphalt and readymix company and lives in Yakima, Washington. Lieutenant Kendig (A 1/3) won the Purple Heart for Operation Buffalo, the Navy Commendation Medal for Operation Shelbyville in September 1967, and the RVN Cross of Gallantry during his third tour, when as XO, D/1/9, he worked with the Vietnamese Marines during the 1972 Easter Offensive. Married, with four children, he retired a major and is presently plant manager for a meat-processing corporation in Lancaster, Pennsylvania. Sergeant Bouchard (A 1/3) won his first Purple Heart when overcome by fumes during his rescue of Captain Jordan. Seriously wounded by artillery shrapnel in the leg during Operation Kentucky (November 1967), he was medically retired as a staff sergeant. Divorced and the father of one, he is now a real estate broker in Newburyport, Massachusetts. Corporal Witkowski (A 1/3) served nearly four months in Vietnam before a booby trap sent him home in August 1967 with a 20 percent disability. Discharged a sergeant and now married with children, he is a postal employee in Mohnton, Pennsylvania. Lance Corporal Lind (A 1/3) left with corporal stripes, and now the father of three is a postal employee in Green Bay, Wisconsin.

Captain Landes (CO, B 1/3) won the Silver Star for Operation Buffalo plus a pair of Bronze Stars during the remainder of his time as company commander before finishing his tour as the S-4. He was XO, 1/9, in 1975 during the evacuations of Phnom Penh and Saigon, and he retired as a colonel to become a computer-software salesman and manager, living with his wife (his three children are grown) in Littleton, Colorado. Private First Class Daley (FO, B 1/3) received the Purple Heart for Operation Buffalo and the Bronze Star for Operation Cochise. Discharged a sergeant, he soon married (and presently has four daughters), and he worked as a police officer while earning his undergraduate degree. Law school followed, then a position in a private law firm, election as a county district attorney, and appointment as a county circuit judge in Janesville, Wisconsin. Lieutenant Norris (B 1/3) eventually won command of the company; but on 30 April 1968, while assaulting a heavily fortified ville above the Cua Viet River, Norris was killed. Staff Sergeant Head (B 1/3) served two combat tours with the battalion, 1965–66 and 1967–68 (winning a Silver Star during Operation Cochise for leading their retake-the-hill charge); he pulled a third tour, 1st MP Battalion, 1970–71, before retiring as a sergeant major. Married, with two children, he is now with nuclear security at a generating station, while living in Oceanside, California. Lance Corporal Dull (B 1/3) was discharged with two Purple Hearts. Presently an operating-room technician in a hospital in Boscobel, Wisconsin, he is married and has three children.

Captain Reczek (CO, C 1/3) won the Bronze Star for Operation Beaver Cage and went on to retire as a colonel. With a wife and two sons, he is now assistant manager of a car dealership and lives in Oceanside, California. Lieutenant Neuss (XO, C 1/3) was killed on 11 October 1967 during a fierce night engagement (Operation Bastion Hill) south of Quang Tri City. Lieutenant Francis (C 1/3) won the Bronze Star during his first tour, but returning as a captain (assigned to a USN Seabee detachment), he was killed on 10 February 1970, reportedly in a helicopter crash. Sergeant Jones (C 1/3) was killed on 16 August 1967 during an open-paddy ambush on Operation Cochise. Lance Corporal Chartier (C 1/3) was discharged a corporal with the Navy Commendation Medal and, following two divorces and two children, is a police officer in Hibbing, Minnesota. Lance Corporal Kalwara (C 1/3) was discharged a corporal, then was married—one child—and divorced. After college came work as a state trooper and homicide investigator, as well as election to city council and registration as a lobbyist with the state legislature. Now, with his second wife, he owns a tool-sharpening business in Juneau, Alaska. Private First Class Pilgreen (C 1/3) was mustered out a lance corporal and, now married and the father of three, is a lead lineman with the power company in Wetumpka, Alabama. Private First Class Steiner (C 1/3) served two tours in Vietnam during 1966–68, the second one ending a bit early when he was shot in the left thigh while a platoon sergeant in the A Shau Valley. Discharged a sergeant with the Navy Achievement Medal and two Purple Hearts, he earned a degree in biology, became an administrator with the fish and wildlife service, and now lives with his wife and two children in Alameda, California. Private First Class Taylor (C 1/3) was discharged a sergeant with three Purple Hearts (in subsequent years, numerous tumors developed, caused, he suspects, by Agent Orange). Married and divorced after the war, he has custody of his two children, plus the two of his second wife, and now owns an insurance agency while living in Hammond, Indiana.

Corporal Brugh (D 1/3) was medically retired with a Purple Heart that cost him ten months in a full-length body cast, more than four years of bed time, and numerous operations over the years. His legs, however, were saved. Still married to the woman he wed just prior to his departure for Vietnam, he is now the father of two and a backhoe operator for the city utilities in Logansport, Indiana. Lance Corporal Fox (D 1/3) was KIA in a shot-down helo on 8 January 1968, immediately prior to his rotation home. Lance Corporal Kelley (D 1/3) rotated with a Purple Heart from Operation Beau Charger, and true to his salty form he was busted down from corporal during his Stateside duty. (Among other things, he neglected to show up for a formation where "they were going to promote a bunch of really punk kids who weren't worth a pisshole in the snow.") Presently suffering from PTSD, he is married, the father of three, and a postal employee in Worcester, Massachusetts. Private First Class Law (D 1/3) was an active member of Vietnam Veterans Against the War following his discharge and, now married with two children, is a licensed practical nurse with the VA hospital. He lives in Chula Vista, California.

Major Beard (CO, BLT 2/3) died of a heart attack following his retirement as a lieutenant colonel. Major Broujos (XO, 2/3) won the Silver Star and Purple Heart as a platoon commander in Korea, retained a Reserve commission as he went on to practice law and get married (he is the father of four), then volunteered to go on active duty to serve in Vietnam, where he earned a Navy Commendation Medal. Retired from the Reserve as a colonel, he is currently an attorney and a state representative in Carlisle, Pennsylvania. Captain Bogard (CO, E 2/3) won the Bronze Star and retired as a colonel. The father of three, now divorced, he is a business-development manager in Alexandria, Virginia. Lieutenant Cannon (XO, E 2/3) won the Silver Star, Bronze Star, and two Purple Hearts and retired as a major. There followed a bout with divorce, alcoholism, and PTSD, steadied by remarriage and college graduation. A real estate broker today, he lives in Los Lunas, New Mexico. Corporal Backus (E 2/3) was wounded three times before discharge as a sergeant. Married and the father of two, he is a middle-school teacher in East Liverpool, Ohio. Lance Corporal Mason (E 2/3) was discharged a sergeant, and now he and his wife have twin girls. Mason is a retail meat cutter in South St. Paul, Minnesota. Captain Sheehan (CO, G 2/3) received the Silver Star and Purple Heart for Operation Buffalo, and after extending his tour to serve on the staff of the 4th Marines he also won a Bronze Star, Navy Commendation Medal, and RVN Cross of Gallantry. Retiring as a colonel, he and his wife live in Chesapeake, Virginia. Sergeant McWhorter (G 2/3) won the Bronze Star for the Battle of 28 February 1967, then served a second tour in the Da Nang rear in the avionics section of MAG-11. Following retirement as a master gunnery sergeant, he was divorced (they had one child) and is currently a car salesman in Las Vegas, Nevada. Corporal Caton (G 2/3) was discharged a sergeant (then joined the Army National Guard, where he is now a staff sergeant/operating room specialist) and went on to get his degree in history. Now the father of two from his first marriage, and of one with his second wife, he is with the state mental hospital and teaches social studies and science to troubled children and adolescents, while living in Yankton, South Dakota. Lance Corporal Huckaba (G 2/3) went home in January 1968, his tour abbreviated by his third Purple Heart (he also won a Bronze Star), and he was discharged a sergeant. Working as a mail carrier while going to night school to earn a two-year degree in personnel management (he was married during this period and eventually divorced), he is now remarried, the father of two, and a postmaster, living in Joliet, Illinois. Captain Culver (CO, H 2/3) won the Silver Star and Purple Heart. Divorced after his tour, he raised their son, and following retirement as a major he became an instructor with a Marine Corps Junior ROTC Unit. His home is in Coeur D'Alene, Idaho.

Appendix

★

Cast of Characters, Operation Buffalo
(2–14 July 1967)

Commanding General, 3d Marine Division: MajGen
    Bruno A. Hochmuth
Assistant Division Commander, 3d Marine Division:
    BrigGen Louis Metzger
Commanding Officer, 9th Marine Regiment: Col George
    E. Jerue

1st Battalion, 9th Marines, 3d Marine Division
    CO: LtCol Richard S. Schening
    XO: Maj D. Curtis Danielson
    S-1: 2dLt Ramirez, until 7 July 67; then 2dLt H. Dugas
    S-2: 1stLt Gatlin J. Howell, until KIA on 7 July 67; then
        1stLt Al Fagan
    S-3: Capt James H. R. Curd, until WIA on 7 July 67;
        then Capt Henry J. M. Radcliffe
    S-4: N/A

    CO, H&S: 1stLt Wallace Dixon, until WIA on 7 July 67
    CO, A: Capt Albert C. Slater, Jr., until rotated on 10
            July 67; then Capt John A. Ryan
    CO, B: Capt Sterling K. Coates, until KIA on 2 July 67;
            then Capt Henry J. M. Radcliffe (acting) until
            10 July 67; then Capt R. C. Wells
    CO, C: Capt Edward L. Hutchinson, until WIA on 4

July 67; then 2dLt. D. M. Telep, until 9 July 67; then 1stLt J. P. Krohn, until 10 July 67; then Capt C. B. Hartzell

CO, D: Capt Richard J. Sasek, until KIA on 6 July 67; then 1stLt S. M. Snyder, until 9 July 67; then Capt Francis L. Shafer, Jr.

3d Battalion, 9th Marines, 3d Marine Division

CO: Maj Willard J. Woodring

XO: Maj J. G. Metas, until 3 July 67; then Maj John C. Studt

S-1: 2dLt H. L. Tieking

S-2: 1stLt H. F. Wright

S-3: Capt George D. Navadel

S-4: Capt Robert Swigart, until replaced on 4 July 67; then 1stLt G. Gudjonson

CO, H&S: 2dLt W. C. Helton

CO, I: Capt Edward H. Coyle, until rotated on 4 July 67; then Capt Robert W. Swigart, until KIA on 4 July 67; then Capt George D. Navadel (acting) until 5 July 67; then Capt William A. Conger.

CO, K: Capt Jerrald E. Giles, until moved to the S-3A position on 11 July 67; then Capt R. L. Close

CO, L: Capt Troy T. Shirley

CO, M: Capt R. B. Johnson

CO, H/2/9 (opcon): Capt Frank L. Southard

Battalion Landing Team 1/3, Special Landing Force A, 9th Marine Amphibious Brigade

CO: LtCol Peter A. Wickwire

XO: Maj Richard W. Goodale

S-1: 2dLt E. W. Sterling

S-2: CWO P. B. Murphy

S-3: Maj Richard C. Ossenfort

S-4: Capt Phillip N. Hendrix

CO, H&S: Capt John H. Mack

CO, A: Capt Charles G. Jordan

CO, B: Capt Burrell H. Landes
CO, C: Capt Gerald F. Reczek
CO, D: Capt Edward P. Aldous

Battalion Landing Team 2/3, Special Landing Force B,
9th Marine Amphibious Brigade
CO: Maj Wendell O. Beard
XO: Maj John H. Broujos
S-I: 2dLt B. L. Heaton
S-2: Capt V. M. Smith
S-3: Maj D. W. Lemon
S-4: Capt R. R. Green

CO, H&S: Capt Raymond C. Madonna
CO, E: Capt Robert N. Bogard
CO, F: IstLt Richard D. Koehler
CO, G: Capt James P. Sheehan, until WIA on 8 July 67;
   then Capt Joseph J. O'Brien
CO, H: Capt Robert N. Culver

Selected Bibliography

★

Books

Bartlett, Tom, ed. *Ambassadors in Green*. Washington, D.C.: Leatherneck Association, Inc., 1971.

Bergsma, Herbert, Cmdr. *Chaplains with Marines in Vietnam 1962–1971*. Washington, D.C.: History and Museums Division, Headquarters, U.S. Marine Corps, 1985.

Boettcher, Thomas. *Vietnam, the Valor and the Sorrow*. Boston: Little, Brown and Company, 1985.

Corson, William, Lt. Col. *The Betrayal*. New York: W. W. Norton & Company, Inc., 1968.

Duncan, David Douglas. *War Without Heroes*. New York: Harper & Row, 1970.

Klein, Joe. *Payback: Five Marines and Vietnam*. New York: Ballantine Books, 1985.

Krulak, Victor, Lt. Gen. *First to Fight: An Inside View of the U.S. Marine Corps*. Annapolis, Maryland: Naval Institute Press, 1984.

Lippard, Karl, Sgt. *The Warriors*. Lancaster, Texas: Vietnam Marine Publications, 1983.

Santoli, Al. *To Bear Any Burden: The Vietnam War and its Aftermath in the Words of Americans and Southeast Asians*. New York: Ballantine Books, 1986.

Sheehan, Neil. *A Bright Shining Lie: John Paul Vann and America in Vietnam*. New York: Random House, 1988.

Shore, Moyers S., Capt. *The Battle for Khe Sanh.* Washington, D.C.: Headquarters, U.S. Marine Corps, 1969.

Simmons, Edwin, Brig. Gen. *The Marines in Vietnam 1954–1973, an Anthology and Annotated Bibliography.* Washington, D.C.: History and Museums Division, Headquarters, U.S. Marine Corps, 1974.

Telfer, Gary, Maj.; Lt. Col. Lane Rogers; and Keith Fleming. *U.S. Marines in Vietnam: Fighting the North Vietnamese, 1967.* Washington, D.C.: History and Museums Division, Headquarters, U.S. Marine Corps, 1984.

Unpublished Manuscripts

Coan, Jim. "Con Thien."

Hendry, David. "An untitled account of B/1/9, 30 June–2 July 67." (1967).

Stubbe Ray, Lt. Cmdr. "The Battle of Khe Sanh; an American Victory in Vietnam." (1973).

Periodicals

"Ambush at Con Thien." *Newsweek,* 17 July 1967, p. 45.

Brey, Ed, Staff Sgt. "NVA Tries Disguise, Tear Gas for Assault." *Sea Tiger* (III MAF), 11 August 1967, p. 5.

Buckley, Tom. "Search for Dead Is Slowed." *New York Times,* 5 July 1967, p. 6.

Hendry, David, Lance Cpl. "AMBUSH!" *True,* September 1968, pp. 28–29, 70–72.

McConnell, Malcolm. "Forever Proud." *Reader's Digest,* November 1988, pp. 65–70.

Warner, Denis. "Bearing the Brunt at Con Thien." *The Reporter,* 19 October 1967, pp. 18–21.

Documents

"Combat After Action Report, Operation 'Buffalo,' 021000H-140900H July 1967, Headquarters, Battalion Landing Team 1/3, 9th Marine Amphibious Brigade."

"Combat After Action Report, Operation 'Beaver Track/Buffalo'; 'Hickory II,' Headquarters, Battalion Landing Team 2/3, 9th Marine Amphibious Brigade."

"Combat After Action Report, 'Buffalo,' Headquarters, 1st Battalion, 9th Marines, 3d Marine Division."

"Combat After Action Report, 'Buffalo,' Headquarters, 2d Battalion, 9th Marines, 3d Marine Division."

"Combat After Action Report, Operation 'Buffalo,' 021000H-140900H July 1967, Headquarters, 3d Battalion, 9th Marines, 3d Marine Division."

"Command Chronology, BLT 1/3, 9th Marine Amphibious Brigade, July 1967."

"Command Chronology, BLT 2/3, 9th Marine Amphibious Brigade, 4–31 July 1967."

"Command Chronology, 9th Marines, July 1967."

"Command Chronology, 1st Battalion, 9th Marines, 3d Marine Division, July 1967."

"Command Chronology, 2d Battalion, 9th Marines, 3d Marine Division, July 1967."

"Command Chronology, 3d Battalion, 9th Marines, 3d Marine Division, July 1967."

"Command Chronology, 3d Tank Battalion, 3d Marine Division, July 1967."

"Operations of U.S. Marine Forces, Vietnam, July 1967."

"U.S. Marine Corps Oral History Program/Interviewee: Lt. Gen. Louis Metzger, 1973."

3d Marine Division Historical Section/Infield Interviews:

Alicna, Adriano, HN, A/1/9 (Camp J. J. Carroll, 27 September 1967)

Burns, Leon, S. Sgt., B/1/9 (Dong Ha, 7 July 1967; and Phu Bai, 5 November 1967)

Christian, Robert, Lt. Col., XO and S-3, SLF Bravo (USS *Tripoli,* 11 August 1967)

Crisan, Thomas, Cpl., A/1/9 (Camp J. J. Carroll, 17 July 1967)

Cromwell, Lawrence, Lance Cpl., B 1/9 (Dong Ha, 7 July 1967)

Cull, Simon, Lance Cpl., B/1/9 (Con Thien, 12 September 1967)

Delaney, William, 1st Lt., B/1/9 (Dong Ha, 7 July 1967)

Dishong, David, Lance Cpl., A/1/9 (Camp J. J. Carroll)

Fazio, Ronald, Cpl., A/1/9 (Camp J. J. Carroll, 29 September 1967)

Fields, Ronnie, PFC, B/1/9 (Con Thien, 12 September 1967)

Francis, Claude, L. Cpl., B/1/9 (Dong Ha, 7 July 1967)

Haggard, Richard, L. Cpl., A/1/9 (Camp J. J. Carroll, 27 September 1967)

Henderson, Dade, PFC, B/1/9 (Balboa Hospital, San Diego, California, 28 September 1967)

Herbert, Harry, Cpl., B/1/9 (Con Thien, 12 September 1967)

Jerue, George, Col., CO, 9th Marines

Lanigan, John, Col., CO, 3d Marines (Camp Smith, Hawaii, 6 July 1967)

Mesa, Ramon, PFC, A/1/9 (Balboa Hospital, San Diego, California, 26 July 1967)

Olson, Charles, LCpl., A/1/9 (Camp J. J. Carroll, 27 September 1967)

Peterson, Sammie, Cpl., A/1/9 (Camp J. J. Carroll, 27 September 1967)

Pitts, Michael, Sgt., B/1/9 (Con Thien, 12 September 1967)

Ragland, Charles, PFC, A/1/9 (Camp J. J. Carroll)

Stockman, James, Col., CO, 3d Marines (Camp J. J. Carroll, 6 July 1967)

Tabor, Claude, PFC, B/1/9 (12 September 1967)

Index

★